AF541123

Backward Class Reservation and Concept of Creamy Layer

Backward Class Reservation and Concept of Creamy Layer

DR. PALLAVI GUPTA
Lecturer
Amity Law School
(Affiliated to GGSIP University, Delhi)
Delhi

Foreword by

DR. M. VEERAPPA MOILY
Former Minister of Law and Justice
Government of India

DEEP & DEEP PUBLICATIONS PVT. LTD.
F-159, Rajouri Garden, New Delhi - 110 027

BACKWARD CLASS RESERVATION
AND CONCEPT OF CREAMY LAYER

ISBN 978-81-8450-402-6

© 2012 PALLAVI GUPTA

All rights reserved with the Publisher, including the right to translate or to reproduce this book or parts thereof except for brief quotations in critical articles or reviews.

Typeset by RAHUL COMPOSERS
358, Pocket-B, Phase-2, Sector-16B, Dwarka, New Delhi - 110 075

Printed in India at MAYUR ENTERPRISES
WZ Plot No. 3, Gujjar Market, Tihar Village, New Delhi - 110 018

Published by DEEP & DEEP PUBLICATIONS PVT. LTD.
F-159, Rajouri Garden, New Delhi - 110 027 • Phone : 25435369, 25440916
E-mail : ddpubs@gmail.com • ddpubs@yahoo.com
Showroom :
2/13, Ansari Road, Daryaganj, New Delhi - 110 002 • Telefax : 23245122

Contents

Foreword

Reservation is one of the many tools that are used to preserve and promote the essence of equality, so that disadvantaged groups can be brought to the forefront of civil life.

Pandit Jawaharlal Nehru, who presided over the Congress Expert Committee emphasized before the Constituent Assembly that the removal of socio-economic inequalities was the highest priority. He believed that only this could make India a casteless and classless society, without which the Constitution will become useless and purposeless.

It is to be understood that "creamy layer" principle has been evolved by the Supreme Court merely to exclude a section of a particular caste on the ground that they are economically advanced or educationally forward.

The author in Chapter 1 has meticulously traced the history of 'backward class' in India. Report of the 'Kaka Kalelkar Commission' and of 'Mandal Commission' has been correctly analyzed.

Constitutional provisions related to 'reservation' and judicial pronouncements have been critically discussed thoroughly. Aspect of 'creamy layer' and its implication has been properly highlighted by the author Dr. Pallavi Gupta. Author has been awarded a degree of doctorate on the topic.

DR. M. VEERAPPA MOILY

Preface

For long, people of backward classes have suffered at the hands of society at large. They have been marginalized by the dominant classes from the mainstream society and also marginalized as objects in a country rather than being treated as its subjects. They have been subjugated at every point in their life. In such circumstances they themselves started to believe that it was their destiny to lead a life full of miseries and degradation. In welfare, democratic, secular and socialist country like India, their statuses need to be uplifted. For this righteous purpose certain stern measures were required for their upliftment and to emancipate themselves further in the mainstream of the country. Accordingly serious and systematic efforts, like reservation in employment, education and political area, had been taken to give them a place into the mainstream of the nation and to overcome from their handicaps.

But Reservation Policy of Government in job and education under Constitutional commitment (also known as, quota system, positive discrimination, reverse discrimination, etc.) of India has resulted in fabulous collative aggression and in litigations. Pro- and anti-reservation stirs and movements have taken revolting figure in different parts of the country. The anti-reservation lists highlights the merit and efficiency theory and they argued from time to time that if any reservation is to be made, it should be on the basis of economic backwardness, not on the caste basis. At first, however, they assented for reservation to the Scheduled Castes and Scheduled Tribes only not to the Socially and Educationally Backward Classes. They argued that Reservation benefit to OBCs is to satisfy only political thrust (vote bank) not for Social Justice to the deprived person of the society and incorporation of the concept of creamy layer is just to cool down the heat of upper class. They further said that reservation, if any, should be given only in the initial stage of appointment not in promotion and benefit of reservation, as held in Indira Sawhney case-1, should be limited upto one generation of deserving candidate. They also want that reservation should be given only to really deserving and needy persons, therefore elite class among SCs and STs should also be excluded like exclusion of creamy layer among OBCs.

The pro-reservationists, on the other hand, argue that caste is a relevant criterion in the determination of backwardness and reservation benefit at promotional level is justified. They further argued that time has not come till yet to stop application of Reservation Policy and to apply the concept of creamy layer on SC/ST. They further said that benefit of reservation for OBCs in education and employment is an intelligent step.

This book relates to reservational justice to be ensured to the backward classes of the society and clinches various issues relating to reservational justice to the OBCs—as the creamy layer formula and other issues in Mandal case lay down for the benefit of deprived section of the society and to bring them back on the track as early as possible. Since reservation for OBCs in the Central Government Services had not been before March 1993 and it had been only for SCs/STs and therefore cases on different issues, though related to SCs/STs, have been discussed at length with a view that similar approach would prevail in cases of reservational justice to OBCs.

The scope of this book is limited to the relevancy of the reservation policy and the application of concept of creamy layer, in the present scenario of privatization and globalisation, the analysis of Constitutional guidelines and its interpretation by the judiciary, efforts of policy or law-maker as well as of the executives in the form of annexure and appendix and the effect of the implementation of reservation policy on the society over all. This book consists of analysis of the various approaches related to the existing reservation policy in India and enshrined recommendations of the Mandal Commission, Kaka Kalelkar Commission (backward commission) and Ramanandan Prasad Commission (on creamy layer). It elucidates the existing job reservation polices for the SCs, STs and OBCs in brief. Besides this, the Indian caste system, caste differences, and caste politics have been discussed at length. This study also comprises bunch of leading Judgments of Hon'ble Supreme Court on reservation issues.

This book provides comprehensive reading material and may initiate a popular and academic debate on the reservation policy in India. This book shall be useful for students, researchers, policy-makers and sociologists as well as academicians.

DR. PALLAVI GUPTA

Acknowledgements

Giving final touches to my book, a very profound sense of joy, contentment and happiness settled inside me and with that comes the subtle realization that how so many considerable people in their own unique ways have contributed to my foundation and have reached out to assist me to go through the completion of my work. I find it very difficult to express my gratitude and thanks in words to all of them, since words have their own limitations but I am sure that in my case they will certainly convey the hidden message of my deepest emotions and feelings. I fully acknowledge that without their support, cooperation and constant encouragement, it would have been just impossible for me to realize my work.

After the almighty, omniscient God, the person who deserves the highest credit for my small achievement is my teacher and well wisher Dr. Preeti Saxena, Head, Dept. of Human Rights Studies, Babasaheb Bhimrao Ambedkar University, Lucknow, for her suggestion and back-up from time-to-time and under whose blessing I could complete my work. I am greatly indebted to Professor (Dr.) S.K. Singh, Vice-chancellor Bhoj (Open) University, Bhopal, for his critical and constructive comments. Their incredible knowledge, immaculate hold over the topic helped me to remain focused and goal-oriented and at no time I found myself going astray or out of context. Therefore, it is my most privilege and foremost duty to express my sincere sense of gratitude to my teachers who have all along been a source of inspiration to me during my work. I have deep regard to the officials and librarians of Indian Law Institute, New Delhi, University of Lucknow, MJP Rohilkhand University, Bareilly, and Bundelkhand University, Jhansi, for their support.

I am thankful to Dr. M. Veerappa Moily, former Minister of Law and Justice, Government of India, for giving a Foreword to my book.

It has been possible to write down this book with the active co-operation and moral support of my husband Dr. Bahadur Singh, Ministry of Law and Justice, New Delhi, who helped me a lot during carrying out work and getting printout.

Last, but not the least, I am thankful to my parents, father Shri Jagadish Prasad Gupta and my mother Smt. Urmila Devi for their love and consistent moral support which inspired me to write this book.

I can not end this acknowledge without expressing my thanks and gratitude to my spiritual Guru Swami Brijanand for ethical support which makes me sturdy and never I feel frustrated during my work. I once again express my sincere sense of reverence to all who made it possible for me to achieve my goal.

My book has meant more to me than just an academic achievement, for me it is a dream come true, a humble aspiration long cherished in my heart finally finding a way out in the sun from the recesses of my heart.

DR. PALLAVI GUPTA

Quotations on the Talk of National Consensus on Reservation, its Objectives and Remedy

1. "A lot of heart burning was caused to the British when they left India. It burns the hearts of all whites when the blacks protest against apartheid in South Africa. When the higher castes constituting less than 20% of the country's population subjected the rest to all manner of social injustice, it must have caused a lot of heart burning to be lower castes. But now that the lower castes are asking for a modest share of the national cake of power and prestige, a chorus of alarm is being raised on the plea that this will cause heart burning to the ruling elite of all the spacious arguments advanced against reservation for backward classes; there is none which beats this one about 'heart burning' in sheer sophistry." (*Report of II B.C.C.*, Vol. I, Chapter XIII (13.8)
2. The Constitutional reservation is the effect and not cause of the social problem. Its root cause lies in unwritten reservation breeding higher caste aggrandizement at the cost of others. Remove the cause, the effect will itself wither away." (Ali Aor. S).

3. "In the Northern states the dominance of upper caste Hindus is so strong that such a policy has either died in its infancy or has to be abandoned in the face of strong opposition. In this context the so called national consensus is nothing but a play of the ruling upper caste elites". (*Ashim K. Roy,* Anti-reservation Movement, *EPW,* 10, 1995).
4. "The road of the abolition of Castes System in India is likely to lie in the caste action". *(Louis Dumot, Homo Hierarchicus,* Granada Publishing Ltd., London, 1972, p. 27).
5. "The compromise between anti-reservation and government on basis of consensus will mean that reservation will have no specific basis, but will be totally *adhoc* and arbitrary, based solely on the agreement among the "Dwijas" on the extent of consensus to be given to the backward castes." *(A.K. Roy,* "Anti-Reservation Movement", *Economic and Political Weekly,* Aug. 10, 1985).
6. "There is no sanction in the Constitution for applying economic criteria, either exclusively or primarily, for reservations. And there seems to be no escape from using caste as a primary criterion for reservations." *(D.L. Seth Reservation:* Changes in Elite Perception, *Financial Express,* June 16-18, 1986).

Abbreviations

Aca.L.R.	Academic Law Review
AIR	All India Reporter
All.	Allahabad
A.L.J.	Allahabad Law Journal
AW.C.	Allahabad Weekly Cases
A.P.	Andhra Pradesh
Art.	Article
B.C.	Backward Classes
B.C.C.	Backward Classes Commission
Bomb.	Bombay
CAD	Constituent Assembly Debates
Cal.	Calcutta
Col.	Column
Del.	Delhi
Doc.	Document
E.P.W.	Economic and Political Weekly
Ed.	Edition/Editor
GO.	Government Order
Gau.	Guwahati
H.P.	Himachal Pradesh
ILR	Indian Law Report
IBR	Indian Bar Review
J.I.L.I.	Journal of the Indian Law Institute

J. and K.	Jammu and Kashmir
Kant.	Karnataka
Ker.	Kerala
Mad.	Madras
M.B.	Madhya Bharat
M.P.	Madhya Pradesh
Mys.	Mysore
N.Y.T	New York Times
Ori.	Orissa
OBCs	Other Backward Classes
P.	Page
PP.	Pages
P. and H.	Punjab and Haryana
Punj.	Punjab
Raj.	Rajasthan
RCSCST	Report of the Commissioner for Scheduled Castes and Scheduled Tribes
Res.	Resolution
S.	Section
Ss	Sections
SCs	Scheduled Castes
SC	Supreme Court
SCC	Supreme Court Cases
SEBC	Socially and Educationally Backward Classes
STs	Scheduled Tribes
U.P.	Uttar Pradesh
U.S.	United States
Vol.	Volume
W.B.	West Bengal

Introduction

Country like India is regarded as a model of pluralistic society, which is reflected in its cultural pluralism of various religions, castes, languages and regions. Its plurality is visible in the four-fold Varna system (Brahmin, Kshatriya Vaishya and Shudra) and about 5,000 castes and sub-castes. Now, the segmental aspects of traditional four-fold Varna system is reflected in terms of four major caste groups created by the modern participatory democratic, political system such as the Scheduled Castes (SCs: 16.73%), the Scheduled Tribes (STs: 7.95%), Other Backward Classes (OBCs: estimated to be 52% according to census of 1931) and the rest regarded as upper castes or forward classes called general category (estimated 23%).

In India social, educational and economic inequalities have existed from time immemorial in different social segments of the society. Early Vedic society was a casteless and classless society. But with the Brahminical culture, caste system came and priests were its strongest supporter. The evil of caste system has been that, "hitherto for centuries, there have been cent percent reservations in practice in all fields, in favour of high castes and classes, to the total exclusion of others. It was a purely caste and class-based reservation". The Scheduled Castes, Scheduled Tribes and Other Backward Classes (broadly known as deprived and downtrodden classes) represent those social groups, suffered through the ages due to caste prejudices, economic inequality, educational backwardness and lagging behind in the field of educational and economic development in comparison to certain advance or the forward castes. To minimize these social, educational, economical as well as political deprivations several provisions have been incorporated in Indian Constitution to safeguard and promoting the interests in various spheres so as to enable them to join the national mainstream alongwith the provision of equality before the law and prohibition of discrimination on grounds of race, religion and caste.[1]

PHILOSOPHY OF RESERVATION

To eradicate the present social, educational and economic disparities caused by purposeful societal discrimination in the past, reservation policy thought to be inevitable and justified for deprived person to give them justice. Therefore, the Constitution of India authorize the state to adopt such affirmative action in the form of reservation, as it deems necessary to uplift the backward classes of citizens to levels of equality with the rest of the countrymen. In the past, the backward classes of citizens have been denied access to government services on account of their inability to struggle effectively in open selections on the basis of merit. It is, therefore opens to the government to reserve a certain number of seats in places of learning and public services in favour of the Scheduled Castes and the Scheduled Tribes and now for Other Backward classes also, to the exclusion of all others, irrespective of merit.[2]

RESERVATION FOR SCs AND STs

Tracing the history of reservation policy, one finds that as for as in 1934 the Government of India issued instruction to give a fair percentage of representation to the *depressed classes*. Since this effort of the Government of India did not yield the desired result, they reviewed the whole issue and passed orders in 1943 to keep 8.33 per cent of the posts reserved for these communities. This percentage was increased to 12.5 per cent in 1946. After independence of India, the whole policy of reservation was laid down by the Government of India in 1950 in pursuance of the prerequisite of Article 16(4), read with Article 335 of the Constitution of India, providing therein reservation of 12.5 per cent of vacancies for Scheduled Castes and 5 per cent of vacancies for Scheduled Tribes. These percentages of reservation were subsequently enhanced in 1970 to 15 per cent and 7.5 per cent for Scheduled Castes and Scheduled Tribes respectively.[3] As displayed in Tables A, B and C.

IMPORTANT ASPECTS OF RESERVATIONS

1. Direct Recruitment

(a) The date of orders/notification and the percentages of reservation Direct Recruitment as fixed are indicated below:

TABLE A

Date of Order	*Recruitment by*	
	Open Competition	*Otherwise*
21.9.47	12-1/2%	16-2/3%
13.9.50	12-1/2%	16-2/3%
25.3.70	15%	7-1/2%

Source : Brochure on Reservation and Concessions for SCs/STs/OBCs, Nabhi Publication, New Delhi, 2004, p. 3.

(b) Normally the reservation is provided according to percentage of population of SCs/STs to the total population at All India level as decided by population census. Hence after every census the reservation rates are expected to be revised.

2. Promotion

The developments in reservation in case of different modes of promotion are indicated in Table B.

TABLE B

Year	Development
1957 4.1.57	The Reservations, for SC & ST in departmental competitive examination was provided.
1963 6.11.63	Reservations in limited departmental examinations to Group B', 'C' and 'D' were provided subjected to a condition that direct recruitment (DR) should not exceed 50%.
1968	Reservations in promotion by seniority-*cum*-fitness was provided subject to the condition that DR does not exceed 50%.
1972 2.11.72	Reservations in promotion by selection from Group 'C' and Group 'B' within Group 'B' and from Group 'B' to lowest rank of Group 'A' were introduced provided the element of Direct Recruitment does not exceed 50%.
1974 20.7.74	The limit on DR was raised from 50% to 66-2/3%.
1976 1989	The limit on DR was raised to 75%
1992	The Supreme Court in Indira Sawhney's case permitted the reservation to continue for a period of 5 years w.e.f. 16.11.92
1997	Article 16(4-A) was incorporated to continue reservations in promotion beyond 15.11.97 were issued on 13.8.97.
2001	Article (4A) amended to provide retention of seniority acquired by SC/ST employees on promotion by virtue of reservation roster.
2005	Article 15(5) was inserted to give reservation in educational institutions for SCs, STs, & OBCs even in unaided-aided educational institutions.
2008	The Supreme Court in Ashok Kumar Thakur's case permitted 27% reservation for OBCs in central educational institution.

Source : Brochure on Reservation and Concessions for SCs/STs/OBCs, Nabhi Publication, New Delhi, 2004, p. 3.

3. Present Percentages of Reservation given in Table C

TABLE C

Mode of Payment	*Percentage fixed for SC*	*Percentage fixed for ST*
I. Direct recruitment on All India basis:	15%	7-1/2%
(a) By open competition (i.e. through UPSC or by means of open competitive test held by any other authority. Otherwise than at (a) above		
II. Direct recruitment to Group C and Group D posts normally attracting candidates from a locality or region	16-2/35—in proportion to the population of SC and ST in the respective States/Union territories	7.1/25—in proportion to the population of SC and ST in the respective States/Union territories
III. Posts filled by promotion in grades or services in which the element of direct recruitment, if any, does not exceed 75%.		
(a) Through limited departmental competitive examination in Groups B, C and D.	15%	7-1/2%
(b) By Selection from Group B to the lowest rung or category in Group A or Groups B, C and D.	15%	15%
(c) On the basis of seniority subject to fitness in Groups A, B, C and D.	15%	15%

Source : Brochure on Reservation and Concessions for SCs/STs/OBCs, Nabhi Publication, N, Delhi, 2004, p. 4.

The State Governments have also passed laws, and issued orders for providing reservation in favour of Scheduled Castes and Scheduled Tribes in services under their control. In the meantime, many concessions and relaxations, including reservation in promotion, etc. have been provided by the Government of India and as well as by the State Governments, to the Scheduled Castes and Scheduled Tribes in services.[4]

The comparative picture of the representation of the SCs/STs in the ministries/departments/officers of the Government of India from 1953 to 1992 is being displayed in Table D.

TABLE D
Representation of SCs and STs in Central Government Service : 1953-92

Year	*Scheduled Castes*				*Scheduled Tribes*			
	CLI	*CLII*	*CLIII*	*CLIV*	*CLI*	*CLII*	*CLIII*	*CLIV*
1953	0.35	1.29	4.52	20.52	0.70	0.24	0.57	1.80
1965	1.64	2.62	8.88	17.75	0.27	0.34	1.14	3.39
1970	2.36	3.84	9.27	18.09	0.40	0.37	1.47	3.59
1975	3.43	4.98	30.71	I8.64	0.62	0.39	2.27	3.99
1979	4.75	7.37	12.3	19.32	0.94	1.03	3.11	5.19
1980	4.83	8.07	11.54	19.16	1.04	1.24	3.04	5.30
1992	9.70	11.60	1530	20.70	2.90	2.40	3.20	6.70

Source : Department of Personnel, Government of India, Report, 1993.

Thus the percentage of representation of the Scheduled Castes and Schcduled Tribes has increased uniformly in all classes from 1953 to 1992. However, it has not reached the prescribed percentage of reservation in Class I and Class II for Scheduled Castes and in all classes for Scheduled Tribes till 1992 although attempts have been made to fill the backlog vacancies.

RESERVATION FOR OBCs

The term 'Other Backward Classes' refers specially to those backward groups other than SCs and STs who are educationally and socially backward in the society. Similarly, some include among backward castes those who are far below the upper cluster, some to those who are just above SCs and STs and some refer to middle cluster of caste hierarchy as backwards.[5] For their upliftment or advancement different states have their own classification of backward class categories, in the same way, to give concession to the right community from backward classes. Karnataka has distinguished between 'backward' and 'more backward', while Bihar and Kerala have made 'backward' and 'most backward'. Such differences are not made by the Government of India.[6] Because of the fact that the Central Government and different State Governments have their own definitions and lists of backward castes, the difference in their population at all-India level seems to be natural. The census of 1951 had estimated the total OBCs population as 18.9 per cent (69 million) of the country's total population. The Planning Commission (1951) had assessed them approximately 20 per cent. According to the Kaka Kalelkar Commission (1953), the total population of the OBCs in India was 31.8 per cent, whereas the Mandal Commission calculated 52 per cent of India's population as OBCs on the basis of census of 1931.

Population data of Scheduled Castes, Scheduled Tribes, Other Backward Classes and Forward Castes[7]

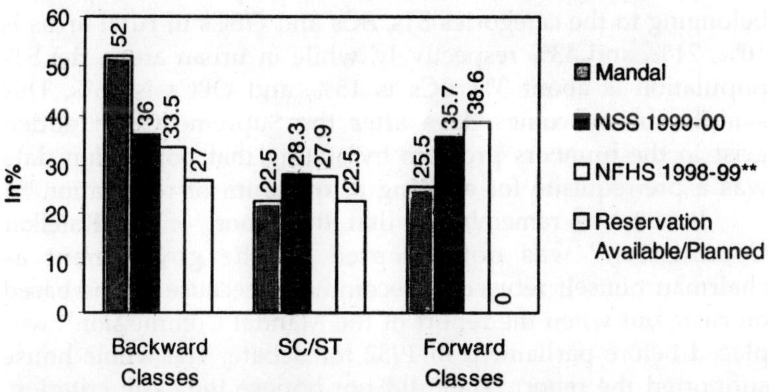

**NFHS Survey estimated only Hindu OBC population. Total OBC population derived by assuming Muslim OBC population in same proportion as Hindu OBC population, SC/ST.

Only SC/ST population details are collected in Indian census. The SC/ST population is 24.4%. After 1931, caste data is not collected for non-SC/ST caste-groups in census. Mandal Commission estimated OBC population based on 1931 census as 52%. There is an ongoing controversy about the estimation logic used by Mandal Commission for calculating OBC population. Famous psephologist and researcher, Dr. Yogendra Yadav of the CSDS [who is a known votary of Affirmative Action] agrees that there is no empirical basis to the Mandal figure.[8]

In 1998 Central Government conducted large nationwide survey for the first time to estimate economical and educational status of various social groups. The National Sample Survey (NSS) puts the figure at 32%. There is substantial debate over the exact number of OBCs in India, with census data compromised by partisan politics. It is generally estimated to be sizable, but lower than the figures quoted by either the Mandal Commission or/and National Sample Survey. Mandal Commission has been criticised of fabricating the data. National surveys indicated that status of OBCs is comparable to Forward castes in many areas.[9]

In 2006 (NSSO) National Sample Survey Organization Survey has claimed that OBCs form 41% of the country's total population. It has quoted OBCs figures at 43% in rural and 36% in urban areas. It claims that proportion of persons belonging to the categories STs, SCs and OBCs in rural areas is 10%, 21%, and 43% respectively, while in urban areas, the STs population is about 3%, SCs is 15%, and OBCs is 36%. This sample survey comes days after the Supreme Court added grist to the numbers problem by stating that population data was a pre-requisite for arriving at quantum of reservation.[10]

It is to be remembered that the report of the Kalelkar Commission[11] was not accepted by the government as chairman himself refused to recommend because it was based on caste but when the report of the Mandal Commission[12] was placed before parliament in 1982 for debate. The whole house supported the report. They did not oppose the caste criterion. The decision to implement the recommendations was a political one. The then Prime Minister and other politicians had taken note of anti-reservation agitations in different parts of the country and were trying to avoid them with the help of national consensus. Thus the matter was left undecided for ten years.

In August 13, 1990, the Government of India issued an Office Memorandum purporting to extend reservations for socially and educationally backward classes (SEBCs now called OBCs) in its services. Accordingly said memorandum reserved 27% of the seats for OBCs in addition to those already reserved for SC and STs.[13] Reservation was to apply in direct recruitment. SEBCs recruited on merit in open competition were not to be compromise castes and communities common to the state-wise lists in the Mandal Commission report and State Government lists. Reservation was extended to public sector undertakings and financial institutions including public sector banks.

The issuance of this memorandum led to widespread protests, self-immolations by the youth. Writ petitions were filed in the Supreme Court questioning the said memorandum. A three judge bench of the Supreme Court comprising *Chief Justice Ranganathan Mishra, Justice K.N. Singh and Justice M.H. Kania*, reviewed its order of September 11, 1990, and refused to interfere on the ground that the matter was a political one. Another petition on behalf of the Supreme Court Bar Association was moved and a five-judge bench of the Supreme Court stayed by its order dated October 1, 1990 the operation of the memorandum dated August 13, 1990 till final adjudication.[14]

In the first half of 1990, a Constitutional bench of the Supreme Court sought to know the clear stand of the new government on the issue. The government indicated its intention to implement the memorandum of August 13, 1990 with certain modifications which it did by issuing another memorandum on September 25, 1991 modifying the earlier one by: (i) introducing the economic: criterion in grant of reservation by giving preference to the poorer sections of the SEBCs in the 27% quota, and (ii) reserving another 10 percent of the vacancies in the civil services for other economically backward sections not covered by any of the existing schemes of reservation which was explained to extend to the poorest among the higher castes and other religions also. The economic criterion was to be specified separately.[15]

The constitutionality of this memorandum was also challenged and a nine-judge bench constituted to hear the matter arising out of it. The economic criterion not having been fixed, the bench by its order of December 12, 1991 rejected to vacate the earlier stay for implementation of the memorandum. The Constitutional special bench of nine-judges became necessary to finally settle the legal position relating to reservations in view of the several earlier judgments of the Supreme Court. Similar questions also arose in respect of implementation of State Commissions Report like those in 1992 which were also directed to the Constitutional bench. *The bench found reservation for OBCs as Constitutionally valid, but asked for the exclusion of creamy-layer from its benefit.*

The Supreme Court, in its majority judgment (six out of nine judges) on November 16, 1992, held the memorandum issued by the Government of India on August 13, 1990, providing for 27% reservation for SEBCs in central civil services and posts, to be valid subject to exclusion of socially advanced persons/sections (creamy-layer) from other backward classes. The Supreme Court also decreed Clause (ii) of memorandum of September 25, 1991 providing for reservation for other economically backward sections as invalid and inoperative on the ground that reservation on the basis of economic criterion is unconstitutional.

In the context of the Supreme Court's direction regarding exclusion of socially advanced persons/sections from OBCs, the Government of India constituted an *expert committee headed by Justice R.N. Prasad* (Retd.) and three other members comprising a social scientist and two officers with wide administrative experience, to recommend the bases to be specified by the Union Government *for exclusion of 'creamy layer' from OBCs.* The committee submitted its report on March 10, 1993 and the same has been accepted by the Government of India.[16] As per the judgment of the Supreme Court, a common list of castes/communities based on castes included in the Mandal Commission report and those included in the respective state list has been finalized. The R.N. Prasad Committee defined *creamy-layer as when a person has been able to shed off the attributes of social and educational backwardness and has secured employment or has engaged himself in some trade/ profession of high status . . . at that stage he is normally no longer in need of reservation for himself.*[17]

On the basis of the Supreme Court judgment and recommendations of Mandal Commission, a fresh reservation order was issued on September 8, 1993 for 27% reservation for OBCs.[18] It seems the OBCs have achieved social justice in the field of public employment after a long battle.

In 2005 when CJI Lohati in *P.A. Inamdar and Others* v. *State of Maharashtra and Others* laid down that reservation policy could not be implemented in private (unaided) educational institutions because we have no law or constitutional provision regarding this. To nullify this judgement parliament has amended the constitution and added Article 15(5) through The Constitutional (Ninety-third) Amendment Act, 2005, to provide reservation to backward classes in education institutions including private educational institutions and to enable states to make law regarding this.

It is noticeable that the Supreme Court in its judgment on November 15, 1992 upheld the reservation policy on caste basis. However in some other cases the Supreme Court has put a cap on reservations by providing that reservations cannot exceed 50% (which it would violate equal access guaranteed by the Constitution). However, there are some State laws which exceed this 50% limit and these are under litigation in the Supreme Court. For example, the caste-based reservation fraction stands at 69% and is applicable to about 87% of the population in the state of Tamil Nadu.[19]

In 2006, parliament enacted The Central Educational Institutions (Reservation in Admission) Act, 2006, to provide reservation for OBCs including creamy layer, in central educational institutions. There was huge opposition across the country and the validity of this Act was challenged in Supreme Court. On April 10, 2008 Supreme Court in *Ashoke Kumar Thakur* v. *Union of India* case upheld the validity of reservation in central educational institutions but excluding creamy layer.

The questions to be discussed today, therefore, are: Is reservation policy, or protective discrimination to backward classes of citizens logical and the useful strategy to ensure justice and equal opportunity to the economically exploited and socially oppressed groups?, Has Supreme Court rightly laid down principle of Concept of creamy layer which found no place in the Indian Constitution?, Is Supreme Court having power to make policy decisions to be imposed on government.

This book is pursuing to study the relevancy of reservation policy even after the 63 year of independence in the era of globalisation and to provide clarification or solutions for several questions arose in my mind, for example—Whether reservation policy has been proved to be winner for achieving its object? Is reservation policy implementing in true sense in various educational institutions as well as in Government services ? Whether benefits of reservation policy are reaching to really needy and deserving deprived applicants? Whether concept of creamy layer could be justified under Indian Concept? Whether this concept of creamy layer should apply on SC/ST also, whether reservation in promotion for SC/ST is justified while it is not available to OBCs? What is the effect of reservation policy on backward society as well as on forward society? What should be the degree or extent of reservation? Whether reservation in services as well as in education institutions should be for ever? With these several quarries I perused to write my book.

References

1. Shyama Nand Singh, "Election and Party Politics in India" in K.L. Kamal (ed. 1944), whither Indian Politics, Printwell (Jaipur), p. 187.
2. Indira Sawhney *versus* Union of India, Supreme Court Judgment, 16 November 1992.
3. Report of the Commission for Scheduled Caste and Scheduled Tribes, Government of India, 1981, p. 227.
4. Shyama Nand Singh, Reservation: Problems and Prospects, Uppal Publications, New Delhi, 1991.
5. Marc Galanter, Competing Equalities; Law and the Backward Classes in India, Oxford (Delhi), 1984, p. 155 and also Law and Society in Modern India, (1992).
6. Shyama Nand Singh, "Background: Reservation Controversy in Andhra Pradesh", *Mainstream*, September 1986, p. 3.
7. www.wikipedia.org.

8. *Ibid.*
9. *Ibid.*
10. November 1, 2006, *Times of India.*
11. Report of the first Backward Classes Commission, of India (Chairman, Kaka Kalelkar), Government of India, 1955, p. vii.
12. Report of the Second Backward Classes Commission, of India (Chairman, B.P. Mandal), Government of India, 1980, p. 58.
13. Office Memorandum of Ministry of Personnel, Government of India, 13 August, 1990.
14. *Indian Express* (New Delhi), 2nd October 1990.
15. Office Memorandum of Ministry of Personnel, Government of India, 25 September 1991.
16. Report of the Expert Committee for specifying the criteria for Identification of Socially Advanced Persons among the Socially and Educationally Backward Classes, (Chairman, R.N. Prasad), Ministry of Welfare, Government of India, 10th March 1993.
17. *Ibid.*, No. 2, p. 472.
18. *Times of India* (New Delhi), February 21, 1994.
19. www.wikipedia.org.

1

History of Backward Class

"Reservations do not perpetuate caste. They destroy its ugly manifestations."

Ramjethmalani, Mandal Revisited IBR
Vols. 17 and 18 (1991) 393 at p. 396

Expression 'Backward Class', which stand for three different categories of castes in 20th century such as Scheduled Castes (SCs), Scheduled Tribes (STs) and Other Backward Classes (OBCs) was used for the first time in 19th century. These three groups in some extent symbolize the fourth Varna (Shudra) and fifth class of ancient Varna System or Caste System. They are considered as socially pedestrian to the first three Varnas, viz. Brahmins, Kshatriyas and Vaishyas. Their low-grade social status pilots to their educational and economic backwardness for centuries and generation after generation.

To comprehend the philosophy, social structure and history of Backward Class it is necessary to sketch out the history of origin of Cast System in India. The History of Backward Class of India, therefore, can be divided into three periods:

(a) Ancient period,
(b) Medieval period, and
(c) Modern period.

HISTORY OF BACKWARD CLASS IN ANCIENT PERIOD OF INDIA

In ancient India 'Caste system' was a legal system[1] and has survived just due to prevention of the masses from the possession of the arms and denying to the masses, the right to property, etc. Caste system was, even now, considered to be divine institution, which support the functional division of the society, and that have exited since the beginning of the society. Evidence shows that in North India before 5000 B.C. Indus valley civilization was in existence and that time society was divided into two classes i.e. Dominant (ruler) class and labour class which were called latter Dasyus as one can found in ancient Vedic literature.

In early Rigvedic period—society was divided into three distinct orders of men; Brahman or priest, Rajan or Kshatriya or noble, Vaishya or tiller of the soil, and Shudra or the service class came into existence as fourth class in Vedic period. There was a great difference between the three and the last. The former are said to be the conquering Aryans and the latter the conquered Shudra or Dasyus. Regarding the manner of the creation of the caste, different stories are prevalent. The most common story, found in the *Purusha Sukta;*[2] *tenth mandal of Rig-Veda* is that, all the four castes are originated from *LORD BRAHMA*, the Supreme Being. The Brahmans came from his mouth, Kshatriya from his arm, Vaishya from his thighs and *the Shudras from his feet*. In the period of *Yajur Vedas and the Brahmans*, the division of the Aryan society is found into four classes with distinct functions. In the *Satapata Brahmana, Taittiriya Brahmana, Vajaseneya Sanhita and the Atharva Veda* account of the origin of the three castes is given as—they sprung from the Vedas. The *Sama Veda* is the source from which the Brahmans sprang. *Yajur Veda* is the womb from which the Kshatriyas were born. And the Vaishya Class was produced from the Rich Verses.[3]

In this period, the first two classes Brahman, Kshatriya were represented broadly the two professions of the poet-priest and the warrior-chief. The third division—Vaishya, was apparently a group comprising all the common people.[4] The reference of four orders (Brahman, Rajan, Vaishya, and Shudra) of the society is available only in the later hymns. The particular limbs associated with these divisions and the order in which they are mentioned, indicate their status in the society of the time.[5] The Brahmans were acknowledged to be the chief, the Rajans as vigorous, Vaishyas as meant to be eaten and the Shudras were considered as servant class. This particular description of the creation not only was the origin of the classes interpreted theologically, but also a divine justification, was sought to be given to their functions and status. God was said to have created certain deities simultaneous with these classes. In the 'Human Sacrifice' the representatives of these orders were dedicated to different deities.[6] But no deities were created along with the Shudra and they were disqualified for sacrifice. Here the social regulation which forbade a Shudra to offer sacrifice was explained as an incidental consequence of the creation.[7]

These classes or orders are repeatedly referred to in later literature as *Varna* popularly known in Hindu religion as *Varnashrama dharma*. Yet in the Rigveda the word *'varna'* is never applied to any one of these classes. While in *Satapata Brahmana* four Classes are described as the four *Varnas*.[8] Initially *'Varna'* means *'colour'*, and was employed in contrasting the Arya and the Dasyu referring to their fair and dark colours respectively and later on, four different colours were assigned to the four classes, by which their members were supposed to be distinguished. Thus Rigvedic literature stresses very strongly the difference between the Arya and the Dasyu, not only in their colour but also in their speech, religious practices and physical features. By the end of this period, this difference appears to have acquired almost all the characteristics of a caste.[9] The first order, Brahman was said to be superior and declared to be God on earth. The second order in the society, the Kshatriya, was known in the later section of Rigveda as the Rajanya. Usually this class is represented as inferior to the Brahmin.[10] Third order in the society was

Vaishya. In comparison with the higher classes, the 'Vaishyas' position was rather insignificant, but marked-off from the Shudra. The name of the fourth class, the Shudra, occurs *only once* in the Rigveda. *This class represented as domestic servants very nearly to the position of slaves. He is described as "the servant of another", "to be expelled at will", and "to be slain at will".*[11] *He is declared to be unfit for sacrifice and not allowed even to be stand in the hall where the sacrifice was being offered. He is untruth itself.*[12]

Besides these four orders, Rigveda mentioned other occupations also like *Blacksmith, leather-worker, barber, physician, goldsmith, merchant, and chariot-builder* which were acknowledged as independent castes or sub-castes.[13] Four other names were also found in the Vedic literature, viz. *Ayogava, Chandala, Niashada, and Paulkasa* and these names often referred to fifth class in the society. The word *'Ayogava'* represents the name of mixed castes. The references of the *Chandala in* Yajurveda *showed to be degraded people*. In next period, Chandala were described as the offspring of a Shudra father and a Brahmin mother. In the *Brihadaranyaka Upanishad* the Paulkasa and Chandala were referred to as *a despised race of men*. Chandala and Paulkasa were sections of the *aborigines who were particularly despised* by the Aryans. *Shudras were systematically debarred from the religious practices of the Aryans.* Here the ideas of *untouchability* were first given literary expression in connection with the Shudra, or fifth class and the sacrifice. There were various inequalities in the matter of religious practices between the other three classes. *Shudras and above mentioned fifth class were denied any justice.*[14]

Purans[15] repeats the same story of origin of caste system but in different version as mentioned in Purusha Sukta. The *Vayu Purana* educates that a thousand pairs of these different castes were formed at once. As Brahma was meditated upon offspring, he created from his mouth a thousand couples of living being who were born with abundantness of goodness, and full of intelligence. He than created another thousand from his breast; they abounded in passion, and were both vigorous and destitute of vigour. After creating from his thighs another pairs in whom both passion and darkness were prevailed, who were descried as active, be formed from his feet yet another thousand pairs, who were full of darkness, disgraceful, and of little vigour'. The *Vishnu Purana* makes the distinction of castes to be the product of character. According to the *Sage Parasera*, "when Brahma became keen to create the world, creatures in whom goodness prevailed sprang from the mouth; others, in whom both passion and darkness were strong, proceeded from his thighs; others created from his feet, whose characteristic was darkness. Another *Purna* text affirmed that owing to character and conduct of the castes in later years men were sub-divided by Brahma.

In the *Krita age*[16] there was no distinctions of Castes. But in *Treata age* they were born again as *Brahma, Kshatriyas, Vaishyas and Shudras. Svayambhu* established division amongst according to their tendencies. Those who were rapacious ordained to be Kshatriyas, protectors of the others. Those who attended on these, speaking the truth and propounding sacred knowledge with exactness were made Brahmans. Those who were previously engaged in slaughter and cultivators of the ground, made Vaishyas; *and those who were addicted to menial tasks, designated as Shudras.*

Narration in the *Ramayana*[17] teaches that the four castes were the offspring of a woman named Manu, the wife of the Kasyapa, a son of Brahma. From an examination of the legends, it is seen that the accounts vary. It is important to note that statements in the *Srauta-Sutra of Drahyana* and in the *Puranas* regarding the function of priests and warriors proved that from the Vedic period to the middle of the Buddhist period, the four-fold division represented *only classes.*

Buddhist literature Jtakas,[18] a collection of folk-tales presents an account of Hindu society. The colour distinction has faded into the background, though it remains with the word *Varna,* used for the social classes namely, Kshatriya, Brahman, Vaishya and Shudra. Here the Kshatriya, heads the list, the Brahman is held in status inferior to the Kshatriya nobility. The Varnas have not yet become castes. The birth qualification has not yet developed to make them close corporations. Vaishyas and Shudras rise to the rank of Kshatriya. Anybody can become a Brahman by becoming a priest there was no endogamous restriction; a Brahman marries a Kshatriya widow. Marriage within the clan was considered preferable to marriage outside it. But the social convention stands in the way of the latter.[19] Below the Varnas there were *hina jatyo, low tribes, of barbers potter or weavers, a remnant of the Dasyus tribes on the outskirts of civilization. The lowest of all are the Chandalas and other outcaste tribes.*[20]

In the Post-Vedic period the Brahminical literature mentions *certain mixed castes (sankara jati) and also a group of outcaste classes (antyavasayin).*[21] Among the four Varnas, the old distinction of Arya and Shudra now appears as *dvija and Shudra*. The first three Vernas were called Divas (twice-born) because they have to go through the initiation ceremony, which was symbolic of rebirth. This privilege was denied to the Shudra who is therefore called *'ekajati'* (once-born).[22] The theory of rebirth was sought to be employed as a sanction for certain rules conduct. The Varna System was deeply rooted in the social life of the people and the poisonous tree of Caste System was growing day-by-day. Whole society was divided into various factions and the practice of discrimination by caste system was in vogue. The word *Jati* is used for Varna but here more often used for the meaning of sub-divisions of the Varna.[23] *In this period the degradation of the Shudras comes out in marked contrast to the growing superiority of the Brahmins.*[24] *It is clear from the data that the Shudra could not perform a sacrifice, could not listen to or recite the Vedic texts nor could be practice austerities. He was categorically denied the right of initiation and consequently the first stage of individual life (ashrama).*[25]

The *Mahabharata* says that the *Shudra can't have absolute property, because his wealth can be appropriated by his master at will.*[26] *If Shudra trying to hear the Vedic texts his ears shall be filled with molten tin or lac; if he recites the Veda his tongue shall be cut off, and if he remembers it he shall be dismembered. If he assumes a position of equality with twice-born men either in sitting, conversing, or going along the road, he shall receive corporal punishment.*[27] *If a Shudra committing adultery with women of the first three castes, shall suffer capital punishment, or shall be burnt alive tied up in straw,*[28] *sometimes shall have his organ cut off and his property confiscated. If he intentionally reviles twice-born men or criminally assaults them, the limb with which he offends shall be cut off.*[29] *It means Shudras had no civil or religious rights.*[30] Theoretically the position of the Shudras was very low, but some evidences show that many of them were well to do[31]. Some of them succeeded in marrying their daughters in royal families. Sumitra, wife of Dasharatha among four wives (Ramayana), was Shudra.[32] In *Mahabharata,* Satyavati wife of Shantanu was daughter of fisherman. Renowned Chandragupta Maurya is known to be a Shudra.[33]

Thus the theories of the divine origin of the four castes were off on repeated with special stress on the origin of the Shudra from the feet of the Creator. However, the Buddhist religions declare that Brahmin, Kshatriya, Vaishya, Shudra and Chandala would be equal in the world of the God.[34]

Great *grammarian Patanjali* applied word 'Jati' to such ethnic groups as the Abhiras. *Shudra too was a 'Jati.'* It seems that other Groups than the four traditional ones were not only in existence but had come to be recognized as 'Jatis'.[35] *Many of the sub-divisions within each Varna had rules of their own for their internal management.*[36] Mixed caste and out castes were also mentioned, but their status in the eye of law and morals was not clearly defined.[37]

Buddhist literatures prove that in this period, Shudras generally were regarded as so low that their food might not be accepted by Brahmin.[38] *The idea that impure persons (outcasted people and Chandalas) impart pollution by their touch and even by their near approach to a member of the first three castes, finds description in law text of this period.*[39]

Patanjali's grammar imparts us the valuable information that the Chandalas were considered to be a variety of Shudra. They were the *'apapatra Shudra'* or simply 'apapatras' a term later used by Manu also about the Chandala. *They were outcaste only as for as the use of their vessels by member of the twice-born orders was concerned is explicitly stated.*[40] This information was corroborated by *Kautilya* in later century.

Some times Dharma Sutra writers designated Chandalas from Shudras. But almost always they were exhorted to be treated like dogs and outcastes.[41] *The outcastes are to live by themselves as a community, teaching each other and marrying among themselves.* Association[42] with them by pure men was prohibited on pain of ex-communication. It *seems that the ideas of pollution had progressed further. Continued use of the water in a well by the Shudras rendered it unfit for religious purpose.*[43]

The lawgiver looks upon marriage in one's own caste among the four orders as the most ideal.[44] The union of higher males and lower female was generally allowed but the unions of males of lower castes with females of higher castes were treated as no marriages at all.[45] *As a matter of fact, the Kauravas and the Pandavas, the heroes of the Mahabharata were represented as the descendants of the line of Satyavati. Though the Kshatriyas were willing to marry females of lower castes and bring up the progeny as their equals, yet they could not tolerate their daughters marrying men of faulty descent. Thus Draupadi at her choice-marriage raised an objection against Karna on the ground of his low birth.* Chandalas—the untouchable and unapproachable class of this period—were represented as the issue of the union of the Shudra male with a Brahmin female.[46]

The information regarding the various classes of Shudras furnished by the Patanjali is very significant. He recognized at least *five varieties of Shudras; First,* Shaka or Yavanas who resided outside Aryavarta, *second,* Chandalas or Domes who resided within the limits of towns but whose food could not be used by the Aryans, *third,* groups like the carpenters, the washermen, the blacksmiths, *fourth,* the weavers whose food could be used by the Aryans, *fifth,* Shudras by implication who could attend sacrificial session and rituals.[47]

In Mauryan period, *Megasthenes,*[48] ambassador in the court of Chandragupta in 300 B.C. analyzed the social system of that day in his literatures. His work present the classification of the people of his day into seven groups viz-the philosophers, the husbandmen, the herdsmen and hunters, the traders and labours, the fighting men, the overseers, the councilors, the judges and administrators. From the above list Brahmans and Kshatriyas are easily identified. The third and fourth groups include Vaishyas and Shudras. Fourth group would include all the guilds of armourers and shipbuilders. The sixth and the seventh groups refer to professional classes. According to *Strabo's*[49] version, "no one is allowed to marry out of his caste or to exchange one profession for another or to follow more than one business, but an exception is made in the case of philosopher". Nevertheless there were violations. During the period between 300 B.C. and 300 A.D. information regarding development of caste is rather scanty. In this period, several invasions of the Sakas, the Yavanas, the Pahlavas and the Kushan were occurred. They left their mark on the Hindu society.[50]

In the early Gupta period[51] (330-450A.D.) Institution of Manu and the chief Purans presented that the Brahmans and Kshatriyas; the sacerdotal and ruling or military castes respectively, are shown as occupational. The Vaishya and Shudra castes are identical probably with trading, industrial and menial classes. Manu's Institution also contains the *Vratya and Vrishala* castes. These castes were the degenerate descendants of the twice-born classes who have neglected to perform the prescribed rites. *These Vratya and Vrishala castes means Khasa, Drivita, Yavana, Saka, Pahlava and China, names of many aboriginal tribes and races; that have partly and wholly merged in the then Hindu tribes and castes. Many tribal castes sprung from foreign invaders, after their adoption of Hinduism.* In this connection, it must be remembered that many of the invaders were barbarous, and their manners and customs would have repugnant to the Hindus.

During the whole Vedic period among the Chaturverna, Brahmans were officiated as priest to the head of the family, the sole master of religious ceremonial, further got supremacy as philosopher and acquired temporal power. In the early Buddhist period the Kshatriyas were become socially supreme. In Manu's account, again supremacy passed to the Brahmans. Till the middle of seventh century A.D. position of Kshatriyas turn out to be low and this lead an opportunity to the Brahmans to increase their authority. Under the Gupta dynasty Brahmans culture was widely diffused but later on both temporally and spiritually revived.

Term 'Visha' or 'Clans' of Vedic period subsequently known as 'Vaishyas'; third classical caste.[52] Expression Vaishya signifies a man who occupies the soil, a cultivator or a merchant. In the Buddhist period Vaishyas and Shudras were not to be found as pure castes, nor did they represents groups anywhere. No particular professional castes belong to either Dasyu Verna or Shudra Verna, were mentioned. The real distinction exited only in the Vedic period. In the early Buddhist period term 'Gahapati' or 'gahapat' referring to landowning and mercantile class, which ranked below

Kshatriya and Brahmans were found gradually the Vaishyas underwent a kind of social degradation. Division of the four castes appeared in the post-Vedic literature does not continue on the same line. There were two groups, one composed of the three higher castes, the other of the Shudras or the lowest. The higher caste constituted the fraternity to which admission was obtained only by religious ceremony of initiation and investment of the sacred thread. *The Shudras were excluded, and take no part in sacrifice. The Shudras were ordained not to wear the sacred thread. Chandalas were the sub-division of Shudras. These Chandalas were the most despised of the Hindu society. They were not allowed to live within the walls of the town.* The Pukkasas were also despised classes. They were excluded from the category of Caste (fifth class). *In the Dharmasastra the occupation of a Chandala was to carry the dead bodies of men who have no relation or friends, and to execute criminals.* In the Madhyadesa five-fold division of society was given viz., Brahman, Kshatriya, Vaishya, Shudra and Niashada. Buddhist literature–Jtakas, also gave the social divisions on the same line. The word Untouchable was a literal translation of the Hindi word 'achhut'. Generally this term applied to the person in the lowest classes (fifth class) of Hindu society.[53]

It is also found that in the early Vedic times, different members of the same family used to undertake different occupations of *'Chaturverna'* (four classes) according to their inclination and abilities. Every member of the family enjoyed the liberty to adopt any profession be liked best. According to Rigveda, no man was considered too high or too low in the society. But in the course of time this healthy sprit of equality resulted in the traditional bound *Caste system* and to the institution of *untouchability,* which divided the Hindus. Traditionally, each caste came to be associated with a profession, administration, trade or manual labour, developed a high degree of exclusiveness among the professional classes. As per the nature of one's work, certain lowest sections of the community acknowledged as *untouchable* and were kept more or less segregated even within villages. By practicing untouchability, the upper caste kept them a subordinate place within the system since they had been traditionally engaged in occupations like shifting of night soil and treatment of hides and skins of animals, which were considered 'unclean' by the upper caste Hindus.

In South India[54] position was different; Brahmans prevented themselves from degeneration into savagery. They stand for civilization and guided human history and human thought for centuries. The concrete expression of their culture was found in:

> (i) The worship of Siva and Vishnu; (ii) Abstinence from animal food; (iii) Prohibition of animal sacrifice; (iv) Infant marriage; (v) Prohibition of the marriage of the widows; (vi) Sraddhas, the annual ceremony in honour of the dead ancestors. These six factors have, by gradual adoption, contributed a great deal to the elevation of lower castes.

The sub-caste connotes no real difference of culture or occupation. They consist of groups within the caste, which marry among themselves. Among the non-Brahmans, *Okkaligas, Reddies and Banajigas* are instances. Sometime adoption of degrading occupation gives rise to a sub-caste within the caste. Its member adopts Brahminical usages. In spite of the rigidity in the caste system, instances of transformation of one caste into another were not rare.

New caste arose because of change in occupation, migration from one place to another and debasement or purification of customs. Other factors responsible to the addition, fission and fusion of caste are conquest, migration, emulation, isolation, separation, occupational, specialization, conversion and sectarianism, and the incorporation of tribal groups.[55]

The two names *'caste' and 'class' are often confused with each other.* They corresponded neither in extent or character, nor in natural tendencies. *The 'class' sub-serves political ambition. The caste obeys narrow scruples, traditional customs and local influence, which have generally no relation to class interests.* The hierarchic division of the population into classes is universal.[56]

The words *'tribe' and 'caste'* are loosely applied to a social group. Tribe is defined as "the largest body of people, and having a common language for themselves as well as a sense of solidarity which express itself in regarding other people as strangers". In its original form, it is an aggregate of persons who have or believe themselves to have a common origin. But its members occupy a definite tract. The modern tendency for such tribe is to be transformed into a caste. Infact, a tribe is a prospective caste.[57]

All the development in this period put forward in favour of the Brahmins. All the three Varnas were exhorted to serve the Brahmin. The Shudra gets socially more degraded. The Shudra was regarded beyond the pale of moral influence. A member of first three castes must not travel in the company of Shudras. It seems that the Shudras were considered to impart some sort of adulteration to objects like bed and seat by their touch. If Shudras calling himself a Brahmin shall have his eyes destroyed by poison or shall pay the heavy fine of eight hundred 'panas'. If he violates a Brahmin female he shall be burnt to death.

In the sphere of religion, a distinction was make between the Shudra who behaved properly according to the Brahmin's ideas, and the Shudra who was slovenly enough not to come up to this standard of conduct—the *'sat' and the 'asat'* Shudra. Only the former class of Shudra was allowed the privilege of the practice of rites and sacraments though without the use of the Vedic formulae.[58] Food offered by a Shudra was generally forbidden to a Brahmin as in the last period but with the difference that there was class of the good Shudras whose food may be accepted.[59] The mixed castes were entitled only to the religious privileges of the Shudras. The issues of the mixed marriage of a hypergamous nature were to be treated as Shudras. The traditional scheme of occupations of the four castes was laid down as usual, but with some modifications. *Yajnavalkaya,* in case of necessity, allows a Shudra to engage in trade or agriculture. The traditional assignment of occupation to the four castes was very largely modified. Vaishyas and Shudras were given common occupations viz agriculture and crafts. The previous job of the Kshatriyas was taken up by other castes as well.

Therefore, after scrutiny of the available evidence of Ancient period in *Rigvedic period,* Backward Class are found in the shape of Dasa or Dasyu, Shudra, blacksmith, leather-worker, barber, physician, goldsmith, merchant, and chariot-builder, Chandalas, Paulkasa, Ayogava, and Niashada, etc. Status of these classes was lower in comparison to other classes like Brahmin, Kshatriya and Vaishya. They were having duties only to serve upper three classes. But in *Post-Vedic Period* several new mixed classes or Jati (Shankar Jati) are born in the form of Abhiras, Shaka or Yavanas, Domes, carpenters, the washermen, and weavers besides the above classes. Now they are turn indirectly in caste and later known as backward classes. In this period they were having no civil status in the society viz. no property rights, no religious rights, no social rights, no educational rights, etc. Their positions turn into very pitiable. Often, term 'Untouchables' were used to these classes by upper classes. In *Dharmashutra period* although Shudras were remaining degraded one but some relaxation was given. They can change their occupation due to the difference between 'sat' and 'asat' Shudra. In brief in ancient period there was no cast only class were prevailed.

HISTORY OF BACKWARD CLASS IN MEDIEVAL PERIOD OF INDIA

10th century A.D. was the beginning of medieval period and it continues till the end of Mughal Regime. This period in Indian History is also called as Muslim period. During this age various travellers and historians like *Xuanzang, Al-Biruni, Duarte Barbosa, Abul Fazal, Moreland, Hamilton,* etc. had visited Indian sub-continental, and gave their descriptions of contemporary Indian society. Medieval history of backward class therefore is drawn out from the accounts of these travelers and other historian of this period.

Xuanzang narrated that, in India there are four castes: first—the pure and ascetic (Brahmanas), second—the nobility (Kshatriyas), third—the merchants (Vaishyas) and fourth—the cultivators (Shudras). Each of these castes forms an exclusive social group.[60] *Al-Biruni* revealed about four Verna System *'by saying that great differences do not exist between the Vaishya and the Shudra'*. Indian commentators of Twelfth-century on Hindu law essentially incorporate in their accounts. Vaishya occupations of cultivator, herder and merchant within the obligations of the Shudra.[61] Today it is normally understood that the Vaishya is the Verna of commerce and that agriculture belongs to the Shudra Verna. From the records of *Xuanzang* it may perceive that such a division of labour between Vaishya and Shudra existed in medieval period has continued till the present day.

During 11th and 12th centuries, the figure of castes, sub-castes and mixed castes increased greatly with the influence of Jainism on the Vaishyas, which were confined mainly to trade, commerce and lending. The position of the Shudra had improved a great deal. As the Vaishyas came under the doctrine of ahimsa, giving up agricultural activities, the *Shudras were nearer true Vaishyas.*[62] *The Shudras gradually improved their economic condition.* Their lot further improved when the reformist movement like Jainism and Saivism welcomed them in their fold, in no way treating them as inferior to the Brahmanas. *But, intellectually they remained rather backward, because higher education was largely restricted to the elite—the Brahmanas and the Kshatriyas.*

The Bhakti saints of this period gave to the backward class Hindus a respectable position in the society. During this period the two mid-Vernas, Kshatriya and Vaishya approximated more towards the fourth Verna, i.e. the Shudra. This process was more pronounced in Bengal than in other parts of the country. According to *Yama* in the Kali Age there were only two Vernas—Brahmana and Shudra.[63] *K.M. Panikkar* points out that "the Shudra seem to have produced an unusually large number of royal families even in more recent times. The Pals of Bengal belonged undoubtedly to that caste".[64] *The difference between the Vaishyas and the Shudras exited in pre-Mauryan period now getting narrower day by day. The occupations of the two Vernas were practically interchangeable. Shudras were permitted to follow the profession of the Vaishya varna.*[65] But later on, Shudras could be found in the professions of cattle breeding and agriculture not only in exceptional circumstances but at all times.[66] Handicrafts passed entirely into the hands of the Shudra verna.[67] *The next step of forbidding the use of sacred thread was practiced in some areas of Bengal and thus the Vaishyas reduced to the rank of the shudras.*[68]

When the Muslims invasion were made in India, the position of these class become worse, because people of one part of the country got separated from those of the others and developed living and food habits which laid a premium on differences and led to the development of further sub-castes and communities.[69] The advent of the Afghans and the Moghuls had a considerable effect on the Hindu social system. An immediate reaction was the emigration of some people to the South. While remained became more exclusive and tried to protect themselves by early marriage and hardening of caste system.

In this age, *various restrictions were imposed on the untouchables especially in south India,* e.g. they could not enter the cities after the sunset lest their shadows may pollute the upper caste persons. There were separate drinking water wells for them in the villages. Some of the prohibitions propounded against the exterior castes were as—that the adi-dravidas shall not wear ornaments of gold and silver; that the male shall not be allowed to wear clothes below their knee or above the hips; that the adi-dravidas shall not use other than earthenware vessels in their homes; that their women shall not be allowed to cover the upper portion of the bodies; that their women shall not be allowed to use flowers or saffron paste; that men shall not use umbrellas for protection against the sun and rain, nor shall they wear sandals.[70]

Literature of this period shows that in some northern parts of the country, orthodox Brahmans were bound to abandon their traditional notions about the Shudra Varna. The village-based brahmanas started conducting ceremonies, beginning with life-cycle and yearly rituals, for local Shudras and became dependent for their livelihood on the remuneration received for these services. A situation arose in which exclusion of Shudras from religious ceremonies, would result in loosing the brahmanas from their means of livelihood. Now brahmanas pressurized to make concessions and compromised with reality by opening the Mahabharata, Ramayana and the Puranas, holy Hindu scriptures to Shudras. *This time Shudras were allowed to hear the lessons of these scriptures taught by the mouth of brahmanas and attend ceremonies at which they could chant the holy mantras taken from them.*

However, only brahmanas were permitted to preside over these rituals.

In the midst of this evolution from Brahmanism to Hinduism, new mantras were given more importance over the, Vedic mantras, and the religious exploitation against the Shudra almost lost effect.[71] In the medieval period, Hindu society (the four-varna-based caste-Hindu society), which accepted the Shudra as members, continued to develop but in this process the number of untouchables excluded from the four Vernas were increased. Several aspects of the social discrimination reserved for the Shudra in ancient Indian society were now transferred into the principles of untouchability. As per Hindu law codes, the Chandala, representative of the untouchables, was the offspring of a Shudra father and a brahmana's mother, considered as offspring of most condemned pratiloma marriage.[72] However, Chandalas came into existence around the dying stages of the Later Vedic Era.

During this period Brahmanas secured the top position in society by virtue of their monopoly of the priesthood like in later Vedic period. This ideological distinction between purity and pollution reached the point of fanaticism among the Brahmanas. This emphasis on purity gave rise to people on the opposite end of society who were considered to be impure or untouchable. The Kshatriyas, ruling class contributing the political ingredient to the development of untouchability. It means untouchables functioned in order to displace the dissatisfaction of the direct producers, Vaishyas and Shudras, within the varna-based society, thus ensuring a stable social order.

The untouchables have been placed outside the framework of the Varna System and have functioned to cement class relations in that society in the form of groups ranked based on their level of purity (or impurity). Most of the untouchables, or those inferiors equated with them, originated in tribal peoples carrying on hunting and gathering in the forests on the periphery of Aryan agrarian society and it was not equated with untouchablity. The Chandala is believed to be the original of one indigenous tribe. As their untouchablity developed with the passage of time, all people associated with their way of life came to be referred to as Chandalas. Some members of Aryan agrarian society were also added to their ranks by virtue of occupation, crime or bohemian attitude.[73] The provisions concerning Chandalas seen in the later Hindu law codes were not very different from those contained in the Manu-Smrti or Dharma sutras. These literature described Chandalas as 'people who will pollute the twice born by either direct or indirect contact'. If one touched by Chandala, he must bathe submerging the entire body.[74] Closer contact, like intercourse with Chandala women, required more difficult penances, including fasting.[75] Chandalas, like Shudras, were totally excluded from the religious practices of the twice born.[76] In this period for the first time a new term *'Asprsya'*, appears for untouchability.

'Asprsya' or 'untouchables' were acknowledged too much degraded person in different stories that the daughter of Brahmana and wealthy merchant washing their eyes after looking upon a Chandala[77] and also that of a Brahmana who was so hungry, he ate food left by a Chandala, then died from embracement.[78] The Chandalas were segregated from the rest of the community, living in groups on the outskirts of cities and villages.[79] It shows that their material lives were of the lowest standards in the society.[80] As the occupations of these classes they were called as hunters, arrowmakers, and woodworkers among their ranks.[81] The task of disposing of dead animals was also of Chandala occupations, as were scavenging and earth working.[82]

Commentator *Vijnanesvara* in his interpretation of the inferior people, listed 14 representative castes including the Chandala, and classifies them two categories depending on their levels of impurity.[83] Here untouchablity becomes more and more complicated. Now the Chandalas are called sinners. They lived isolated from the rest of society, and when they enter a city, they must sound an alarm by striking a piece of wood to warn everyone of their presence and enable the citizens to avoid running into them. The Chandalas, fishermen, and hunters are the only sellers of animal flesh.[84]

Al-Biruni, narrates that there were eight castes *(fullers, shoemakers, acrobats, basket weavers, sailors, fishermen, hunters and cloth-weavers)* called *'antyaja'*, who were considered inferior to the Shudra. They lived outside of the towns and villagers where those of the four Vernas resided. Four other castes were, including the Chandala, considered even more inferior. They were the *entertainers, executioners and slaughterers*, and the like.[85] The untouchable and other inferior groups, living on the periphery of agrarian society were also caught up within this village reorganization, moving to the outskirts of individual collages and maintaining their tribal organization in the form of castes. Strata of inferior castes and artisans were designated as untouchable. Moreover, stratification occurred among the old and new untouchable castes based on differing degrees of pollution, resulting in exclusionary behaviour among them.[86]

Al-Biruni grouped together Dom and Chandala as "not reckoned among any caste or guild. They are occupied with dirty work, like the cleansing of the villages and other services. They are considered as one sole class, and distinguished only by their occupation". As per Al-Biruni's information there were other two classes of people, the first was formed by people following certain crafts, were grouped together *as 'Antyajas'*. This group, with eight guilds, had to live near but outside the villages and the towns of the four castes, there were two sub-divisions. *Jugglers, basket and shied-makers, sailors, fishermen, and hunters of wild animals and birds,* could freely intermarry though they belonged to separate guilds. But none of their members would condescend to have anything to do with the fuller, the shoemaker, and the weaver (which formed second sub-division of the Antyajas). The sixth class of people had four named groups among them, of which two were, viz. dome and Chandala as untouchable.[87]

Hem Chandra, during the regime of Rajpoot Raja used *desi* word *Dumba* or *Dom* for *Svapacha*. Further he narrate that the Chandalas carried a stick in their hands to warn people to avoid their touch, which receive a specific *desi* name, i.e. *'jhajjhari'*. In the time of *Kalhana* (1150 A.D.) the people of Kashmir were not much scandalized by either the touch of Dombas or Svapachas or even by the acceptance of the food of the aristocratic ones among them. And even they tolerated the visits of the Dumba queen to their temples, it means in their view the royal status of a person removed all traditional and hereditary disabilities from him. During this time the reference is also found about the *Svapaka* as soldier and his exploits in archery. The *ashmirians* were willing to give scope to the abilities of a person of unknown parentage and of known Shudra and Chandala fosterage.[88]

Duarte Barbosa speaks of eighteen castes, having separate customs and idol-worship of its own.[89] *Abul Fazal* remarks that the Vaishya and the Shudra were divided into numerous branches.[90] *Moreland* rightly summarizes the position of caste at the end of Akbar's regime in the following words: "Among the Hindus the Caste system existed substantially as it exists today and the differences among caste and races were such that we find travelers speaking of the 'Baniyas' or of 'Gujaratis' as 'nations' distinct from Brahmins or Rajputs".[91] In the period of Jahangir, the Baniyas of Gujarat had numerous sub-divisions neither they would eat nor drink with others.[92] Hamilton in the middle of the 18th century mentions sixty-five divisions of the Baniyas of Surat.[93]

In first half of medieval age *'Chamar'* Caste marking it off from the other untouchable classes. In Kashmir in the region of king Chandrapida the *Chamar* was boldly sought and got the audience of the King. In Bengal the Chamar, trace their decent from *Raidas,* a well-known saint and a disciple of the more famous Brahmin saint *Ramananda*. Many Chamar in Uttar Pradesh and Bihar were embracing *Raidasism,* a person who is described as *Mochi,* member of a section of Chamars, is recorded to have built a temple of Vishnu at Raipur in A.D. 1415. *Hide and leather working* has been traditional occupation of some group of Chamars in the South. Several alternative words were used by this caste as *Ramdasia, Ruidas, Rabidas, Satnami, Raidasi Rohit, Rohidas, Raidas, Ramnami and Rishi.* Though the Chamar is counted among the unclean untouchables because of the fact that the flesh of the dead animals or beef or both entered in his diet yet in some parts of the country he used to be served by some kind of a Brahmin. Such are the principal castes that made up the group of untouchable and aloof. The list of groups considered to have been the result of mixed unions turn out to be very large and includes almost all the groups, occupational or otherwise as behaving like unit castes.[94]

During the Peshwa rule the caste supremacy of Brahmins was in vogue. The other castes were treated as inferior. This particular class dominated the lower castes. On the other hand, the condition of the subordinate caste became very critical. The upper caste people treated the lower caste badly. They had no political rights to exercise. They were not allowed to use water from public wells, lakes and ghats. Their conditions were horrible than that of slaves. Shudras were not at all on equal footing with three upper castes. Even within the folds of new creeds like devotional Vaishnavism, the Shudra's inferiority is taken for granted and even acted upon. It is precisely because Ramananda was insulted by his brethren for his social inferiority that he traveled northward and established a new sect.

The religious upheaval in Maharastras, start in the beginning of the thirteenth century, produced considerable appreciation in the religious position of the Shudra.[95] There flourished a number of Shudra saint of outstanding personality. They explored easy method of salvation for the Shudras and freed the Shudras from the Brahminical domination in their spiritual life. But they upheld the old order of the four castes including their own status of inferiority in the scheme. With its peculiar practices and beliefs, the Hindu society developed in itself a more dreadful form of untouchability in the course of time and the traditional untouchability of certain communities persisted in all over India in such a large amount, that the practice of untouchability became a permanent character of the Hindu communities.[96] The Caste Hindu who became polluted by their touching with untouchable, could be purified by adopting purificatory prescriptions. But as for the untouchables they could never be made pure because, "they were born impure, they remain impure while they live, they die and the death of the impure, and give birth to children who are born with the stigma of untouchablity affixed to them. It is a case of permanent, hereditary stain which nothing can cleanse.[97]

Literature of this period mentioned the *Mahars, Mangs* and *Chambers or Chamars or Chamahars*. Sometimes the Mahar was called as *Dher "Bhoomia"* or guide, *Yeshkar* or watchman, *"Taral"* or gatekeepers. Sometimes the Mang was also known as *Vajantri* or musician. Records of this age also refer to the *Mangavargant snake charmers*. The charmers were known as

Mochis (shoe-makers), *Jingar* (Saddle-makers), etc. Among all this, Mahars are the principal untouchable community in Maharastras. The single largest untouchable community found in Maharastra is Mahar. During the era of Peshwas, Mahars, Mangs and the Chamahars were forced to live outside the village. Various duties were assigned to untouchables to perform. Their main duty was the service of the twice born as given by Manu. Another important duty of Mahar was to watch over the boundaries of both, the village lands and of each individual's field, to give evidence in cases of boundary disputes, and to watch over the crops. He carried the news of death to the relatives of the deceased person from one village to another and conveyed the death information from the military camps to the relatives of the dead and also to the Government. He rendered services in disposing of the dead persons and dead animals. Besides these services several professions have been considered in certain circumstances fit for the Ati-shudras. The works such as of man hanging and man killing were also used to be assigned to them. They made all leather pickets, halters, whips, popes and bonds for agricultural purposes. These professions were the part of the multiple economic activities in which their lives were moulded and made their position worst. An untouchable was harassed by caste Hindus if he tried to adopt a new profession, which was not assigned to him traditionally or by Hindu lawgivers.[98]

Under the regime of Peshwas "a greater distinction was made in awarding the punishment on account of the castes of the culprits rather than the nature of the crime." The untouchables or lower castes were awarded punishment of damaging their limbs and wholesale capital punishments were inflicted on criminals convicted for murder, treason or dacoity. There is a long list of convicts condemned to lose their hands and feet. During this period adultery was such an offence about which punishment was death for untouchables. Murder of the Brahmin was considered the highest heinous crime. Peshwas were very particular to follow the traditional pattern of socio-religious rules and regulations formulated in the laws of Manu. Therefore, Brahmins had been assured the highest social status by expressly forbidding lower caste to initiate usages and customs practiced by the former. For instance, lower castes were prohibited to wear the sacred thread and to perform certain specific rites both of which were entitled only to Brahmins. Marriages of the untouchable were not officiated by the Brahmins but by untouchable priests themselves still remain. Their demand to officiate by Brahmin was rejected by the priest but by supported by local bureaucrat and forcibly attached the office of the Brahmin priests.[99]

Thus in this medieval period concept of untouchability get the shape of big tree and its *shadow roofed all the sub-class or caste including fifth class*. Due to this untouchability concept degrees of social restrictions were high. Caste systems become rigid. Although some religious reformist tried to reform the situation of these lower class.

HISTORY OF BACKWARD CLASS IN MODERN PERIOD OF INDIA

As regard with the history of Backward Class in modern period, it starts from the end of Mughal Empire regime. This is the period when Britishers, French and Portuguese were trying to become ruler of India. During this period the present day vernaculars of India were being evolved. A fresh religion and ethnic stock, accounting for many of our present day political and social problems were also introduced during this age. In this period the old village economy, which had given so much strength to the caste system, became disrupted under British Rule. The land policy of British ruler created a new class of landlords and drove millions into the ranks of tenants and agricultural labourers.[100]

With the advent of the Britishers, Portuguese, French and Duchess, social position of the untouchables recorded some high improvement. The Christian missionaries found, among the untouchables a fertile ground for conversion. These missionaries used both, their social inequality and economic misery to get new recruits particularly from the lowest rungs of the Hindu society.[101] It was, however, the education policy and social reform of the British ruler, more than the work of missionaries which paved the way for the mitigation of their social misery. British educational system created a new generation of intellectuals and reformers who were imbedded with liberalistic ideas like Raja Ram Mohan Roy, Keshav Chandra, Ram Krishna Paramahansa, and Swami Dayananda, etc. Their aim was to sanitize the evil of Hindu society and to elevate the status of lower caste.[102]

Evidence shows that in the census of 1901,[103] Chandalas were known as *Namashudras* being the largest caste of East Bengal. They had low status in social scale, being considered to be clean untouchable group. It had eight main functional divisions, which neither ate nor intermarried among themselves. The agricultural section stood out pre-eminent and the boating division followed. The caste was not served by community barbers but by their own caste-men working in that capacity. In other part of India, Doms have been carrying on as village sweepers and as workers in cane. They live by agriculture and village handicrafts. In some part they form migrant caste introduced them for the specific purpose of the filthiest of work. The Doms ate all manner of unclean food. For them no Brahmin could be found to administer their religious needs; neither would the common barber nor the common washerman work for them. The Dom was only one of the castes traditionally concerned with scavenging. In census of 1951, Dom, an unclean untouchable group, alternatively called Chandala.

The other castes like the Chuhra, the Bhangi Mehtar, the Bhuinmali, the Hari, the Haddi, the Mala, and the Paraiyan were also carried on scavenging. Yet the Namashudras is one of the Scheduled Castes of the Government of India's Order. They are now mostly occupied in cultivation and boat-playing. Some of them are carpenters, traders and shopkeepers. "A considerable number now follow the various so-called learned professions". Yet their social position as a caste is very low.

In Maharastra, the Mahar, because of their village menial status are grouped together as field-labourers, conveyed pollution without touch, either at a specific distance or by their shadow and were classed as impure untouchables. Drumming and playing on pipe-music is one of the needs of the village life. No boundary dispute in a village could be finally settled without the help of these castes in their respective regions. More often than not, disposing of the dead cattle of the village was also their duty. They cannot use the water of common well. The largest group appearing under a single name, being represented over the whole of the Indo-Aryan area is the Chamar or the Chambhar, whose name proclaims him to be a worker in leather. Manu speaks of two group or caste concerned with leather working, both of them being very mixed in origin, named Karavavra and Dhigvana. Karavavra is described in occupational terms as Charmakara, 'cutter of hide', and the origin of the current terms Chamar, for the leather-working caste in the Indo-Aryan regions. The Dhigvana's occupation that of working in leather and trading in leather products is represented in recent and contemporary society in the above-mentioned regions by the Mochi or Muchi. The Chamar has been one of the village menials in the traditional village economy, entitled to his customary share at the harvest. Though his chief contribution to the life of the village was through his hide and leather working yet he played no mean part in it, as a field-labour. Chamar was the largest single group going under one name next only to the Brahmin.

Jotiba Phooley of Poona was pioneer to improve the condition of and to secure social equality to the erstwhile untouchable and aloof classes. R.G. Bhandarkar, V.R. Shinde, and other reformers endeavored a lot for the social and educational upliftment of these lower or untouchable strata. As a result with the help of British Government, special efforts to encourage the education of the depressed classes were made. The educational progress of these classes has to be start with the primary education.

Sometimes various horrible events happened in the village against Scheduled Caste reveal the persistence of the occasional but darkest feature of the situation of the Scheduled Caste. The efforts taken by the social reformers and the government to abolish untouchablity and the Caste system did not yield much result. In order to eradicate the evil of caste system, the great saints of the Bhakti cults and some Britishers made attempts in this direction. The untouchables themselves were also at the forefront in removing the stigma. It was no doubt this is the beginning of creating a new social order in India. Efforts had been taken to make legislation for abolishing the practice of aloofness and for upliftment of lower caste improve their status in the form of various Commissions and Acts.

Reform movements had a constructive effect of cleansing the Hindu social order of some of its undesirable features, narrowing down the class and caste distinctions and changing the attitude of the high caste people towards the untouchables, who not only mixed with the lower castes but also worked for their uplift. The growth of towns, contributed to the relaxation of caste prejudices. New economic activities taken by the States gave birth to numerous non-caste occupations. The establishment of civil arid criminal courts also robbed the caste-system.[104]

In this period, new economic system introduced new occupations and old traders attracted new workers. It is observed in 1934 that the Chamars, a caste extremely low in the Hindu hierarchy, had gained considerable prestige because the sale of hides to European countries had produced a new source of wealth. Similarly, the teli (oil pressers) of Bengal had profited greatly from the new markets and many of their members become wealthy bankers and merchants.[105]

In pursuance of 'divide and rule' policy, Britishers introduced separate electorates, and gave special recognition to non-Brahmin castes in South, this contributed to the disruption in India and also hardened the caste distinctions because it divide and sub-divide the people at whatever level possible. This ensured formation of new castes, mainly untouchables, incorporated in the Schedule by the British Government. A striking feature of the caste system in the pre-British period was its local character. But British rule destroyed the local character of the caste system.[106] It was in this manner that the institution of caste became more rigid than before in the period of British rule.[107]

In pre-independence period the National Congress also took up the work of uplifting of the depressed class on a national scale.[108] It was only after Gandhi this matter received any momentum. He called them 'Harijan', children of God—and organized a network of agencies to work for their cause. Campaigns also carried out by him, against untouchablity through the press, pulpit and platform.[109]

Dr. B.R. Ambedkar, who himself was an untouchable, played a very significant role in the movement of Harijan upliftment. His emphasis was not only social, but political also. He declared that unless and until the untouchables enjoy political power, they would not be able to lift themselves up. He argued that the depressed classes should be entitled to special protection more than any other religious minority in the country.[110]

Since the Government of India Act of 1858, 1861, 1892 and 1909 did not mention any references of the Scheduled Castes and Scheduled Tribes. They were so far un-heard and un-sung. Indian Constitutional account disclosed that the history of representation of depressed classes or untouchables (now known as the Scheduled Caste[111]) in services or Indian legislature is of recent origin.

For the first time the term *Depressed Classes* was discussed in the *Indian Legislative Council* in 1916 and decided to include under this term all the criminal and wandering tribes, aboriginal tribes and the untouchables. *Sir Hennery Sharply* explained this term to include the classes, pursuing 'unclean profession' and whose touch or even shadow is polluting, those *classes* who were backward and educationally poor and despised and *certain classes* of Mohammedans also. However, the *Southborough Committee, 1919,* defined 'Depressed Classes' applying the criteria of untouchability and excluded primitive or aboriginal tribes and economically backward classes. But in South India expression 'Depressed or Backward Classes' indicate all castes and communities except Brahmins.

In Indian Constitutional and legal history for the first time *the existence of depressed classes was recognized under the Government of India Act, 1919.* It was provided that in Central Legislative Assembly among the fourteen nominated non-official members, one shall be the representative of depressed classes. In Provincial Legislative the depressed classes were represented by four nominations. It was after the *Government of India Act, 1919,* the Scheduled Castes, previously known as depressed classes or fifth order of the four-fold Hindu society, became a *political entity* for consideration in future set-up of constitutional reform.[112]

Due to the pressures exerted by the different depressed class organization, *Simon Commission* in 1927 suggested to reserve ten seats for the depressed classes. The Simon Commission prescribed 13 tests for including a caste in the Scheduled list. Some of these tests were:

(i) Whether caste in question pollutes high castes by their touch or proximity; whether caste in question is denied entry into temples; whether caste in question is denied the use of public places like schools, wells, etc.;

(ii) Whether caste in question can be served by Brahmins as purohits; Whether caste in question can be served by tailors (darjis), barbers (nais), washer men (dhobis), water-carriers, etc.;

(iii) Whether caste in question is one from whose hands a caste Hindu can take water;

(iv) Whether in ordinary social intercourse, a well educated member of the caste in question will be treated as an equal by high caste man;

(v) Whether caste in question is merely 'depressed' on account of its own ignorance;

(vi) Illiteracy or poverty and but for that would be subject to no social disability;

(vii) Whether caste in question is 'depressed' on account of the occupation followed; and

(viii) Whether but for that question, it would be subject to no social disability like—Chuhra, Bhangi, Chamar, Dom, Pasi, Raigar, Mochi, Rajbansi, Dosadh, Shanan, Thiyan, Paraiyan and Kori.[113]

D.N. Majumdar summarized the position of the depressed castes by maintaining that these castes are not depressed in all states; the same caste may be depressed in one area but may not suffer from any social and political disability in another. The disability are rigid where the depressed castes are numerically small, and fewer or on the decline where they are numerically strong.[114] It was supposed that the scale of reserved category representations as recommended was to secure a substantial increase in the number of members of legislative Councils drawn from the depressed classes.

In 1928 the term 'Backward Class' was identified as those Castes or Classes which were *educationally backward and depressed classes, aboriginal, hill tribes and criminal tribes*. In 1929 the list of backward class was expanded by *Indian Central Committee* even to include the *less advanced* of the inhabitants of British India. This time the Depressed Classes were excluded. It leads the view that backward classes were distinguished from untouchables since former include only backward communities.

In 1930 a *Bombay committee* insisted that the term *"Depressed Classes"* should include only untouchables and the larger group may be designated as *"Backward Classes"*. It further recommended the division of this larger group into three sub-headings—Depressed Classes (Untouchables), Aboriginal and Hill Tribes and Other Backward Classes (including wandering tribes). Besides this different other terms such as *Backward Classes, Backward Communities, Forward Non-Brahmin Communities, Backward Hindu, etc. were used*. The expression *Scheduled Castes* coined by the Simon Commission for the cases of depressed or backward Classes or untouchables now finally embodied in the Government of India Act, 1935, under section 309 and the term *'Scheduled Tribes'* for *tribals* also included.

The bold fight of Dr. Ambedkar on the behalf of the untouchables of India in 3rd Round Table Conference resulted in tremendous revolutionary changes. This round table conference was very historic because it recommended that special provisions should be made in the Federal Legislature for the representation of the depressed classes. Dr. Ambedkar took all the pain to fight for the representation of depressed classes in the services. Keeping in view the demonstration of Ambedkar the conference passed resolution for the safeguard of depressed classes in India in services, which envisaged; (a) no person shall be under any disability for the country merely by reason of community caste creed or race; (b) membership of any community, caste and creed or race shall not be a ground for promotion or suppression in any public service.

The Poona Pact was manifestation of material advantage to the depressed classes, which provide the basis for their representation in the Government of India Act, 1935. By the end of 1940 the preferential treatment of the schedule Castes through the policy of reservation, had become a hard reality. In 1942 the Government of India decided to fix a certain percentage of jobs for depressed classes. In 1943 the Government of India reserved 8.2% seats in services subject to increase in the case of available qualified candidates.[115]

In the first meeting of *Constituent Assembly* on December 9, 1946 Jawaharlal Nehru moved a resolution later called *'Objective Resolution'*, to initiate the procedure of providing Constitutional remedy in the form of reservations for the scheduled castes. This resolution affirmed that adequate safeguard should be provided for depressed classes and backward classes.[116]

An Advisory Committee was established on January 24, 1947 which further appointed a Sub-Committee to report on this crucial point. This sub-Committee submitted its report to the Advisory Committee on July 1947. The Advisory Committee drafted the report and sent to the Constituent Assembly.[117] The Draft Constitution, prepared by the constitutional advisor in October 1947. It prohibited *discrimination* on the grounds of religion, race, caste or sex and assured access to the shops and places of public resorts and provides reservation of posts in favour of *any classes of citizen* who, in the opinion of the state were not adequately represented in the service under the state.[118]

The Draft Constitution with minor modification was submitted to the President of the Constituent Assembly on February 21, 1948. It contain the provisions regarding prohibition of discrimination on the grounds of religion, race, caste or sex and provided for reservation of posts in favour of any backward classes of citizens who, in the opinion of the state were not adequately represented in the service under the state. Here the Drafting Committee inserted the word *'backward' before the word 'class of citizen'*.

This Draft Constitution was introduced for discussion on November 4, 1948. It contained several provisions for the Scheduled Castes and Scheduled Tribes.[119] At the meeting of the Constituent Assembly the Advisory Committee recommended to kept reservation only for scheduled castes and scheduled tribes.[120] The Constituent Assembly had taken decision to retained, reservation of seats in favour of Scheduled Castes and Scheduled Tribes. It was indeed a very crucial momentous and historical decision in relating reservation of seats to the schedule Castes. In defending the policy of reservation in favour of backward classes as embodied in the draft constitution it is argued that it reconciled three points of observation expressed in the Constituent Assembly :

> "the first is that there shall be *equality of opportunity* for all citizens. It is the desire of numerous members of this house that every individual who is eligible for a particular post should be free to apply for the post, to sit for examinations and to have his qualifications tested so as to determine whether he is fit for the post or not and that there ought to be no barrier in the operation of the principle of equality of opportunity. Another view, mostly shared by a section of this house, is that this principle is to be operative... there ought to be no reservations of any sort for any class or community at all, that all citizens if they are not qualified, should be placed on the same footing of equality so far as the public services are concerned . . . then we must have a massive opinion which insists that there shall be a provision made for the entry of certain communities which have so far been outside the administration".[121]

Thus the Constitution while adopting the general principle of non-discrimination based on religion, castes, etc. has made an exception in so far Scheduled Castes and Scheduled Tribes and Backward classes were concerned. The term 'Schedule Castes' indicate 'Depressed Classes' which means such castes, races or tribes corresponding to the classes of person formerly known as the depressed classes (as used in the Government of India Act, 1935). Mahatma Gandhi had designated them with the word "Harijan". But the framers of Indian Constitution adopted the term and as in the sense as coined by the Simon Commission. The Indian Independence Act, 1947 continued this meaning even after the independence of India.

The Constitution of India, 1950 *defines the Scheduled Castes* in terms of castes, race and tribes. They have been provided with special privileges in the matter of recruitment in services as well as with special representation in the legislative bodies. Although Article 341(a) of Indian Constitution empowers the President, after consulting the head of particular State, to notify "the *castes, races or tribes or parts of or groups within castes, races or tribes which shall be deemed to be Scheduled Castes in relation to that State*". Article 341(b) empowers Parliament to pass a law *to include in or exclude* from the list so notified by the President *"any caste, race or tribe"* therefore the Scheduled Castes may be define as those groups which are named in the Scheduled Castes Order in force for the same being.

In India the *'Other Backward Classes'* category is formed in late 20th century after Indra Sawhney case on the recommendations of Mandal Commission. All those castes that were thought to be the part of the Shudra Verna according to the Hindu Verna system now the core of the Other Backward Classes. It consists of peasant caste of various descriptions, and they have generally lagged behind the higher castes in education and consequently in professions and government vocations.[122]

Galanter remarked, that the question *'who are the Backward Classes'* is a post-independence question which answered after a long debate, by including all deprived, downtrodden, living outside village persons, Untouchables, Out-Caste and socially and educationally Backward Classes, declared to be mention by the Parliament and State Legislative Assembly. *At present, the term 'Backward Classes' denotes three different categories of castes such as Scheduled Castes (SCs), Scheduled Tribes (STs) and Other Backward Classes (OBCs).*

Notes and References

1. Sarajit Kumar Chatterjee, The Scheduled Castes in India, Vol. 1. Pub. Gyan Publishing House, N. Delhi, ed. 1996.
2. Vedic index, ii, pp. 247, 257.

3. G.S. Ghurye, 'Caste and Race in India', Pub. Popular Prakashan, Bombay, pp. 43-44, Ed. 1969 (Rpt.).
4. *Ibid.*, at p. 44.
5. *Ibid.*
6. G.S. Ghurye, 'Caste and Race in India', Pub. Popular Prakashan, Bombay, pp. 44-45, Ed. 1969 (Rpt.).
7. Muir, p. 16.
8. Vedic index, ii, p. 247.
9. G.S. Ghurye, 'Caste and Race in India', Pub. Popular Prakashan, Bombay, p. 46, Ed. 1969 (Rpt.).
10. Compare Satapatha Brahman, v, pp. 3, 4, and 20.
11. G.S. Ghurye, 'Caste and Race in India', Pub. Popular Prakashan, Bombay, pp. 49-50, Ed. 1969 (Rpt.).
12. Eggling's trans., pt. v, p. 446.
13. G.S. Ghurye, 'Caste and Race in India,' p. 51, Ed. 1969 (Rpt.), Pub. Popular Prakashan, Bombay.
14. *Ibid.*, at pp. 52-54.
15. Manu, xii, 54-80, ix, 322.
16. *Ibid.*, at 15.
17. Sarajit Kumar Chatterjee, The Scheduled caste in India ed. 1996, Vol. 1, Pub. Gyan Publishing House, New Delhi.
18. Prof. Ramesh Chandra and Dr. Sanghmitra, Dalit Identity in New Millenium, ed. 2003, p. 186, Pub. Commonwealth, Daryaganj, New Delhi.
19. *Ibid.*
20. *Ibid.*
21. G.S. Ghurye, 'Caste and Race in India', p. 55, Ed. 1969 (Rpt.), Pub. Popular Prakashan, Bombay.
22. Vasishtha, p. 9.
23. G.S. Ghurye, 'Caste and Race in India', p. 56, Ed. 1969 (Rpt.), Pub. Popular Prakashan, Bombay.
24. *Ibid.*
25. *Ibid.*, at 60.
26. Mahabharata, Shanti Parva, 39, 59.
27. Apastamba, 165, Gautama, p. 236.
28. Apastamba, p. 165; Vasishtha, pp. 109-10, Baudhayana, p. 233.
29. Gautama, p. 236.
30. G.S. Ghurye, 'Caste and Race in India', p. 62, Ed. 1969 (Rpt.), Pub. Popular Prakashan, Bombay.
31. Compare the Allusion to Paijavana and other wealthy Shudras in the Mahabharata.
32. *loc. cit.*, 1, 2, 72.

33. G.S. Ghurye, 'Caste and Race in India',p. 63, Ed. 1969 (Rpt.), Pub. Popular Prakashan, Bombay.
34. *Ibid.,* at 64.
35. Vyakaranamahabhshya, I, 2, 72.
36. G.S. Ghurye, 'Caste and Race in India', p. 75, Ed. 1969 (Rpt.), Pub. Popular Prakashan, Bombay.
37. *Ibid.,* at 76.
38. *Ibid.,* at 78.
39. *Ibid.,* at 79.
40. *Ibid.,* at 80.
41. Vyakaranamahabhshya, II, 4,10; Apastamba, 1, 7, 21; 1, 5, 16; II, 7, 17; Vasishtha, XX, 16; Baudhayana, 1, 21, 15; II, 2,13. N.B.: R.G. Bhandarkar first drew attention to the important passage in Patanjali's Mahabhashya in his social history of India in 1901. He commands on it thus: "Patanjali mentions carpenters and blacksmiths as belonging to the Shudra class. The lowest of them, the Chandalas were in the same degraded condition as they are now" (collected works), Vol. II, p. 450. V.P. Kane in his History of Dharmashastra, Vol. II, pt. I (1941) observes: "therefore it follows that Panini and Patanjali included candelas, and mritapas among Shudras" (p. 168).
42. Baudhayana, p. 220; Vasishtha, p. 5.
43. G.S. Ghurye, 'Caste and Race in India', p. 80, Ed. 1969 (Rpt.), Pub. Popular Prakashan, Bombay.
44. *Ibid.,* at 83.
45. Gautama, p. 197.
46. G.S. Ghurye, 'Caste and Race in India', p. 86, Ed. 1969 (Rpt.), Pub. Popular Prakashan, Bombay.
47. Vyakaranamahabhshya, II, 4, 10; N.B. V.P. Kane in his History of Dharmashastra, (Vol. I, Pt. I, p. 121), observes on the passage: "Shudras were divided into numerous sub-castes. But there were two main divisions. One was 'aniravasita Shudra' (such as carpenters and blacksmiths) and the other 'niravasita Shudras' (like candelas)".
48. Prof. Ramesh Chandra and Dr. Sanghmitra, Dalit Identity in New Millenium, ed. 2003, p. 186, Pub. Commonwealth, Daryaganj, New Delhi.
49. Prof. Ramesh Chandra and Dr. Sanghmitra, Dalit Identity in New Millenium, ed. 2003, pp. 186-87, Pub. Commonwealth, Daryaganj, New Delhi.
50. Prof. Ramesh Chandra and Dr. Sanghmitra, Dalit Identity in New Millenium, ed. 2003, p. 187, Pub. Commonwealth, Daryaganj, New Delhi.
51. *Ibid.*

52. *Ibid.*, at 189.
53. *Ibid.*, at 191, (Manu 4 et seq).
54. *Ibid.*, at 199.
55. *Ibid.*, at 201.
56. *Ibid.*, at 198.
57. *Ibid.*
58. G.S. Ghurye, 'Caste and Race in India', pp. 92-93, Ed. 1969 (Rpt.), Pub. Popular Prakashan, Bombay.
59. *Ibid.*, at p. 96.
60. T. Waters, tr., On Yuan Chwang's Travel in India, Delhi, 1961, Indian edn., p. 168.
61. E.C. Sachau, ed. and tr., Al-Beruni's India, Delhi, 1983, Indian Edn., p. 100.
62. Dr. B.N., Sharma, *op. cit.*, p. 28.
63. Srinivas, *op. cit.*, pp. 25-26.
64. K.M. Panikkar, Hindu society at cross-roads, Bombay, 195, p. 8.
65. Yajnavalkaya Smriti, 1.120.
66. Kautilya Arthasatra, 1.3.
67. Gautama Dharmasutra, x: Vishnu Purana II.
68. Dutt, *op. cit.*, Vol. II, p. 135.
69. Sharma, Dr., B.N., *op. cit.*, p. 176.
70. *Ibid.*
71. P.V. Khane, History of Dharmashutra, Vol. I, pp. 839-96; Vol. II, pp. 155-59, 198-99; Vol. v, pp. 920-30, 1641-42.
72. Gaunt, iv, 17-18. vas. xviii, 1. Baudh. 1, 8, 16, 8; 1, 17, 7 Manu x, 12, 16. *Ibid.*
73. Sanjay Paswan and Paramanshi Jaideva, Encyclopedia of Dalits in India, Ed. 2002, Pub. Kalpaz Publication, New Delhi, Vol. 14, pp. 19-20.
74. Ap. II, 1, 2, 8-9.
75. Gaunt, XXIII, 32-34. vas. XX, 16; XXIII, 39-41. Baudh. II1. 2, 13-14; II, 2, 4, 12-13.
76. Ap. 1, 3, 9, 14-18. vas. XXIII, 33-35.
77. Jat. iv, pp. 376, 390-91.
78. Jat. II, pp. 82-84.
79. Jat. IV, pp. 200, 376-77, 390; VI, p. 156.
80. MN. III, pp. 169-70. SN. I, pp. 93-95, p. 107; 1185-86; III, pp. 385-86.
81. Taisho IV, p. 304. Apadana II, p. 377.
82. Taisho IV, pp. 298, 352, 495.
83. Mitaksara on Yaj. III, 260, 265.

84. S. Beal, tr., The Travels of Fah-Hian and Sung-Yum, London, 1964, 2nd ed., p. 55.
85. E.C. Sachau, al-Beuni's India, pp. 100-2.
86. Sanjay Paswan and Paramanshi Jaideva, Encyclopedia of Dalits in India, Ed. 2002, Pub. Kalpaz Publication, New Delhi, Vol. 14, p. 25.
87. G.S. Ghurye, Caste and Race in India, Ed. 1969 (Rpt.), Pub. Popular Prakashan, Bombay, p. 78.
88. *Ibid.*, at pp. 98-101
89. The Book of Durate Barbosa by M. Longworth Dames, Vol. ii, (1921), pp. 7, 37, 60.
90. Ain-i-Akbari, translated by Jarett, Vol. iii, (1894), p. 118, and Vol. ii, pp. 129, 131, 161, 162-3, 164-8, 177, 182, 184, 187, 189, 191, 198, 204-5, 255, 290.
91. India at the death of Akbar (1920), p. 23.
92. Jehangir's India, by Moreland and Geyl, (1925), p. 76.
93. A new account of the East Indies, by Capt. Alexander Hamilton, Vol. I, (1740), p. 151.
94. G.S. Ghurye, Caste and Race in India, Ed. 1969 (Rpt.), Pub. Popular Prakashan, Bombay, p. 80.
95. Sanjay Paswan and Paramanshi Jaideva, "Encyclopedia of Dalits in India", Vol. 6, Ed. 2002, Pub. Kalpaz Publication, New Delhi, p. 31.
96. *Ibid.*, at p. 40.
97. *Ibid.*, at Vol. 14, p. 28.
98. *Ibid.*, at Vol. 6, pp. 35-36.
99. *Ibid.*, at Vol. 6, pp. 42, 43 44, 45.
100. Report of the first Backward Classes Commission, 1955, p. 23, Para 44-45.
101. Depressed and Oppressed, B.S. Murthy, 1972, p. 44.
102. Scheduled Castes and Welfare Measures, R. Santhakumari, (first Ed.), p. 5.
103. Caste and Race in India, G.S. Ghurye, ed. 1969 (Rpt. 1999), p. 317 Pub. Popular Prakashan Pvt. Ltd., Bombay.
104. Sarajit Kumar Chatterjee, the Scheduled Castes in India, ed. 1996, Pub. Gyan Publishing House, New Delhi, Vol. 1, p. 77.
105. Buchanan, Daniel H., The Development of Capitalist Enterprises in India, New York, 1934, p. 24.
106. Sarajit Kumar Chatterjee, the Scheduled Castes in India, Vol. 1, p. 79.
107. Sovani, N.V., Non-Economic Aspects of Economic Development, in Administration and Economic Development, ed., *op. cit.*, p. 268.
108. Scheduled Castes and Welfare Measures, R. Santhakumari, (first Ed.), p. 5.
109. The Depressed Classes in India, O.P. Ralhan, 1987, p. 1.

110. Scheduled castes and welfare Measures, R. Santhakumari, (first Ed.), p. 5.
111. The term 'scheduled caste' 'is the standardized in the Constitution of Republic of India. The expression thus standardized by the constitution was first coined by the Simon Commission and finally embodied in the Government of India Act 1935, in section 309.
112. Mr. Gandhi and Economic Position of Untouchables, Dr. B.R. Ambedkar, 1943, p. 13.
113. Ram Ahuja, Indian Social System, ed. 1993, pp. 364-65.
114. Ram Ahuja, Indian Social System, ed. 1993, p. 367.
115. Round Table Conference Proceeding of Sub-committee, Vol. viii, pp. 231-33.
116. Report of the Commissioner for Scheduled Castes and Scheduled Tribes, 1951, p. 23.
117. C.A.D., Vol. II, pp. 332-33.
118. C.A.D., Vol. I, p. 200.
119. The Framing of Indian Constitution, B. Shiva Rao, p. 3.
120. *Ibid.*, pp. 630-34.
121. C.A.D., Vol. III, p. 330.
122. The Framing of Indian Constitution, B. Shiva Rao, p. 3.

2

Classification of National Backward Class Commissions

"The chief merit of reservation is not that it will introduce egalitarianism among OBCs when the rest of the Indian society is seized by all sorts of inequities. But reservation will certainly erode the hold of "Higher castes on the services and enable OBCs in general to have a sense of participation in running the affairs of their country".

(Mandal Commission's Report)

It is well settled that the expression "backward class of citizens" in article 16(4) means the same thing as the expression "any socially and educationally backward classes of citizens" in article 15(4).[1] But this term "backwardness, has not been defined anywhere in the Constitution of India. It is wide enough to include all kinds of backwardness—social, educational, economic or of any other kind.

In *Triloki Nath Tikku* v. *State of Jammu and Kashmir case*[2] it is argued that mere under representation of certain classes in the state government services was a conclusive evidence of their backwardness for the purposes of article 16(4). Rejecting this argument Subba Rao, C.J., observed that if the argument based upon inadequate representation was accepted, "it would really exclude the backward classes from the benefit of article 16(4) and confer benefits only on a class of citizens who though rich and cultured have taken to other avocations of life".[3] He ruled that in order to invoke article 16(4) two conditions must be satisfied:

(a) a class of citizens is socially and educationally backward as explained in *Balaji's case;* and
(b) the said class is not adequately represented in the services under the state.[4]

The test of under representation of certain classes in the State services is only one of the many attributes of backwardness. This test is often applied along with other relevant tests, for the purposes of delineating socially and educationally backward classes.

Before the commencement of Indian Constitution, demand of Backward Class leader for the benefits similar to those granted to Scheduled Caste and Scheduled Tribes was not accepted in the Constituent Assembly[5] of India, because it was presumed that the 'backward classes' were sufficiently potent and politically powerful to look after their own interests at the local level and there is no need for any central control to ensure the inculcation of all deprived classes of people in the category of backward classes. But after the enforcing of Indian Constitution it was made obligatory for the government to appoint a Backward Classes Commission within ten year of the Commencement of the Constitution.[6]

Answer the question that who is "Backward Class" was not simple. This question was answered by National Backward Class Commission which was appointed to identify 'backward class of citizens' as contemplated under Article 16(4) for the purpose of making reservation of appointments or posts in the government services. This Commission was first National Backward Class Commission named as Kaka Kalelkar Commission, appointed in 1953, second National Backward Class Commission was Mandal Commission appointed in 1980.

FIRST BACKWARD CLASS COMMISSION

First National Backward Classes Commission under the Chairmanship of Kaka Saheb Kalelkar[7] was constituted under Article 340 on 29.1.1953. Other members of National Backward Class Commission were as under :

1.	Shri Kaka Saheb Kalelkar	Chairman
2.	Shri Narayan Sadoba Kajrolkar, (M.P.)	Member
3.	Shri Bheeka Bhai, (M.P.)	Member
4.	Shri Dayal Singh Chaurasia	Member
5.	Shri Rajeshwar Patel, (M.P.)	Member
6.	Shri Abdul Qayum Ansari, (M.L.A., Bihar)	Member
7.	Shri T. Mariappa, (M.L.A., Mysore)	Member
8.	Shri Lala Jagannath	Member
9.	Shri Atma Singh Nambhari (M.P.)	Member
10.	Shri N.R.M. Swami, (M.P.)	Member
11.	Shri Arunomghrhu Dey	Secretary

The job of First National Backward Class Commission was as follows:

(a) to *determine the criteria* to be adopted in considering whether any section of the people in the territory of India (in addition to the Scheduled Castes and Scheduled Tribes specified by notifications, issued under Articles 341 and 342 of the Constitution) should be treated as socially and educationally backward classes, and in accordance with such criteria prepare a list of such classes setting out also their approximate members and their territorial distribution,

(b) to *investigate the conditions* of all such socially and educationally backward classes and difficulties under which they labour and make recommendations :

(i) as to steps that should be taken by the Union or any State government to remove such difficulties or to improve their condition;

(ii) as to the grants that should be made for the

purpose by the Union or any State government and the conditions subject to which such grants should he made;

(iii) to investigate such matters as the President may hereafter refer to them; and

(iv) to present to the President a report setting out the facts as found by them and making such recommendations as they think proper.

After employing two year labour fruits of the Commission were as following :

1. The Commission used the term *'classes'* as if it were synonymous with 'castes' and 'communities' and prepared a list of backward classes on the basis of the *caste*. The Commission listed *2,399* backward castes and communities out of which *837* castes as *'most backward castes'* for the purpose of development and upliftment and remaining *1562 castes* as *only backward castes*. Out of these 2,399 castes only *913 castes* accounted for an estimated population of 115 millions (about 32% of the total population of India).[8] About 70% of India's population was considered as backward. Commission recommended various measures to be taken for their economic and social advancement.
2. Commission identified various causes of educational backwardness among backward communities, as under :

(i) Traditional lack of interest for education, on account of social and environmental conditions or occupational handicaps;

(ii) Poverty and lack of educational institutions in rural areas;

(iii) Living in inaccessible areas;

(iv) Lack of adequate educational aids such as free studentships, scholarships and monetary grants.

(v) Lack of residential hostel facilities.

(vi) Unemployment among the educated which acts as a damper on the desire of the members to educate their children.

(vii) Defective educational system which does not train students for appropriate occupations and professions.[9]

3. The Commission laid down the following four tests or criteria for classifying socially and educationally backward classes—[10]

   (i) Low social position in the traditional caste hierarchy of Hindu Society;

   (ii) Lack of general educational advancement among the major section of a caste or community;

   (iii) Inadequate or no representation in government services; and

   (iv) Inadequate representation in the field of trade, commerce and Industry.

4. Commission suggested following measures for eradication of evils of backwardness as under :

   (a) A clear enunciation and effective implementation of the policy of social solidarity and national progress;

   (b) Necessary legislation on marriage and inheritance;

   (c) Prohibition of social disabilities by law;

   (d) Arrangement for production and distribution of literature on social problems;

   (e) Liberal use of the press, films, platforms and radio for removal of social evils;

   (f) Prohibition of all observances tending to promote caste feelings in governmental activities;

   (g) Reorganization of the educational system with special emphasis on the dignity of the manual labour;

(h) Full assistance to promote education as speedily as possible among the backward classes;

(i) Adequate representation in government service and government controlled establishments of these sections who had no chance so far; and

(j) Encouragement of art, literature, special cultural groups and assistance and promotion of cultural activities with this social end in view.[11]

5. Important recommendations made by the Commission are as under:

(a) The government of India should undertake *caste-wise* record of population in the census of 1961;

(b) It should seek to relate *social backwardness* of a class to its low position in the traditional caste hierarchy of Hindu society;

(c) *All women* should be treated as *'backward'* and subject to great social hardships, the Commission recommended the following measures for their upliftment :

(i) Free education at all levels to all girls whose parent's income is less than Rs. 3000 per annum;

(ii) Scholarship for girls belonging to the backward classes;

(iii) Residential Hostels for girl students, with priority for girls of the backward classes;

(iv) Samta Ashrams for girls of all communities to be run by trained staff of women and men;

(v) Creation of special facilities for girls to study medicine, home sciences and other subject specially;

(vi) More facilities for training women in the fine arts and in social services;

(vii) Reformative measures for women, rescue homes and social workers' involvement in tackling women problems to be encouraged.[12]

(d) Reservation of 70% seats in all medical, scientific and technical and professional institutions for qualified students of backward classes;[13]

(e) Minimum reservation of vacancies in all government services and local bodies for the listed backward classes and communities on the following scale:

At least 25% in class I,
33.5% in class II, and
40% in class III.[14]

6. The Commission suggested the creation of a *separate ministry for Welfare Backward Classes.*[15]

Criticism: The Commission's task was, however, complicated without the availability of adequate data even on caste lines. Caste-wise literacy figure was available only upto year 1941 because in 1951 the caste enumeration in the census records was abandoned. Even the caste-wise data on income and occupation was not available to the Commission. Nor was the information regarding the inadequacy of representation in services forthcoming. The absence of adequate data led the Commission to remark:

"In the absence of reliable facts and figures, the only course open to us was to rely on the statistics available from various governments and previous census report, and to go by the general impression of government officers, leaders of public opinion and social workers".[16]

The Commission based its conclusions on the then existing list of backward classes.[17] It included in the list even those communities regarding whom it had no data at all and thus gave them "the benefit of doubt". Not only this, the

Commission included in its list even few financially well-off communities on the ground of their educational backwardness.

The commission realized that the problem of backward classes was really the problem of rural India.[18] Majority of the members of Commission overemphasized the importance of 'caste' in any classification of the other backward classes. The sole criterion applied by it was the position of a caste in social hierarchy. It realized that "our society was not built essentially on an economic structure but on the—medieval ideas of 'varna', caste and a social hierarchy".[19]

Following the analogy of the maxim viz., *"using the thorn to remove a thorn"*, the Commission concluded that the evils of caste could be removed by measures which could be considered in terms of caste alone.[20] However, the Commission was itself disturbed over the exclusive reliance on *caste criteria*. It observed:

> "We are not less concerned to eradicate the evils of caste-system nor are we keen to perpetuate caste-system. We tried to avoid caste in the present prevailing conditions. We wish it were easy to (disassociate) separate caste from social backwardness at the present juncture".[21]

For using caste as a criterion of backwardness commission took into account the position or standing of the castes and communal groups in the social hierarchy and it treated a caste as a whole as backward. The Commission thought that its task was to demarcate those social categories or groups who were suffering disabilities and backwardness due to genetic or heredity reasons and whose backwardness was associated with the discrimination caused by the hierarchy of caste. It, therefore, concentrated on collective backwardness not of individual's backwardness. The groups to be drawn for the purposes of State preferences therefore could not be merely the economic groups or even the social classes. It believed that real social equality could be achieved in India only by eliminating the hierarchy of caste and of its consequent social discrimination. And the evils of caste-system could be eliminated only by taking caste into account.[22]

Three of the members (Anup Singh, Arungshu De and P.G. Shah) were opposed to one of the most crucial recommendations of the commission, i.e. *the acceptance of caste* as a criterion for determining the social backwardness and reservation of posts in government services on that basis.[23]

Last minute disclaimer of Chairman's regarding Commission's work changed the whole picture. In his belated clarification Kaka Kalelkar observed,

> "My eyes were, however opened to the dangers of suggesting remedies on caste basis when I discovered that it is going to have a most unhealthy effect on the Muslim and Christian sections of the nation".[24]

> Repudiating the caste criterion the Chairman observed:

> "Once we eschew the principle of caste it will be possible to help the extremely poor and deserving from all communities. Care of course must be taken to give preference to those who come from traditionally neglected classes".[25]

The Chairman felt that backwardness could be determined by factors other than cast, such as poverty, residence and occupation. He made a strong case for de-classifying those members of the once-designated backward classes who have attained sufficient economic and educational advancement.[26] He not only rejected 'caste' as a criteria for determining backwardness but also the use of 'caste' as a unit for classification. He found 'caste' criteria as repugnant to democracy and inimical to the creation of a casteless and classless society.[27]

When the report of the Commission was laid before the Parliament on September 3, 1956, it met with many objection or criticism by the Government.[28] The use of caste test was described as generative of "the dangers of separatism[29] and "the greatest hindrance in the way of the country's progress towards an egalitarian society".[30]

The report of Kaka Kalelkar Commission was placed before both Houses of Parliament on 3rd September, 1956 along with a memorandum explaining the action taken on it. It was explained in the memorandum that if the bulk of the country's millions were to be regarded as backward classes, no useful purpose would be served by a separate enumeration of such classes.[31] Even the Report spoke of divided opinions, 5 out of 11 members recorded their dissent; Dr. Anup Singh, Sri Arungshu De and Sri P.G. Shah dissented on the point of treating caste as basis of measuring backwardness. On the other hand in his 67 pages dissent Shri S.D. Chaurasia made strong plea of the acceptance of caste as criterion of backwardness and that too those which are equal to Scheduled Caste/Scheduled Tribe. Mr. T. Mariappa concerned himself to inclusion of a couple of castes, i.e. Urban Lingayats and Vokkalingas in the list of Backward Class. Chairman's forwarding letter itself amounted to a dissent against treating caste as measure of backwardness.

Govind Ballabh Pant, then Home Minister in the Government of India, was totally against caste-based reservation. He observed: "it cannot be denied that the caste system is the greatest hindrance in the way of progress towards an egalitarian society, and the recognition of the specified castes as backward may serve to maintain and even perpetuate the existing distinctions on the basis of caste".[32] The usefulness of the Report was also spoiled by the expansiveness of the list with result being that 'really needy would be swamped by the multitude and hardly receive any attention'.[33]

Since the Commission had failed to provide 'positive and workable criteria'.[34] Further investigation was thought to be imperative and therefore, the State Governments were requested to undertake adhoc surveys to determine number of backward classes and in meantime to give "all facilities" to backward classes "in accordance with their existing lists and also to such others who in their opinion deserve to be considered as socially and educationally backward in the existing circumstances".[35]

The report of Kaka Kalelkar Commission was finally discussed in 1965 where the Government once again condemned caste criteria as repugnant to the Constitution.

And the Centre decided not to draw up any list of "Backward Class/Other Backward Classes". The States were advised to draw their own lists using economic test rather than to go by caste[36] because for this it had support of the judiciary.[37]

SECOND BACKWARD CLASS COMMISSION

In post-emergency period once again, it was the Janta Party regime, when the interest in finding out an acceptable criteria for defining backward classes was revived under second National Backward Class Commission. This commission was appointed by the President in exercising the powers conferred under Article 340 of the Indian Constitution, to investigate the conditions of socially and educationally backward classes within the territory of India. This Commission also called Mandal Commission.

This commission[38] was constituted on 20.12.1978 under the chairmanship of B.P. Mandal and the composition of the Commission with other members was as follows :

1.	Mr. B.P. Mandal (Ex-M.P.)	Chairman
2.	Mr. Dewan Mohan Lal	Member
3.	Mr. Justice R.P. Bhole	Member
4.	Mr. K. Subramaniam	Member
5.	Mr. Din Bandhu Saha/L.R. Naik (Ex-M.P.)	Member
6.	Mr. S.S. Gill	Secretary

Task of the Mandal Commission was as follows :[39]

(A) (i) to determine the criteria for defining the socially and educationally backward classes;

(ii) to recommend steps to be taken for the advancement of the socially and educationally backward classes;

(iii) to examine the desirability or otherwise of making provision for the reservation of appointments or posts in favour of such backward classes of citizens which are not adequately represented in public services and posts in connection with the affairs of the Unions or any State; and

(iv) to present to the President a Report setting out the facts found by them and making such recommendations as they think proper.

(B) In this connection, the Commission was also advised to examine the recommendations of the other Backward Classes Commissions appointed earlier and the considerations which stood in the way of the acceptance of its recommendations by Government.

Report of Mandal Commission was, submitted on December 31, 1980, divided into VII Volume. Vol. I is related with main report and recommendations; VII is related with composition and terms of reference of the First Backward Class Commission; Vol. III is related with study prepared by the Indian Law Institute; Vol. IV is related with analysis of the Court and legislative debates leading to the first amendment of the Indian Constitution, summary of cases under article 15(4), Constituent assembly debates and summary of Court cases under Article 16(4), and analysis of cases under article 15(4); Vol. IV is related with report of the State Backward Class Commission, summary and conclusions; Vol. V is related with socio-educational survey tables; Vol. VI is related with state-wise list of other backward classes; Vol. VII is related with minute of dissent.

IDENTIFICATION OF OBCs

Main assignment of the commission was to identify the backward classes. A search team was appointed by the Commission for this job. Finally, a large number of castes were identified as backward among Hindu as well as non-Hindu in each State as a result of the Socio-Educational Survey.

The Mandal Commission evolved 11 'indicators' or criteria for determining social and educational backwardness among Hindu. These 11 indicators were grouped under three broad heads, i.e., Social, Educational and Economic.[40]

Social indicators are as :

(i) Castes/classes considered as socially backward by others;
(ii) Castes/classes which mainly depend on manual labour for their livelihood;
(iii) Castes/classes where the percentage of married women below 17 is 25% above the State average in rural areas and 10% in urban areas; and that of married men is 10% and 5% above the State average in rural and urban areas respectively; and
(iv) Castes/classes where participation of females in work is at least 25% above the State average.

Educational indicators[41] are as:

(v) Castes/classes where the number of children in the age group of 5 to 15 years who never attended school is at least 25% above the state average;
(vi) Castes/classes where the rate of student drop-out in the age group of 5-15 years is at least 25% above the state average;
(vii) Castes/classes amongst whom the proportion of matriculates is at least 25% below the state average.

Economic indicators[42] are as:

(viii) Castes/classes where the average value of family assets is at least 25% below the state average;
(ix) Castes/classes where the number of families living in *kachcha* houses is at least 25% above the state average;
(x) Castes/classes where the source of drinking water is beyond half a kilometer for more than 50% of the households;
(xi) Castes/classes where the number of the house-holds having taken a consumption loan is at least 25% above the state average.

Commission remarks, as the above three groups are not of equal importance for our purpose, separate weight was given to indicators in each group. All the *social indicators* were given a weight of three points each, *educational indicators* a weight of two points each, and *economic indicators* a weight of one point each. Economic indicators were considered more important as they directly flowed from social and educational backwardness. This also helped to highlight the fact that socially and educationally backward classes are economically backward too.[43]

It will be seen that from the values given to each indicator the total score adds up to 22. All these 11 indicators were applied to all the castes covered by the survey for a particular state. As a result of this application, *all castes which had a score of 50 percent (i.e. 11 points) or above were listed as socially and educationally backward and the rest were treated as advanced.*[44]

The Mandal Commission has also considered that there is no doubt social and educational backwardness among non-Hindu communities is more or less of the same order as among Hindu communities.[45] The set of eleven Indicators (criteria), being caste-based, could not be applied to non-Hindu communities. In view of this, *a separate set of criteria was evolved for the identification of non-Hindu backward communities. Rough and ready criteria for identifying non-Hindu OBCs is as under:*

(i) all untouchables converted to any non-Hindu religion, and

(ii) such occupational communities as are known by the name of their traditional hereditary occupation and whose Hindu counterpart have been included in the list of Hindu OBCs (e.g., Dhobi, Teli, Dheemar, Nai, Gujar, Kumhar, Lohar, Darzi, Badhai, etc.)[46]

Estimated Population of OBCs

On the basis of the available census data, evidence, personal knowledge of the population of Hindu and non-Hindu OBCs was estimated to be 52 per cent of the total population of India. This is in addition to the population of Scheduled Castes and Scheduled Tribes which amounts to 22.5 per cent.

The Mandal Commission gathered caste/community-wise population figures from the census records of 193I and then grouped them into broad caste—clusters and religious groups. These collectivities were subsequently aggregated under five major heads:

(i) SCs/STs;
(ii) Non-Hindu communities, religious groups, etc.;
(iii) Forward Hindu castes and communities;
(iv) Backward Hindu castes and communities, and
(v) Backward non-Hindu communities.

Results of this exercise are contained in Table A on the next page and a look at it will indicate the broad classification adopted by the Mandal Commission.[47]

As table shows that the population of Hindu OBCs could be derived by subtracting from the total population of Hindus, the population of Scheduled Castes, Scheduled Tribes and communities and that of forward Hindu Castes and communities and it worked out to 52%. But the same approach could not be adopted in respect of non-Hindu OBCs. Assuming that roughly the proportion OBCs amongst non-Hindu was of the same order as amongst the Hindus, population of non-Hindu OBCs was also taken as 52% of the actual proportion of their population of 16.16%, or 8.40%. Thus the total population of Hindu and non-Hindu OBCs added up to nearly 52% (43.70%+8.40%) of the country's population. Therefore, overall OBCs constitute nearly 52% of the Indian Population by excluding both the Scheduled Caste and Scheduled Tribes.[48]

The Mandal Commission prepared a consolidated list of BCs, and identified *3,943 castes covering 52% of the population of India as OBCs*. This Commission identified comparatively more castes as OBCs in each State than the earlier Kaka Kalelkar Backward Classes Commission. Backward Classes Commissions appointed by the various States added yet many more castes to their respective lists of OBCs. Commission

TABLE A
Percentage Distribution of Indian Population by Caste and Religious Groups

Sl. No.	*Group Name*	*Percentage of Population Total*
I.	**Scheduled Castes and Scheduled Tribes**	
A-1.	Scheduled Castes	15.05
A-2.	Scheduled Tribes	7.51
	Total of 'A'	22.56
II.	**Non-Hindu Communities, Religious Groups, etc.**	
B-1.	Muslims (Other than STs)	11.09(0.02)
B-2.	Christians (Other than STs)	2.16(0.44)
B-3.	Sikhs (Other than STs)	1.67(0.22)
B-4.	Buddhists (Other than STs)	0.67(0.03)
B-5.	Janis	0.47
	Total of 'B'	16. 16
III.	**Forward Hindu Castes and Communities**	
C-1.	Brahmins (Including Bhumihars)	5.52
C-2.	Rajputs	3.90
C-3.	Marathas	2.21
C-4.	Jats	1.00
C-5.	Vaishyas-Bania, etc.	1.88
C-6.	Kayasthas	1.07
C-7.	Other forward Hindu Caste/groups	2.00
	Total of 'C'	17. 58
	Total of 'A', 'B' and 'C'	56 .30
IV.	**Backward Hindu Castes and Communities**	
D.	Remaining Hindu castes/groups which come in the category of OBCs	43.70
E.	52 percent of religious groups under section 'B'. They also be treated as OBCs	8.40
F.	The approximate derived population of other Backward classes including non-Hindu communities (Aggregate of D & E rounded)	52%

* This is derived figure.

** Figures in brackets give the population of SCs and STs among these non-Hindu communities.

Source : Report of the Backward Classes Commission, 1980, Part 1, p. 56.

found that the representation of the backward classes (other than the SC/ST) in the Central services in different categories is less than that of the SC/ST, although the population of these OBCs is more than double of the SC and ST. A better representation of SCs and STs in the services and education is entirely due to the reservation policy. It therefore recommended reservation for these OBCs in proportion to their populations. However, in view of the legal constraint that total reservation should not exceed 50% for all categories, it limited this reservation to 27% in government services and in educational institutions. Therefore, the castes whose name appeared in Mandal as well as the State lists are getting benefits of 27% reserved posts.

Recommendations : In the report commission alleged, it may appear that the upliftment of OBCs is part of the larger national problem of the removal of mass poverty. This is only partially correct. The absence of OBCs is very special case of the larger national issue: here the basic question is that social and educational backwardness and poverty is only a direct consequence of these two crippling caste-based handicaps. As these handicaps are implanted in our social structure, their removal will require extensive *structural changes*. No less importance will be changes in the perception of the problems of OBCs by the ruling classes of the country.[49] Therefore, for the upliftment of OBCs Commission suggested certain recommendation as under:

(a) Reservation in Government services and educational institutions for the candidates of OBCs. By favoring reservation, Commission believed that it is not at all our argument that by offering a few thousand jobs to OBC candidates we shall be able to make 52 per cent of the India population as forward. But we must recognize that an essential part of the battle against social backwardness is to be fought in the minds of the backward people in India. Government service has always been looked upon as a symbol of prestige and power. By increasing the representation of OBCs in Government services, we give them an immediate feeling of participation in the governance of this country. When a backward class

candidate becomes a Collector or a Superintendent of police, the material benefits accruing from his position are limited to the members of his family only. But the psychological spin off of this phenomenon is tremendous; the entire community of that backward class candidate feels socially elevated. Even when no tangible benefits flow to the community at large, the feeling that now it has its "own man" in the "corridors of power" acts as moral booster.[50]

In the democratic set-up every individual and community has legitimate right and aspiration to participate in ruling this country. Any situation which results in a near-denial of this right to nearly 52 per cent of the country's population needs to be urgently rectified. The chief merit of reservation is not that it will introduce egalitarianism amongst OBCs when the rest of the Indian society is seized by all sorts of inequalities. But reservation will certainly erode the hold of higher castes on the services and enable OBCs in general to have a sense of participation in running the affairs of their country.[51]

Quantum of Reservation:[52] Regarding quantum of reservation Commission argued that Scheduled Castes and Scheduled Tribes constitute 22.5 per cent of the country's population. Accordingly a pro-rata reservation of 22.5 per cent has been made for them in all services and public sector undertakings under the Central Government. In the States also, reservation for SCs and STs is directly proportional to their population in each State. Since the population of OBCs is around 52% of the total population of India, accordingly 52% of all posts under the Central Government should be reserved for them. But this provision may go against the law laid down in a number of Supreme Court judgments wherein it has been held that the total quantum of reservation under Articles 15(4) and 16(4) of the Constitution should be below 50%. In view of this, the proposed reservation for OBCs would have to be hanged at a figure which, when added to 22.5% for SCs, STs, remains below 50%. In view of this legal constraint, the Commission is obliged to recommend a reservation of 27% only, even though their population is almost twice this figure. States which have already introduced reservation of OBCs exceeding 27% will remain unaffected by this recommendation.

With the above general recommendation regarding the quantum of reservation the Commission proposes the overall scheme of reservation for OBCs as under:[53]

1. Candidates belonging to OBCs recruited on the basis of merit in an open competition should not be adjusted against their reservation quota of 27 per cent;
2. The above reservation should also be made applicable in promotion quota at all levels;
3. Reserved quota remaining unfilled should be carried forward for a period of three years and dereserved thereafter;
4. Relaxation in the upper age limit for direct recruitment should be extended to the candidates of OBCs in the same manner as done in the case of SCs/STs candidates.
5. A roster system for each category of posts should be adopted by the concerned authorities in the same manner as presently done in respect of SCs/STs candidates.

The above scheme of reservation in its toto should also be made applicable to recruitments to public sector undertakings both under the Central and State Governments as also to nationalized banks. All private sector undertakings which have received financial assistance from the Government in one form or the other should also be obliged to recruit personnel on the aforesaid basis. All universities and affiliated colleges should also be covered by the above scheme of reservation.

To give proper effort to those recommendations, it is imperative that adequate statutory provisions are made by the Government to amend the existing enactments, rules, procedures, etc to the extent they are not in consonance with the same.

Educational Concessions: Commission cited that it is well known, most backward class children are irregular and indifferent students and their drop-out rate is very high. There are two main reasons for this. First, these children are brought up climate of extreme social and cultural deprivation and a proper motivation for schooling is generally lacking. Secondly, most of these children come from very poor homes and their parents are forced to press them into doing small chores from a very young age.

Commission, therefore, recommended that Special educational facilities designed for upgrading the cultural environment of the students should be created in a phased manner in selected areas containing high concentration of OBCs. Special emphasis should be placed on vocational training. Separate coaching facilities should be provided in technical and professional institutions to OBCs students to enable them to craft up with students from open quota.

It is also obvious that even if all the above facilities are given to OBCs students, they will not be able to compete on an equal footing with others in securing admission to technical and professional institutions. In view of this it is *recommended that seats should be reserved for OBCs students in all scientific, technical and professional institutions run by the Central as well as State Governments*. This reservation will fall under Article 15(4) of the Constitution and the quantum of reservation should be the same as in the Government services i.e., 27 per cent. Those States which have already reserved more than 27 per cent seats for OBCs students will remain unaffected by this recommendation.[54]

While implementing the provision for reservation it should also be ensured that the candidates who are admitted against the reserved quota are enabled to derive full benefit of higher studies. It has been generally noticed that these OBCs students coming from an impoverished cultural background, are not able to keep shoulder to shoulder with other students. It is, therefore, very essential that *special coaching facilities* are arranged for all such students in our technical and professional institutions. The concerned authorities should clearly appreciate that their job is not finished once candidates against reserved quota have been admitted to various institutions. In fact, the real task starts only after that. Unless adequate follow-up action is taken to give special coaching assistance to these students, not only these young people will feel frustrated and humiliated but the country will also be landed with ill-equipped and sub-standard engineers, doctors and other professionals.

Financial Assistance: Special programmes for *upgrading the skills of village artisans* should be prepared and subsidized loans from financial institutions granted to them for setting up small scale industries. To promote the participation of OBCs in the industrial and business life of the country, a separate network of financial and technical institutions should be creased by all State Governments.

The share of OBCs in the industrial and business life of the country is negligible and this partly explains their low-income levels. As a part of its overall strategy to uplift the backward classes, it is imperative that all State governments are suitably advised and encouraged to create a separate network of financial and technical institutions to foster business and industrial enterprise among OBCs.

Structural Changes: Under the existing *scheme of production-relations* Backward Classes comprising mainly small landholders, tenants, agricultural labour, village artisans, etc., are heavily dependent on the rich peasantry for their sustenance. In view of this, OBCs continue to remain in mental and material bondage of the dominant castes and classes. Unless these production-relations are radically altered through structural changes[55] and progressive land reforms implemented strictly all over the country, OBCs will never become truly independent. In view of this, higher priority should be given to radical land reforms by all the States.

The Commission, therefore, strongly recommended that all the State Governments should be directed to enact and implement progressive land legislation so as to effect basic structural changes in the existing production relations in the countryside. At present surplus land is being allotted to SCs and STs a part of the surplus land becoming available in future as a result of the operation of land ceiling laws, etc. should also be allotted to be OBC landless labour.

Backward Class Development Corporations should be set up both at the Central and State level to implement various Socio-educational and economic measures for their advancement.

A separate Ministry/Department for OBCs at the Centre and the States should be created to safeguard their interests.[56]

With a view to giving better representation to certain very backward sections of OBCs like the Gaddis in Himachal Pradesh, Neo-Buddhists in Maharastra, Fishermen in the Coastal areas, Gujjars in J & K It is recommended that areas of their concentration may be carved out into separate constituencies at the time of delimitation.

Central Assistances: At present no Central Assistance is available to any State for implementing any welfare measures for Other Backward Classes. It is, therefore, recommended that welfare programmes specially designed for OBCs should be financed by the Central Government in the same manner and to the same extent as done in the case of SCs and STs.[57]

Regarding the period of operation of the Commission's recommendations, the entire scheme should be reviewed after twenty years. We have advisedly suggested this period of one generation, as the raising of social consciousness is a generational progress.[58]

The report of the Mandal Commission was placed before parliament in 1982 for debate. All political parties supported the report. They did not oppose the caste criterion. The Ministry of Home Affairs, Government of India then created a Backward Classes Cell which consisted of five officers, and is concerned, not with the implementation of the recommendations of the report, but the preparation of replies to questions rose in parliament. On 13th August 1990, the V.P. Singh government issued an executive order to reserve 27% posts in central services for OBCs.[59] It led to strong anti-reservation agitation. Writs were filed in the Supreme Court which stayed the government order till its final judgment of 16th November 1992. The Supreme Court with its majority Judgement, found the 13th August, 1990 order as constitutional and subsequently the Mandal Commission report was executed with effect from 8th September, 1993.

Minute of dissent : L.R. Naiku, a member of the Commission, was not agree with the recommendation of the Commission only with reference to categorization of socially and educationally backward classes of citizens, identified by the Commission in terms of references made to them.

Therefore, he wrote a separate minute of dissent. He held very sincerely that castes/classes mentioned in the common list, each having homogeneous and cohesive characteristics, are not at the same degree and educational backwardness. He alarm that the safeguards recommended for their advancement will not penetrate to less unfortunate sections among them and the constitutional objectives proclaiming and establishment of an egalitarian society will remain a myth.

He suggested that a separate list be prepared for each state and that each list should be in two parts—one part detailing the *intermediate backward classes*[60] and the other enumerating the *depressed backward classes*.[61] Entries in depressed backward classes fully indicate their social and educational backwardness and therefore, should have been proposed by the founding fathers of our Constitution as in case of the Scheduled Castes and Scheduled Tribes for the purpose of specification. This lapse on the part of our Constitution-makers has resulted in a serious constraint in establishing an egalitarian society based on justice; social, economical and political. In view of the fact that the 'Depressed Backward Classes' are comparable in matters of backwardness to those of the Scheduled Castes and Scheduled Tribes, I recommend 15 per cent reservation for them out of 27 per cent both in public services and educational institutions as mentioned above. For all other concessions they should be treated on par with SC/ST. I refrain from recommending political reservation.[62]

But the Commission did not accept this suggestion; it even cited the judgment of the Supreme Court of the India in *Balaji* v. *State of Mysore*,[63] which had, *inter alia* stated:

> "In introducing two categories of backward classes, what the impugned order, in substance, alleged to do is to devise measures for all the classes of citizens who are less advanced compared to the most advanced classes in the State, is not the scope of Article 15(4)."

A Critical Study of the Two National Commission's Reports: Kaka Kalelkar Commission did not provide any positive recommendation to view of the last minute *volte-face* of its Chairman, when he virtually repudiated the Commission's work with conclusion that "it would have been better if we could determine the criteria of backwardness on principles other than caste".[64] He found caste test as repugnant to democracy and inimical to the creation of "a casteless and classless society. Mr. Marc Galanter very rightly comments,[65] "The Chairman's last-minute desertion foreshadow the negative reception that awaited the Report.[66]

The disturb elements in the report were two — (i) about 70 per cent of India's population considered as backward, and (ii) Caste was made sole criteria of backwardness. The Chief merit of the Kaka Kalelkar Commission may viewed as its recommendation to divide backwards into backward and most backward—out of 2399 castes identified as backward castes 837 were treated as most backward and remaining 1562 castes were declared to be backward castes.

In such a situation Mandal Commission presents improvement upon Kaka Kalelkar Commission. It identified 52% of population as backward. It used economic and educational indicators in addition to caste as criterion for identification of backwardness. It also took care of backward Muslims which were left outside by Kaka Kalelkar Commission. What the Commission did not look into was the division of backwards into backward and most backward. It was so because the Commission itself recommended periodic review of backward classes. It was also so because the emphasis of Commission through reservation was not on services but on balance in control of levers of power. It observed:

> "The Chief merit of reservation is not that it will introduce egalitarianism among OBCs when the rest of the Indian Society is seized by all sorts of inequalities. But reservation will certainly erode the hold of higher caste on the services and enable OBCs in general to have a sense of participation in running the affairs of the country."

The identification of the backward classes by the Mandal Commission is not with a seal of perpetual finality but on the other hand it is subjected to reviewability by the Government. The Mandal Commission has itself suggested that, "the entire scheme should be reviewed after 20 years". Therefore, it is for the Government to review the lists at any point of time and take a decision for the exclusion of any pseudo community or caste suggested into the backward class or for inclusion of any other community which in the opinion of the government suffers from social backwardness.[67]

> "A lot of heart burning was caused to the British when they left India. It burns the hearts of all whites when the blacks protest against apartheid in South Africa. When the higher castes constituting less than 20% of the country's population subjected the rest to all manner of social injustice, it must have caused a lot of heart burning to be lower castes. But now that the lower castes are asking for a modest share of the national cake of power and prestige, a chorus of alarm is being raised on the plea that this will cause heart burning to the ruling elite of all the spacious arguments advanced against reservation for backward classes; there is none which beats this one about 'heart burning' in sheer sophistry."
>
> Report of II B.C.C., Vol. I, Chapter XIII (13.8).

Notes and References

1. Janki Prasad *v.* State of Jammu & Kashmir AIR 1973 SC 930, 936.
2. AIR 1967, SC 1283, 1286.
3. *Ibid.*, at 1286.
4. *Ibid*, State of Jammu & Kashmir v. Jagananth, AIR 1958.
5. CAD, Vol. VII.
6. Article 340 of Indian Constitution, article 340(3) declares: the president shall cause copy of report, explaining the action taken thereon, to be laid before each House of Parliament.
7. Reservational Justice to other backward Classes (OBCs): Theoretical and practical issues, Anirudh Prasad, Deep and Deep Publications, New Delhi (ed. 1997), p. 30.
8. Report of the Commission for the Scheduled castes and Scheduled Tribes 10th report part I, p. 317 (1960-61). The lists of backward

Classes were specified in Vol. II of the Report of BCC. Gazette of India, Extraordinary dt. 31.1.1953.

9. *Ibid.*, at 30-31.
10. *Ibid.*, at 31.
11. Backward Classes Commission Report, Vol. 1, pp. 106-7).
12. Reservational Justice to Other Backward Classes (OBCs): Theoretical and practical issues, Anirudh Prasad, Deep and Deep Publications, New Delhi (ed. 1997), p. 32.
13. Ist BCC at p. XIII, p. 125.
14. *Ibid.*, at 140, the Commission prepared only one list both for the purposes of articles 15(4) and 16(4).
15. *Ibid.*, at 143.
16. Ist BCC at 8, 47.
17. *Ibid.*
18. Ist BCC at 55.
19. *Ibid.*, at 39.
20. Ist BCC at p. XIII (Extract of the following letter of the Chairman).
21. *Ibid.*, at 41.
22. In certain writing on the work of the Backward Classes Commission also the similar views have been expressed. Like Nirmal Kumar Bose, "who are the Backward Classes", 34(2) man in India 89, 98 (2954); Nabendu data Majumdar, 'the Backward Classes Commission and its work' in social welfare in India (issued by the Planning Commission), New Delhi (1960).
23. Report of the Backward Classes Commission, (Chairman B.P. Mandal), Parts I, II, New Delhi, 1981, p. 1 (hereinafter cited as Mandal Commission Report).
24. Ist BCC at VI.
25. *Ibid.*, at VII.
26. *Ibid.*, at VIII.
27. *Ibid.*, Besides the Chairman, three members also repudiates the Caste criteria and favoured economic test, Anup Singh, 3 BCC at 4, Arunghshu De *Ibid.*, at 5, P.G. Shah *Ibid.*, at 7.
28. Government of India: Ministry of Home Affairs, Memorandum on the Report of the Backward Classes Commission; 1-5 (1956).
29. *Ibid.*, at 3-4.
30. *Ibid.*, at 3.
31. N. 7, p. 2.
32. Memorandum on the report of the Backward Classes Commission: Ministry of Home Affairs, Government of India, New Delhi, 1956, p. 2.
33. Ministry of Home Affairs, 1956:4.
34. *Ibid.*

35. *Ibid.*, pp. 4-5. Letters of Ministry of Home Affairs to Chief Secretaries of all State Governments/Union Territories, Aug. 14, 1961.
36. Government of India: Ministry of Home Affairs, 38 (1962).
37. E.G. Balaji *v.* State of Mysore, Chitralekha *v.* State of Mysore, A.I.R. 1964 S.C., 1823.
38. Reservation for Backward Classes, Mandal Commission Report of the Backward Classes' Commission, 1980, Pub. Akalank Publication, Mori Gate, Delhi, p. iv.
39. *Ibid.*
40. *Ibid.*, Chapter xi, at p. 56.
41. *Ibid.*, at p. 57.
42. *Ibid.*
43. *Ibid.*
44. *Ibid.*
45. *Ibid.*, at Chapter XII, p. 60.
46. *Ibid.*, at p. 61.
47. *Ibid.*
48. *Ibid.*
49. *Ibid.*, at Chapter XII, p. 62.
50. *Ibid.*
51. *Ibid.*
52. *Ibid.*, at p. 63.
53. *Ibid.*
54. *Ibid.*, at p. 64.
55. *Ibid.*, at p. 65.
56. *Ibid.*
57. *Ibid.*
58. *Ibid.*
59. Official Memorandum of Ministry of Personnel, Government of India, 13 August, 1990.
60. The 'Intermediate Backward Classes', in my opinion are those whose traditional occupation had been agriculture, market gardening, beetle leaves growers, pastoral activities, village industries like artisans, tailors, dyers and weavers, petty business-*cum*-agricultural activities, heralding, temple service, toddy selling, oil mongering, combating, astrology, etc., who have co-existed since times immemorial with upper castes, N. 7, p. IV.
61. Depressed Backward Classes' whose mixture with the Indian society either denied, prohibited and even segregated obviously on account of stigma of the traditional occupations stigma of criminality, stigma of nomadism resulting in their abysmally low social status. They, generally, are ex-criminal tribes, nomadic and

wandering tribes, earth diggers, fishermen, boatmen and palanquin bearers, salt-makers, washermen, shepherds, barbers, scavengers, basket-makers, furriers and tanners, landless agricultural labourers, watermen, toddy tappers, camel-herdsmen, pig-keepers, pack bullock carriers, collectors of forest produce, hunters and fowlers, corn parchers, primitive tribes (not specified as Scheduled Tribes), exterior classes (not specified as Scheduled Castes), begging communities, etc.

62. Reservation for Backward Classes, Mandal Commission Report of the Backward Classes' Commission, 1980, Pub. Akalank Publication, Mori Gate, Delhi, Vol. VII, pp. 355-57.
63. AIR 1967 SC 1283.
64. I.B.C.C. XIV.
65. Marc Galanter, Competing Equalities, 1984, p. 172.
66. In addition to the Chairman's repudiation, three other members of the Commission, including the secretary field minutes of the dissent objecting to the caste basis of classification (Minutes of Dissent of Dr. Anup Singh, Shri Arungshu De, Shri P.G. Shah). Two other members dissented on the ground that the commission not gone for enough. Shri T. Mariappa merely objected to the failure in include urban Lingayats Vokalingas in Mysore, Shri S.D. Singh Chauraisa set forth a detailed proposal for equating Backward (with Shudras). The various Minutes of Dissents is complied in Vol. III of the Report.
67. Indra Sawhney Case, 1993, AIR SC at Para 353.

3

Constitutional Commitment for Backward Class

"Democracy is not just a ballot box and a government. The saga of democracy is the saga of human dignity. If one person's boot is on the other person's head wherein is democracy? If one is discriminated by birth wherein is equity? If we carry the hatred of a thousand years in our hearts wherein is fraternity? To get human dignity, equality to all and fraternity reservation is obligatory".

(Anirudh Prasad, Reservational Justice to OBCs)

Objective of the Preamble of Indian constitution[1] is to secure to every citizen *Justice*—social, economic and political: *Equality* of status and opportunity: and to promote among them all. It contained the concept of brotherhood of man and gives realistic shape by abolishing title, untouchablity, and other social evils which influenced the social arena of Indian society. 'Liberty, Equality, and Fraternity' which the Constitution seeks to secure for the people of India are to serve the primary objective of ensuring social, economic and political justice egalitarian society.

Indian Constitution is a social document. Its maximum provision aimed at achieving the goals of the socio-economic revolution and the core of the commitment to the social revolution lies in the Fundamental Rights and Directives Principles of State Policy.[2] Since founding fathers of the Indian Constitution were very much aware about the upliftment and advancement of deprived and backward classes, therefore, advocated certain safeguards for their upliftment under Indian Constitution.

To achieve social justice, social disabilities or ills have to remove or abolish. For this purpose Indian Constitution provides for:

(1) Abolition of untouchablity (Article 17);
(2) Throwing open of Hindu religious institutions of a public character to all classes and sections of Hindus [Article 25(2)(b)];
(3) Prohibition of traffic in human beings and forced labour (Article 23); and
(4) Prohibition of employment of children in factories (Article 24).

To achieve Educational and Economic justice Indian Constitution provides:

(1) Special provisions for the advancement of any socially and educationally backward classes of citizens or for the Scheduled Castes and the Scheduled Tribes. [Article 15(4)];
(2) Promotion of educational and economic interest of Scheduled Castes, Scheduled Tribes and other weaker sections (Article 46);
(3) Provision for reservation in services and post for backward class of citizens [Article 16(4)]; and
(4) Claims of Scheduled Castes and the Scheduled Tribes to services and posts (Article 335).

And to achieve political justice Indian Constitution provides certain political safeguards :

(1) Reservation of seats for Scheduled Castes and the

Scheduled Tribes in the House of the People (Article 320).

(2) Reservation of seats for Scheduled Castes and the Scheduled Tribes in the Legislative Assemblies of the states (Article 332).

(3) Reservation of seats shall cases to have effect on the expiration of fifty years from the commencement of Indian Constitution (Article 334).

(4) Appointment of National Commission for Scheduled Castes and the Scheduled Tribes, etc. (Articles 338, 340) and Other Backward Classes.

Above mentioned safeguards are further classified into various head, i.e. (a) Fundamental Rights, (b) Directive principal, and (c) other special Constitutional provisions.

CONSTITUTIONAL COMMITMENT FOR BACKWARD CLASSES UNDER FUNDAMENTAL RIGHTS (Articles 14, 15, 16, 17, 25)

Indian Constitution being a social document is the guarantee for political democracy as well as social democracy. It has opened up new vistas of growth through an assortment of rights and privileges incorporated to the citizens in general and backward classes in particular. The objectives of the Indian Constitution find a paramount place in expressions—*Justice, Liberty, Equality, Fraternity and Dignity* proclaimed in the preamble.

The expression *justice* is currently used in two senses: as presenting, on the one hand, the faithful realization of existing laws as against any arbitrary infraction of it; and as representing, on the other, the ideal element in all laws—the 'idea' which the law tends to subserve.[3] The preamble of Indian Constitution gives accent to justice in the social, economic and political sphere. *Social justice* demands the eradication of inequalities based on caste, colour, race, creed, etc. *Economic justice* rules out distinction from man to man from the point of view of economic values. Every man is awarded according to his labour. *Political justice* refers to the absence of arbitrary treatment of citizens in the political sphere—the right to exercise franchise and enter legislatures. It has been realized that political freedom alone would be futile in the absence of social and economic justice and so they have guaranteed justice in all three spheres.[4] To achieve this triple field justice Fundamental Rights are enshrined in the constitution.

Liberty defined as affirmation by an individual or group of his or its own essence,[5] liberty means freedom, the negation of unreasonable restrictions. Liberty sounds very significant in the sense that, citizens cherished the idea of liberty. Here *Pt. Nehru* remarked: *"Civil liberty is not merely for us an airy doctrine or a pious wish, but something which we consider essential for the orderly development and progress of a nation."*[6]

"Fraternity" postulates human values by respecting the dignity of human personality. Article 17 of the Indian Constitution, which refers to the abolition of untouchablity and secured to the millions of citizens' equality of status as human being, is an illustration of the advocacy of the concept of fraternity.[7]

Term *"Dignity"* denotes a quality of being worthy or honourable. It suggests a high rank or a position of distinction in community.[8] The human dignity consists in man's ability to experience self-awareness and to think rationally. Dignity means 'Maryada' and 'Maryada' means behaving in rightful manner.[9] The Epic of Mahabharata narrates 'Maryada' means a dignity lies in righteous conduct and its characteristic is to control or to limit or to restrain.[10] Dignity is a social thing. It involves one's ability to hold some kind of rank in social arrangement. Reputation, honour and social position are thought to be hallmark of a person's dignity. It may be said that human dignity only presents when a person is allowed to make his own decisions and determination. To enslave, imprison or otherwise deprive someone of his freedom, is to rob him his essential human worth and dignity. Human dignity is, thus a concept, which applies to whole community of persons—not merely to fragment of person.[11] A person is said to suffer indignity if he is treated as a subject or object only by others. In this perspective one's dignity or indignity depends upon other's action rather than his own.[12] The preamble of the Constitution embodies certain human values, cherished principles and spiritual norms and recognizes and holds the dignity of man. It accepts individual as a focal point of all development.

"Equality" means all human beings are born free and equal in dignity and rights. They are gifted with reason and conscience and therefore should act towards others in a spirit of brotherhood. Equality does not mean that we are all the same. Each of us is different in our own special way. But we also have the common qualities that make us all humans. So each of us should be treated with respect and dignity and treat others in the same way.[13] All persons have the right to live their lives free from tyranny, persecution, harassment or any conspiracy of discrimination by a person or institution against any person because of sex, sexuality, gender, marital status, race, color, ethnicity, chronological age, nationality, descent, heritage, religion, creed, or handicap, that is designed to deny that person the equal protection of one's rights under law.[14]

Traditional view of equality remained, for long, as an individual-oriented view of equality by the application of the formula that equals must be treated equally, unequals unequally. It was not viewed as a means to redress rooted inequalities by positive measures, giving unequal benefits to the disadvantaged group of a society. But according to new approach, justice demands "equality of result" which can be attained only by the mitigation of inequalities of men by positive State action.[15] It was realized that the "claim of equality is in fact protest against unjust, undeserved and unjustified inequalities. Equality is a symbol of man's revolt against chance, fortuitous disparity, unjust power and crystallized privileges".[16]

Notion of equality represents two ideas, numerical (or literal or formal) equality and proportional equality. According to numerical equality each individual is to receive numerically identical amount of benefits being distributed the public sector.[17] If all men were equal and similar in every respect expect that they were distinct individuals, formal equality would have been sufficient. But men are not equal in their physical characteristics, native endowments, social and economic position, subjective preferences, values and tastes. It requires an appeal to empirical realities and adoption of a value system, which considers similarities and differences between different persons.[18]

According to proportional equality all will receive the same consideration but the amount may differ. It demands a differential and separate treatment to those who are unequal. The standard of proportional equality requires the distribution of benefits according to 'merit' or 'need'. Both the merit principle and need principle is consistent with constitutional equality.[19] Therefore, principle of proportional equality should be tested on reason justifying different treatment to historically depressed classes, who are economically and socially unequal. They should be given share according to need.[20]

"*Equality*" in the preamble of Indian Constitution is not only equality in general but equality of Status and opportunity.[21] Equality is cherished words of passion and power and it find paramount place in the preamble and in the whole body of the Indian Constitution.[22] *Equality*, the keynote of democratic institutions, does not mean the leveling down of people, but only an equal treatment of citizens in the enjoyment of rights.[23]

The framer of the Indian Constitution were sentient of the prevailing miserable and appalling conditions of the backward groups who had remained far behind and segregated from national and social life and had continued to be socially oppressed and economically exploited for centuries due to various type of disability. It became imperative, therefore, to adopt a policy of 'compensatory' or 'protective discrimination' as an equalizer to those who were made too weak to compete with the advanced sections of the society in the race of life.[24] They took positive initiative to uplift the downtrodden, untouchable and his assimilation into the society on equal footing and made social justice a founding faith and built into it humanist provisions to lift the level of the lowly backward classes to make democracy viable and equal for all.[25]

Consonant with Constitution's resolve in the preamble to secure to all citizens; "justice, social, economic and political . . . equality of Status and opportunity", the Constitution guarantees to every person right to, "equality before the law and equal protection of law".[26] In order to give effect to general right to equality the Indian Constitution secures to all its citizens a freedom from discrimination on grounds of religion, race and caste.[27] In the specific application of this guarantee of equality, the State is further forbidden to discriminate against any citizen on grounds of place or birth,[28] residence,[29] descent,[30] class,[31] languages[32] and sex.[33] Untouchability has been abolished[34] and the citizens are protected against discrimination even on the part of private persons and institutions.[35] Indian Constitution secures political equality to all citizens by providing special privileges to the politically powerless groups in the legislative bodies such as Scheduled Caste and Scheduled Tribes.[36] Reservation in the legislatures for these desperate groups is in the spirit of real equality of opportunity to those people who are lacking in political consciousness and political experience.

Among various fundamental rights guaranteed to the citizens, the first and foremost is *"right to equality"*. *Doctrine of equality* has many facets and alive under Articles 14-18 of the Indian Constitution.

Article 14 affirms that the state shall not deny to any person equality before the law or the equal protection of law within the territory of India.[37]

This doctrine of natural equality[38] affirmed: "Men are born and always continue free and equal in respect of their rights." The same ideal[39] was again proclaimed as "we hold these truths to be self-evident, that all men are created equal. . . ." It got a patronage in the Declaration[40] "All are equal before the law and are entitled without any discrimination to equal protection of the law. All are entitled to equal protection against any discrimination in violation of this declaration and against any incitement to such discrimination." The two phrases in the article—*"Equality before the law"* and *"the equal protection of the laws"*, may be better described as a harmonious fusion of the American Constitutional safeguard and the Dicean concept of the Rule of law in England.[41]

Expression *"equality before the law"*,[42] means a Court administering justice is not concerned with the status or position of the parties appearing before it; the law is no respecter of persons" and declares that no one can claim special privileges and all classes are equally subject to the ordinary law of the land. It is said that state should not differentiate between the citizens either in the promulgation or application of the law." It is the negation of differential treatment and impartiality in the adjustment of justice.

Ivor Jennings marvelously inform that, "*Equality before the law*" means among equals, the law should be equal and should be equally administered, that like should be treated alike".[43] If all men were created equal and remained equal, it would mean the guarantee of the same laws for all. But the political theory of equality gets confronted with the natural fact of inequality. Complete equality among all men and women is not possible therefore theory of classification has been adopted as a necessary consequence of the concept underlying the equality clause that a law must operate alike on all people under like circumstance.[44]

In *Dalmia Cement (Bharat) Ltd. v. Union of India*[45] case, the concept of equality in its proper spectrum encompasses social and economic justice in a political democracy. Doctrine of *equality before law* has many facets. . . . In a society if glaring inequalities of income, social injustice and exploitation, inequality of status and opportunity exit, there is no room for equality before law. This doctrine is co- relative to the concept of rule of law for all round evaluation of healthy social order. A basic postulate of the rule of law is that "justice should not only be done but it must also seem to be done".[46]

The expression "*the equal protection of the laws*" means if all men were created equal, and remained equal throughout their lives, then the same would apply to all men. It postulates the application of the same laws alike and without discrimination to all persons similarly situated. It denotes equality of treatment in equal circumstances. It implies that among equals the law should be equal and equally administered, that the like should be treated alike without distinction of race, religion, wealth, social status or political influence.[47] But we know that men are unequal by nature, attainment or circumstances; consequently, a right conferred on persons that shall not be denied.

The "equal protection of the laws" cannot mean the protection of the same laws for all; it must mean the protection of equal laws for all persons similarly situated.[48] *Ivor Jennings* explained that "equal protection of the laws" means equal treatment should be meted out in like circumstances irrespective of any consideration whatever. The law of the land should be the same to the highest and the lowest.[49]

Mahajan J., in the *State of West Bengal v. Anwar Ali*[50] case interpreted, "right to equality is a principle of Republicanism and Article 14 enunciates this quality principle in the administration of justice. In its application to legal proceedings the article ensures to everyone the same rules of evidence and modes of procedures". This principle, however, does not mean that every law must have universal application for all persons who are not by nature, attainment or circumstance in the same position and varying needs of different class of persons often require separate treatment. Further held that the principle of equality does not take away from the State the power of classifying persons for legislate purposes. If a law deals equally with members of a well-defined class, it is not obnoxious and it is not open to the charge of denial of equal protection on the ground that it has no application to other person.[51]

Mukherjea J., construed the concept of equality in case of *Kathi Raning Rawat v. The State of Saurashtra*,[52] as equality prescribed by the constitution would not be violated if the statute operates equally on all persons who are included in the group, and the classification is not arbitrary or capricious, but bears a reasonable relation to the objective, which the legislation has in view.[53]

In *Narain Das v. Improvement Trust* case Hon'ble SC held that Article 14 requires, that all person are equally subject to the law and have a right to equal protection in similar circumstances both as regards privileges conferred and liabilities imposed by laws.[54] In *Sri Srinivasa Theatre v. Government of Tamilnadu*[55] it was held that there shall be no privileged person or class and that none shall be above the law. In *Ramesh Kumar Singh v. State of Bihar* case SC held that Equality is for equals, that is to say, those who are similarly circumstanced are entitled to an equal treatment but the principle of equality under Articles 14 and 16 cannot be carried beyond a point.[56]

In *Royappa's*[57] case it was held that equality is antithetic to arbitrariness from a "positivistic point of view". Equality and arbitrariness are sworn enemies; one belongs to the rule of law in a republic while the other, to the whim and caprice of an absolute monarch. If an act is arbitrary it is unequal both according to political logic and constitutional law. This Article strikes at arbitrariness in State action and ensures fairness and equality of treatment. Equality requires that State action must be based on valid relevant principles applicable alike to all . . . and must not be guided by any irrelevant considerations because that would be denial of equality.

In *Manaka Gandhi* case[58] the Court held that equality is a dynamic concept with many aspects and dimensions and cannot be "cribbed, cabined and confined or imprisoned" within traditional and doctrinaire limits. The principle of reasonableness, legally and as well as philosophically, is an essential element of equality. In "*Sholapur Mills* case[59] it was held that the principle of equality does not mean that every law must have universal application for all persons who are not by nature, attainment or circumstances in the same position, and the very needs of different classes of persons often require separate treatment.

In *Air India* v. *Nargesh Meerza*[60] case the Supreme Court formulated a propositions that article 14 is certainly attracted where equals are treated differently without any reasonable basis. In the very nature of things the society being composed of unequals, a welfare State will have to strive by legislative, executive and judicial action to help the less fortunate in the society to ameliorate their conditions so that the social and economic inequality in the society may be bridged.[61]

Article 14 (general equality) is founding faith of the Indian Constitution and pillar on which the foundation of our democratic republic rests and therefore it must not be subjected to narrow, pedantic approach because equality is a dynamic concept with many aspects and dimensions. Equality clause requires the State in framing the legislation to take into account the private inequalities of wealth, education and other circumstances.[62] Equilibrium in human terms emerges from release of the handicapped and from social disadvantage, to discriminate positively in favour of the weak, may be sometimes by promotion of genuine equality before the law. One law for the Lion and an Ox is oppression.[63]

Thus the Constitution of India ensures social and economic equality and distributive justice to the people. The root cause of the existence of inequalities is the glaring social and economic inequalities prevailing in the society. Treatment with the backward classes and their position in the society is against the principle of equality under Article 14. Equality before law means, equality of basic human rights, economic equality, equality of opportunity or equality of consideration for all persons but the position of backward classes is contrary to the growth of humanity at equal footing. The victims of inequality are deprived of every right in this unequal society and are entitled for equal treatment under Article 14. The doctrine of equality is a necessary corollary to the high concept of the rule of law accepted by our constitution. This concept made a specific Constitutional guarantee for the purpose of creating men equal even though they are born unequal.[64] *Therefore, provision of reservations for backward classes to bring them in the mainstream of nations is not discrimination.*

Article 15[65] provides Constitutional protection against discrimination on grounds of religion, race, caste, etc.

Article 15 owes its origin to article 9 of the Draft Constitution and originally enacted only three sub-clauses. When on November 29, 1948, the Constituent Assembly took up the consideration of Draft Article 9; *Prof. K.T. Shah* brought an Amendment No. 323, for extending the advantage or safeguards to the *Scheduled Castes and backward tribes.*[66] He argued:

> "I read it that this is a provision for discrimination in favour of women and children, to which I have added the Scheduled Castes or backward tribes. This discrimination is in favour of particular classes of our society, which, owing to an unfortunate legacy of the past, suffer from disabilities or handicaps. Those, I think, may require special treatment; and if they do require it, they should be permitted special facilities for some time so that real equality of citizens be established.
>
> In regard to the Scheduled Caste and backward tribes, it is an open secret that they have been neglected in the past; and

their rights and claims to enjoy and capacity to enjoy as equal citizens happens to be denied to them because of their backwardness. I seek therefore by this motion to include them also within the scope of this sub-cause (2), so that any special discrimination in favour of them may not be regarded as violating the basic principles of equality for all classes of citizens in the country. They need must be given, for some time to come at any rate, special treatment in regard to education, in regard to opportunity for employment, and in many other cases where their present inequality, their present backwardness is only a hindrance to the rapid development of the country.

As section of the community which is backward must necessarily impede the progress of the rest; . . . we should provide facilities so that they may be brought up-to-date so to say and the uniform progress of all be forwarded.

I have, of course not included in my amendment the length of years, the term of years for which some such special treatment may be given. That may be determined by the circumstances of the day. I only want to draw your attention to the fact that there are some classes of our citizens who may need, through no fault of theirs, some special treatment if equality is not to be equality of name only or on paper only, but equality of fact. I trust this will commend itself to the House and the amendment will be accepted".[67]

With this amendment of K.T. Shah, Dr. Ambedkar was not agreed and he rejected it to accept. Further he pointed out that *'it may have just the opposite effect'*. Elaborating this point he said:

> "The object which all of us, have in mind is that the Scheduled Caste and Scheduled Tribes should not be segregated from the general public.[68]

Thus initially Article 15 was not having any specific provision for backward classes, only it prohibits any kind of discrimination based on the grounds mentioned under Article 15(1). But within sixteen months from the commencement of the Indian Constitution, as a result of the decision of apex Court in *Madras* v. *Champakam Dorairajan*,[69] case Article 15 was amended for the addition of sub-clause (4).

In that case, the Hon'ble Court struck down the "Communal G.O." of Madras Government, as violating Article 15 or Article 29(2). As it held that any reservation for backward classes in educational institutions was invalid because of the provisions in clause (2) of the Article 29 which provided that, "No citizen shall be denied admission into any educational institution maintained by the State or receiving aid out of State funds on grounds of only of religion, race, caste, language or any of them."

To meet out the problem raised in *Champakam* case a new clause (4) was inserted by an amendment[70] and permits the State to make specials provisions for the educational and social advancement of backward classes or SC and ST. The special provision may be by way of reservation of seats for them, or to grant them fee concession; in public educational institutions.[71] Thus this fourth clause has been added so as to give special recognition to backward classes, Scheduled Castes and Scheduled Tribes and considered as an exception to the general rule lay down in clauses (1) and (2) of Article 15. Therefore, object of this clause is to bring Articles 15 and 29 in line with Articles 16(4), 46 and 340, and to make it for the State to reserve seats for backward classes of citizens SC/ST in the public educational institutions[72] as well as to make other special provisions as may be necessary for their advancement. The immediate effect of this amendment was to override the decision given in *Champakam* case to the effect that Article 29(2) do not controlled by Article 46 and that the Constitution does not intend to protect the interest of the backward classes in the matter of admission to educational institutions. But though the amendment would validate reservation for the backward classes and scheduled castes and tribes, it would not support the distribution of seats according to communities so as to discriminate between classes who are not backward, *inter se*, in short, the amendment would not sanction any communal order. This Article is also in the nature of an exception to clause (2) of Article 29.

The SC and ST being mentioned together with the 'backward classes' in Article 15(4), it is evident that by the expression 'backward classes' the clause refers to classes of persons other than the members of SC/ST.[73]

Supreme Court has emphasized that Article 15(4) 'does not speaks of Castes, but only speaks of Classes', and that 'caste' and 'classes' are not synonymous. Exclusion of caste to ascertain backwardness does not vitiate classification if it satisfies other tests.[74] Though discrimination on the ground of caste only is prohibited by clause (1) of Article 15, it would be permissible under clause (4) for the State to make special provision for three categories of person i.e.

(i) Socially and educationally backward classes of citizens,
(ii) Scheduled castes, and
(iii) Scheduled tribes.[75]

Therefore on the one side, general provision of Article 15(1) and (2) "forbids discrimination on ground of race, caste or religion etc., so that the old iniquitous situation may not be continued, on the other side it permits, [Article 15(4)] these very criteria for correcting evil consequences flowing from their past misuse".[76] This view was supported by Judiciary where it held that the State is authorized to use caste as an index of social and educational backwardness for making preferences of course, subject to the rider that caste cannot be the sole or dominant test (although it can be used in conjunction with other relevant consideration like poverty, occupation, place of habitation etc.).[77]

Article 15(4) at the first sight appear to be a blanket provision, protecting any kind of beneficial discrimination in the nature of special provisions for the benefit of the classes mentioned therein, but unreasonable discrimination will not be permitted at any cost. Hence reservation of an excessively high percentage of seats in technical institutions for each class would be void, because it will violate the general principle of equality under Article 14.[78] In *Mohan Bir Singh* v. *Punjab University*[79] SC upheld University-wise preference if it valid, domicile-wise reservation if it does not exceed reasonable limits, but college-wise reservation is held bad.

The word 'discrimination' used in this article is very crucial, it means 'making an adverse distinction with regard to' or distinguishing unfavourable from others, and other crucial word is 'only', it means if the discrimination is based on some ground not connected with religion, etc., but with some other rational factor, the discrimination would be valid.[80]

By virtue of Article 15(4), in building of reservation by executive order the State has to take care that it is not unduly wide. Apart from Scheduled Caste, Scheduled Tribes, the other classes, eligible for reservation if made by the State, is the category of "socially and educationally backward classes of citizens". Under Directive Principles it is the obligation of the State to promote with special care the educational and economic interests of "the weaker sections of the people".[81] It is also provided[82] that the claims of the members of the SC and ST shall be taken into consideration consistently with the maintenance of efficiency in the administration, in the making of appointments to services and posts in connection with the affairs of the Union or of a State. But this article does not mention about backward classes.[83]

In Chitralekha R. v. *State of Mysore*[84] it was pointed out that Article 15(4) does not speak of caste but only of classes. The juxtaposition of the expression "backward classes" and scheduled castes in Article 15(4) also leads to the reasonable inference that the expression "classes" is not synonymous with castes. While this observation is correct the conclusion that caste cannot be the sole or dominant criterion for ascertaining the class to which a person belongs is not correct after the Mandal case. But there can be a sincere attempt to promote the welfare of backward classes and weaker section, weightage should not be given to progressive sections of society under the false colour of caste. In *Balaji's* case,[85] it was held that though caste is a relevant factor, its importance should not be exaggerated and it cannot be the sole basis for determining the backwardness of a particular group or class of citizens. But in a subsequent decision, it was held that if a caste as a whole is socially and educationally backward, it could be the basis for reservation under Article 15(4).[86]

The innovation of Article 15(4) is wholly unjustified in granting remission to the convicted prisoners belonging to SC/ ST as it is no measure for their 'advancement'. However, benefit obtained was permitted to be retained.[87]

There is no constitutional or legal bar on State to categorizing backward classes as backward and more backward. While Article 16(4) recognizes only one class namely "backward class of citizens"; it does not speak separately of Scheduled Castes and Scheduled Tribes as does Article 15(4). Even though SCs/STs are included in the expression "backward classes", separate reservation can be provided in their favour. The backward classes referred to in Article 16(4) has a much wider scope than Article 15(4).[88] In the *Mandal* case[89] after referring earlier decision on the subject it was held that Article 15(4) speaks of "adequate representation" and not "proportionate representation" which has been accepted only for a limited period. It is reasonable to state that reservation should not exceed 50% of the appointments or posts barring extraordinary situation.

A division bench of the Supreme Court has held that when a part of a State is socially and educationally backward, with reference to another part, the inhabitants of that part may be considered as a 'backward class', so that it would be permissible for the state to offer reservation or weightage to that backward area in the matter of admission to an educational institution which is common to both parts.[90]

In *State of M.P. v. Nivedita Jain,*[91] judiciary held that they (SCs/STs) constitute a protected class, apart from any condition of backwardness as specified in Article 15(4). Hence, the State is entitled to do everything for the upliftment of member of these Castes, and Tribes, to make reservations for their admission to educational institutions and to impose such conditions as would make the reservation effective. It follows that government may make relaxation of the rules for admission to such institutions or for selection to Government employment, say, by lowering the minimum qualifying marks or other conditions; or by offering them two avenues for promotion in place of one for the rest of the people or reservation of selection posts for them.[92] A Scheduled Caste is not a 'caste' within the meaning of that word in Article 15(1) and 16(2). It has a special meaning, namely, a caste as notified by the President under Article 366(25).[93]

Reservations are to ensure the advancement of socially and educationally backward citizens to make them equal with other segments of the community. Reservations should and must be adopted to advance the prospects of weaker sections of society but while doing so, care should be taken not to exclude the legitimate expectation of other segments of the community.

Government should not act on the assumption that once a class is considered backward it should continue to be backward for all times. If once a class appears to have reached a stage of progress from which it could be safely inferred that no further protection is necessary, the State would do well to review such cases and suitably revise the list of the backward classes.[94]

It is manifest that as per provisions of under Article 15(4) reservation is applicable only in Government aided Institutions not in private Institutions or private job. Recently Supreme Court delivered an unanimous judgement by Chief justice *R.C. Lahoti* with 7 judges Bench (*Justices Y.K. Sabharwal, D.M. Dharmadhikari, Arun Kumar, G.P. Mathur, Tarun Chatterjee and P.K. Balasubramanyan)* in the case of *P.A. Inamdar & others* v. *State of Maharashtra & others* declaring that the State can't impose its reservation policy on minority and non-minority unaided private colleges, including professional colleges (engineering and medical colleges). This judgement was an attempt to bring clarity to two previous judgements by the Supreme Court.[95] One of them is the judgement delivered on October 31, 2002 by 11 judges in the case of *Pai Foundation* case[96] with multiple opinions—a majority opinion by the 5 judges—*G.B. Pattanaik, S. Rajendra Babu, K.G. Balakrishnan, P. Venkatarama Reddi & Arijit Pasayat* with a separate but concurring opinion by the Chief Justice *V.N. Khare,* and three separate opinions by *S.N. Variava, Ashok Bhan and Syed Shah Mohammed Quadri.* The other is the judgement delivered on August 14, 2003 by a constitution bench that interpreted the Pai Foundation judgement in the case of *Islamic Academy of Education,*[97] again with multiple opinions—a majority opinion by the 4 judges—*CJI V.N. Khare, S.N. Variava, K.G. Balakrishnan & Arijit Pasayat* and a separate opinion by *S.B. Sinha.*

The Supreme Court in its judgement on August 12, 2005 ruled on reservation policy, in relation to minority and non-minority unaided higher education institutions. It held that neither the policy of reservation can be enforced by the State nor any quota or percentage of admissions can be carved out to be appropriated by the State in a minority or non-minority unaided educational institution. So far as appropriation of quota by the State and enforcement of its reservation policy is concerned, we do not see much of difference between non-minority and minority unaided educational institutions. The State cannot insist private educational institutions which receive no aid from the State to implement State's policy of reservation for granting admission on lesser percentage of marks, i.e. on any criterion except merit.

It is observed,

> "that merely because the resources of the State in providing professional education are limited, private educational institutions, which intend to provide better professional education, cannot be forced by the State to make admissions available on the basis of reservation policy to less meritorious candidate. Unaided institutions, as they are not deriving any aid from State funds, can have their own admissions if fair, transparent, non-exploitative and based on merit."

The apex court for the first time, allowed a 15 per cent quota for NRIs in professional institutions. It, however, made it clear that the higher fee charged from such students should be used for thc benefit of students of economically weaker section.

To nullify this decision of Apex court, Parliament has passed an The Constitutional (93rd Amendment) Act, 2005 by which Article 15(5)[98] has been incorporated to pave the way and widen the scope of reservation for SCs, STs and other backward class by extending it to not just in aided professional educational institutes but all the unaided educational institutions also. The repercussions of this would be felt by private schools and other institutions which have never been brought under the reservation umbrella. In the case of *Ashoke Kumar Thakur* v. *Union of India*,[99] Supreme Court upheld the constitutionality of Article 15(5). Now State would have to come up with enabling legislations to enforce the constitutional amendment in any private educational institution. The rational behind this is private institutions can not escape from their liability to provide social justice.

Article 16 endow with right to equal opportunity in matters of public employment and further provides not to make discrimination on the grounds mentioned under clause (2) of Article 16.[100]

The main object of Article 16 is to create a Constitutional right to equality of opportunity and employment in public offices. In a sense the scope of the right to equal opportunity in matters of employment guaranteed by Article 16(1) appears to be more fully defined when read with the governmental obligation to promote the educational and economic interests of the weaker section. Article 16 is a spread of Article 14. Hence non-arbitrariness is a part and parcel of Article 16.[101]

Clauses (1) and (2) of Article 16 endow with equality of opportunity to all its citizens in matter of appointment to any office or any other employment under the State. Citizens can not be discriminated against or be ineligible for any employment or office under the state on grounds only of religion, race, caste, sex, descent, place of birth or residence. Here two new grounds 'descent' and 'residence' are included in clause 2 of Article 16. But it should be remembered that under Article 16 the guarantee against discrimination is limited to 'employment and appointment' under the State, while Article 15 is more general and deals with all cases of discrimination which do not fall under Article 16.[102]

The words 'employment or appointment' are wide enough to include tenure, duration emoluments and duties and obligations, whether the employment is temporary or permanent. They cover amongst themselves not merely the initial appointment, but also salary, increments, revision of pay, promotion, gratuity, leave, pension and age of superannuation.[103]

Article 16(3) is an exception to clause (2) of this Article. This article empowers parliament to regulate by law the extent to which it would be permissible for a State to depart from the above principle. In exercise of powers conferred Parliament has passed the Public Employment (Requirement as to Resident) Act, 1957; it provides that no one will be disqualified on the ground that one is not the resident of a particular state. However, the Act makes an exception for employment in Himachal Pradesh, Manipur, Tripura, and Telangana. This exception is because of the backwardness of these areas.[104]

Article 16(4) authorizes State to make special provisions for reservation in appointments or posts but applies only when if two conditions are satisfied that :

(i) the class of citizen is backward; and
(ii) the said class is not adequately represented in the services of the state.

It is justified with the discussion held in the Constituent Assembly on 30th November 1948. As we know that this Article owes its origin in Draft Article 10. During discussion on the amendments about Article 10, Hon'ble Dr. B.R. Ambedkar observed,

> ". . . as I said, the Drafting Committee had to produce a formula . . . firstly, that there shall be equality of opportunity, secondly that there shall be reservation in favour of certain communities which have not so far had a 'proper look-in' so to say into the administration. If honourable members will bear these facts in mind—the three principle had to reconcile, they will see that no better formula could be produced than the one that is embodied in sub-clause (3) of Article 10 of the Constitution; they will find that there shall be equality of opportunity, has been embodied in sub-clause (1) of Article 10. It is a generic principle, at the same time, as I said, we had to reconcile this formula with the demand made by certain communities that the administration which has now—for historical reasons—been controlled by one community or a few communities, that situation should disappear and that the others also must have an opportunity of getting into the public services. They will find that there shall be equality of opportunity, has been embodied in sub-clause (1) of Article 10. It is a generic principle. At the same time, as I said, we had to reconcile this formula with the demand made by certain

communities that the administration which has now—for historical reasons—been controlled by one community or a few communities, that situation should disappear and that the others also must have an opportunity of getting into the public services. Therefore, the seats to be reserved, if the reservation is to be consistent with sub-clause (1) of Article 10, must be confined to a minority of seats. It is then only that the first principle could find its place in the constitution and effective in operation. If honourable members understand this position that we have to safeguard two things, namely the principal of equality of opportunity and at the same time satisfy the demand of communities which have not had so far representation in the state, than I am sure they will agree that unless you use some such qualifying phrase as "backward" the exception made in favour of reservation will ultimately eat up the rule altogether. Nothing of the rule will remain. That is the justification why the drafting Committee undertook on its own shoulders the responsibility of introducing the word 'backward' which I admit, did not originally find a place in the fundamental rights in the way in which it was passed by this Assembly. But I think honourable members will realize that the Drafting committee which has been ridiculed on more than one ground for producing something a loose draft, something which is not appropriate and so on, might have opened itself to further attack that they produced a draft Constitution in which the exception was so large, that it felt no room for the rule to operate. I think this is sufficient to justify why the word 'backward' has been used".[105]

While in *Indra Sawhney* v. *Union of India*,[106] SC held that Article 16(4) is not an exception to Article 16 as held in some cases.[107] But an instance of classification permitted under cls. 1 and 2 and the concession in favour of backward class have to be reconciled in such a manner that it does not unreasonable encroach upon the field of equality.[108] Like Article 14, Article 16(4) permits of reasonable classification. This provision actually effectuates the constructional mandate engrafted in Article 16(1) as it would offer equality of opportunity in the matters relating to employment and it would not be monopolized by a specified category of persons in the feeder category to get promotions.[109]

Cls. (4) is exhaustive of the concept of reservation in favour of backward classes. It does not follow however that cls. (1) does not permit of any reservation for any class other than backward. But in the latter case, the reservation will be valid if it satisfies the test of reasonable classification and the state shall have to satisfy that such a provision was necessary in the public interest to redress an exceptional situation.[110]

The word 'provision' used in cls. (4) of Article 16, is distinguished from the word 'law' used in cls. (3) of Article 16, it means that reservation under Article 16 may be made not only by statute but also by an executive order.[111] The word 'any provision' is wide enough to include not only reservation but other supplemental and ancillary provisions such as exemptions, concessions, which are necessary for the upliftment of the backward classes; of course consistently with Article 335.[112]

Term 'backward classes' used in Article 16(4) have the same sense as used in Article 15(4) and includes the educationally and socially backward classes or Scheduled Castes and Scheduled Tribes. Thus to qualify for being called a 'backward class citizen' under Article 16(4), one must be a member of a socially and educationally backward classes. The expression 'backward class' is not synonymous with 'backward caste' or 'backward community'.

To determine whether a section of population forms a 'backward class' for purpose of Article 16(4), a test solely based on caste, community, race, religion, sex, decent, place of birth or residence cannot be adopted.[113] But it should be remember that determination of backwardness by the executive is not a matter of subjective satisfaction but must be founded on objective test, e.g., social and other relevant criteria, and will be subject to judicial review.[114] In the case of a particular backward class, the Government may be of the opinion that it would not be necessary to provide for reservation and that it would be sufficient if a certain preference or concession is made in their favour.[115]

Under Article 16(4), reservation in government services is permissible not only at the initial stage of recruitment, but also permissible in the matter of promotion from a lower to a higher post or cadre. Selection posts could also be reserved for backward classes.

The right to consider for promotion is a fundamental right guaranteed to Scheduled Castes and Scheduled Tribes in fulfilment of the mandate under Article 16(1) read with Article 46 of the Constitution to render Socio-economic justice.[116] But when the quota for SCs/STs has already been completed, promotion cannot be claimed merely on the basis of being SC/ST candidates.[117] It is also held that in preparing the select panel of Scheduled Caste candidates for promotion, the criterion should be seniority. However, Scheduled Caste candidates, who are outstanding, in their selection test, have to be given preference.[118]

> "The purpose of keeping reservations even in favour of the socially and educationally backward classes under clause (4) is not to alleviate poverty but to give it an adequate share in power." [Per Sawant, J., *Indra Sawhney* v. *Union of India,* AIR 1993 SC (Para 492)].

Thus it is said that :

> "The objective behind the Article 16(4) is empowerment of the deprived backward communities—to give them a share in the administrative apparatus in the governance of the community.
>
> *[Majority Judgment in Mandal Case (Para 694)].*

In the case of *Bijoy Prasad v. Union of India & others*[119] it was held that when minimum service is prescribed for promotion, a candidate of reserved community should be promoted against reserved vacancy from the date of completion of such minimum service. If such candidates becomes eligible for promotion later on, meanwhile post should either be kept vacant or filled up by a person of other category on *ad hoc* basis. But in no case the post should be filled up on regular or permanent basis.

So far as provision for lower qualifying marks or lesser level of evaluation in the matter of promotion is concerned, it is not permissible under Article 16(4) in view of the command in Article 335 of the Constitution.[120]

The object of reservation as judiciary held is to provide socio-economic equality to the disadvantaged. Judiciary certified that reservation in appointment is the part of Constitutional scheme as a positive facility and opportunity to backwards to improve excellence in a service or post. Reservation for backward class normally implies a separate quota which is reserved for a special category of person.[121]

The implementation of Article 16(4) works under a rider or we could say that clause 4 is subject to safeguard, for this Supreme Court laid down that this article has to be interpreted in the light of Article 335,[122] virtually, the Hon'ble Court has held the element of efficiency of administration as a limitation on Article 16(4). This incidentally calls upon the judiciary to read together Articles 14, 46, 335.[123] Hence, clause 4 of Article 15 regarding backward class of citizens seems to possess a double character. As regards persons not belonging to such class, may appears to be discriminatory for special reason, but as regards the backward classes themselves, they view it as a corrective to remedy the imbalance which has resulted from historical causes. Broadly speaking, it may be stated that reservation in excess of 50% may be, prima facie, regarded as discriminatory.[124] In *Ram Bhagat Singh* v. *State of Haryana apex Court* held relaxation in shape of lower standards of eligibility is permissible for SC candidates etc., but also held that relaxation should be consistent with eligibility.[125]

As per the nature of Article 16(4) it, neither confers a constitutional right upon any member of backward class nor impose a Constitutional duty on the government to make a reservation for any one in public services. It is merely an enabling provision and confers a discretionary power on the State to reserve appointment in favour of certain classes of citizens.[126] Though Article 16(4) does not confer any fundamental right upon any individual, it enjoins the State to take positive action to alleviate inequality or, in other words, it confers power couples with duty.[127] As Article 16(4) says that reservation could be made to the post in favour of Scheduled Castes and the Scheduled Tribe, which in the opinion of the State are not adequately represented in the services under the state.

Reservation and Promotion: Since ruling of Apex Court in *Indra Sawhney* case approved that reservation in appointments or posts under Article 16(4) is confined to the initial appointment and cannot extend to reservation in the matter of promotion. This ruling was considered to adversely affect the interests of SCs and STs. It was thought that since the representation of SCs and STs in services in States had not reached the required level, so it is necessary to continue the existing dispensation of providing reservation in promotion to protect the interest of SC and ST. Therefore, the *Sub-clause 4A*[128] *has been inserted by 77th Constitutional Amendment Act, 1995 to provide reservation in promotion to SCs and STs. The 85th Constitutional Amendment Act, 2001*[129] *has been enacted to provide reservation* in favour of SCs and STs in promotion with *consequential seniority also (w.e.f. 1995).*

In *Ajit Singh* v. *State of Punjab* case[130] bench held that Article 16(4) and Article 16(4-A) do not confer any fundamental rights nor do they impose any constitutional duties but are only in the nature of enabling provision vesting a direction in the State to consider providing reservation of the circumstances mentioned in those articles so warranted. In *General Manager, Southern Railway* v. *Rangachari*[131] it was settled that the words 'employment' 'or 'appointment' are wide enough to include the matter of promotion, including promotion to selection post.

In *Kuldeep Kumar Gupta* v. *Himachal Pradesh State Electricity Board*[132] case apex court was of the view that this in the largest interest of the administration that it is the employer, who is best suited to decide the percentage of posts in the promotional cadre, which can be earmarked for different category of persons. This provision actually effectuates the constitutional mandate engrafted in Article 16(1), as it would offer equality of opportunity in the matters relating to employment and it would not be the monopoly of a specified category of persons in the feeder category to get promotions. There is no infraction of the constitutional provision engrafted Article 16 (4) while providing a quota in promotional cadre.

Sub-clause 4B was inserted through 81st Constitutional Amendment Act in 2000[133] *to consider unfilled reserved vacancies for backward classes, as a separate class.* It shall not be considered together with the vacancies of the year in which they are being filled up to determine the ceiling of 50% of the total vacancies of that year.[134]

Therefore want of Articles 15(4) and 16(4) arose in order to counter the prohibitions contained in Articles 15(1) or 16(2) and 29(2). *In Kathi Ranning* v. *State of Saurashtra* case,[135] Patanjali Shashtri, C.J. said that discrimination against involves an element of unfavourable bias against other on the grounds only of caste; religion, etc. and such discrimination will incur condemnation whenever such unfavourable bias is disclosed. Apparently, the compensatory discrimination in favour of backward classes is not tainted with unfavourable bias nor is it a discrimination against only on grounds of caste, religion or race. A valid compensatory discrimination is based on social, economic, or educational backwardness of certain groups. It is discrimination in favour of certain groups marked out by multiple criteria of backwardness such as caste, religion, poverty, occupation and so on. These provisions authorize the State to depart from uniform equality for favouring the backward groups. Articles 15(4) and 16(4) enable the State to act positively in the direction of uplifting the weaker elements in the society by making a reasonable classification

But it should be remember that when a member is transplanted into SC/ST or OBCs, he/she must also, of necessity, have had undergone the same handicaps and must have been subjected to same disabilities, disadvantages, indignities or sufferings so as to entitle him/her to avail the facility of reservation. Therefore, a candidate for a post who had the advantageous start in life being born in forward caste and had march of advantageous life but transplanted in Backward Caste by adoption or marriage or conversion, does not become eligible to the benefit of reservation either under Article 15(4) or 16(4), as the case may be. Acquisition of the status of Scheduled caste, etc. by voluntary mobility into these categories would play fraud on the Constitution, and would frustrate the benign constitutional policy under Articles 15(4) and 16(4).[136]

Article 17 endow with Constitution guarantee for abolition of untouchablity.[137]

The expression 'Untouchablity' is generally used with reference to those persons who are born in those castes and communities that are classed as Harijans or outcastes. It refers to those social disabilities historically imposed on certain classes of people solely by reason of their birth in certain castes which preclude them from any kind of intercourse with people belonging to the so-called higher classes or castes. This expression include those persons also who are made untouchable even though they might have been born in a higher caste. In Hindu Dharmashastra there was always a sharp distinction between 'Jathi Chandalas' (born untouchables) and 'Karma Chandalas' (those who became Chandalas on account of their own bad conduct). If a person born in a higher caste is effectively ex-communicated he becomes for all practical purpose an 'untouchable' and has no place in the society in which he is born in consequence of which all other members of his caste exclude him from joining in any social or religious ceremony. Article 17 prohibits this form of untouchability also.[138]

Before 800 B.C. the idea of ceremonial purity almost full-fledged and even operative in relation to the despised and degraded group of people, called Chandala, and to the fourth order of the society, the Shudras. During the period of Dharmasutrakars and Kautilya, Chandalas are declare to be the progeny of the most hated of the reverse order of mixed unions, that of a Brahmin female with a Shudra male. Breed of the Chandalas is a degraded one and is ranked with that of the dog and the pig. Some times Chandalas treat themselves as Shudras, but the Shudras treated them too low. Reference of Antyavasayin, progeny of a Vaishya female by a Shudra male is also found. During the time of Manu, Antyavasayin was of much more depraved origin. Other degraded castes called Sepaka, progeny of Kshatri male and augra male and Pandusopaka, are also mention. *Great Patanjali* (150 B.C.) speaks of Mritapas in combination with Chandalas as a variety of Shudra. They are rigorously excluded from all social contacts, residence were prescribed them outside the village. Although some time they resided within the limits of towns and villages of the Aryans as, other Shudras like carpenters, blacksmiths, washermen, weavers, did. The social distinction on status between groups as carpenters, blacksmiths, washermen, weavers, etc. on the one hand, and the Chandalas and the Mritapas, on the other hand, made only in the use of the meal-vessels of these people.

Chandalas and Mritapas were technically 'apapatras' or 'untouchables'. Apapatras are not permitted to see the performance of a funeral sacrifice. Brahmins are exhorted not to recite the Veda within hearing or sight of Shudras or Apapatras. In the age of Manu and onwards they were assigned duties and perquisites, it shows that they were looked upon as vile specimens of humanity.

Article 17 knocks the whole problem of untouchablity at the very bottom and throws it out lock, stock and barrel. Article does not stop with a mere declaration but announces that this forbidden 'untouchablity' is not to be henceforth practiced in any form. If it were so practiced it shall be dealt with an offence punishable in accordance with the law.[139] However, 'untouchablity' in the constitution is nowhere defined in the Constitution; in 1947 in the Constituent Assembly Rohini Kumar Chaudhry defined untouchablity as,

> 'Untouchablity' means any act committed in exercise of discrimination on grounds of religion, caste or lawful vocation of life'.[140]

Thus the principal object of this Article is to ban the practice of untouchability in any form. This expression refers to the social disabilities imposed on certain classes of persons by reason of their birth in certain castes and does not cover social boycott based on conduct.[141] Under the protective umbrella of Article 35 Parliament empowers to make laws for prescribing punishment for the acts, which are declared to be offences under Part III (Fundamental Rights) of the commission. In exercise of this power, parliament has enacted in 1955 the Untouchablity (Offences) Act, 1955 which prescribed punishment for the practice of untouchablity and for the enforcement of any disability arising thereform and for the matters connected therewith.[142]

Article 25 provides constitutional right to freedom of religion to all the citizens.[143]

This right is considered for the social advancement of backward classes. Objective of this Article is to abolish religious restrictions which were imposed in ancient time on certain class since their birth and saves the power of the state to regulate secular activities associated with the religious practice.[144] Under this article every person has a fundamental right under Indian Constitution not merely to entertain such religious belief as may be approved of by his judgment or conscience but to exhibit his belief and ideas in such overt acts as are enjoined or sanctioned by his religion and further to prorogate his religious views for the edification of other.

Article 25(2)(b) gives a Constitutional guarantee that all laws enacted before the commencement of the Constitution for social welfare and reform or for throwing open of Hindu religious institutions of a public character to all classes and sections of Hindus would not be invalidated. This sub-section also entitles the States to legislate on matters of social welfare and reform or for throwing of Hindu religious institutions of a public character to all classes and sections of Hindus. For the purpose of this section only, Hindus would mean Sikhs, Jains and Buddhist as well.[145] Consequently, their religious institutions of a public character should be thrown open to all sections of the Hindu instead of being confined to members of their own sects or denominations.

CONSTITUTIONAL COMMITMENT FOR BACKWARD CLASSES UNDER DIRECTIVE PRINCIPLES (Articles 38, 39, 39A, 46)

The directive principles have been scribed as forerunners of the U.N. Convention on Right to Development as an inalienable human right.[146] During the adoption of Indian Constitution, with reference to Directive Principles, Dr. Ambedkar said,

> "We must our political democracy a social democracy as well. Political democracy cannot last unless lies at the base of it social democracy. . . . We must begin by acknowledging the fact there is complete absence of two things in Indian society. One of these is equality. On the social plane, we have in India a society of graded inequality, which means elevation of some and degradation of others. On the economic plane, we have a society in which there are some who have immense wealth as against many who live in abject poverty.
>
> On the 26th January 1950, we are going to enter into a life of contradictions. In politics we will have equality and in social and economic life we will have inequality . . . we must remove this contradiction at the earliest possible moment or else those who suffer from inequality will blow up the structure of political democracy which this assembly has so laboriously built up".[147]

Further he said,

> ". . . there can be no democracy without social and economic justice to common man, to create socio-economic conditions in which there can be social and economic justice to everyone is the theme of the Directive Principles".[148]

Social justice is an objective of the Indian constitution . . . it demands preferential treatment to the weaker sections to correct the imbalance existing in the society. When justice is administered, 'equal' treatment is likely to result in injustice. Social justice therefore requires special treatment for the backward peoples. It helps in carrying on a just society by removing imbalance in social, educational, economic and political life of the people. It may be defined as the right of the weak, aged, destitute, and others underprivileged persons to those who are socially higher, economically richer, politically in authority and educationally advanced.

At the same time the Supreme Court held that Directive Principles are positive aspect. It can be held to supplement fundamental rights in achieving a welfare state. Parliament can amend fundamental rights for implementing the Directives. Legislation enacted to implement the Directive principles should be upheld, as for possible. Even legislative entries may be given a wide interpretation for effecting Directive Principles.[149]

Indian Constitution directs the State Governments to take positive action to strengthen the social, economic and educational status of deprived, week, or backward classes and to provide social, economic and political justice among the backward section of the society. To achieve this object numerous Articles are enshrined in the form of Directive Principles, because framers of the Constitution were very much cognizant of the existing socio-economic situation and aims at bringing about radical transformation in that situation.

Directive Principles are as follows:

Firstly; Indian Constitution directs the state government to secure a Social Order for the promotion of welfare of the people under Article 38.[150]

This article envisages not only legal justice but socio-economic-political justice as well. This enjoins the State to strive to promote the welfare of the people by securing and promoting, as effectively as it may, the social order in which justice—social economic and political—it shall, inform all the institution of national life striving to minimize inequalities in income and endeavour to eliminate inequalities in status, facilities, opportunities among individuals and group of people residing in different areas or engaged in different avocations.[151] The provision of the Act, which is to social measure, should be interpreted in the light of the public law principles viz. Articles 14, 15, 21, 38, 39, 39A, and 46.[152]

To secure justice to its people under the law, courts with broad power established in the country.[153] Judiciary aims equality in all spheres of life. It therefore, enables the state to have a national policy on wages and eliminate inequalities in various spheres of life.[154]

Article 39[155] *in its principles embodies the jurisprudential doctrine of 'Distributive Justice'.*

The concept of 'distributive justice' in the sphere of law making connote, *inter-alia*, the removal of economic inequalities and rectifying the injustice resulting from dealing or transactions between unequals in society.[156] Various clauses of Article 39 contain one main objective, namely, the building of a welfare State and an egalitarian social order[157]—to fix certain social and economic goals for immediate attainment by bringing about a non-violent economic and social revolution.[158] The social revolution was to mean to remove caste and communities hurdles, while economic revolution was intended to bring about, 'transition from primitive economy to scientific and planned agriculture and industry.[159] Through such revolutions Constitution seeks to fulfil the basic need of the common man and to change the structure of the society,[160] without which political democracy has no meaning.[161]

Under Article 39(a) it is the obligation of the State to implement its policy towards securing right to adequate means of livelihood. Right to livelihood is an important feature of right to life because no person can live without means of living that is means of livelihood.[162] Other objectives of Article 39 may be achieved by the State by differential taxation, giving debt relief, distribution of property owned by one to many who have none by imposing ceiling on holdings or by direct regulation of contractual transactions by forbidding certain transactions.[163] This Article has been described as having the object of securing a welfare State and may be utilized for construing provisions as to fundamental rights.[164] These principles are regarded as a dependable index of a 'public purpose'. If a law is enacted to implement the socio-economic policy laid down in directive principles, it must be regarded as one for public purpose. In *Kameshwar Singh's* case, the SC relied on Article 39 to decide that the law to abolish Zamindari had been enacted for public purposes within the meaning of Article 31.[165]

Under Article 39A[166] Constitution pursuant to the new policy of the Government to give *legal aid to economically backward classes* of people, it puts stress upon. This direction necessitates or obligates the State to secure that the operation of the legal system promotes justice, on a basis of equal opportunity and shall, in particular, provide free legal aid, by suitable legislation or scheme or in any other way, to ensure that opportunities for securing justice are not denied to any citizen just due to their backwardness or merely because of economic or other disability. In *Prem Chand Garg* v. *Excise Commissioner*[167] Hon'ble Supreme Court held that Court also comes under the definition of State, therefore courts are under an obligation to provide legal assistance and justice. Supreme Court has taken a lead in this respect and is doing tremendous job in providing free legal aid and justice. Supreme Court at various occasions has treated even a post card as writ petition.

Indian Constitution also declares that objective of the State is to promote the Educational and Economic Interests of Scheduled Caste, Scheduled Tribes and Other Weaker Sections under Article 46.[168]

This article does not confer any justiciable right, like others Directive Principles. Hence a member of backward class could not obtain relief from the Court when he is denied any concession in school fees.[169] But by virtue of the amendment made in 1951[170] *teeth* are given to these principles. It will now be possible for the state to make special provisions, viz., to construct a State colony for the habitation of Harijans, notwithstanding the bar against discrimination on the ground of caste.[171] An Act made under Article 46, to protect and preserve the economic interests of persons belonging to the Scheduled Castes and Scheduled Tribes and to prevent their exploitation; would not infringe Article 47.[172] An Act passed by Maharastra legislature to prohibit alienation of agricultural lands by members of the Scheduled Tribes to persons not belonging to the Scheduled Tribes was held valid.[173]

In view of the economic empowerment of the dalits and tribals under Article 46, the Supreme Court directed the Government to regularize their possession on the uncultivable wasteland, granted to them on lease as per policy then in vague when the Government sought their eviction on the expiry of the lease period.[174] The State is under an obligation to provide SCs/STs the facilities and opportunities for their economic empowerment[175] as it is their fundamental right.[176] An employee belonging to backward classes has a fundamental right to be considered for promotion on the basis of Article 16 read with 46.[177] Similar view was taken in

Omprakash v. *State of Punjab*[178] where reservation system in favour of the Scheduled Castes in educational institutions was upheld on the ground that Article 46 must be taken as an exception to Article 29(2) . . ." and that the state was authorized to adopt a system of reservation by making a proper classification to promote the educational and economic interest of the weaker sections.

Regarding the expression, "weaker section of the society", the Supreme Court has directed the central government to lay down appropriate guideline.[179] In *Indra Sawhney*[180] case the Supreme Court clarified that the expression "weaker Section" is wider than the expression 'backward classes' of citizens. Term 'weaker section' does not necessarily refer to a group or a class. A division bench has held that poor fishermen by traditional implements are member of 'weaker section' under Article 46 so that the State is under an obligation to protect their interests.[181]

Above discussion shows that directive principles are enshrined as a path for the State to make available social justice, educational and economic justice to all backward classes of citizens including other category of weaker section. These directives principles are considered as *'Gangotri'* of Social justice. All canals of social measures took birth from this Gangotri. The Indian Constitution declares these principles as fundamental in the Governance of the country and the 'state' has been placed under an obligation to apply them in making laws. The directive principles lead the exercise of legislative power.[182]

CONSTITUTIONAL COMMITMENT UNDER OTHER CONSTITUTIONAL PROVISIONS

Besides the Fundamental Rights and Directive Principles some other special provisions are also enshrined under XVI of the Indian Constitution for socially and educationally advancement of Backward Classes or Scheduled Castes and Scheduled Tribes as follows.

Reservation in Lok Sabha and State Assemblies: Article 330[183] make available political safeguard or justice in the form of reservation of seats for Scheduled Castes and Scheduled Tribes in the House of the People (Parliament) and State Assembly under Article 332.[184]

The number of seats reserved in any State/UT bears the same proportion to the total number of seats allotted to that State/UT in the House of People (Lok Sabha) as the population of SC and ST bears with the total population of State/UT as per 1991 census (until the figures of Census 2026 are available).

The effect of reservation of seats for the Scheduled Castes and Scheduled Tribes in the parliament or State legislature as the case may be, is to guarantee a minimum number of seats or the members of the SCs and STs, but it does not deprive a member of a Scheduled Caste of his right to contest from a general seat, on which every adult citizen could possess, and every citizen can contest for a general seat on the strength of the very nomination for a reserved seat.[185] For instance when Meera Kumar daughter of ex-Minister Jagjeevan Ram, had contested election for the reserved seats from Shahjahanpur district of U.P., it was challenged on the ground that she is disqualified to contest the election from the reserved seat because when she got married with the person belonging to non-Scheduled Caste, she has lost the degree of reserved category. Allahabad High Court held that benefit of reservation remains with the person even if she/he being SC/ST category since birth but get marriage with non-SC/ST. It does not affect the status. The reservation of seats expressly provided under Article 332 cannot be challenged on the ground of right to equality guaranteed under Article 14.[186] But it should be remember that benefits of reservation of seats for STs/SCs in Parliament or State Assembly are not permanent. Because Article 334[187] says reservation of seats and special representation is subject to cease after seventy years although initially it was for only 10 year after the commencement of Indian Constitution.

It also should notice that this benefit is provided only the members of Scheduled Castes and Scheduled Tribes not to the members of socially and educationally backward classes.

In the Legislative Assemblies of Arunachal Pradesh, Mizoram, Nagaland and Meghalaya, if on the commencement of the Constitution (57th Amendment) Act, 1987, they were having all members as STs, they shall continue to have all but one seats reserved for STs. Otherwise number of reserved seats to total seats shall have the same proportion as the number of ST members in the existing assembly bears to the total number of seats.

Article 334 provides reservation in the Lok Sabha and legislative Assemblies in State/UT except in the autonomous district of Assam, the reservation shall cease after 60 years from the commencement of the Constitution, i.e. on 25th January 2010. But this will not affect the composition of the House or Legislative Assembly, existing just before completion of 60 years, until that House or Assembly is dissolved. Earlier, the provision of reservation was to cease on 25th January, 2000. The same was extended to 25.10.2010.[188]

Claims of Backward Class: Article 335[189] provides Constitutional guarantee to protect the claims of Scheduled Castes and Scheduled Tribes to Services and Posts.

It is the Constitutional duty of the State to take into consideration the claims of the members of the Scheduled Castes and Scheduled Tribes in matter of appointment.[190] Article 335 is to be read with Article 46, which provides that the State shall promote with special care the educational and economic interest of the weaker section of the people and, in particular, of the Scheduled Castes and Scheduled Tribes and shall protect them from social injustice and all forms of exploitation.[191] This article extends to agencies of the State under Article 12.[192] When by way of discharging the aforesaid duty, Government issues an administrative instruction, but a Department fails to comply with such instruction, the court may issue direction, even though it is non-statutory.[193]

It has been seen that there is some overlapping between the Article 335 and Article 16(4), inasmuch as the reservation for 'backward classes' in Article 16(4) obviously includes reservation for members of the Scheduled Castes and Tribes but not for other backward classes while wide interpretation of the term 'backward classes' includes SCs/STs/OBCs.[194] The fact that Article 335 is outside the part of fundamental rights and directive principles, does not matter much since Article 16(4) is also an enabling provision.[195] However, this overlapping has been eliminated by the Supreme Court by holding that Article 335 operates as a limitation to the provision contained in Article 16(4), does 'not specifically refer to Article 335 or raise any question of maintenance of efficiency of the administration.[196] A reservation for the backward classes will, thus, be struck down as violative of Articles 14 and 16(1), if it is unreasonably excessive.[197]

About other backward classes, in *Mandal Commission case* Supreme Court had examined the implication of Articles 14, 15, 16, 335, etc., at length. According to the majority judgment there is a need to maintain a balance between reservation and efficiency not only with reference to Scheduled Castes and Scheduled Tribes but also with reference to other Backward Classes. Since sacrifice of merit may have to be made for social justice.[198] Ordinarily, a reservation in excess of 50% would be considered excessive,[199] but there is no invariable formula on this point; a reasonable balance has to be struck between several relevant circumstances.[200] Reasonableness should, however, be determined with reference to the circumstances of each case and the 50% should be applicable in the absence of extraordinary situations.[201] Whether a particular class is adequately represented in the services under the State or not, is a matter within the subjective satisfaction of the appropriate government based on the materials in the possession of the government and the existing conditions in the society.[202]

Permanent Commissions: Article 338[203] and Article 338A[204] provides constitutional guarantee to hear/protect the voice of Scheduled Caste and Scheduled Tribes by appointing Commissions for them.

Before the 65th (Amendment) Act, 1990, this article provided for a special officer for the Scheduled Caste and Scheduled Tribes to investigate all matters relating to the safeguards provided for the Scheduled Caste and Scheduled Tribes under the Constitution and to report to the president on their working. It was felt that a high level five member—commission will be a more effective arrangement in respect of the Constitutional safeguards for the Scheduled Caste and Scheduled Tribes than a single special officer. It was also felt it was necessary to elaborate the function of the said Commission so as to cover measures that should be taken by the Union or any State for the effective implementation of those safeguards and other measures for the protection, welfare and socio economic development of the Scheduled Caste and Scheduled Tribes and to entrust to the commission such other functions in relation to the protection, welfare and development and advancement of the Scheduled Castes and Scheduled Tribes as the president may specify. Article 339[205] mentions special provision for the protection of Scheduled Tribes by authorizing the President of India to appoint a commission to give report on the administration of Scheduled area and the welfare of ST.

Article 340[206] makes sure the appointment of a Commission to investigate the conditions of backward classes.

After the decision of 9 judges' bench in *Indra Sawhney* case[207] and the power conferred under Article 340, the president was bound to appoint Backward Class Commission. Parliament has enacted the National Commission for Backward Classes Act, 1993, for the identification of the backward classes and to make special provisions relating to such backward classes and their reservation for appointment or posts under the Government of India. Thus in 1993 permanent Backward Class Commission in centre and State came into existence.

Under this article assignment of composition of the Commission and initial identification were left on the Central Government. Functions of the Commission shall be to entertain the applications for the inclusion of other classes in the lists of OBCs and the hearing of complaints relating to such lists. Though its functions are advisory but its advice shall ordinarily be binding upon the central government and when the government does not accept any such advice, the government has to report such reasons to Parliament.

Definitions: Article 341[208] and Article 342[209] gives constitutional definition of Scheduled Castes and Scheduled Tribes respectively. And both the Articles 341 and 342 is reconfirms by Article 366[210]

The object of these articles is to provide additional protection to the member of the Scheduled Castes and Scheduled Tribes. It is obvious that in specify castes, races or tribes, the President has been authorized to limit the notification to parts or groups within the castes, etc., and that must mean after examination of the social and educational backwardness of a caste, etc., the President may well come to the conclusion that not the whole race, caste or tribe but parts or groups within them should be specified. Similarly, the President may specify castes etc., or part thereof in relation not only to the entire State, but in relation to parts of the State where he is satisfied that the examination of the social and educational backwardness of the race, caste or tribe justifies such specification.[211]

Another object of this article is to avoid all disputes as to whether a caste is a Scheduled Caste or not, for the purpose of the constitution and it is the president notification issued, to determine who is to be deemed to be a member of a Scheduled Caste.[212] In absence of which a non-ST Candidate cannot get the said status by merely interpolating the documents.[213]

The Scheduled Caste Order, 1950, has been promulgated by the President under this power. In order to determine whether a particular caste is a 'Scheduled caste' within the meaning of Article 341, one has to look to the terms of this order.[214] Once the parliament includes in or excludes from any race, caste, tribe, parts of or groups within any caste, race, or tribe, the president thereafter shall have no power to vary it by any subsequent notification.[215] The Court is also devoid of power to include in or exclude from or substitute or declare synonyms to be of a scheduled caste or Scheduled tribe or parts thereof.[216] The list of Scheduled Tribes is now contained in the Constitution (Scheduled Tribes) Order, 1950, as amended by the Scheduled caste and scheduled tribes Order (Amendment) Act 63 of 1956, 108 of 1976, 18 of 1990. The entries in the presidential order have to be taken as final. The Order is made after detailed inquiry as to the economic status, the level of education and the necessity of protection, inclusion into or exclusion from the order. If any change is needed in the list appended to the president's order that can be made by law of Parliament.

The courts have no power to go behind this order or to hold any inquiry or to let in any evidence to determine whether or not any particular community falls within the order or not.[217] It is now well established that where a person belonging to a Scheduled Caste or Scheduled Tribes of one State migrates to another state, he will not be entitled to claim the privileges or benefits admissible to a member of Scheduled Caste or Scheduled Tribes, even though there may be a Scheduled Caste or Scheduled Tribes of the same nomenclature in the latter State.[218]

Where the respondent obtained the caste certificate from the state of W. Bengal wherein his parents were ordinarily residing, though he was born and received education upto graduation level and his parents had some property in the state of Bihar. His caste was recognized a Scheduled Caste in the state of W.B. but not in the State of Bihar. He obtained the said certificate as per "instruction to the candidates" and was accepted by the UPSC and was selected but its validity was doubted while he was in service. On consideration of relevant provisions and the place where his parents were ordinarily residing, it was held that he belonged to Scheduled Caste.[219]

CONCLUSION

Thus in brief, Articles 330 and 332 provide reservation of seats in the Lok Sabha and state Assemblies for the Scheduled Caste and Scheduled Tribes. Under 334, period for reservation is fixed for sixty years. This provision was initially for a period of ten years. Regarding this Article a protected debate has taken place in the constituent assembly on the desirability of restricting the concession to a period of ten years. One point of view was expressed by *Shibban Lal Saxena:* "in ten years time even the Harijans will be in a position to rise to the occasion and give up the right of reservation. Then everybody will get proper representation without distinction of caste and religion. At that time, service merit and ability will alone will votes, and all relics of out past slavery will have been buried deep."[220] Ambedkar however, preferred a more flexible policy, one that favoured a longer time frame to do the necessary leveling. But he accepted the existing position and observed, "if at the end of the ten years, the scheduled castes find that their position has not be improved or that they want further extension... it will not be beyond their capacity to invent new ways of getting the same protection which they are promised here." [221]

Article 335 stipulates that the claims of the scheduled caste and the scheduled tribes shall also be taken into consideration, consistent with the maintenance of efficiency of administration, in the making of appointments to services and posts in connection with the affairs of the union or of a state." Articles 338 and 338A provide for a commission for scheduled caste and scheduled tribes respectively, to be appointed by the president. For the purpose of Article 338, references to Scheduled Caste and scheduled tribes are to be construed as including references to such other backward classes as may be specified by the president on receipt of a report from the commission, which may be appointed under Article 341(1). Article 339 provides for the appointment of a commission to report in regard to the administration of the scheduled areas and the welfare of the scheduled tribes. Article 340(1) provides for the appointment of a commission to investigate the condition of socially and educationally backward classes within the territory of India and which they labour and to make recommendations as to the steps that should be taken by the union or any state to remove such difficulties and to improve there condition, etc.

Reservation in Panchayat and Municipal Corporation: Beside reservation in Lok Sabha and State Assemblies Article 243D provides reservation of seats and officers for Scheduled Caste/ Scheduled Tribe in every Panchayat.[222]

Article 243 T provides for reservation of seats and officers for SC/ST in Municipal Corporation.[223] In the recent case of *Meera Kawaria* (Decided in December 2005) female of Rajpoot cast (Sunita) married with the male of scheduled caste in Dec. 2000 by performing Hindu custom. She got SC certificate and on the basis of SC certificate she fought election and won with 14757 votes from Delhi Nagar Nigam Ward No. 20. But when her election was challenged, district judge declared her election as illegal. When appeal was made before Delhi High Court it was held that there is no need to perform special kind of marriage ceremonies for a high caste member to become member of Scheduled Caste and further held that law for reservation in service is different and the law to fight election from reserved constituency. But in Supreme Court Bench of Justice S.B. Sinha and P.K. Balaramanyam by disapproving judgement of Delhi High Court held that female of high cast Hindu does not automatically become entitle to the benefit of reservation just after marrying with the male of scheduled caste and even accepting by family of her husband. On this ground apex court cancelled election of a lady (who does not belong to reserved category) from the reserved constituency. But further held if she is accepted by whole of the community she would becomes be entitle to get the benefit of reservation.[224]

Articles 244 and 244A provides for specific provisions for administration of *Scheduled Tribal Areas*.[225] The word 'administration' is wide enough to embrace the exercise of government power of every description—executive, legislative and judicial.[226]

Article 164 provides that in the States of Bihar, Madhya Pradesh and Orissa there shall be a *Minister for Tribal Welfare of SCs*, who may also be in charge of welfare of SCs, backward classes and any other work.[227]

Notes and References

1. We, the people of India, having solemnly resolved to constitute India into a sovereign socialist secular democratic republic and to secure to all its citizens: justice social, economic and political; liberty of thought, expression, belief, faith and worship; equality of status and of opportunity; and to promote among them all; fraternity assuring the dignity of the individual and the unity and integrity of the nation, in our constituent assembly this twenty-sixth day of November 1949, do hereby adopt, enact and give to ourselves this constitution. P.M. Bakshi, the Constitution of India, ed. 2002, p. 1, Pub. Universal law Publishing Co. Pvt. Ltd.
2. Minerva Mills Ltd. *v.* Union of India, (1980) 3 SCC 625 at 704-5.
3. Georges Gurvitch, Encyclopedia of the Social Sciences, Vol. 8, 1949, p. 509.
4. Ratna, G. Revankar, The Indian Constitution—A case study of Backward Classes, Fairleigh Dickinson University Press, p. 40.
5. Harold J. Laski, Encyclopedia of the Social Sciences, Vol. 9, 1949, p. 444.
6. The Jawaharlal Lal Nehru, The Unity of India, 1948, p. 67.
7. Ratna, G. Revankar, The Indian Constitution—A case study of Backward Classes, Fairleigh Dickinson University Press, p. 39.
8. Joyce, M. Hawkins, Oxford Minidictionary, (S.K. Mookerjee, Oxford University Press, New Delhi 1981), p. 118.

9. William M.M. English Sanskrit Dictionary, p. 182.
10. Mahabharata 15-22-25 (Poona: Bhandarkar institute, 1944).
11. Misra, Govind, "The Concept of Human Dignity and the Constitution of India" in M.P. Singh, Comparative Constitutional Law, (Eastern Book Company, Lucknow 1989), p. 357.
12. *Ibid.*
13. www. libertocracy.com.
14. *Ibid.*
15. Dr. Parmanand Singh, 'Equality, Reservation and Discrimination in India', p. 17, ed. 1985, Pub. Deep & Deep Publications, New Delhi.
16. Mathew, J. in State of Kerala *v.* N.M. Thomas, AIR 1976 SC 513 Bennet Coleman *v.* Union of India, AIR 1973 SC 106, 141.
17. Dr. Parmanand Singh, 'Equality, Reservation and Discrimination in India', p. 17, ed. 1985, Pub. Deep & Deep Publications, New Delhi.
18. *Ibid.*
19. *Ibid.*, at p. 18.
20. *Ibid.*, Article 14 enshrines the principles of equality both positively and negatively, i.e. where equality is achieved to some extent by removing inequality e.g. slavery (which was the most flagrant denial of equality of human beings in U.S.A.), and 'untouchablity' (in India) the abolition of 'untouchablity' or 'slavery' secured to the careers of Indians, equality of status as human beings.
21. H.M. Seervai, Constitutional Law of India, Universal Law, New Delhi, 1999, Vol. 1, p. 937 (N.M. Tripathy, Bombay, 1983).
22. Articles 14-18 of the Indian constitution.
23. Ratna, G. Revankar, The Indian Constitution—A case study of Backward Classes, Fairleigh Dickinson University Press, p. 39.
24. Dr. Parmanand Singh, 'Equality, Reservation and Discrimination in India', p. 21, ed. 1985, Pub. Deep & Deep Publications, New Delhi.
25. State of Kerala *v.* N.M. Thomas (1976) 2 SCC 310 at 344.
26. Article 14.
27. The State is Discrimination on grounds of race, religion and caste is prohibited generally by Article 15(1) and more specifically by Article 16(2) (in regard to state employment), Article 23(2) (in regard to compulsory public service), Article 29(2) (in regard to state-run and state-sided educational institutions).
28. Articles 15(1) and 16(2).
29. Article 16(2).
30. *Ibid.*
31. Article 23(2).
32. Article 29(2) Cf. Article 30(2), 29(1) and Article 350.
33. Articles 15(1), 16(2) and 325.

34. Article 17.
35. Articles 15(2), 28(3) and 29(2).
36. Articles 330, 332, 333, and 334.
37. P.M. Bakshi, The Constitution of India, ed. 2002, p. 16, Pub. Universal Law Publishing Co. Pvt. Ltd., New Delhi.
38. First found its expression in the declaration of Rights of men, 1789, proclaimed by the National Assembly of France.
39. Echoed in the American declaration of independence.
40. Article 7 of Declaration of Human Rights 1948.
41. Wade and Phillips, constitutional and Administrative Law, 87 (1977).
42. First limb of Article 14.
43. Ivor Jennings, Law of the Constitution, 3rd ed., p. 49.
44. State of Bengal *v.* Anwar Ali Sarkar; AIR 1962 SC 75.
45. 1996 10 SCC 104.
46. Justice Hewart.
47. State of Uttar Pradesh *v.* Deoman Upadhyaya, AIR 1960 SC 1960, SC 1125, 1134, decenting judgment as per Subba Rao, Jagananth prasad *v.* Uttar Pradesh, AIR 1961 SC 1245, Mohd. Shaheb Mahboob *v.* Dy. Custodian, AIR 1961 SC 1657.
48. H.M. Seervai, Constitutional Law of India, pp. 438-39, ed. 4th, Vol. 1, Pub. Universal Book Traders, N. Delhi.
49. Ivor Jennings, Law of the Constitution, 3rd ed., p. 49.
50. AIR 1952 SC 75.
51. AIR Vol. 39, 1952, para 35, P.S.C. 85; Fazl Ali, J., State of Bombay and another *v.* F.N. Balsara AIR; Chiranjit Lal Chowdhury *v.* The Union of India and Others, AIR 1951 SC 41.
52. AIR 1952, SCR 435; AIR 1952 SC 123, para 32.
53. S.K. Singh, 'Bonded Labour', ed. 1994, Pub. Deep & Deep Publication, N. Delhi, p. 172.
54. AIR 1972 SC 865, 871.
55. AIR 1992 SC 999, 1004.
56. AIR 1978 SC 327, 331.
57. E.P. Royappa *v.* State of Tamilnadu, AIR 1974 SC 555; Ramana Dayaram Shetty *v.* Union of India, AIR 1979 SC 1628; Express Newspapers Pvt. Ltd *v.* Union of India.
58. Maneka Gandhi *v.* Union of India, AIR 1978 SC 597,624; Ajay Hasia *v.* Khalid Mujib (81) A.SC 487; Paradise Printers *v.* Union territory of Chandigarh AIR 1988 SC 354.
59. Charanjit Lal *v.* Union of India, AIR 1951 SC 41.
60. (1981) 4 SCC 335.
61. D.S. Nakara *v.* Union of India, (1983) 1 SCC 305 at 318.

62. Dr. Parmanand Singh, 'Equality, Reservation and Discrimination in India', p. 21, ed. 1985, Pub. Deep & Deep Publications, New Delhi.
63. *Ibid.*
64. Ratna, G. Revankar, The Indian Constitution—A case study of Backward Classes, Fairleigh Dickinson University Press, p. 48.
65. (1) The State shall not discriminate against any citizen on grounds only of religion, race, caste, sex, place of birth or any of them. (2) No citizen shall, on grounds only of religion, race, caste, sex, place of birth or any of them, be subject to only disability, liability, restriction or condition with regard to : (a) access to shops, public restaurants, hotels and places of public entertainment; or (b) the use of wells, tanks, bathing ghats, roads and places of public resort maintained wholly or partly out of state funds or dedicated to the use of the general public. (3) Nothing in this article shall prevent the State from, making any special provision for women and children. (4) Nothing in this article or in clause (2) of Article 29 shall prevent the State from making any special provision for the advancement of any socially and educationally backward classes of citizens or for the Scheduled Caste and Scheduled Tribe.
66. His amendment was for addition of some words, "That at the end of the clause (2) of Article 9, the following be added—or for Scheduled caste or backward tribes, for their advantage, safeguard or betterment". Thus wording of the clause would as, "Nothing in this article shall prevent the state from making any special provision for women and children". The Intention was to give special facilities to the Scheduled caste and backward tribes for some time so that real equality of citizens be established, 11 C.A.D., Vol. VII, pp. 655-56.
67. C.A.D., Vol. VII, pp. 655-56.
68. C.A.D., Vol. VII, p. 661. The underlying idea of draft Article 9 was to ensure that the citizens were not discriminated on grounds of caste, sex, birth, etc. And it was renumbered as Article 15, thus became one of the Fundamental Rights enshrined in the Constitution;
69. 1951, SCR 525; (51) A.SC 226.
70. The Constitutional Amendment Bill, 1951; this proposed amendment was debated in the Parliament at different stages. The main criticism was that in the absence of a definition of the "backward classes" this provision might be abused when attempts would be made to bring in new communities under this class by the backdoor and that the very purpose of the amendment would be defeated unless clause (2) of Article 19 was also amended. Most of the members were agreed for insertion of the following words at the end of clause (3) of Article: *"or for the educational, economic or*

social advancement of any Backward class of citizens". But the select committee redrafted it and made it an independent clause as follows; "Nothing in this Article or in clause (2) of the Article 29 shall prevent the State from making any special provision for the advancement of any socially and educationally backward classes of citizens or for the Scheduled Caste and Scheduled Tribes."

71. Sarajit Kumar Chatterjee, The Scheduled Castes in India, Vol. 4, p. 509, Gyan Publishing House, New Delhi, 1996.
72. Sudarshan Puppala *v.* State of A.P., AIR 1958 569.
73. Mandal case AIR 1993 SC 477; Ajay Kumar Singh *v.* State of Bihar, 1994 4 SCC 401.
74. M.P. Jain, Indian Constitutional Law, Wadhwa and Company Law Publisher, New Delhi, 1987; Reprint 1994, p. 501.
75. Encyclopedia of Dalits in India: Reservation, Sanjay Paswan and Paramanshi Jaideva, Kalpaz Publications, 2002, p. 245.
76. R.K. Gupta, 'Justice: Unequal But Inseparate' 11 J.I.L.I. 811969, Mark Galanter, 'Protective Discrimination—For Backward Classes in India' 3 JILI 39, 55 1961. He says the history of Articles 15(4) and 16(4) indicates that they included with this purpose; CAD, Vol. 7, 673702;
77. Balaji *v.* State of Mysore, AIR 1963 SC 649; H. Janardhan Subbaraya *v.* State of Mysore, AIR 1963 SC 701; Chitralekha *v.* State of Mysore, AIR 1964 SC 1823; P. Rajendran *v.* State of Madras, AIR 1968 SC 1012; State of A.P. *v.* P. Sager AIR, 1968 SC 1379; Jaishree *v.* State of Kerala, AIR 1976 SC 2381.
78. State of Uttar Pradesh *v.* Balram, AIR 1972, SC 1395; Rajendran *v.* Union of India, AIR 1968 SC 507; Balaji *v.* State of Mysore, AIR 1963 SC 649, 612; Anil *v.* Dean, Govt. Medical College, Nagpur, AIR 1985 Bom 153.
79. AIR 1997 SC 788.
80. Kathi Raning Rawat *v.* State of Saurashtra, 1952 SCR 435, 442.
81. Article 46.
82. Article 335.
83. K.C. Vasanth Kumar *v.* State of Karnataka, AIR 1985 SC 1495; Comptroller and Auditor General *v.* Jagmohan, AIR 1987 SC 537.
84. AIR 1964 SC 1823.
85. AIR 1963 Sc 649.
86. Rajendran, P. (Minor) *v.* State of Madras, AIR 1968 SC 1012; Periakaruppan, A. *v.* State of Tamilnadu, AIR 1971 2303, Triloki Nath Tikku *v.* State of Jammu and Kashmir, AIR 1969 SC 1, Vasanta Kumar K.C. *v.* State of Karnataka, AIR 1985 SC 1495.
87. State of M.P. *v.* Mohan Singh (1995) 6 SCC 32 (Para 12).
88. Indra Sawhney Case, AIR 1993 SC at 586.

89. *Ibid.*
90. State of Kerala *v.* Roshna T.P. Kumari, 1979 1 SCC 572.
91. State of A.P. *v.* Balram U.S.V., AIR 1972 SC 1375.
92. Sharma, S.S. *v.* Union of India, AIR 1981 SC 588.
93. State of Kerala *v.* N.M. Thomas, AIR 1976 SC 490; Bhaiyalal *v.* Harikishan, AIR 1965 SC.
94. AIR 1981 SC 2045; 4 SCC 296.
95. August 12, 2005 *Hindustan Times*, www.ndtv.com,www.judis.nic.in
96. T.M.A. Pai Foundation & Ors. *v.* State of Karnataka & Ors, 2002.
97. Islamic Academy of Edn. & Anr. *v.* State of Karnataka & Ors, 2003.
98. Article 1595—Nothing in this article or in sub-clause(g) of clause (1) of Article 19 shall prevent the state from making any special provision, by law, for the advancement of socially and educationally backward class of citizens or for scheduled cast or scheduled tribes in so far as such provisions relate to their admission to educational institutions including private educational institutions, whether aided or unaided.
99. (2008) 6 SCC 1.
100. (1) There shall be equality of opportunity for all citizens in matters relating to employment of appointment to any office under the State. (2) No citizen shall, on grounds only of religion, race, caste, sex, descent, place of birth, residence or any of them, be ineligible for, or discriminated against in respect of any employment or office under the State. (3) Nothing in this article shall prevent Parliament from making any law prescribing in regard to a class or classes of employment or appointment to an office under the Government of, or any local or other authority within a state or union territory, any requirement as to residence within the state union territory prior to such employment or appointment. (4) Nothing in this article shall prevent the state from making any provision for the reservation of appointment or post of any backward class of citizens, which, in the opinion of the State, is not adequately represented in the services under the State. (5) Nothing in this article shall effect the operation of any law, which provides that the incumbent of an office in connection with the affairs of any religious or denominational institution of any member of the governing body thereof shall be a person professing a particular religion or belonging to a particular denomination.
101. D.T.C. *v.* Mazdoor Congress, AIR 1991 SC 101.
102. J.N. Pandey, Constitutional Law of India, Central Law Agency, ed. 1994, p. 106.

103. Champakam *v.* Union of India, AIR 1964 SC 1854; Shin Charan *v.* State of Mysore, 1965 SC 280, 282; Union of India *v.* Kashikar, AIR 1986 SC 210.
104. *Ibid.*, at p. 106.
105. C.A.D., Vol. VII, pp. 701-02.
106. AIR 1993 SC 477.
107. Rajendran, C.A. *v.* Union of India, AIR 1968 SC 507; Devadasan T. *v.* Union of India, AIR 1964 SC 179.
108. Post-Graduate Institute of Medical Education and Research, Chandigarh *v.* Faculty Association, 1998 4 SCC 1.
109. Indra Sawhney *v.* Union of India, AIR 1993 SC 477.
110. *Ibid.*
111. *Ibid.*, at 55, 56.
112. *Ibid.*
113. M.P. Jain, Indian Constitutional Law, Wadhwa and Company Law Publisher, New Delhi, 1987; Reprint 1994, pp. 517-18.
114. Indra Sawhney *v.* Union of India AIR 1993 SC 477, para 55, 56.
115. Indra Sawhney *v.* Union of India AIR 1993 SC 477, para 58.
116. Municipal Corporation of Greater Bombay & Others *v.* Mrs. Kalpana Sadhu Kanihie & Others (1988) Supp. 2 SCR 679; 1988 (2) ATJ 544 and Vishwas Anna Sawant & Others *v.* Municipal Corporation of Greater Bombay & Ors. C.A. No. 4073 of 1994 decided on 22.4.1994 (SC).
117. Ghansham Singh & Others *v.* Union of India and others decided on 4.2.1992 (CAT-Bombay).
118. Ram Kumar *v.* UOI & Others, O.A. No. 1790 of 1992 decided on 21.2.2002 (CAT-Allahabad).
119. O.A. No. 109 decided on 1.9.1992 (CAT-Patna).
120. S. Vinod Kumar and Anothers *v.* Union of India & Others (1996) 6 SCC 580, and Balbir Singh *v.* Union of India & others decided on 15.4.1997 (CAT-Chandigarh).
121. State of U.P. *v.* Dr. Dina Nath Shukla, 1997 9 SCC 662; Government of A.P. *v.* P.B. Vijaykumar, AIR 1995 SC 1648.
122. Which says that, the claims of the Scheduled Castes and the Scheduled Tribes shall be taken into consideration consistently with the maintenance of efficiency of administration.
123. Devadasan *v.* Union of India, AIR 1985 SC 983; Balaji *v.* State of Mysore, AIR 1963 SC 649, 664; State of Kerala *v.* N.M. Thomas, AIR 1976 SC 490; K.C. Vasanthkumar *v.* State of Karnataka, AIR 1985 SC 537.

124. General Manager *v.* Ranhuchari, AIR 1962 SC 36; Rajendran *v.* Union of India, AIR 1968 SC 507; Triloki Nath *v.* State of Jammu & Kashmir, AIR 1967 SC 1283; Peria Karuppan *v.* State of Tamilnadu, 1971 SCR 430.
125. AIR 1997 2 SCC 417.
126. Indra Sawhney *v.* Union of India, AIR 1993 SC 477; Perriakurrapan A. *v.* State of T.N., 1971 SCR 430; P. & T. Assocn. *v.* Union of India, 1998 4 SCC 147; Ajit Singh *v.* State of Punjab, AIR 1999 SC 3471. M.P. Jain, Indian Constitutional Law, Wadhwa and Company Law Publisher, N. Delhi, 1987; Reprint 1994, p. 518.
127. Indra Sawhney *v.* Union of India, AIR 1993 SC 477 Para 56, 57, 94A, 292.
128. Section 2 of this Act empowering the State to make a provision for reservation in matters of promotion to any class or classes of posts in the services under the state in favour of SC and the ST which in the opinion of the state, are not adequately represented in the services under the state, notwithstanding anything contrary contained in Article 16.
129. Article 16 (4A) Nothing in this article shall prevent the state from making any provision for reservation in matters of promotion, with consequential seniority, to any class or classes of posts in the services under the state in favour of Scheduled Castes and the Scheduled Tribe, which in the opinion of the State are not adequately represented in the services under the state.
130. AIR 1999 SC 3471.
131. AIR 1962, SC, p. 36; Ajit Singh (II) *v.* State of Punjab, 1999 7 SCC 209.
132. AIR 2001 SC 308.
133. (4B) Nothing in this article shall prevent the state from considering any unfilled vacancies of a year which are reserved for being filled up in that year in accordance with any provision for reservation made under clause (4) or clause (4A) as a separate class of vacancies to be filled up in any succeeding year or years and such class of vacancies shall not be considered together with the vacancies of the year in which they are being filled up for determining the ceiling of 50% reservation on total number of vacancies of that year.
134. D.D. Basu, Shorter Constitution of India, Wadhwa and Company Law Publisher, N. Delhi, ed. 13th (Rp. 2004), p. 142.
135. AIR 1952, SCR 435; AIR 1952 SC123, para 32.
136. Valsamma Pal *v.* Cochin University, 1996 3 SCC; REVERSING Public Service Commission *v.* Dr. Kunjamma Alex 1981 KLT 24 and over-ruling Kunjamma case 1980 KLT and Khazan Singh *v.* Union of India, AIR 1980 Del 60.

137. 'Untouchablity' is abolished and its practices in any form are forbidden. The enforcement of any disability arising out of "Untouchablity" shall be an offence punishable in accordance with law.
138. Hadtbanow Behra *v.* Benamalt Sahu, AIR 1961 Ori 33.
139. Sarajit Kumar Chatterjee, the Scheduled Castes in India Gyan Publishing House, New Delhi, 1996 Vol. 4, p. 389.
140. *Ibid.*, at pp. 395-96.
141. Devarajiah *v.* Padmanna, AIR 1961 Mad 35, 39.
142. Sarajit Kumar Chatterjee, the Scheduled Castes in India, Gyan Publishing House, New Delhi, 1996, Vol. 4, pp. 395-96.; Although title of the Act was changed in 1976 as the protection of Civil Rights Act, 1955.
143. Freedom of conscience and free profession, practice and propagation of religion (1) Subject to public order, morality and health and to the provisions of this apart, all persons are equally entitled to freedom of conscience and the right freely to profess, practice and propagate religion. (2) Nothing in this article shall affect the operation of any existing law or prevent the state from making any law—(a) regulating or restricting any economic, financial, political or other secular activity which may be associated with religious practice; (b) providing for social welfare and reform or the throwing open of Hindu religious institutions of a public character to all classes and sections of Hindus, Article 25(2)(a).
144. Ratilal *v.* State of Bombay, 1954 SCR 1055.
145. Sarajit Kumar Chatterjee, the Scheduled Castes in India, Vol. 4, p. 408, Gyan Publishing House, New Delhi, 1996.
146. Air India Statutory Corporation *v.* United Labour Union, AIR 1997 SC 645 Para 38 (observation that they stand elevated to human rights).
147. C.A.D. VII.
148. Keshavanand Bharti *v.* State of Kerala, 1973 4 SCC 225.
149. Chandra Bhavan *v.* State of Mysore, AIR 1970 SC 2042, Para 13; State of Kerala *v.* N.M. Thomas, AIR 1976 SC 496; Lingappa *v.* State of Maharastra, AIR 1985 SC 389; Manchegowda *v.* State of Karnataka, AIR 1984 SC 1151. Chief Justice *v.* Dikshitutu, (1979) 2 SCC 34; Jalan Trading Co. *v.* Aney, AIR 1985 SC 233; Mukesh *v.* State of Madhya Pradesh, AIR 1987 SC 232; A.B.K. Singh *v.* Union of India, AIR 1981 SC 298, 335.
150. Article 38(1) The State shall strive to promote the welfare of the people by securing and protecting as effectively as it may a social order in which justice: social, economic and political shall inform all the institutions of the national life. (2) inserted in 1978, The State shall, in particular strive to minimize the inequalities in income and

endeavor to eliminate inequalities in status, facilities and opportunities not only amongst individual but also amongst groups of people residing in different engaged in different vocations. P.M. Bakshi, The Constitution of India, ed. 2002 (Rp. 2004), p. 86. Pub. Universal Law Publishing Co. Pvt. Ltd.

151. Dalmia Cement (Bharat Ltd.) *v.* Union of India, (1996) 10 SCC 377.
152. All India Statutory Corporation *v.* United Labour Union, 1997 2 SCC 377.
153. M.P. Singh, Indian Constitutional Law, ed. 4th, 1987, p. 742.
154. J.N. Pandey, Constitutional Law of India, ed. 27th, 1994, p. 269.
155. Article 39 : State shall, in particular direct its policy towards securing—(a) that the citizens, men and women equally, have the right to an adequate means of livelihood; that the ownership and control of the material resources of the community are so distributed as best to sub serve the common good; (b) that the operation of the economic system does not result in the concentration of wealth and means of production to the common detriment; that there is equal pay for equal work for both men and women; that the health and strength of workers men an women and the tender age of children are not abused and that citizen are not forced by economic necessity to enter avocations unsuited to there age or Strength; that children are given opportunities and facilities to develop in a healthy manner and in condition of freedom and dignity and that childhood and youth are protected against the exploitation and against moral and material abandonment;
156. J.N. Pandey, Constitutional Law of India, ed. 27th, 1994, p. 271.
157. Keshavanand Bharti *v.* State of Kerala, 1973 4 SCC 225.
158. *Ibid.*
159. Minerva Mills Ltd. *v.* Union of India (1980) 3 SCC 625 at 704-5.
160. Keshavanand Bharati *v.* State of Kerala, 1973 4 SCC 225.
161. *Ibid.*
162. Maneka Gandhi *v.* Union of India 1978 1 SCC 248; Francis Coralie Mullin *v.* Administrator, Union Territory of Delhi and others 1981 1 SCC 608; Peoples Union for Democratic Rights *v.* Union of India, 1982 3 SCC 161; Neerja Chaudhary *v.* State of M.P., 1984 3 SCC 243; Olga Tellis *v.* Bombay Municipal Corporation, 1985 3 SCC 545.
163. Lingappa Pochanna *v.* State of Maharastra, AIR 1985 SC 389.
164. Srinivasa *v.* State of Karnataka, AIR 1987 SC 1518; Heshvan and Bharati *v.* State of Kerala (1973) 4 SCC 28; AIR 1973 SC 1461; State of Tamilnadu *v.* Abu, AIR 1984 SC 326; Sanjeev Coke *v.* Bharat Cooking Cool, AIR 1983 SC 239.
165. State of Bihar *v.* Kameshwar Singh, AIR 1953 SC 252.

166. Article 39A—The State shall secure that the operation of the legal system promotes justice on a basis of equal opportunity, and shall, in particular, provide free legal aid, by suitable legislation or schemes or in any other way to ensure that opportunities for securing justice are not denied to any citizen by reason of economic or other disabilities. P.M. Bakshi, The Constitution of India, ed. 2002 (Rp. 2004), p. 88, Pub. Universal Law Publishing Co. Pvt. Ltd.
167. AIR 1963 SC 996.
168. The State shall promote with special care the educational and economic interests of the weaker sections of the people, and, in particular, of the Scheduled Castes and Scheduled Tribes, and shall protect them from social injustice all forms of exploitation.
169. *In re,* Thomas, AIR 1952 Mad. 21.
170. 1st Indian Constitutional Amendment Act 1951.
171. Cf. Jagwant Kaur Kesarsing Dang *v.* State of Bombay.
172. Bhanu Ram *v.* Hills Division, AIR 1957, Ass. 182, 188.
173. Lingappa Pochanna *v.* State of Maharastra, AIR 1985 SC 389.
174. Charan Singh *v.* State of Punjab, (1997) 4 SCC 565 (Para 10).
175. Panchayat Varga Sharmajivi Samudaik Sahakari Khedut Cooperation Society *v.* Haribhai Mevabhai, (1996) 10 SCC 320 (paras 6, 10 & 14).
176. Tara Chand Vyas *v.* Chairman & Disciplinary Authority, (1997) 4 SCC 565 (Para 2).
177. Vishwas Anna Sawant *v.* Municipal Corporation of Greater Bombay, IT 1994 (3) SC 573.
178. AIR 1951 Punj. 93, AIR 1996 11 SCC 399.
179. Shantistar Builders *v.* Narayan Khimalal Totame, AIR 1990 SC 630, Para 12.13.
180. Indra Sawhney *v.* Union of India, (1992) Supp. SCC 217, 1993 SC 477.
181. State of Kerala *v.* Joseph Antony, AIR 1994 SC 721.
182. Deep Chand *v.* U.P., AIR 1959 SC 648, 664.
183. (1) Seats shall be reserved in the House of the People for-the Scheduled Castes; the Scheduled Tribes except the Scheduled Tribes in the autonomous districts of Assam; and the Scheduled Tribes in the autonomous districts of Assam. (2) The number of seats reserved in any State or union territory for the Scheduled Castes or the Scheduled Tribes under clause (1) shall bear as nearly as may be, the same proportion to the total number of seats allotted to that State or union territory in the House of the People as the population of Scheduled Castes in the State or Union territory or part of the Scheduled Tribes in the State or Union territory or part of the State or Union territory as the case may be, in respect of

which seats are so reserved, bears to the total Population of the state or Union Territory. (3) Notwithstanding anything contained in clause (2), the number of seats reserved in the Parliament for the Scheduled Tribes in the autonomous districts of Assam shall bear to the total number to seats allotted to that State a proportion not less than the population of the Scheduled Tribes in the said autonomous districts bears to the total population of the State. Here expression 'population' means the population as ascertained at the last preceding census of which the relevant figure has been published. It is provided that the reference to the last preceding census of which relevant figure has been published shall be construed as a reference to the 2001 census, until the relevant figures for he first census taken after the year 2026 have been published;

184. Seats shall be reserved for the Scheduled Caste and Scheduled Tribes, except the Scheduled Tribes in the autonomous districts of Assam, in the Legislative Assembly of every State. (2) Seats shall be reserved also for the autonomous districts in the Legislative Assembly of the State of Assam. (3) That number of seats reserved for the Scheduled Castes or the Scheduled Tribes in the Legislative Assembly of any State under clause (1) shall bear, as nearly as may be, the same proportion to the total number of seats in the Assembly as the population of the Scheduled Castes in the State or of the Scheduled Tribes in the State or part of the State as the case may be in respect of which seats are so reserved, bears to the total population of the State. (3A) Notwithstanding anything contained in clause (3), until the re-adjustment under Article 170 takes effect, on the basis of the first census after the year 2026, of the number of seats in the legislative Assemblies of the States of Arunachal Pradesh, Meghalaya, Mizoram and Nagaland, the seats shall be reserved for the Scheduled Tribes in the Legislative Assembly of any such State shall be : (a) if all the seats in the Legislative Assembly of such State in existence on the date of coming into force of the Constitution (Fifty-seventh Amendment) Act, 1987 are held by members of the Scheduled Tribes, all the seats expect one; (b) in any other case, such number of seats as bear to the total number of seats, a proportion not less than the number of members belonging to the Scheduled Tribes in the existing Assembly bears to the total number of seats in the existing Assembly. (3B) Notwithstanding anything contained in clause (3), until the taking effect, under Article 170, of the re-adjustment, on the basis of the first census after the year 2026, of the number of seats in the Legislative Assemblies of the States of Tripura, the seats which shall be reserved for the Scheduled Tribes in the Legislative Assembly, shall be, such number of seats as bears to the total number of seats, a proportion not less the number, as on the date of coming into

force of the constitution (seventy-second Amendment) Act, 1992 of members belonging to the Scheduled Tribes in the Legislative Assembly in the existence on the said date bears to the total number of seats in the Assembly. (4) The number of seats reserved for an autonomous district in the Legislative Assembly of the State of Assam shall bear to the total number of seats in that Assembly a proportion not less than the population of the district bears to be total population of the State. (5) The constituencies for the seats reserved for any autonomous district of Assam shall not comprise any area outside the district. (6) No person who is not a number of a Scheduled Tribe of any autonomous district of the State of Assam shall be eligible for election to the Legislative Assembly of the State from any Constituency of that district. It is provided that for elections to the legislative assembly of the state of Assam, the representation of the scheduled tribes and non-scheduled tribes in the constituencies included in the Bodoland territorial areas District and existing prior to the constitution of the Bodoland territorial Areas District, shall be maintained.

185. Giri, V.V. *v.* Dora Dippala Suri, AIR 1959 SC 1318.
186. Poudyal, R.C. *v.* Union of India, 194, Supp. (1) SCC 324.
187. Notwithstanding anything in the foregoing provisions of this part, the provisions of this Constitution relating to—(a) the reservation of seats for the Scheduled Castes and the Scheduled Tribes in the Parliament and in the Legislative Assemblies of the States...shall cease to have effect on the expiration of a period of seventy years (inserted by 95th Constitutional Amendment Act, 2010) from the commencement of this Constitution. But this article shall not effect any representation in the Parliament or in the Legislative Assembly, until the dissolution of the then existing house or Assembly as the case may be.
188. The Constitutional (79th Amendment) Act, 1999.
189. The claims of the members of a Scheduled Castes and the Scheduled Tribes shall be taken into consideration, consistently with the maintenance of efficiency of administration, in the making of appointments to services and posts in connection with the affairs of the Union or of a State. It is provided that this Article shall not prevent in making of any provision in favour of the member of the scheduled castes and scheduled tribes for relaxation in qualifying marks in any examination or lowering the standards of evaluation, for reservation in matters of promotion to any class or classes of services post in connection with affair of the Union or of a State;
190. Comptroller *v.* Jagannathan, AIR 1987 SC 537, paras 21 & 22.
191. *Ibid.*
192. *Ibid.*

193. Comptroller and Auditor General of India, Gian Prakash *v.* K.S. Jagannathan, AIR 1987 SC 537.
194. Devadasan T. *v.* Union of India, AIR 1964 SC 179.
195. Cf. Balaji, M.R. *v.* State of Mysore, AIR 1963 SC 649.
196. Devadasan T. *v.* Union of India, AIR 1964 SC 179.
197. Cf. Balaji, M.R. *v.* State of Mysore, AIR 1963 SC 649.
198. Indra Sawhney *v.* Union of India, 1992, Supp. (3) SCC 217.
199. Devadasan T. *v.* Union of India, AIR 1964 SC 179.
200. Cf. Balaji, M.R. *v.* State of Mysore, AIR 1963 SC 649.
201. Indra Sawhney *v.* Union of India, 1992, Supp. (3) SCC 217.
202. *Ibid*.
203. (1) There shall be a National Commission for the Scheduled Castes to be known as the National Commission for the Scheduled Castes. (2) The Commission shall consist of a Chairperson, Vice-Chairperson and five other Members and the condition of services and tenure of offices of the Chairperson, Vice-Chairperson and other Members so appointed shall be such as the President may by rule determine. (3) The Chairperson, Vice-Chairperson and other Members of the Commission shall be appointed by the president by warrant under his hand and seal. (4) The commission shall have the power to regulate its own procedure. (5) It shall be the duty of the Commission to investigate and monitor all matters relating to the safeguards provided for the Scheduled Castes under this Constitution or under any law for the time being in force or under any order of the Government and to evaluate the working of such safeguards; (b) to inquire into specific complaints with respect to the deprivation of rights and safeguards of the Scheduled Castes; (c) to participate and advise on the planning process of socio-economic development of the Scheduled Castes and to evaluate the progress of their development under the Union and any State; (d) to present reports to the President, Upon the working of those safeguards, annually and at such other times as the Commission may deem fit; (e) to make in such reports recommendations as to the measures that should he taken by the Union or any State for the effective implementation of those safeguards and other measures for the protection, welfare and socio-economic development of the Scheduled Castes; and (f) to discharge such other functions in relation to the protection, welfare and development and advancement of the Scheduled Castes as the President may specify. (6) The President shall cause all such reports to be laid before each House of Parliament along with a memorandum explaining the action taken or proposed to be taken on the recommendations relating to the Union and the reasons for the non-acceptance if any, of any of such recommendations. (7) Where any such report, or any

part thereof, relates to any matter within which any State Government is concerned, a copy of such report shall he forwarded to the Governor of the State who shall cause it to be laid before the Legislature of the State along with a memorandum explaining the action taken or proposed to be taken on the recommendations relating to the State and the reasons for the non- acceptance if any, any of such recommendations. (8) The Commission shall while investigating any matter referred to in sub-clause (a) or inquiring into any complaint referred to in sub-clause (b) of clause (5), have all the powers of a civil court trying a suit and in particular in respect of the following matters, namely: (a) summoning and enforcing the attendance of any person from any part of India and examining him on oath; (b) requiring the discovery and production of any documents; (c) receiving evidence on affidavits; (d) requisitioning any public or copy thereof from any court or office; (e) issuing commissions for the examination of witnesses and document; (f) any other matter which the President may by rule, determine. (9) The Union and every State Government shall consult the Commissions on all major policy matters affecting Scheduled Castes. (10) In this article, references to the Scheduled Castes shall be construed as including references to such other backward classes as the president may, on receipt of the report of a Commission appointed under clause (l) of Article 340 by order specify. Substituted by the Constitution (89th Amendment) Act, 2003.

204. Article 338A—There shall be a National Commission for the Scheduled Tribes to be known as the National Commission for the Scheduled Castes. (2) The Commission shall consist of a Chairperson, Vice-Chairperson and five other Members and the condition of services and tenure of offices of the Chairperson, Vice-Chairperson and other Members so appointed shall be such as the President may by rule determine. (3) The Chairperson, Vice-Chairperson and other Members of the Commission shall be appointed by the president by warrant under his hand and seal. (4) The commission shall have the power to regulate its own procedure. (5) It shall be the duty of the Commission—(a) to investigate and monitor all matters relating to the safeguards provided for the Scheduled Tribes under this Constitution or under any law for the time being in force or under any order of the Government and to evaluate the working of such safeguards; (b) to inquire into specific complaints with respect to the deprivation of rights and safeguards of the Scheduled tribes; (c) to participate and advise on the planning process of socio- economic development of the Scheduled Tribes and to evaluate the progress of their development under the Union and any State; (d) to present reports to the President, Upon the working of those safeguards, annually

and at such other times as the Commission may deem fit; (e) to make in such reports recommendations as to the measures that should he taken by the Union or any State for the effective implementation of those safeguards and other measures for the protection, welfare and socio-economic development of the Scheduled tribes; and (f) to discharge such other functions in relation to the protection, welfare and development and advancement of the Scheduled tribes as the President may specify. (6) The President shall cause all such reports to be laid before each House of Parliament along with a memorandum explaining the action taken or proposed to be taken on the recommendations relating to the Union and the reasons for the non-acceptance if any, of any of such recommendations. (7) Where any such report, or any part thereof, relates to any matter within which any State Government is concerned, a copy of such report shall he forwarded to the Governor of the State who shall cause it to be laid before the Legislature of the State along with a memorandum explaining the action taken or proposed to be taken on the recommendations relating to the State and the reasons for the non-acceptance if any, any of such recommendations. (8) The Commission shall while investigating any matter referred to in sub-clause (a) or inquiring into any complaint referred to in sub-clause (b) of clause (5), have all the powers of a civil court trying a suit and in particular in respect of the following matters, namely: (a) summoning and enforcing the attendance of any person from any part of India and examining him on oath; (b) requiring the discovery and production of any documents; (c) receiving evidence on affidavits; (d) requisitioning any public or copy thereof from any court or office; (e) issuing commissions for the examination of witnesses and document; (f) any other matter which the President may by rule, determine. (9) The Union and every State Government shall consult the Commissions on all major policy matters affecting Scheduled Tribes.

205. (1) The President may at any time and shall, at the expiration of ten years from the commencement of this Constitution, by order appoint a Commission to report on the administration of the scheduled areas and the welfare of the scheduled tribes in the State. . . . The order may define the composition, powers and procedure of the commission and may contain such incidental or ancillary provisions as the President may consider necessary or desirable. (2) The executive power of the union shall extend to the giving of directions to a State . . . as to the drawing up and execution of schemes specified in the direction to be essential for the welfare of the scheduled tribes in the State.

206. (1) The President may appoint a Commission consisting of such persons as he thinks fit to investigate the conditions of socially and educationally backward classes within the territory of India and the difficulties under which they labour and to make recommendations as to the steps that Should be taken by the Union or any State to remove such difficulties and to improve their condition and as to the grants that should be made for the purpose by the Union or any state and the conditions subject to which such grants should be made, and the order appointing such Commission shall define procedure to be followed by the Commission. (2) A Commission so appointed shall investigate the matters referred to them and present to the President a report setting out the facts as found by them and making such recommendations as they think proper. (3) The president shall cause a copy of the report so together with a memorandum explaining the action taken thereon to be laid before each House of Parliament.

207. AIR 1993 SC 477.

208. (1) The president may, with respect to any State or Union territory, and where it is a State after consultation with the Governor thereof, by public notification, specify the castes, races, or tribes or parts of or groups within castes, races or tribes which shall for the purposes of this Constitution be deemed to Scheduled Caste in relation to that State or Union Territory, as the case may be. (2) Parliament may by law include in or exclude from the list of Scheduled Castes specified in a notification issued under clause (1) any caste, race or tribe or part of or group within any caste, race or tribe, but save as aforesaid a notification issued under the said clause shall not be varied by any subsequent notification.

209. (1) The President may with respect to any State or Union territory, and where it is a State after consultation with the Governor thereof, by public notification specify the tribes or tribal communities or parts of or groups within tribes or tribal communities which shall for the purposes of this Constitution be deemed to be Scheduled Tribes in relation to that State or Union Territory, as the case may be. (2) Parliament may by law include in or exclude from the list of Scheduled Tribes specified in a notification issued under clause (1) any tribe or tribal community or part of or group within any tribe or tribal community but save a aforesaid a notification issued under the said clause shall not be varied by any subsequent notification.

210. Article 366(24)—"Scheduled Castes" means such castes, races or tribes or parts of or groups within such castes, races or tribes as are deemed under Article 341 to be Scheduled Castes for the purpose of this Consultation; Article 366(25)—"Scheduled Tribes" means such tribes or tribal communities or parts of or groups within such

tribes or tribal communities as are deemed under Article 342 to be Scheduled Tribes for the purposes of this Constitution.

211. Bhaiyalal *v.* Harikishan Singh, AIR 1965 SC 1557.
212. *Ibid.*
213. S. Narayan *v.* District Collector, Salem, 1997 2 SCC 571.
214. Bhaiyalal *v.* Harikishan Singh, AIR 1965 SC 1557.
215. A. Chinappa *v.* V. Venkatamuni (1996) 3SCC 585.
216. Nityanand Sharma *v.* State of Bihar, 1996, 3 SCC 576.
217. Palghat Jila Thandan Samrakshna Samiti *v.* State of Kerala (1994) 1 SCC 359.
218. Action Committee *v.* Union of India (1994) 5 SCC 244.
219. Union of India *v.* Dudh Nath Prasad (2000) 2 SCC 20.
220. Ramesh Chandra and Sanghmitra, "Dalit Identity in the New Millennium", Vol. 9, Commonwealth Pub., ed. 2003, p. 174.
221. *Ibid.*, at 175.
222. Durga Das Basu, Shorter Constitution of India, 13th Edition, 2001, Reprint 2004, Wadhwa and Company Law Publishers, New Delhi at p. 1115.
223. *Ibid.*, at p. 1125.
224. *Amar Ujala*, Thursday, 16 December 2005.
225. *Ibid.*, at pp. 1137-38.
226. Hota Venkata Surya Sivaram Sastry *v.* State of A.P., AIR 1967 SC 71.
227. Durga Das Basu, Shorter Constitution of India, 13th Edition 2001, Reprint 2004, Wadhwa and Company Law Publishers, New Delhi, p. 71.

4

Judicial Hunch for Backward Class Reservation

Social justice as visualized by the Indian Constitution implies a reduction of social and economic inequalities. It is distributive justice which involves distribution of resources, benefits and burdens in society according to needs, worth merit and work. In India professional education and governmental jobs constitute important aspects of distributive justice. Hence seats and posts are reserved in educational institution and government services for the deprived social sections. It is based on two premises: *first;* that an egalitarian society is a worthy ideal; *second;* that reservation is an efficient means to achieve an egalitarian society, and that this policy will in course of time bring the deprived classes up to a reasonable level of equality when compared to the rest of the society. Articles 15(4) and 16(4) of the Indian Constitution convey constitutional ethics of compensatory or protective discrimination for the leveling up of backward classes, namely, Scheduled Caste, Scheduled Tribes and Other Backward Classes (Caste).

Since the day of the commencement of Indian Constitution, Judiciary is playing a crucial role in interpreting and protecting the interest of various backward sections of the society in accordance with the constitutional mandate. During last 58 years, Judiciary has been enthusiastically discharging its constitutional responsibilities to accomplish the goals enshrined in the Preamble, Fundamental Rights and Directive Principles of the Indian Constitution. To realize social and economic justice, judiciary has contributed more. In number of cases, the State Government's policy of reservation in jobs and educational institutions has been challenged. The main problem in the various cases was related to determine the criteria of backwardness. Whether it should be caste basis or economic status basis.[1] Later in subsequent cases it was challenged on the other ground that what should be the total extent or limit of Reservation. Could limits of reservation be fixed up to 50% or more? It is also questioned, could reservation given to SCs and STs in promotion is justiciable.

This chapter discussed significant elucidation of reservation policy given by the highest law adjudicating agency of India, i.e. Supreme Court of India. In variety of cases Hon'ble Supreme Court proceeds :

(i) as a liberator of backward class,
(ii) as a protector of backward class, and
(iii) as a harbinger of backward class.

JUDICIARY AS LIBERATOR OF BACKWARD CLASSES

Liberator means the one, who can provide liberty. Liberty means freedom from restraint under conditions essential to equal enjoyment of the same right by others.[2] In its most signification liberty is said to be a power to do as one thinks fit, unless restrained by the law of the land.[3] Liberty means freedom from restraint, it means freedom to go where one may wish and to act in such manner, non-inconsistent with the equal right of others, as one's judgment may dictate for the promotion of one's happiness, that is to pursue such profession and avocation as may be most suitable to develop one's capacities and to give them their highest enjoyment. Liberty as far as backward classes is concerned, means backward classes must be freed from any other those obligations which could slow down them to bring social justice and obstruct their upliftment. They therefore, should be given an opportunity to lead a life like other free human being.[4]

In India, hon'ble Supreme Court is doing excellent job to liberate the backward classes. In numerous writ petitions it issued various directions to the Central and State Governments for the upliftment of backward classes and liberating them from the clutches of backwardness. Judiciary decided in number of case that generally discrimination is not allowed on the ground mention in Article 15 but for the advancement of backward classes and to carry social justice, positive discrimination in their favour is to be allowed, and therefore it leads to liberty from the restrictions.

Smt. Champakam Dorairajan v. Sate of Madras[5] case was the first judicial pronouncement or interpretation about reservation policy of the government (rule to bringing social justice through quotas) in this line. In this case through communal order reservation was made for different communities on the basis of religion, race and caste. This was challenged as unconstitutional and *ultra-vires*. It was defended under Article 46 to promote with special care the educational and economic interests of the weaker sections of the people. Supreme Court with the bench of *Kania C.J., Fazal Ali, Patanjali Shastri, Mahajan, B.K. Mukherjea, S.R. Das & Bose JJ.* struck down the reservation made by the State and held that it was unconstitutional as it classified students on the basis of caste and religion which are prohibitory grounds under Article 15(1) of the Constitution. Here the court pointed out positively that reservation in appointments or posts could be made in favour of any backward classes of citizens, which are not adequately represented in the services under Article 16(4) by the State. It is also held that the "omission of such an express provision from Article 29 cannot be regarded as significant. It may well be that the intention of the Constitution was not to introduce at all communal considerations in matters of admission into any educational institutions maintained by the State or receiving aid out of State funds". Hon'ble court observed that the chapter of fundamental rights is sacrosanct and not liable to be abridged by any legislative or executive order, except to the extent provided in the appropriate Article in part III. The Directive Principle of State policy under article 46 cannot override the provisions found in part III, but it has to confirm and run as subsidiary to the chapter of Fundamental Rights.

To nullify this decision and to protect the interest of the weaker sections, the Government of India, therefore, preferred the Constitutional amendment to verify the judicial intervention in the reservation policy and subsequently clause 15(4)[6] was introduced in the Constitution of India. *This clause gives liberty from the restrictions mentioned in Articles 15(1) and 16(2) for the upliftment of any socially and educationally backward classes or for SCs/STs by authorizing State to make special provisions.*

In M.R. Balaji v. *The State of Mysore*[7] is another case when the court scrutinized various issues concerning reservation policy, *first;* whether the criteria applied for preparing the lists of backwardness is proper and valid. *Second;* whether the protection contemplated in clause 15(4) can be given only to those classes of citizens who are both socially and educationally backward or whether it can be given to classes which are backward in any of the two respects. *Third;* what is meant by the expression 'classes of citizens' in Article 15(4), and *fourth;* how the social and educational backwardness has to be determined. *Fifth;* what should be the limit to provide reservation.

In this case Government order to provide job reservation for Backward Classes was challenged on the two grounds, *firstly;* that the lists of backward classes were prepared only on the caste basis that is unconstitutional and clear violation of Article 15. *Secondly;* it was challenged that the 68% reservation was excessive and unreasonable in protecting the interest of the candidates coming under the merit pool.

Regarding meaning of *'Classes of Citizens'* the 6 judges' bench of Supreme Court (B.P. Sinha C.J., P.B. Gajendragadkar, K.N. Wanchoo, K.C. Das Gupta, & J.C. Sash, JJ.) observed as:[8]

> ". . . the groups of Citizens to whom Article 15(4) applies are described as 'classes of citizens' and not as castes of citizens. A class, according to the dictionary meaning,

shows division of society according to status, rank or caste. In the Hindu social structure, caste unfortunately plays an important part in determining the status of citizen. The history of growth of caste system shows that its original function and occupational basis was later on over burdened with considerations of purity based on ritual concepts, and led to its ramifications which introduced inflexibility and rigidity, and to foster narrow caste loyalties. Therefore, in dealing with the question as to whether any class of citizens is socially backward or not, it may not be irrelevant to consider the caste of the said group of citizens. It is, however, necessary to bear in the mind that the special provision is contemplated for classes of citizens and not for individual citizens as such, and so, though the caste of the group of citizens may be relevant, its importance should not be exaggerated. If the classification of the backward classes of citizens was based solely on the caste of the citizens it may not always be logical and may perhaps be contain the voice of perpetuating the castes themselves".

Further judiciary said that we think therefore that though castes in relation to Hindu may be relevant factor to consider in determining the social backwardness of groups or classes of citizens, it cannot be the sole or the dominant test in that behalf. Social backwardness is on the ultimate analysis, the result of the poverty to a very large extent. The classes of citizens who are deplorably poor automatically become socially backward.

The court finally held that occupations of citizens may also contribute to make classes of citizens socially backward. There are some occupations which are treated as inferior according to conventional beliefs and classes of citizens who follow these occupations, are apt to become socially backward. The place of habitation also plays a part in determining the backwardness of a community of persons. Further held that sociological, social and economic considerations also come into play in solving the problem and evolving proper criteria for determining which classes are socially backward it is obviously a very difficult task. In a sense, the problem of social backwardness is the problem of rural India and in that behalf, 'classes of citizens' occupying a social backward position in rural area, fall within the purview of Article 15(4).

Balaji case is regarded as a landmark case, in the struggle for equality by backward classes, the principle points enunciated in the judgment may briefly be summarized as below:

(1) The classification of backward classes into backward and more backward is not permissible. It is not so warranted by Article 15(4).
(2) Relative test would result in identifying several layers or strata of backwardness and each of them may have to be included under Article 15(4).
(3) The backwardness must be both, social and educational not either social or educational.
(4) The bracketing of the backward classes with the scheduled castes and scheduled tribes in Article 15(4) indicates that backwardness must be comparable to the Scheduled Castes and Scheduled Tribe.
(5) Only such castes and communities, those are well below the state average in education could be classified as educationally backward.
(6) The groups of citizens under Article 15(4) are classes of citizens and not caste of citizens. It is therefore, clear that the term 'Classes' demonstrate the division of the society, on status and ranks basis not on caste basis.
(7) Special provisions are indicated for classes of citizens and not for individuals.
(8) The caste of the group of citizens may be relevant, but its importance should not be exaggerated.
(9) If the test of caste is emphasized, it may not be logical and may perhaps contain the vice of perpetuating the castes themselves.
(10) Caste is a relevant factor in Hindu social structure, but it should not be the sole or dominant factor in determining backwardness.
(11) The caste would breakdown in respect of communities that do not recognize the caste system.

The exclusion of muslims, christians, jains and even lingayats from such test would hardly be justifiable.

(12) Social backwardness was in the ultimate analysis the result of poverty to a very large extent and likely to be aggravated by consideration of caste. This shows the relevancy of both caste and poverty in determining the backwardness.

(13) Occupation followed by certain classes may also contribute to social backwardness.

(14) Place of habitation may also be relevant for backwardness.

(15) Classes of citizens' occupying a socially backward position in rural areas fall within the purview of Article 15(4). The problem of determining who socially backward classes are undoubtedly is very complex question and very difficult to resolve. It will need an elaborate investigation and collection of data and examining the said data in a rational and scientific way. That, however, is a function of the state which purports to act under Article 15(4).

(16) For determining the educational backwardness, test has been put high by the *Nagan Gowda Committee.* However, it would not be justifiable to treat those whose educational average was slightly above, or very near, or just below the State average as educationally backward. Only average that can properly be regarded as educationally backward.

(17) Reservations have the inevitable effect of lowering the quality of education and the services. Thus special provision like reservation of posts and appointments contemplated by Article 16(4) must be within reasonable limits. The interests of weaker section of society which are a first charge have to be adjusted with the interests of the community as a whole. Speaking generally and in a broad way, reservation should be less than 50%, how much less than 50% would depend upon the relevant prevailing circumstances in each case. Reservation, therefore, of 68% is inconsistent with the concept

authorizes by Article 15(4).[9] Thus Court has put 50% cap on reservations.

(18) Article 15(4) is an enabling provision; it does not impose an obligation, merely leave it to the direction of the appropriate government to take suitable action, if necessary.[10]

When Article 15(4) contemplates that the State can make the special provision in question, the said provision can be made by an executive order, and legislation for the purpose is not necessary. But it is necessary for the State to remember that the policy that is intended to be implement, is the policy, which has been declared by Article 46 and the preamble of the Constitution. It is for the attainment of the social and economic justice that Article 15(4) authorizes for making the special provisions for the advancement of the communities, contemplated even if such provisions may be inconsistent with the fundamental rights guaranteed under Article 15 or Article 29(2). The context therefore, requires that the executive action taken by the State must be based on an objective approach, free from all extraneous pressures. The said action is intended to do social and economic justice and must be taken in a manner that justice is and should be done.[11]

At present regarding limit for reservation almost all states except Tamil Nadu (69%, under 9th schedule) and Rajasthan (68% quota including 14% for forward castes, post-Gujjar violence, 2008) has not exceeded 50% limit. Tamil Nadu exceeded limit in 1980. Andhra Pradesh tried to exceed limit in 2005 which was again stalled by High Court.

In *Chitralekha* case[12] observation of *Balaji's* case was followed by bench of *B.P. Sinha C.J., K. Subba Rao, Raghubar Dayal, N. Rajagopala Ayyangar and J.R. Mudholkar, JJ*. In this case it is assumed that a government order, making a classification of socially and educationally backward classes on the basis of economic condition only, is not bad because it had been done by taking into consideration the caste also. The authority concerned may take caste into consideration in ascertaining the backwardness of a group of persons; but if it does not, its order will not be bad on that account, if it can ascertain the backwardness of a group of persons on the basis of other relevant criteria.[13] Caste is only a relevant and not a compelling circumstance in ascertaining the backwardness of a class and where it can be done the social backwardness of a group of citizens could be determined without references to caste at all.[14] Articles 46, 341, 342 and 15(4) form a group which have relevance in making of special provisions for advancement of any socially and educationally backward classes of citizens in the matter of admissions to colleges. Hon'ble Court pointed out two principles, namely:

(1) the caste of a group of a citizens may be a relevant circumstances in a ascertaining their social backwardness; and
(2) though it (caste) is relevant factor to determine the social backwardness of a class of citizens, it cannot be the sole or document test in that behalf.[15]

Judgment given by the bench of *A.N. Rao C.J., H.R. Kania, K.K. Mathew, M.H. Beg, V.R. Krishna Iyer, A.C. Gupta, and S. Murtaza, Fazal Ali JJ.* in *State of Kerala V.N.M. Thomas*[16] case shows two logics. *First;* in favour of caste as a determinant factor of backwardness and *second;* if everyone in any case is socially and educationally backward, the whole caste be regarded as backward. *In this case Supreme Court said that classification made on the caste basis is not against Article 16(2) and upheld the caste-based reservation policy. It concludes that the aim of the constitution is to eliminate caste from the State's affairs. Yet, certain backward castes have to be recognized and classified for compensatory measures.*

Judiciary held that the classification of employees belonging to Scheduled Castes and Scheduled Tribes for allowing them an extended period of two years for passing the special tests for promotion is a just and reasonable classification having rational nexus to the object of providing equal opportunity for all citizens in matters relating to employment or appointment to public offices.[17] The temporary relaxation of test qualification made in their favour is warranted by their inadequate representation in the services and their overall backwardness. A rule in favour of an under-represented backward community specifying the basic needs of efficiency of administration will not contravene Articles 14, 16(1) and 16(2). It is aim of our Constitution to bring them up from handicapped position to improvement. *If classification is permissible under Article 14 it is equally permissible under Article 16, because both the Articles lay down equality. The quality and concept of equality is that if persons are dissimilarly placed they cannot be made equal by having the same treatment.*

V.R. Krishna Iyer, J. observed,

> "Scheduled Castes and Scheduled tribes are no castes in the Hindu fold but an amalgam of castes, races, groups, tribes, communities or parts thereof found on investigation to be the lowliest and in need of massive State aid and notified as such by the president. To confuse this backward most social composition with castes is to commit a constitutional error, misled by a compendious appellation. So that, to protect Harijans is not to prejudice any caste but to promote citizens solidarity. Article 16(2) is out of the way and to extend protective discrimination to this mixed bag of tribes, races, groups, communities and non-castes outside the fourfold Hindu division is not to compromise with the acceleration of Castelessness enshrined in the sub-article. Article 16(4) serves not as an exemption but as an emphatic statement of backward people and the opportunity for the free competition the forward selections are ordinarily entitled to".[18]

The Principles laid down by the Supreme Court in this case on the relevance of caste may be summarized as under;

(a) Articles 15(4) and 16(4) speak classes of citizens and not caste of citizens, class is wider expression than caste and is not synonymous with it.

(b) Caste is a relevant factor in determining social backwardness of a class or group of citizens but it cannot be the sole or dominant consideration.

(c) While caste may be considered in ascertaining the social backwardness of a class, if it is not, it will not bad, if the backwardness of the class can be ascertained on the basis of other relevant criteria.

(d) A caste is also a class of citizens and if a caste as a whole is socially and educationally backward, reservation can be made in favour or such a caste on the ground of its social and educational backwardness.

In *the state of Andhra Pradesh and others* v. *U.S. Balram*[19] case divisional Bench of *C. A. Vaidialingam and K.K. Mathew, JJ.* by negating observation of *Thomas case* held that Article 15(4) has to be read as a *proviso or exception* to Articles 15(1) and 29(2). Therefore the conditions which justify the departure from Article 15(1) must be strictly shown to exist. The backward classes for those improvements special provision are contemplated by Article 15(4) *must be in the matter of their backwardness and be comparable to Scheduled Castes and Scheduled Tribes*. However, social and educational backwardness need not be exactly similar in all respects to that of Scheduled Castes and Scheduled Tribes.[20]

In the case of *A. Periakaruppan* v. *State of Tamilnadu and others*[21] Hegde J. with J.C. Sahai and A.N. Grover, JJ. observed that *Rjendran's*[22] *case is an authority for the proposition that the classification of backward classes on the basis of caste is within the purview of Article 15(4) if those caste are shown to be socially and educationally backward*. No further material has been placed before us to show that the reservation for backward classes is not in accordance with Article 15(4). There is no gainsaying the fact that there are numerous castes in this country which are socially and educationally backward. To ignore their existence is to ignore the facts of life. Hence we are unable to ignore to uphold the contention that the impugned reservation is not in accordance with Article 15(4).

In the case of *Heggade Janardhan Subbaraya* v. *the State of Mysore and others,*[23] judiciary followed the decision of *Balaji* v. *State of Mysore,* and held that order for reservation of seats fixed in educational institutions for student of SCs and STs has always remained the same and it can't be deemed to have been affected. It is consistent with Article 15(4).

In Indra Sawhney & etc. v. *Union of India and others,*[24] *B.P. Jeevan Reddy J, on behalf of C.J. and M.N. Venkatachaliah and A.M. Ahmadi, JJ. with concurring judgment of S. Ratnavel Pandian and*

P.B. Sawant, JJ. observed that Article 16(1) does permit reasonable classification for ensuring attainment of the equality of opportunity assured by it. For assuring equality of opportunity, it may well be necessary in certain situations to treat unequally situated persons unequally. Not doing so perpetuate and accentuate inequality. Article 16(4) is an instance of such classification, put in to place the matter beyond controversy. They further held that the, "backward classes of citizens" are classified as a separate category deserving a special treatment in the nature of reservation of appointments/posts in the services of the State. Clause (4) of Article 16 is not an exception to clause (1) of Article (16), followed observation of Thomas case. It is an instance of classification implicit in and permitted by clause (1). Clause (4) of Article 16 is a provision which must be read along with and in harmony with clause (1) of Article 16. Indeed, even without clause (4), it would have been permissible for the State to have evolved such a classification and made a provision for reservation of appointment/posts in their own favour. Clause (4) merely puts the matter beyond any doubt in specific terms". Judiciary therefore gave the way for the implementation of separate reservation for other backward classes in central government jobs

Further judiciary held that aim should be to ensure a balance between cls. (1) & (4) of Article 16. Clause 4 should be construed strictly and in a manner that does not render the guarantee in cls. (1) altogether nugatory or illusory. Thus in the interests of the backward class of citizens the state cannot reserve all the appointments under the state or even a majority of them, viz the doctrine of equality of opportunity (cls. 1) shall be reconciled in favour of backward classes (cls. 4) in such a way that the latter while serving the cause of backward classes shall not unreasonably encroach upon the field of equality.[25] The Supreme Court laid down a scheme for reservation in direct recruitment to post of professor, Readers and lecturers in universities/colleges.[26]

It is not correct to say that a class cannot be treated as a backward class under Article 16(4) unless its backwardness is comparable to that of the SC/ST. For, if a class is situated similarly to the Scheduled Caste, it may have a case for inclusion in that Scheduled Caste, but there is no warrant for the proposition that there cannot be any other backward class. Scheduled Caste and Scheduled Tribes are evidently backward but the category of OBC is wider. There may be caste and occupational groups who are backward having regard to the entire populace and will come under the category of OBC.[27]

In the case of *Ram Bhagat Singh* v. *State of Haryana,* apex court of the country held that lower qualifying marks/ standard of eligibility must be prescribed and relaxation in age be considered for the persons belonging to the SC/ST or backward classes without affecting efficiency required for the job or administration. The government was directed to make a conscious decision objectively as to what should be the minimum percentage of marks necessary for administration.[28]

In *Haridas Perdesia* v. *Urmila Shakya* case judiciary held that relaxation in qualifying marks is available to the reserved candidates not only when such candidates are competing with general candidates but also when only reserved candidates are appearing in the examination.[29]

Judiciary endorse in *R. Chitralekha* v. *State of Mysore case* that these provisions recognize the factual existence of backward classes in our country brought about by historical reasons and make a sincere attempt to promote the welfare of the weaker sections thereof. They shall be so construed as to effectuate the said policy but not to give weightage to progressive sections of our society under the false colour of caste which they happen to belong.[30] It is also cleared by bench that while Article 16(4) is limited by Article 335, no such limitation applies to admission to educational institutions under Article 15(4).[31]

It is provided that for any person to be entitled to the benefits as SC/ST/OBC he has to obtain a certificate in the prescribed form, from the prescribed authority to show that he belongs to SC/ST/OBC. This certificate is a merit for appointment and admission in Government/PSUs, etc. against reserved posts. Where a candidate finds difficulty in obtaining a caste certificate, it is incumbent on the Government to verify the matter through the District Magistrate or collector insisting that the latter should either issue a certificate or clearly record a finding that the applicant dos not belong to SC or ST as the case may be.[32] In *G. Ayyanar* v. *Union of India*[33] Judiciary held that appointment of a candidate cannot be kept pending due to delay in verification of his community certificate. The applicant if otherwise eligible should be provisionally appointed subject to final verification of the community.

In *Union of India and others* v. *Dudh Nath Prasad* [34] Supreme Court held that where the parents residing in District Howrah in west Bengal for more than 30 years, they should be treated to be 'ordinarily residing' in that district and the mere fact that they were born in a village in District Siwan in the State of Bihar and that they owned some property there also, would not affect their status.

In *Rajendra Kumar Gour and others* v. *Union of India and others*[35] it was held that if there is only one post in the cadre, there could be no reservation under Article 15(4) of the Constitution. In the case of *Purna Chandra Modi* v. *Union of India*[36] it was decided that there is no question of reservation when the appointment is expressly ad hoc and stopgap and is likely to be reverted at any time. The principle is that, reservation percentage operates to posts in a cadre, but not to purely ad hoc and stopgap arrangement. In the case of *All India Non-SC/ST Employees association (Railway)* v. *V.K. Aggarawal and others*[37] it was held that if as a result of reclassification and readjustment there are no additional posts which are created and it is a case of upgradation, then the principle of reservation will not be applicable.

Where the total number of posts remains unaltered, through in different scales of pay as a result of regrouping and the effect of which may be that some of the employees who were in the lower scale will go into higher scales, it would be case of upgradation of post and not a case of an additional vacancy or the post being created to which the reservation principle would apply. It is only if in addition to the total number of existing posts, some additional posts are created that in respect of those additional posts the reservation will apply.

In the case of *R.K. Sabharwal & Ors.* v. *Union of India*[38] it was decided that if more than the requisite percentage of SC/ ST candidate are already appointed/promoted in a cadre on their own merit/seniority by competing with the general category candidates, then the proper interpretation of reservation policy does not imply that the purpose of reservation in the particular cadre has consequentlly been achieved and that the Government rules/instructions pro reservation would become inoperative. In other words, if a candidate belonging to SCs/STs /OBCs has got a promotion in his own merit by competing with general category candidates, then such promoted person shall be treated as a general category candidate for next higher promotions irrespective of the fact member of SC/ST/OBC.

Regarding the issue of reservation in promotion Supreme Court held in the cases of *General Manager, S. Rly.* v. *Rangachari,*[39] *State of Punjab* v. *Hiralal,*[40] *Akhil Bharatiya Soshit Karamchari Sangh (Railway)* v. *Union of India*[41] that reservation of appointments or posts under Article 16(4) included promotions also. This was overruled in *Indira Sawhney & Ors* v. *Union of India*[42] and held that Reservations cannot be applied in promotions. But to make this judgment invalid 77th Constitutional amendment Act, 1995 was enacted to introduced. [Article 16(4A)] for providing reservation in promotion also in favour of SCs and STs. In 2001 by 85th Constitutional amendment, Consequential Seniority was inserted in Article 16(4)(A) to be effective from 1995. In 2000 Article 15(4B) was introduced by 81st constitutional amendment Act 2000.

In the case of *M. Nagaraj and Others* v. *Union of India and Others,*[43] the validity, of (i) the Constitution (Seventy-Seventh Amendment) Act, 1995, the Constitution (Eighty-first Amendment) Act, 2000, the Constitution (Eighty-second Amendment) Act, 2000, and the Constitution (Eighty-fifth Amendment) Act, 2001 was challenged. After hearing *Five judges bench (Y.K. Sabharwal, K.G. Balakrishnan, S.H. Kapadia, C.K. Thakker & P.K. Balasubramanyan)* held that the impugned constitutional amendments by which Articles 16(4A) and 16(4B) have been inserted flow from Article 16(4). They do not alter the structure of Article 16(4). They retain the controlling factors or the compelling reasons, namely, backwardness and inadequacy of representation which enables the States to provide for reservation keeping in mind the overall efficiency of the State administration under Article 335. These impugned amendments are confined only to SCs and STs. They do not destroy any of the constitutional requirements, namely, ceiling-limit of 50% (quantitative limitation), the concept of creamy layer (qualitative exclusion), the sub-classification between OBC on one hand and SCs and STs on the other hand.[44]

However, regarding the "extent of reservation" it was held that the concerned State will have to show in each case the existence of the compelling reasons, namely, backwardness, inadequacy of representation and overall administrative efficiency before making provision for reservation. As stated above, the impugned provision is an enabling provision. The State is not bound to make reservation for SC/ST in matter of promotions. However, if they wish to exercise their discretion and make such provision, the State has to collect quantifiable data showing backwardness of the class and inadequacy of representation of that class in public employment in addition to compliance of Article 335. It is made clear that even if the State has compelling reasons, as stated above, the State will have to see that its reservation provision does not lead to excessiveness so as to breach the ceiling-limit of 50% or obliterate the creamy layer or extend the reservation indefinitely.

Subject to above therefore, apex court upholds the constitutional validity of the Constitution (Seventy-seventh Amendment) Act, 1995, the Constitution (Eighty-first Amendment) Act, 2000, the Constitution (Eighty-second Amendment) Act, 2000 and the Constitution (Eighty-fifth Amendment) Act, 2001 and laid down following principles :

1. Article 16(4)(A) and 16(4)(B) flow from Article 16(4). Those constitutional amendments do not alter structure of Article 16(4).
2. Backwardness and inadequacy of representation are the controlling/compelling reasons for the state to provide reservations keeping in mind the overall efficiencies of state administration.
3. Government has to apply cadre strength as a unit in the operation of the roaster in order to ascertain whether a given class/group is adequately

represented in the service. Roaster has to be post specific with inbuilt concept of replacement and not vacancy based.

4. If any authority thinks that for ensuring adequate representation of backward class or category, it is necessary to provide for direct recruitment therein, it shall be open to do so.
5. Backlog vacancies to be treated as a distinct group and are excluded from the ceiling limit of 50%.
6. If a member from reserved category gets selected in general category, his selection will not be counted against the quota limit provided to his class and reserved category candidates are entitled to compete for the general category post.
7. The reserved candidates are entitled to compete with the general candidates for promotion to the general post in their own right. On their selection, they are to be adjusted in the general post as per the roster and the reserved candidates should be adjusted in the points earmarked in the roster to the reserved candidates.
8. Each post gets marked for the particular category of candidate to be appointed against it and any subsequent vacancy has to be filled by that category alone.

In 1996 in the case of *S. Vinodkumar* v. *Union of India*[45] supreme court held that relaxation of qualifying marks and standard of evaluation in matters of reservation in promotion was not permissible. To invalidate this decision by the Constitution (82nd) Amendment Act, 2000, a proviso was inserted at the end of Article 335. *M. Nagraj & Ors.* v. *Union of India and Ors.*[46] held the amendments constitutional.

In 1994 Supreme Court advised Tamilnadu to follow 50% limit in reservation because Tamilnadu exceed the limit and put the reservations under 9th Schedule of the Indian Constitution. It was challenged as unconstitutional. In the case of *I.R. Coelho (Dead) by LRS.* v. *State of T.N*[47] Supreme Court held, that Ninth Schedule law has already been upheld by the court, it would not be open to challenge such law again on the principles declared by this judgment. However, if a law held to be violative of any rights in Part III is subsequently incorporated in the Ninth Schedule after 24 April, 1973, such a violation/infraction shall be open to challenge on the ground that it destroys or damages the basic structure as indicated in Article 21 read with Article 14, Article 19 and the principles underlying thereunder. Action taken and the transactions finalized as a result of the impugned Acts shall not be open to challenge.

In the case of *P.A. Inamdar and Others* v. *State of Maharashtra and Others,*[48] issue—Can State enforce its policy of reservation or any quota in admissions to unaided educational institutions was raised? Supreme Court with 7 judges bench (R.C. Lahoti (CJI), Y.K. Sabharwal, D.M. Dharmadhikari, Arun Kumar, G.P. Mathur, Tarun Chatterjee & P.K. Balasubramanyan) held that neither the policy of reservation can be enforced by the State nor any quota of admissions can be carved out to be appropriated by the State in a minority or non-minority unaided educational institution.

In 2005 to make this judgment invalid 93rd Constitutional Amendment Act, 2005, was enacted to introduce Art 15(5). Its validity was challenged in *Ashoka Kumar Thakur* v. *Union of India and Others,*[49] and several issues arose :

(i) Whether Ninety-Third Amendment of Constitution is against the "basic structure" of the Constitution?;
(ii) Whether Article 15(4) and 15(5) are mutually contradictory, hence Article 15(5) is to be held ultra vires?;
(iii) Whether exclusion of minority educational institutions from Article 15(5) is violative of Article 14 of Constitution?;
(iv) Whether the Constitutional Amendment followed the procedure prescribed under Article 368 of the Constitution?;
(v) Whether the Act 5 of 2007 is constitutionally invalid in view of definition of "Backward Class" and whether the identification of such "Backward Class" based on "caste" is constitutionally valid?;

(vi) Whether "Creamy Layer" is to be excluded from SEBCs?; What should be the para-meters for determining the "creamy layer" group?;

(vii) Whether the "creamy layer" principle is applicable to Scheduled Tribes and Scheduled Castes?;

(viii) Whether the principles laid down by the United States Supreme Court for affirmative action such as "suspect legislation", "strict scrutiny" and "compelling State necessity" are applicable to principles of reservation or other affirmative action contemplated under Article 15(5) of the Constitution?;

(ix) Whether delegation of power to the Union Government to determine as to who shall be the backward class is constitutionally valid?;

(x) Whether the Act is invalid as there is no time limit prescribed for its operation and no periodical review is contemplated?;

(xi) What shall be the educational standard to be prescribed to find out whether any class is educationally backward?;

(xii) Whether the quantum of reservation provided for in the Act is valid and whether 27% of seats for SEBC was required to be reserved?

Supreme Court with Five judges bench (K.G. Balakrishnan (CJI), Dr. Arijit Pasayat, C.K. Thakker, R.V. Raveendran & Dalveer Bhandari) laid down following principles :

1. The Constitution (Ninety-third Amendment) Act, 2005 does not violate the "basic structure" of the Constitution so far as it relates to the state maintained institutions and aided educational institutions. Question whether the Constitution (Ninety-third Amendment) Act, 2005 would be constitutionally valid or not so far as "private unaided" educational institutions are concerned, is left open to be decided in an appropriate case, because issue was not arose in this case.

2. "Creamy layer" principle is one of the parameters to identify backward classes. Therefore, principally, the "Creamy layer" principle cannot be applied to STs and SCs, as SCs and STs are separate classes by themselves.
3. Preferably there should be a review after ten years to take note of the change of circumstance.
4. A mere graduation (not technical graduation) or professional deemed to be educationally forward.
5. Principle of exclusion of "creamy layer" is applicable to OBCs.
6. The Central Government shall examine as to the desirability of fixing a cut off marks in respect of the candidates belonging to the Other Backward Classes (OBCs) to balance reservation with other societal interests and to maintain standards of excellence. This would ensure quality and merit would not suffer. If any seats remain vacant after adopting such norms they shall be filled up by candidates from general categories.
7. So far as determination of backward classes is concerned, a Notification should be issued by the Union of India. This can be done only after exclusion of the creamy layer for which necessary data must be obtained by the Central Government from the State Governments and Union Territories. Such Notification is open to challenge on the ground of wrongful exclusion or inclusion. Norms must be fixed keeping in view the peculiar features in different States and Union Territories. There has to be proper identification of Other Backward Classes (OBCs). For identifying backward classes, the Commission set up pursuant to the directions of this Court in Indra Sawhney-1 has to work more effectively and not merely decide applications for inclusion or exclusion of castes.
8. The Parliament should fix a deadline by which time free and compulsory education will have reached every child. This must be done within six months, as the right to free and compulsory education is

perhaps the most important of all the fundamental rights [Article 21(A)]. For without education, it becomes extremely difficult to exercise other fundamental rights.

9. If material is shown to the Central Government that the Institution deserves to be included in the Schedule (institutes which are excluded from reservations) of The Central Educational Institutions (Reservation in Admission) Act, 2006 (No. 5 of 2007), the Central Government must take an appropriate decision on the basis of materials placed and on examining the concerned issues as to whether Institution deserves to be included in the Schedule of the said act as provided in Section 4 of the said act.
10. Held that the determination of SEBCs is done not solely based on caste and hence, the identification of SEBCs is not violative of Article 15(1) of the Constitution.

JUDICIARY AS PROTECTOR OF BACKWARD CLASSES

To renovate and reshuffle Indian judicial system time has come so that injustices do not occur and disfigure the fair and shining face of our budding democracy. There is urgent necessity of introducing a dynamic and comprehensive legal service programme with a view of reaching justice to the downtrodden or poor people.[50]

The poor in their contact with the legal system has always been on the wrong side of the line. They have always come across the law for the poor rather than the law of the poor. The law is regarded by them as something mysterious and forbidding, always taking something away from them and not as a positive and constructive social device for changing the social economic order and improving their life conditions by conferring rights and benefits on them. The result is that the legal system has lost it's credibility for the weaker section of the community.[51] In such a situation the Supreme Court of India has injected the concept of equal justice by creating judicial radicalism and has set a new constitutionalism at a time when there was lack of concern on the part of State for human values.[52]

Courts have protected the backward Classes (SCs, STs and OBCs) in various ways, e.g. (i) it has deviated from the old and stereotyped procedure to help backward classes, (ii) it has removed the obstacle of locus-standi for the path of backward classes, and (iii) it has construed the various Articles of the Constitution in a liberal way to help the backward classes.

Locus-Standi means a right of appearance in the court of justice.[53] According to this doctrine only persons can approach the court whose rights were violated. In 1981 this doctrine was diluted in judge's case.[54] The court took the view that where a person or class of persons to whom legal injury is caused by reason of violation of fundamental rights, is unable to approach the court for judicial redress on account of poverty or disability or socially or economically disadvantaged position, any member acting bonafide can move the Court for relief under Article 32 and Article 226.[55] The Court again deviated from the doctrine in *Asiad* case,[56] to bring justice within the reach of poor masses, and held:

> ". . . Courts are not meant only for rich and well do, for the business magnate and the industrial tycoon, but they exist also far poor and downtrodden, the have-nots and handicapped and the half hungry millions of our countrymen".[57]

Hon'ble Supreme Court in *B. Venkataramana* v. *State of Madras*[58] case held that Article 16(4) makes provision for reservation of appointments in favour of any backward class of citizens, who are not adequately represented in the services of the State; hence reservation of posts in favour of any backward class of citizens couldn't be regarded as unconstitutional. Further held that the communal G.O. of the Madras Government, which, besides making reservation of post for Harijans and backward Hindus, as sanctioned by Cls. (4) of the Article 16, also make reservation of posts for other communities viz., Muslims, Christians, Non-Brahmins Hindu and Brahmins which is repugnant to the provisions of Article

16, is as such void and illegal. The contention that the non—brahmins Hindus are protected by the list of backward classes maintained by the State was not accepted.

Commenting on this Supreme Court judgment, *Dr. Ambedkar* remarked,

> "it was utterly unsatisfactory and was not in consonance with the Articles of the Constitution".[59] He further stated that Article 46 directed the State to protect the interests of weaker sections.

In *Thomas case*[60] the Supreme Court has stated that classification of people can be made under Article 16(1), 29(2) and Article 14, in order to achieve equality through protective or compensatory discrimination. Article 15 was amended by adding it nearly a similar way to Article 16(4). It says, "Nothing in this Article or in clause (2) of Article 29 shall prevent the State from making any special provision for the advancement of any socially and educationally backward class of citizens or for the Scheduled Castes and Scheduled Tribes".[61]

Stressing on the need for amendment, then Prime Minister *Jawaharlal Nehru* stated,

> "We have to deal with the situation where for variety of reasons for which the present generation is not to blamed the past . . . there are groups, classes, communities who are backward. They are backward in many ways economically, socially, and educationally. Some they are backward in one of these respects and yet backward in another to these matters we had to do some thing special for them".[62]

In the case of *P. Rajendran* v. *State of Madras*[63] Chief Justice K.N. Wanchoo with the bench of R.S. Bachawat, J.M. Shelat, G.K. Mitter, C.A. Vaidialingam, JJ. observed that a cast is also a class of citizens and if the caste as a whole is socially and educationally backward, reservation can be made in favour of such a caste on the ground that it is a socially and educationally backward classes of citizens within the meaning of Article 15(4). Though the list in the Appendix is nothing but a list of certain castes, the castes included therein are, as a whole educationally and socially backward. Hence neither the list nor rule is violative of Article 15.[64]

Here court also held that under Article 16 of the constitution, there shall be equality of opportunity for all citizens in matters relating to employment or appointment to any offices under the State or promotion from one office to a higher office there under. Further said, that Clause (4) of article 16 does not cover the entire field covered by cls. (1) and cls. (2) of that Article. The only matter which cls. (4) Cover is a provision for the reservation of appointment in favour of a backward class of citizens. Articles 14, 15 and 16 are form part of the same constitutional code of guarantees and supplement with each other. It follows therefore that there can be a reasonable classification of the employees for the purpose of appointment and promotion. To put it differently, the equality of opportunity means equality as between members of the same class of employees, and not equality between members of separate, independent class.

In *State of Andhra Pradesh* v. *P. Sager*[65] case *justice J.C. Shah with Ramaswamy and G.K. Mitter, JJ.* observed that the expression "class" in Article 15(4) means a homogenous section of the people group together because of certain likenesses or common traits and who are identifiable by some common attributes such as status, rank, and occupation, residence in a locality, race, religion and the like. In determining whether a particular section forms a class, caste cannot be excluded altogether but in the determination of a class a test solely based upon the caste or community cannot also be accepted. The parliament has attempted to balance by enacting cls. (4) as against the right to equality of citizens, the special necessities of the weaker sections of the people by allowing a provision to be made for their advancement. In order that effect may be given to cls. (4), it must appear that the beneficiaries of the special provision are the classes which are backward socially and educationally and they are other than the scheduled castes and scheduled tribes, and that the provision made is for their advancement. The criterion for determining the backwardness must not be based solely on religion, race, caste, sex, or place or birth, and the backwardness must be similar to the backwardness from which the Scheduled castes and scheduled tribes suffer.[66] ·

Justice Shah by delivering order with *M. Hidayatullah C.J., S.M. Sikri* v. *Ramaswamy and V. Bhargava JJ. in Triloki Nath Tikku & another* v. *The State of Jammu and Kashmir*[67] *case* held that the difference in the phraseology used in Article 15(4) and Article 16(4) namely, socially and educationally backward classes in the former and backward classes in the latter, leads to the inevitable conclusion that "backward class" of citizens in Article 16(4) are only such class of citizens who are not adequately represented in the services of the State. Tests to satisfy conditions laid down in Article 16(4) are to see whether (i) the class of citizens is backward, say (ii) socially and educationally represented in the services under the state. The second alone can be the sole criterion.

Hon'ble Shah further held that Article 16 in the first instance prohibits discrimination by clause (2) on the ground interalia, of religion, race, caste, place of birth, residence and permits an exception by clause (4) to be made in the matter of reservation in favour of backward classes of citizens. The expression "backward class" is not used as synonymous with backward caste or "backward community". The members of an entire caste or community may in the social, economic and educational scale of values at a given time be backward and may on that account be treated as a backward classes but that is not because they are members of a caste or community, but because they form a class.[68]

In its ordinary connotation the expression "class" means a homogenous section of the people grouped together because of certain likeness or common traits, and who are identifiable by some common attributes such as status, rank, occupation, residence in a locality, race, religion and the like. But for the purpose of Article 16(4) in determining whether a section forms a class, a test solely based on caste, community, race, religion, sex, descent, and place of birth or residence cannot be adopted, because it would directly offend the constitution.[69] Clause 4 of Article 16 provides a limited exception to the operation of the other clause of Article 16.[70] Therefore, claim of petitioner that they are discriminated against in the matter of promotion to the gazetted cadre, solely on the ground of religion and place of residence[71] are allowed and held such discrimination void. The promotion granted are accordingly declared contrary to the provisions of Articles 16(1) and (4) of the constitution and therefore void. This will not however prevent the State from devising a scheme, consistent with the Constitutional guarantees, for reservation of appointments, posts or promotions in favour of any backward class of citizens which in the opinion of the State is not adequately represented in the services under the State.

In the case of *State of Kerala* v. *N.M. Thomas*[72] judiciary (with majority view of A.N. Ray, C.J., H.R. Kania, K.K. Mathew, V.R. Krishna Iyer, A.C. Gupta, and S. Murtaza, Fazal Ali, JJ.) treated Article 16(4) as a means to bring social justice and decided that this article acts *as proviso* of Articles 16(1) and (2) in the interest of downtrodden or backward classes. By upholding the action or order taken under this article authority of interpreting law observed,

> ". . . that because of their backwardness those sections of the population would not be in a position to compete with advanced section of the community who had all the advantages of affluence and better education. The fact that the doors of the competition were open to them would have been a poor consolation to the members of the backward classes because the chances of their success in the competition were far too remote on account of the inherent handicap and disadvantage from which they suffered. The result would have been that, leaving aside some exceptional cases; the members of backward classes would have hardly got any representation in jobs requiring educational background. It would have thus resulted in virtually repressing those who were already repressed. The framers of the Constitution being conscious of the above disadvantages from which backward classes were suffering enjoined upon the State in Article 46 of the Constitution to promote with special care, educational and economic interests of the weaker sections of the people, in particular of the Scheduled castes and Scheduled tribes, also protect them from social

injustice and all from exploitation. To give effect to that objective in the field of public employment, a provision was made in Article 16(4). Under the above clause, it is permissible for the State, in case it finds the representation of any backward class of citizens in the State services to be not adequate, to make provision for the reservation of appointments or posts in favour of that backward class of citizens. Such prefential treatment is plainly a negation of the equality of opportunity for all citizens in matters relating to employment or appointment to an office under the State. Clause 4 of Article 16 has, therefore, been construed as a proviso or exception to clause (1) of that Article".[73]

Chief Justice Ray stated[74] that Article 16(4) clarifies and explains that classification on the basis of backwardness does not fall within Article 16(2) and is legitimate for the purpose of Article 16(1) if preference shall be given to a particular under represented community other than a backward class or under represented state in an All India Services such a rule will contravene Article 16(2). A similar rule giving preference to an under-represented backward community is valid and not will contravene Articles 14, 16(1) and 16(2).[75]

Further held, that the power to make reservation which is conferred on the State under Article 16(4) can be exercised by the State in a proper case not only by providing for reservation of appointments but also by providing for reservation of selection posts.[76] The special treatment accorded to the Scheduled Castes and Scheduled Tribes in Government services which had become part and parcel of the conditions of services over the long periods amply justify the classification of the members of the Scheduled castes and Scheduled tribes as a whole by rule and Government Orders. These rules and Government orders are related to the constitutional mandate also under Article 335.[77] The historical background of these rules justifies the classification of the personnel of the Scheduled castes and Scheduled tribes in services for the purpose of granting them exemption from special tests with a view to ensuring them the equality of treatment and equal opportunity in matters of employment having regard to their backwardness and under representation in the employment of the state.[78] From the point of time a differential treatment is given to the members of Scheduled Castes and Scheduled tribes for the purpose of giving them equality consistent with efficiency.[79]

M.H. Beg, J. observed,

> "As a reservation of post under Article 16(4) for employees of backwards classes can include complete reservation of higher posts to which they can be promoted, it can also be partial or for a part of the duration of service and hedged round with the condition that a temporary promotion would operate as a complete and confirmed promotion only if the temporary promotee satisfied some tests within a given time. If both rule and order....could satisfy the requirements of substantial equality in keeping with Article 335, and meet the demands of equality and justice liked at from the broader point of view of Article 46 of the Constitution, they could also be justified under Article 16(4)".[80]

Equality of opportunity need not be confused with absolute equality. Article 16(1) does not prohibit the prescription of reasonable rules for selection to any employment or appointment to any office. In regard to employment, like others terms and conditions associated with and incidental to it, the promotion to a selection post is also included in the matters relating to employment.[81] All legitimate methods are available for equality of opportunity in services under Article 16(1). Article 16(1) is affirmative whereas Article 14 is negative in language. Article 16(4) indicates one of the methods of achieving equality embodied in Article 16(1).[82]

Bench of Hon'ble *C.A. Vaidialingam and K.K. Mathew, JJ.* held in the case of *State of Andhra Pradesh and others* v. *U.S. Balram*[83] that caste is a fact, found to be socially and educationally backward classes by their caste name and is not violative of Article 15(4). A caste is also a class of citizens and a caste as such may be socially and educationally backward. After collecting the necessary data if it is found that the caste as a whole is socially and educationally backward the reservation made of such persons will have to be upheld notwithstanding the fact that a few individuals in that group may be both socially and educationally above the general average.[84] For determination of backward classes Supreme Court held that it is not axiomatic that the educational average of the class should not be calculated on the basis of the student population in the last three high school classes. Nor that only those classes whose average is below the States average that can be treated as educationally backward.[85] Further held, that determination of certain classes as belonging to backward classes by a commission appointed for that purpose does not become invalid on ground that the Commission has used its personal knowledge for the purpose of charactersing a particular group as backward.[86]

It is also held that admission to the reserved seats of backward classes is not affected by some of the candidates belonging to these classes getting admission on their own merit. Judiciary has taken a slightly different view. If a situation arises wherein the candidates belonging to the groups included in the list of backward classes, are able to obtain more seats on the basis of their own merit, we can only state that it is the duty of the government to review the question of further reservation of seats for such groups. The government should not act on the basis that once a class is considered as a backward class. It should continue to be backward for all time.[87]

In the case of *Akhil Bhartiya Soshit Karamcharari Sangh (Railway)* v. *Union of India,*[88] *V.R. Krishana Iyer and Chinnappa Reddy, JJ.* observed that

"the State may classify, based upon substantial differentia, groups or classes and this process does not necessarily spell violation of Articles 14 to 16. The fundamental right to equality of opportunity has to be read as justifying the categorization of SCs and STs separately for the purpose of "adequate representation" in the services under the State. The object is constitutionally sanctioned in terms, as Articles 16(4) and 46 specificate. The classification is just and reasonable. The court may however, have to test whether the means used to reach the end era reasonable and do not outrun the purposes of the classification. Of course, apart from Article 16(1), Article 16(2) expressly forbids discrimination on the ground of Caste. Even assuming that SCs and STs are castes, classification, if permitted, will validate the differential rules for promotion, moreover, Article 16(4) is an exception to Article 16(2) also."

In this case by upholding carry forward rule, it was further observed that, "the carry forward rule by being increased to 3 years is not going to confer a monopoly upon the SC and ST candidates and deprive others of their opportunity for appointment. Going by the actual no serious infraction of any individual's fundamental right under Article 16(1) takes place and no monopoly is conceivably conferred on SCs and STs Candidates. They are not available in sufficient numbers to reach anywhere near the percentage reserved.

Unlimited reservation of appointments may be impermissible because it renders article 16(1) nugatory. At the same time Article 16(4) calculated to promote social justice and expressive of the deep concern of the constitution for the limping bracket of Indians, must be given full pay. The problem of giving adequate representation to backward classes under Article 16(4) is a matter for the government to consider, bearing in mind the need for a reasonable balance between the rival claims.[89]

In *Indra Sawhney case* apex court held that Cls.4 is applicable only to backward classes. Classes other then OBCs have to look to cls. (1) for reservation, if any.[90] Where the test of 'backwardness' in cls. (4) is not satisfied or there is no other test in accordance with cls. (4), a distribution of posts on basis of community or place of residence shall be violative of cls. (1) of this article. In *Chairman & Managing Director, Singareni Collieries Co. Ltd.* v. *M. Naresh Chander case*[91] it was held that no quota can be created in the common pool for the candidates other than those covered under this clause. Hence reserving a quota for internal candidates in direct recruitment in impermissible.

Regarding scientific and technical post in *P.G.I. of Medical education & Research* v. *K.L. Narasimhan case*[92] it was held that those posts which were not accorded cannot be excluded from reservation unless specifically approved by the government. Statutory bodies are bound by the reservation policy.

Regarding limit of reservation hon'ble court held in *Indra Sawhney case*[93] that limit of 50 percent is applicable only to 'reservation' and cannot be applied to exemptions, concessions or relaxations, if any, provided to backward classes, under Article 16(4).

In the latest case of *Meera Kawaria* Supreme Court Bench of *Justice S.B. Sinha and P.K. Balaramanyam* by rejecting judgement of Delhi High Court held that female of high cast Hindu does not automatically become entitle to get the benefit of reservation just after getting marriage with the male of scheduled caste and on even accepting her by family of her husband. On this ground apex court cancelled election of the lady who won election from the reserved constituency. Further held although if she is accepted by whole of the community she would become entitle to the benefit of reservation.[94]

In a latest case of *R.K. Sabharwal and others* v. *Union of India*[95] Judiciary held that reservation is with reference to the total number of posts in a cadre and not with reference to the vacancy. Once the total number of posts in a cadre is filled up and the posts earmarked in the roster for SC/ST and OBC are duly filled, the purpose of reservation provided for reserved categories is achieved and that thereafter the roster does not survive. Any post falling vacant in the cadre thereafter will be filled from amongst the category of persons to whom the reserved post belongs.

It is said that to give effect to the reservation policy, every appointing authority should maintain a reservation roster as per prescribed instructions. But prior to 1997 the reservation roster were based upon the vacancies. In the case of *R.K. Sabharwal* v. *State of Punjab and J.C. Mallick* v. *Ministry of Railways*,[96] vacancy based roster was challenged, court held that : (i) the reservation of posts for SC/ST/OBC should apply to posts and not to vacancies; (ii) vacancy based roster can operate only thel time as the representation of persons belonging to the reserved categories, in a cadre, reaches the prescribed percentage of reservations; (iii) thereafter, the rosters cannot operate and vacancies released by retirement, resignation, promotion, etc. of the persons belonging to the general and the reserved categories are to be filled by appointment of persons from the respective category so that the prescribed percentage of reservation is maintained; (iv) person belonging to the reserved categories, who are appointed on the basis of merit and not on account of reservation—are not to be counted towards the quota meant for reservation.

Judiciary further held that the roster is implemented in the form of running account from year to year. The purpose f running account is to make sure that the SC/ST and OBC get their percentage of reserved posts. The only way to assure the proper the representation of ST/SC and OBC is to permit the roster to operate till the time the respective appointees/promotee occupy the posts meant for them in the roster.

In case of *Bhup Singh* v. *State of Haryana and others*[97] it was held that utility of roster is to provide a guideline for filling up the reserved quota for different groups *vis-a-vis* the candidate from the general category. Once the quota is achieved as for one or the other group of communities entitled to reservation, the roster will cease to have utility for that community because the guidelines would have already been followed.

In the case of *C.C. Jacob & others* v. *Collector of Customs, Cochin*[98] it was held that 'Quota' is the law and 'roster point' is the mechanism/guideline to achieve the quota. 'Quota' refers to the limit in law, whereas 'roster' indicates the point through which it is to be attained. For 'quota' to be achieved, roster refers to a reserved point in the 'running register' and acts as a day to day watchdog.

In the case of *Ram Singh v. Union of India & Ors.*[99] It was held that when a candidate belonging to a reserved category, who has availed relaxation of age, with regard to eligibility criteria, was necessarily to be adjusted against the reserved share of vacancy inspite of the fact that he had secured a position for selection on his own merit alongwith candidates of other communities of unreserved category.

Reservation meant for a Scheduled Tribe candidate can be exchanged for a Scheduled Caste candidate in the third recruitment year and *vice versa*.[100]

In the case of *Union of India & others* v. *Hari Singh Barkodia & others* it was decided that if post reserved for candidate of Scheduled Tribe couldn't be filled up for want of availability of candidates then in the third recruitment year that pot would be concerted as a post reserved for Scheduled Caste and a candidate belonging to that cast would be entitled to be appointed thereto. However, a Scheduled Caste candidate shall have no right to be appointed till the time for conversion of the post from Scheduled Tribe to Scheduled Caste has arisen.[101]

The *full Bench of Andhra Pradesh High Court* quashes the ordinance of State Government on for providing 5 percent reservations to the Muslim community in jobs and educational institutions in the State under Articles 15(4) and 16(4) of the Constitution on 7 November 2005 by saying that it is against Article 14 which provide equality before law and 15 which prohibit discrimination on the ground of religion. Another reason was that by giving 5% reservation to Muslims community it exceeds the limit of reservation (50%). Court also pulled up the state backward class commission, whose report had formed the basis for the quota policy, observing that the commission had given "defective advice" to evolve reasonable criteria to categorize Muslims as backward class. The High Court had further said that the commission did not do its job properly and could not produce sufficient material to suggest that the entire Muslim community was socially and educationally backward.[102]

In appeal under special leave petition to the Supreme Court, bench comprising *Y.K. Sabharwal C.J., C.K. Thakker and R.V. Raveenderan, JJ.* upheld the decision of High Court that had declared as unconstitutional a law providing reservations in jobs and educational institutions. The bench however granted limited relief by ensuring that admissions already made under the law passed by the state government would not be disturbed. Further considering the fact that important question of are involved in this matter, Chief Justice Y.K. Sabharwal referred the matter for hearing by a five-member Constitutional bench of the apex court.[103]

THE JUDICIARY AS HARBINGER TO SOCIAL REFORM AND SOCIAL EQUALITY FOR BACKWARD CLASS

Our legal system was established by Britishers who had come to rule this country and harvest the full advantage by exploiting the people of this country. British aristocracy was responsible for the creation of legal system and they had created it for the welfare of elite classes. The judges, who belonged to elite classes, interpreted the Constitution in favour of vested interests and individual rights.[104] The procedure used in the court was so complex and confusing, that justice could be obtained, only by engaging advocates and paying them a handsome amount as their fee, which was beyond the reach of poor. The judicial system was not in a position to bring changes in the life conditions of the poor. Our courts have become courts for the poor rather than the court of poor. In Asiad[105] case the court observed:

> ". . . the courts have been used only for the purpose of vindicating the rights of wealthy and the affluent. It is only these privileged classes which have been able to approach the courts for protecting their interests. It is only the moneyed who have so far had the golden key to unlock the doors of justice".

Millions of people belonging to the deprived and vulnerable sections of humanity are looking to the courts for improving their life conditions and making basic human rights meaningful for them. The courts are not meant only for the rich and well to do, for the landlords and business magnate, but they exist also for the poor and downtrodden, the have-nots and handicapped. Therefore, when the fundamental rights of poor are flouted, when atmosphere of exploitation, torture and fear is created,[106] when the basic element of care, comfort, necessaries to sustain life is refused, when injustice and inhumanity emerge and the legislative protection is ignored, it will become the constitutional obligation of the court as a guardian of fundamental rights of the people to break the fetters to right the wrong[107] and to restore justice to them.

The court also owes a duty to the society to help people in distress. It is the duty of the court to help the poor and indigent, to protect the health and strength of its inhabitants and to promote positive good for them by providing favourable social and economic conditions in the society. In a welfare democratic state, it is the society which has to develop its welfare means. No society can have welfare out-look unless; it gears up on the basis of amity, friendship, co-operation, consideration and compassion. If everyone living in India is willing to believe in the 'live and let live' principle, he would be prepared to devote the same attention to people around him as he is willing to devote for himself.[108]

Judges, though brought up and trained in western style are also product of our society where these inequalities flourish. They are very much sensitized towards the social evils. Therefore they have come up to the occasion where there is violation of human rights,[109] where there is torture and ill treatment,[110] where human being are treated like animals[111] and denied justice. Courts have helped these downtrodden and backward classes directly and indirectly by issuing many directions to stop ill treatment and to provide good for them and favourable social educational and economical condition in the society in the shape of reservation in education, employment or services and post.[112]

The question of reservation has become a very knotty socio-politico issue of the day. Because of keen completion for limited opportunities available in the country, government is pressurized to indulge in all kinds of reservations for all categories of groups apart from reservations for Scheduled Caste and Scheduled Tribe. Basically any positive action like reservation is discriminatory for reservation means that as between two candidates of equal merits, the candidate belonging to the reserve quota. Many deserving candidates thus feel frustrated because of reservation for the less deserving persons and they seek to challenge the scheme of reservation as unconstitutional.

A number of cases as violative of Articles 14, 15 and 16 have arisen recently around the question of reservation. The courts had to draw a balance in the area so as to discourage excessive or extreme form of reservations. The test applied to adjudge the validly of any reservation is whether it is based on any rational and relevant principle. The Court accepted limited reservation designed to remove backwardness and infirmities from certain section of society but they are very reluctant to accept reservations on other grounds.

In the case of *Heggade Janardhan Subbaraya* v. *the State of Mysore and others*[113] *Gajendragadkar, J.* observed that the State Government would be justified in giving effect to the reservation made in respect of the SCs/STs".[114]

In the case of *C.A. Rajendran* v. *Union of India and Others*[115] it is well settled that cls. (4) of article 16 *is an exception clause, not independent provision,* therefore it has to be strictly construed. It is also apparent that the language of Article 16(4) has to be interpreted in the context and background of Article 335 of the Constitution.[116]

In *State of Kerala* v. *N.M. Thomas*[117] case it was held that the power to make reservation, conferred on the State under Article 16(4), can be exercised by the State in a case not only by providing reservation in appointments but also by providing reservation in selection posts.[118] But at the time of providing reservation in appointments or posts under Article 16(4) the State has to take into consideration the claims of the backward classes consistently with the maintenance of the efficiency of administration.[119]

In the case of *Govt. of A.P.* v. *P.B. Vijaykumar,* bench held that Reservation normally implies a separate quota which is reserved for a special category of persons.[120] In the case of *K. S. Jaysree* v. *the State of Kerala and others,*[121] judiciary observed that,

> "in ascertaining social backwardness of a class of citizens it may be relevant to consider the caste of the group of citizens. Caste however, cannot be made the sole or dominant test. Social backwardness which results from poverty, in its ultimate analysis, is likely to be aggravated by considerations of their caste. This shows the relevance of both, caste and poverty in determining the backwardness of citizens. Poverty by itself is not the determining factor of social backwardness but it is relevant in the context of social backwardness. *It is*

declared that basis of the reservation is not income but social and educational backwardness, determined on the basis of relevant criteria."

Judiciary further stated that problem of determining, *who socially and educationally backward classes are,* is undoubtedly not simple. Sociological and economic considerations come into play in evolving proper criteria for its determination. This is the occupation of the state. The court's jurisdiction is to decide whether the test applied is valid or not. For a test applied, to be proper and valid, the classification of socially and educationally backward classes based on the test will have to be consistent with the requirements of Article 15(4). The commission has found on applying the relevant tests that the lower income groups of the communities named in Appendix VIII of the report, constitute of socially and educationally backward classes.[122]

In dealing with the question as to whether any class of citizens is *socially backward* or not, apex court held that caste of the said group of citizens may be irrelevant to consider because it should remember that social provision is contemplated for classes of citizens and not for individual citizens as such. Though the caste of the group of the citizens may be relevant, its importance should not be exaggerated. If the classification is based solely on caste of the citizens, it may not be logical, social backwardness is the result of the poverty to a very large extent. *Caste and poverty are both relevant for determining the backwardness.* Neither cast alone nor poverty alone will be the determining tests. When the commission has determining a class to be socially and educationally backward, it is not on the basis of income alone but the determining is based on the relevant criteria also laid down by the court. Since Article 15(4) also speaks of Scheduled Caste and Scheduled Tribe, therefore socially and educationally backward classes of citizens in Article 15(4) couldn't be equated with castes. In *Chitralekha case* this court said that the classification of backward classes based on economic conditions and occupation does not offend Article 15(4).[123] *Eventually here the court held that educational backwardness is mirrored to a certain extent by the economic conditions of the group. Thus exclusion of candidates belonging to families whose annual income is Rs. 10,000 or above, from the reservation of seats for backward (i.e. socially and educationally) classes on the basis of commission report is not violative of Article 15.*[124]

In the case of *Akhil Bhartiya Soshit Karamcharari Sangh (Railway)* v. *Union of India*[125] *Pathak, J.* observed on the limit of reservation that

> 'quota of the posts may be reserved in favour of a backward class of citizens, but the interests of an efficient administration requires that at least half the total number of the posts be kept open to attract the best of the nation's talent and not more than half be made the sum of reserved quotas would convert the state services into a collective membership predominantly of backward classes. This will be inconsistent with the all-important goal of maintaining the efficiency of administration'.[126]

A Bench comprising *V.R. Krishna Iyer, R.S. Pathak, and O. Chinnappa Reddy, JJ.* held that apart from the impact that an excessive reservation in a particular year is bound to have on the general community of citizens, there is the further far-reaching significance this assumes in the context of Article 335. The maintenance of efficiency of administration is bound to be adversely affected if general candidates of high merit are correspondingly excluded from recruitment because the large bulk of the vacancies, numbering anything over 50% for reserved quota. It was held that a maximum number of 50% for reserved quotas in their totality is a rule which appear fair and reasonable, just and equitable and violation of which would contravene Article 335'.[127]

In *State of A.P.* v. *Balram U.S.V. case*[128] Hon'ble C.A. Vaidialingam and K.K. Mathew, JJ. held that in making reservations for the backward classes, the State cannot ignore the fundamental rights of the rest of the citizens. A special provision under Article 15(4) must, therefore, strike a reasonable balance between several relevant considerations and proceed objectively. Further judiciary follows that in making special provision for the weaker sections for higher education; the State cannot weaken standards of education or lower the efficiency of scholars to the detriment of national interests. Hence in *Fazal Gafoor* v. *Union of India and Preeti srivastava* v. *State of M.P. case*[129] held that there should be no reservation for *taking admission in the highest technical courses,* called 'super-specialties'.

Case of *Indra Sawhney etc.* v. *Union of India and others*[130] is measured as an authority in various issues. By giving a landmark decision 9 judges bench judiciary *(M.H. Kania, C.J., M.N. Venkatachaliah, S.R. Ratnavel Pandian, Dr. T.K. Thommen, A.M Ahmadi, Kuldip Singh, P.B. Sawant, R.M. Sahai and B.P. Jeevan Reddy, JJ.)* observed,

> "doctrine of equality[131] are to be understood in the light of articles contained in Part IV of constitution.[132] As claims of scheduled castes and scheduled tribes in public employment are to be considered consistently with maintenance of efficient. Similar consideration will also apply while considering claims of other backward classes and other weaker sections".[133]

By approving the decision of *State of Andhra Pradsh* v. *Balram, AIR 1972 SC 1375, B.P. Jeevan Reddy, M.N. Venkatachaliah and A.M. Ahmadi, JJ.* expressed their opinion that,

> "in spite of best efforts that any commission may make in collecting data, its conclusion cannot be always scientifically accurate in such matters. Therefore, the proper approach, in our opinion should be to see whether the relevant data and materials referred to in the report of the commission justify its conclusions. In our opinion, there was sufficient material to enable the commission to be satisfied that the persons included in the list are really socially and educationally backward. No doubt there are few instances where educational average is slightly above the State average, but that circumstance by itself is not enough to strike down the entire list. Even assuming there are few categories which are like above the stage average, in literacy, that is a matter for the State to take note of and review the position of such categories of persons and take a suitable decision".[134]

They held that provision for reservation of appointments or post in favour of backward classes of citizens, contemplated by Article 16(4) cannot only be made by the parliament/ legislature but by the executive wing also in respect of Central/State services and also by the local bodies and 'other authorities' contemplated by Article 12. Therefore, *an executive order made in terms of Article 16(4) is effective and enforceable by itself.*[135]

Article 16(4) is not an exception; B.P. Jeevan Reddy, on behalf of *C.J. and M.N. Venkatachaliah and A.M. Ahmadi, JJ.* with concurring judgment of *S. Ratnavel Pandian and P.B. Sawant, JJ.* observed that,

> "Article 16(1) does permit reasonable classification for ensuring attainment of the equality of opportunity assured by it. For assuring equality of opportunity, it may well be necessary in certain situations to treat unequally situated persons unequally. Not doing so perpetuate and accentuate inequality. Article 16(4) is an instance of such classification, put in to place the matter beyond controversy."

Therefore the "backward class of citizens" is classified as a separate category deserving a special treatment in the nature of reservation of appointments/posts in the services of the State. *Clause (4) of Article 16 is not an exception to clause (1) of Article (16) but is an instance of classification implicit in and permitted by clause (1).* Clause (4) is such a provision which must be read along with and in harmony with clause (1). *Indeed, even without clause (4), it would have been permissible for the State to have evolved such a classification and made a provision for reservation of appointment/posts in their own favour.* Clause (4) merely puts the matter beyond any doubt in specific terms. They held that the law lay down in the *case of Balaji (AIR 1963, SC 649) and Devadasan (AIR 1964, SC 179) are not good but they approve the decision held in Thomas case (AIR 1976 SC 490).*[136]

While *Ratnavel Pandian, J.* observed that clause (4) of Article 16 is not an exception to Article 16(1) and (2) but is an enabling provision and permissible in character overriding Article 16(1) and (2); besides it, this is a source of reservation for appointment or posts in the services so far as the backward classes of citizen is concerned and under cls. (1) of Article 16 reservation for appointments or posts can be made to other sections of the society such as physically handicapped, etc.[137]

P.B. Sawant, J. also opinioned that,

> "clause (4) of Article 16 is not an exception to clause (1) thereof, but is merely an emphatic way of stating what is implicit in cls. (1). Equality postulate not merely legal equality but also real equality. The equality of opportunity has to be distinguished from the equality of results". The various provisions of the Constitution like 38, 46, 335, and 340 together with the preamble, show that the right to equality enshrined in our Constitution is not merely a formal right or a vacuous declaration. *It is positive right, and the State is under an obligation to undertake measures to make it real and effectual"*.[138]

He stated that to enable all to compete with each other on equal plane, it is necessary to take positive measures to equip the disadvantaged and the handicapped to bring them to the level of the fortunate advantaged. Articles 14 and 16(1) no doubt would by themselves permit such positive measures in favour of the disadvantaged to make real the equality guaranteed by them. Thus, what was otherwise clear in clause (1) where the expression *"equality of opportunity"* is not used in a formal but in positive sense was made explicit in clause (4) so that there was no mistake in understanding either the real import of the *"right to equality"* enshrined in the constitution or the intention of the constitution framers in that behalf. *The purpose of the cls. 4 was to emphasis that, "there shall be reservation in favour of certain communities which have not so far had a proper look in the administration"*.[139]

He further said that,

> " . . . there would be no other classification permissible under cls. (1), and cls. (4) would be deemed to exhaust all

the exceptions that can be made to cls. (1). It would then not be open to make provision for reservation in services in favour of say, physically handicapped, army personnel and freedom fighters and their dependents, project affected persons, etc. The classification made in favour of persons belonging to these categories is not hit by cls. (2). Apart from the fact that they cut across all classes, the reservations in favour are made on considerations other than that of backwardness within the meaning of cls. (4). Some of them may belong to the backward classes while some may belong to forward classes or classes which have an adequate representation in the services. They are, however, more disadvantaged in their own class whether backward or forward. Hence, even on this ground it will have to be held that Article 16(4) carves out from various classes, for whom reservation can made, a specific class viz, the backward class of citizens, for emphasis and to put things beyond doubt".[140]

For the very reasons, it will be said that so far as "backward classes" are concerned, the reservation for them can only be made under cls. (4) since they have been taken out from the classes for which reservation can be made under cls. (1). Hence Article 16(4) is exhaustive of all the reservations that can be made for the backward classes as such, but is not exhaustive of reservations that can be made for classes under Article 16(1). So no reservation can be made Article 16(4) for classes other than "backward classes" implicit in that Article.[141]

Various form of reservation; Judiciary interpreted the phrase, "*provision for the reservation of appointments or posts*" in Article 16(4) as such that the constitutional scheme and context of Article 16(4) make it clear this phrase do not contemplate only one form of provision namely reservation (highest form of special provision) but it take other forms of special provisions like preferences, concessions, relaxations and exemptions (lesser types of special provisions). Therefore, larger concept of reservations takes within its sweep all supplemental and ancillary provisions consistent no doubt with the requirement of maintenance of efficiency of administration (Article 335).[142] *Hence, it may be stated that reservation can take various forms whether they made for backward class or other classes. They may consist of preferences, concessions exemptions, extra facilities, etc. or of an exclusive quota in appointments.* Whatever the form of the reservation, the backward classes have to look for them to Article 16(4) and the other classes to Article 16(1).[143]

Reservation may be under Article 16(1) as well as under Article 16(4). S. Ratnavel Pandian and P.B. Sawant, JJ. with majority view said reservation may be provided under Article 16(1) but it is in very exceptional situations, and not for all and sundry reasons. Although in such situation State has to satisfy, that making such a provision was necessary to redress a specific situation.[144]

While *Kuldeep Singh and R.M. Sahai, JJ.* with minority view said that Article 16(4) being part of equality doctrine, is exhaustive of reservation, therefore, no reservation is permissible under article 16(1). Article 16(4) completely overrides Article 16(1) in the matter of job reservations. Any reservation for any class other then backward class would be, contrary to constitutional objective and thus invalid.[145]

Caste is socially homogeneous or occupational group, apex court held that interpretation of the word "caste" can not be concluded either that "class" is antithetical to "caste" or that a caste cannot be a class or that a caste as such can never be taken as a backward class of citizens. There are various reasons why the constitution could not have used the expression "castes" or "caste" in Article 16(4) and why the word "class" was the natural choice in the context. The Constitution was meant for the entire country and for all time to come. Non-Hindu religions like Islam, Christianity and Sikh did not recognize caste as such though castes did exist even among these religions to a varying degree. The word "class" in Article 16(4) is used in the sense of social class and not in the sense it is understood in marxit jargon.[146]

A caste is nothing but a social class—a socially homogeneous class. It is also an occupational grouping with this difference that its membership is hereditary . . . to repeat; it is a socially and occupationally homogenous class. Endogamy is its main characteristic. Its social status and standing depend upon the nature of the occupation followed by it. In rural India, occupation—caste nexus is true even today. A few members may have gone to cities or even abroad but when they return—they go into the same fold again. It does not matter if he has earned money. He may not follow that particular occupation. Still, the lebel remains. His identity is not changed. For the purpose of marriage, death and all other social functions, it is his social class—the caste—that is relevant.[147]

As *Dr. Ambedkar* observed, during the Constituent Assembly speech that, "a caste is an enclosed class" and he used the word "communities". This expression includes not only the castes among the Hindus but also several other groups. The word "community" is clearly wider than "caste"—and "backward communities" meant not only the castes—wherever they may be found—but also other groups, classes and sections among the populace.[148]

For identification of backward Classes *B.P. Jeevan Reddy, S. Ratnavel Pandian and P.B. Sawant JJ.* with majority view held that—*if backwardness is found in a caste, any other group, section or class, it can be treated as backward.* They observed that,

> "For identification of backward classes one has to begin some where—with some group, class or section. Article 16(4) seeks to ameliorate social backwardness. There is nothing unconstitutional with it, more so when caste, occupation, poverty and social backwardness are so closely intertwined in our society. Therefore, if a Commission/Authority begin its process of identification with castes and occupational grouping among others, it cannot be said to be constitutionally or legally bad. But there is no set or recognized method, no rule of law or other statutory instrument prescribing the methodology that a test to be applied for identifying backward classes should be only one and or uniform. In a vast country like India, it is simply not practicable. If the real object is to be discover and locate backwardness, if such backwardness is found in a caste, it can be treated as backward, if it is found in any other group, section or class, they too can be treated as backward".[149]

Further they take plea that reservation is not being made

under Clause (4) of Article 16 in favour of 'caste' but a 'backward class'. But once a caste satisfies the criteria of backwardness, it becomes a backward class for the purpose of Article 16(4), besides it, it must be further found that backward class is not adequately represented in the services of the State. In such a situation the bar of cls. 2 of Article 16 has no application whatsoever.[150]

In the field of identification of socially and educationally backward classes' it may be stated *that caste neither can be the sole criterion nor can it be equated with 'class' for the purpose of Article 16(4) for ascertaining the social and educational backwardness of any section or group of people so as to bring them within the wider connotation of 'backward class'*. The cast system, however, is predominantly known in Hindu society and runs through the entire fabric of social structure. Therefore, the caste criterion cannot be divested from the other established and agreed criteria in identifying and ascertaining the 'backward classes'. A caste becomes a 'backward class' provided that caste satisfies the test of backwardness.[151]

As *P.B. Sawant, J.* observed

> "What is, however, required to be done for the purpose of Article 16(4) is not classification but identification. The identification of the backward class of citizens . . . Any factor—whether caste, race, religion, occupation, habitation etc. which may have been responsible for the social and educational backwardness, would naturally also supply the basis for identifying such classes not because they are socially and educationally backward classes".[152]

While *Kuldip Singh, J.* with minority view opinioned, *"Class" under Article 16(4) cannot read as "caste"*. Caste cannot be adopted as collectives for the purpose of identifying the "backward class" under Article 16(4). Occupation (plus income or otherwise) or any other secular collectivity can be basis for the identification of "backward classes".[153] Further he said that "Not adequately represented in the services under the State" is the only test for the identification of a class under Article 16(4). Thereafter the "backward class" has to be culled out from out of the classes which satisfy the test of inadequacy. Once, such classes are identified then the reserve posts are to be offered to the backward sections of those classes".[154]

Dr. T.K. Thommen, J. said separately that reservation is provided exclusively for the Harijans, the Advasis, the Dalits or other like "depressed" classes. As he observed,

> "reservation is meant exclusively for the Harijans, the Girijans, the Advasis, the Dalits or other like "depressed" classes or races or tribes most unfortunately referred to in the past as the "untouchables" or the "outcastes" by reason of their being born in what was wrongly regarded as low castes and associated with what was equally wrongly treated as demeaning occupations, or any other class of citizens afflicted by like degree of poverty and degradation caused by prior and continuing discrimination and exploitation, whatever be their professed faith, religion or caste".[155]

While *R.M. Sahai, J.* observed,

> "expression 'backward class' is of wider import . . . it should be understood in its broader and normal sense. Backward class under Article 16(4) is not confined to erstwhile Shudras or depressed classes or intermediate backward classes amongst Hindus only. The principle of identification has to every community and not only to those who are either converts from Hinduism or some of whom who carry same occupation as some of the Hindus".[156]

"Similarly identification of backward class by such factors as dependence of group or collectivity on manual labour, lower age of marriage, poor schooling, living in *kuccha* house etc. and applying it to caste would be violative of Article 16(2) not only for being caste based but also for violation of Article 14 because it excludes other communities in which same factors exist only because they are not Hindus. While identification of a group or collectivity by any criteria other than castes, such as, occupation cum social cum educational and economic criteria ending in castes may not be invalid".[157]

B.P. Jeevan Reddy, S. Ratnavel, Pandian Kuldip Singh and P.B. Sawant, JJ., with majority view overruled the decision of AIR 1973 SC 930, AIR 1963 SC 649 AND AIR 1985 SC 1495 and held *that the backwardness contemplated by Article 16(4) is mainly social backwardness. It would not be correct to say that the backwardness under Article 16(4) should be both social and educational.* They observed that,

> "Clause (4) of Article 16 does not contain the qualifying words "socially and educationally" as does clause (4) of Article 15, Article 340 does employ the expression "socially and educationally backwardness" and yet that expression does not find place in Article 16(4). The reason is obvious: "backward classes of citizens" in Article 16(4) takes in scheduled tribes, scheduled castes and all other backward classes of citizens including the socially and educationally backward classes. Thus certain classes which may not qualify for Article 15(4) may qualify for Article 16(4). In identifying and classifying a section of people as a backward class within the meaning of Article 16(4) for reservation of appointments or posts, the 'social backwardness' plays a predominant role. Therefore, the degree of importance to be attached to social backwardness is much more than the importance to be given to the educational backwardness and the economical backwardness."

About Creamy Layer majority view of *B.P. Jeevan Reddy, J., (for behalf and on behalf of M.H. Kania, C.J. and M.N. Venkatachaliah, A.M. Ahmadi, JJ., with P.B. Sawant,* observed that,

> "When reservations are making for backward classes Creamy layer can be and must be excluded. After excluding them alone would the class be a compact class. In fact such exclusion benefits the truly backward. The Supreme Court therefore directed the Government of India to specify the basis of exclusion—where on the basis

> of income, extent of holding or otherwise—of creamy layer.[158]

and held that after exclusion of Creamy layer reservation is valid."

But *S. Ratnavel Pandian, J.* was *against any test of Creamy Layer* as he observed,

> "No section of the SEBCs can be excluded on the ground of creamy layer till the Government takes a decision in this regard on a review on the recommendations of a Commission or a committee to be appointed by the government.[159]

He further said that,

> "the office memorandum on the basis of Mandal Commission report does not speak of any "creamy layer test". Therefore, the Supreme Court is not called upon to lay a test or give any guideline as to who are all to be eliminated from the listed groups of the Report, there is no necessity to lay any test much less "creamy layer".[160]

While as per observation of *Kuldip Singh, J.*

> ". . . It is, therefore, necessary that the benefit of the reservation must reach the poorest and the weaker section of the backward class. . . . Means test is imperative to skin-off the affluent sections of the backward classes".[161]

R.M. Sahai, J. observed in support of *exclusion* of creamy layer that,

> "while reserving posts for backward classes the departments should make a condition precedent that every candidate must disclose the annual income of the parents beyond which one could not be considered to be backward. What should be that limit can be determined

by the appropriated State. Income apart provision should be made that ward of those backward classes of persons who have achieved a particular status in society either political or social or economic or if their parents are in higher services then such individuals should be precluded to avoid monopolization by the services reserved for backward classes by a few. And once a group or collectivity itself is found to have achieved the constitutional objective then it should be excluded from the list of backward class. Creamy layer amongst backward class of citizens must be excluded by fixation of proper income, property or status criteria".[162]

Economic criterion is no exclusive area; Majority view with *B.P. Jeevan, J.* held that, "A backward class cannot be determined only and exclusively with reference to economic criterion. It may be consideration or basis along with and in addition to social backwardness, but it can never be the sole criterion".[163]

Inadequacy must exist at the time of making reservation; R.M. Sahai, J. observed that,

> *"the importance of word "is"* in article 16(4) should not be lost of. Backwardness and inadequacy should exist on the date the reservation is made. Reservation for a group which was educationally, economically and socially backward before 1950 shall not be valid unless the group continues to be backward today. The group should not have suffered only but it should be found to be suffering with such disabilities. If a class or community ceases to be economically and socially backward or even if it so it is adequately represented then no reservation can be made as it no more continues to be backward even though it may not be adequately represented in services or it may be backward but adequately represented".[164]

Reservation cannot exceed 50%; Majority view with *Dr. T.K. Thommen and Kuldip Singh, JJ.* held that the power conferred by clause 4 of Article 16 should also be exercised in a manner and within reasonable limits—that reservation under cls. 4 of Article 16 shall not exceed 50% of the appointments or posts, barring certain extraordinary situations. This Clause speaks of *adequate representation and not proportionate representation* and adequate representation cannot be read as proportionate representation.[165]

They observed that,

> "the principal aim of Articles 14 and 16 is equality and equality of opportunity and that clause 4 of Article 16 is but a means of achieving the very same objective. Clause 4 is not an exception of clause 1 but a special provision. Both the provisions have to be harmonized keeping in mind the fact that both are restatements of the principle of equality enshrined in Article 14. The provision under Article 16(4)—conceived in the interest of certain sections of society—should be balanced against the guarantee of equality enshrined in clause (1) of Article 16 which is a guarantee held out to every citizen and to entire society".[166]

But, in concurring opinion, *P.B. Sawant, J.* held that ordinarily, the reservations kept both under Article 16(1) and 16(4) together should not exceed 50% of the appointments in a grade, cadre or services in any particular year. *It is only for extraordinary reasons that this percentage may be exceeded.* However, every excess over 50% will have to be justified on valid grounds which grounds will have to be specifically made out.[167] He observed that,

> "the adequacy of representation is not to be determined merely on the basis of the over all numerical strength of the backward classes in the services. For determining the adequacy, their representation at different levels of administration and in different grades has to be taken into consideration and not the total number which determines the adequacy of representation".[168]

While *S. Ratnavel Pandian, J.*, in giving dissenting opinion, held that, "*no maximum ceiling of reservation can be fixed under Article 16(4) of the Constitution for reservation of appointments or posts in favour of any backward class of citizens in the services under the State*".[169] He relied on the decision of *AIR 1976 SC 490 and AIR 1981 SC 298*, observed that,

> "Any reservation of excess of 50% for "backward classes" will not be violative of Articles 14 and 16 of the Constitution. But at the same time such reservations made either under Article 16(4) or under Article 16(1) cannot be extended to the totality of 100%. As to what extent the proportion of reservation will be so excessive as to render it bad must depend upon adequacy of representation in a given case. Therefore, the decisions fixing the percentage of reservation only up to the maximum of 50% are unsustainable. The percentage of reservation at the maximum of 50% is neither based on scientific data nor on any established and agreed formula. *In fact, Article 16(4) itself does not limit the power of the Government in making the reservation to any maximum percentage; but it depends upon the quantum of adequate representation required in the Services*".[170]

If there is only one post in the cadre, no reservation with reference to that post can be made. Reservation presupposes availability of at least more than one post in the cadre[171] but subsequently it was held that provision for reservation in promotion to such a post by rotating the vacancies as per the roster point would not violative of Article 16(1).[172]

There shall be no reservation in Promotion; With majority view *S. Ratnavel Pandian, T.K. Thommen, and R.M. Sahai, JJ.*, held that *Article 16(4) does not contemplate or permit reservation in promotions as well.* It is true that the expression "appointment" takes in appointment by direct recruitment, appointment by promotion and appointment by transfer. It may also be that Article 16(4) contemplates not merely quantitative but also qualitative support of backward class of citizens. But this question has not to be answered on a reading of Article 16(4) alone but on a combined reading of Article 16(4) and Article 335 and overruled decision held in AIR 1962 SC 36.[173] They observed that,

> "Reservation of appointments or posts theoretically and conceivably means some impairment of efficiency. There can be no justification to multiply 'the risk' by holding that reservation can be provided even in the matter of promotion".[174]

Further they opinioned that,

> ". . . At the initial stage of recruitment reservation can be made in favour of backward class of citizens but once they enter the service, efficiency of administration demands that these members too compete with others and earn promotion like all others; no further distinction can be made thereafter with reference to their "birth—mark". It is wrong to think".[175]

P.B. Sawant, J. observed that,

> "the reservation in promotions are inconsistent with the efficiency of administration and are impermissible under the Constitution. Because "consistently with the maintenance of efficiency of administration" (under Article 335) is related not only to the qualification of those who are appointed, it covers all consequences to the efficiency of administration on account of such appointments. They would necessarily include the demoralization of those already in employment who would be adversely effected by such appointments and its effect on the efficiency of administration".[176]

Denying reservation in matter of promotion does not have the effect of confining the backward class of citizens to the lowest cadres. It is well known that direct recruitment takes place at several higher levels of administration and not merely at the level of class IV and class III.[177] It would be permissible for the state to extend concessions and relaxations to members of reserved categories in the matter of promotion without compromising the efficiency of the administration. However, it would not be permissible to prescribe lower qualifying marks or a lesser level of evaluation for the members of reserved categories since that would compromise the efficiency of administration.[178]

By overruling the judgment of the case AIR 1962 SC 36, it is held that *Article 16(4) permits reservation of appointments or posts in favour of any backward class of citizens only at the initial stage of entry into the state services.* It does not permit reservation either to the selection posts or in any other manner in the process of promotion. It is a settled proposition of law that right to promotion is a condition of service. Once a person is appointed he is governed by the conditions of the services applicable thereto. Appointment and conditions of services are two separate incidents of services. Conditions of services exclusively come within the expression "matters relating to employment" and are covered by Article 16(1) and nor by 16(4). When all conditions of services fall out—side the purview of Article 16(4) then where is the justification to bring promotion within Article 16(4) by giving strained—meaning to the expression 'posts'".[179]

But in the case of *State of Punjab* v. *G.S. Gill*[180] reservation in promotion to a single post is not unconstitutional. Implementation of the reservation policy in the upgraded posts after restructuring of the cadres whether *'en masse'* or on partial or on partial basis is not tenable in the eye of law.

If no eligible person within the zone of consideration for being considered against a reserved point was available, it was held appropriate to get that vacancy deserved and to appoint/ promote a person belonging to the general category.[181] But a general category applicant has no right to force the authorities to deserve a post which is otherwise meant for the SC candidate 6.[182]

Regarding rule of carry forward; he held that, limit of 50% in reservation does not apply to exemption; concession etc. Also the concession cannot be give retrospectively.[183] Rule of carry forward to unfilled vacancies in state services is not unconstitutional. However, operation of such rule should not result in breach of 50% rule.[184] By overruling the decision of AIR 1976 SC 490, he held that rule of 50% limit is to be applied by taking a year as the unit not the entire strength of cadre/services as the case may be, it would not be consistent with Article 16 and overruled the decision of AIR 964 SC 179.[185]

Types of reservation quota; B.P. Jeevan Reddy, J. observed that there are two types of reservations, "vertical reservations" and 'horizontal reservations'. The reservation in favour of scheduled castes, scheduled tribes and other backward classes [(under Article 16(4)] may be called *vertical reservations* whereas reservations in favour of physically handicapped (under clause 1 of Article 16) can be referred to as *horizontal reservations*. The person selected against quota will be placed in the appropriate category; if he belongs to open competition (O.C.) category, he will be placed in that category by making necessary adjustments, the percentage of reservations in favour of backward class of citizens remains—and should remain the same".[186]

Exception—reservations are not available in some posts and services., e.g. B.P. Jeevan Reddy, J. held that, "in matter of appointment Government cannot say that there shall be no minimum qualifying marks for Scheduled Caste and Scheduled Tribes candidates while prescribing a minimum for others. Reservation has to be consistent with requirements of efficiency of administration".[187] With majority view *S. Ratnavel Pandian, J.* observed,

> "There are certain services and positions where either on account of the nature of duties attached to them or the level at which they obtain, merit alone counts. In such situations, it may not be advisable to provide for reservations. Following are such services and posts where rule of reservation are not applicable—*(i) Defence services* including all technical posts therein but excluding civil posts. *(ii) All technical posts* in establishments engaged in Research and Development including those connected with atomic energy and space and establishments

engaged in production of defence equipment. *(iii) Teaching posts of Professors*—and above, if any, *(iv) Posts in super-specialties* in medicine, engineering and other scientific and technical subjects, *(v) Posts of pilots (and co-pilots) in Indian Airlines and Air India.* The list given above is merely illustrative and not exhaustive".[188]

Jurisdiction of judiciary: As per view of *S. Ratnavel Pandian, J.*, the action of the Government in making provision for the reservation of appointments or posts in favour of any "backward class citizens" is a matter of policy of the Government. What is best for the 'backward class' and in what manner the policy should be formulated and implemented bearing in mind the object to be achieved by such reservation is a matter of decision exclusively within the province of the Government and such matters do not ordinarily attract the power of judicial review or judicial interference except on the grounds which are well settled by a catena of decisions of Supreme Court.[189] As per view of *P.B. Sawant, J.* Judicial scrutiny would be available (i) if the criterion inconsistent with the provisions of Article 16 is applied for identifying backward class for giving special benefits. (ii) If the classes who are not entitled to the said benefit are wrongly included in or excluded from the list of beneficiaries. (iii) If the percentage of reservations is either disproportionate or unreasonable so as to deny the equality of opportunity to the unreserved classes.[190]

As per view of *R.M. Sahai, J.* Reservation in public services either by legislative or executive action is neither a matter of policy nor a political issue. The higher courts in the Country are constitutionally obliged to exercise the power of judicial review in every matter which is constitutional in nature. Reservation of appointments and posts under Article 16(4) can be challenged if it is constitutionally invalid or disturbed three balance of equality guaranteed under Article 16(1) for being unreasonable or arbitrary.[191]

After considering the fact *majority view held that, cls. (1) of amended O.M. dated 25/09/1991 classifying backward classes into backward classes and poorer sections of backward classes and giving preference to poorer sections is not unconstitutional.* Here words 'poorer section' mean not economically poorer but those who are socially and economically more backward and having regard to the fact that the backward classes are sought to be divided into two sub-categories, viz. backward and more backward. And the word 'preference' would mean equitable appointment of vacancies amongst the two sub-categories.[192]

It was also held with majority view of *S. Ratnavel Pandian and T.K. Thommen, JJ.* that, clause (ii) of amended O.M. dated 25/09/1991, i.e. *reservation of 10% seats in favour of economically backward section among open competition category is not permissible* under Article 16(1) and memorandum liable to be quashed.[193]

For the identification of backward classes, a permanent body to examine compliant of wrong inclusion or non-inclusion of groups in list of backward classes should be constituted under Article 16(4) read with Article 340.[194]

The *recommendations of the Mandal Commission Report*, based on deeply consideration of social, educational and economical backwardness of various classes of citizens of our country in the light of the various propositions and tests laid down by this court and on *the ground of 1931 census are valid.*[195]

Reservation is justified for getting social justice; The purpose of cls. (4) of Article 16 is to ensure the benefits flowing from the fountain of this clause on the beneficiaries, i.e. backward classes—who in the opinion of the constitution makers would have otherwise found it difficult to enter into public services, competing with advanced classes and who could not be kept in limbo until they are benefited by the positive action schemes and who are suffered and are still suffering from historic disabilities arising from past discrimination or disadvantage or both.

However, unfortunately all of them had been kept at bay on account of various factors, operating against them inclusive of poverty. They continue to be deprived of enjoyment of equal opportunity in matters of public employment despite there being sufficient statistical evidence in proof of manifest imbalance in Government jobs which evidence is sufficient to support an affirmative action plan. If candidates belonging to SEBCs (characterized as mediocre by anti-reservationists) are required to enter the open field competition, along with the candidates belonging to advanced communities without any prefential treatment in public services in their favour and go through a rigid test mechanism being the highly intelligence test and professional ability test as conditions of employment, certainly those conditions would operate as "built-in headwinds" for SEBCs. It is therefore in order to achieve equality of employment opportunity; cls. (4) of Article 16 empowers the State to provide permissible reservation to SEBCs in matters of appointment or posts as a remedy so as to set right the manifest imbalance in the field of public employment.[196]

Therefore, *S. Ratnavel Pandian, J.* observed that,

> "implementation of recommendations of Mandal Commission about reservation for socially and educationally backward classes would not result in demoralization and discontent. It would not curtail concept of equality enshrined under Article 14 or destroy basic structure of constitution".[197]

P.M. Sahai, J. viewed that, *no period for reservation is provided*. However every State must keep on evaluating periodically if it was necessary to continue reservation, and to whom.

In *E.V. Chinnaiah* v. *State of A.P., (2005) 1 SCC 394*[198] case again Articles 15(4), 16(4), 14, 341, 342 and Ch. XVI were considered by apex court of land and held with majority to capture measures to be taken to ensure success of reservation. *N. Santosh Hegde, J.* held that further sub-classification of Scheduled Castes, for apportioning the quota/seats already reserved for Scheduled Castes, is not a permissible remedy.

S.N. Variava and B.P. Singh, JJ., held that if benefits of reservation are not percolating to them equitably, measures should be taken to see that they are given such adequate or additional training as to enable them to compete with the others.

S.B. Sinha, J. with concurring decision enumerated essence of reservation and accordingly held that instead of the sub-classification of Scheduled Castes what is necessary is to provide scholarships, hostel facilities, special coaching, etc. to the groups found most backward so that they could be brought on the same platform as the relatively more advanced Scheduled Castes. Unless children of the said groups are educated, reservation in both higher education and public service would be a myth for them, and ultimately, the benefit of reservation specifically apportioned to them would go to other categories anyway.

N. Santosh Hegde, S.N. Variava and B.P. Singh, JJ., held *reservation to a backward class is not a constitutional mandate, but a prerogative of the State.* They further held that under the State's (State of A.P.) reservation policy the backward class consists of Other Backward Classes, Scheduled Castes and Scheduled Tribes. Such a class cannot be sub-divided so as to give more preference to a minuscule proportion thereof in preference to other members of the same class.

S.B. Sinha, J. with concurring judgement held that backward class which may be given benefit of Article 15(4) or 16(4) must consist of a homogenous group—while reasonable classification is permissible, micro-classification or mini-classification is not. Such sub-classification or micro-classification would be violative of Article 14 and violative of the doctrine of reasonableness.

H.K. Sema, J. concurring, held further classification and/or regrouping of the Scheduled Castes would tantamount to discrimination in reverse and would attract the wrath of Article 14—Justice to one group at the cost of injustice to another group is another way of perpetuating injustice.

Again *S.B. Sinha,* J. *concurring,* held the State cannot take away benefit of reservation on the premise that one or the other group amongst the Scheduled Castes has advanced and thus, is not entitled to the entire benefit of reservation.[199] Further *S.B. Sinha, J. concurring,* held responsibility of improving the lot of Scheduled Castes has been entrusted to National Commission and Parliament—Whenever a situation arises in respect of Scheduled Castes wherein a "creamy layer" amongst them needs to be demarcated, it will be Parliament alone that may take the necessary legislative steps in terms of Article 341(2).[200]

Judgment in *Indra Sawhney case (Mandal Commission case),* 1992 Supp (3) SCC 217, clarified, that sub-division of Other Backward Classes contemplated therein is not applicable to

Scheduled Castes and Scheduled Tribes.[201] *S.B. Sinha, J.* held that a person does not even cease to be a Scheduled Caste automatically even on his conversion to another religion, (2005) 1 SCC 394.[202]

S.B. Sinha, J., held that "Backward class of citizens" includes Scheduled Castes and Scheduled Tribes both.[203]

Though the courts have taken much pain for the social reforms from time to time, but it has certain limitations, it can not monitor every welfare scheme, its registry has congestion. To get attention for a matter of human welfare, courts are bound to take help of executive.

In the case of *P.A. Inamdar & others* v. *State of Maharashtra & others*[204] *Chief Justice R.C. Lahoti* declare with unanimous judgement of 7 judges Bench that the State can't impose its reservation policy on minority and non—minority unaided private colleges, including professional colleges (engineering and medical colleges). This judgement was an attempt to clarify that reservation policy is applicable only on Government or Government-aided institutions.

In another resent significant judgement[205] *Allahabad High Court* ruled that if a candidate from the reserved category applies for an appointment in the general category, he cannot apply for the reserved category and *vice versa*. The court further said that any other interpretation of UP SC/ST and OBC Reservation Act, 1994 , will not only disturb the balance of the extent of reservation provided under the Act, but will also upset interest of other claimants of the society—namely the general category.

Recently, selections on posts and adjustment of OBC candidates in general categories misinterpreting sub-section (6) of section 3 of the UP Act 1994 raised the serious issues, dividing society. Appointing authorities, in order to please political bosses, are further dividing the society on caste lines, remarked the court.

The constitution benches of the Supreme Court have repeatedly held that reservation should not be stretched too far to break down social structure, the court said, "it has therefore become absolutely necessary for this court to decide and hold that sub-section (6) of section 3 of the UP Act, 1994 cannot be interpreted in a manner that those who have competed in their own reserved categories are entitled to be adjusted with general category candidates if they have secured higher marks on merits. *Justice S. Ambawani* delivered this judgement, while dealing with the selection and appointment held in 1999 for a village development officer (VDO) in the rural department of UP government.

On 4th January 2006 a division bench of the *Allahabad High Court*[206] has dismissed appeals by HRD minister and affirmed judgment given by a single judge (Arun Tandan, J.) of the Court, (on last October 2005) holding that Aligarh Muslim University is not a minority institution. The single judge had also quashed an HRD Ministry notification (dated February 25, 2005) permitting AMU to reserve 50 percent in admissions seats for Muslim students in admissions as unconstitutional.

The division bench said the students who had been given admissions earlier under the quota system and who were studying at AMU would continue to do so. But the court made it clear that from 2006-07 admissions at AMU will be "free to all". There shall be no reservation on the ground of religion. The bench comprising *Chief Justice A.N. Ray and Justice Ashok Bhushan*—struck down sections 2(L) and 5(2)(C) of the Aligarh Muslim University (Amendment) Act, 1981 which granted minority institution status to the university. The court said the sections were ultra vires to the Constitution. The high court passed the judgment on special appeals filed by the HRD Ministry and AMU. Further division bench also refused to give special leave petition against this decision to Supreme Court.

In these, the HRD ministry and AMU had challenged the verdict given by the single judge in October, declaring that AMU was not a minority institution.

NOTES AND REFERENCES

1. Shyama Nand Singh, Reservation: Problems and Prospects, Uppal Publication, New Delhi, 1991, p. 74.
2. National survey on the incidence of Bonded Labour, (New Delhi 1978), p. 730.
3. *Ibid.*
4. Prof. S.K. Singh, "Bonded Labour and the Law", Deep & Deep Publication, N. Delhi, 1995, p. 230.

5. AIR 1951 Mad 120, AIR 1951 SCR 525, AIR 1951 SC 226.
6. Added by First Constitutional Amendment Act 1951;
7. AIR 1963 SC 649.
8. *Ibid.*, at 650 Para 20-25.
9. *Ibid.*, at Para 35.
10. *Ibid.*, at p. 652, (Para 37)
11. *Ibid.*, at p. 652 (para 35).
12. R. Chitralekha *v.* State of Mysore, AIR 1963, p. 1823.
13. *Ibid.*, at para 15.
14. *Ibid.*, at para 15.
15. *Ibid.*, at para 19.
16. AIR 1976 SC, p. 490.
17. *Ibid.*, at p. 490.
18. *Ibid.*, at 492, Para (160, 161).
19. AIR 1972, SC, 1375.
20. *Ibid.*, at 1394 Para 80.
21. AIR 1971 SC, p. 2303.
22. AIR 1968 SC, p. 507.
23. AIR 1968 SC, p. 507.
24. AIR 1993 SC, 477.
25. *Ibid.*, Para 57, 58, 94A, 292, 396, 399-400.
26. State of U.P. *v.* Dr. Dina Nath Shukla, 1997 9 SCC 662 (Paras 9, 10 and 13).
27. AIR 1993 SC 477 (Para 410) overruled decision of Balaji M.R. *v.* State of Mysore, 1963 and Gandhi *v.* State of J.K., AIR 1973. But approved the decision of vasantha Kumar, K.C. *v.* State of Karnataka, AIR 1985.
28. (1997) 11 SCC 417 paras 5 and 7.
29. 2000 1 SCC 81.
30. AIR 1963, at para 19.
31. Ajay Kumar Singh *v.* State of Bihar, 1994 4 SCC 401 paras 8, 13.
32. Rajagopal Ramraj *v.* Union of India, M.P. 1993.
33. 1993 CAT Madras.
34. 2000 SCC.
35. 2001 CAT, Smt. G.D. Chatterjee *v.* Union of India, 2001 (CAT Lucknow) Smt. Chetna Dilip Motghare *v.* Bhide Girls Educational Society, Nagpur and Others 1995 Supplement (1) SCC.
36. 1996 CAT.
37. 2001, G.N. Rao and Others *v.* Union of India and others, 2001 CAT—Mumbai.
38. 1995 (1) ATJ 410 and Santi Nath Bose & Others *v.* Union of India & Others decided on 26.10.1995 (CAT-Calcutta).

39. 1970(3) SCC 567.
40. (1981) 1 SCC 246.
41. AIR 1993 SC 477: 1992 Supp (3) SCC 217.
42. 1997 (5) SCC 201.
43. 2006 (8) SCC 212.
44. Indra Sawhney *v.* Union of India, AIR 1993 SC 477.
45. 1996 6 SCC 580.
46. AIR 2007 SC 71.
47. 2007 (2) SCC 1 : 2007 AIR (SC) 861.
48. 2005 (6) SCC 537.
49. SCC (6) 2008 1.
50. Hussainara Khatoon *v.* Home Secretary, State of Bihar, (1980) 1 SCC 81 at p. 84.
51. Prof. S.K. Singh, Bonded Labour and the Law, Deep & Deep Publication, N. Delhi, 1994, p. 221.
52. Y.R. Hargopal Reddy, "Supreme Court on Bonded Labourers: Future of New Constitutionalism" (1984) 8 CULR, pp. 541-42.
53. National Survey on the incidence of bonded labour, (New Delhi 1978) at 751.
54. S.P. Gupta *v.* Union of India, 1981 Supp. SCC 87. Hereinafter referred as Judge's case.
55. *Ibid.*, at 210.
56. Bonded Labour System (Abolition) Act 1976, Sec. 2(d).
57. *Ibid.*, at 242.
58. AIR 1951 SC 229.
59. Dhananjaykee, Dr. Ambedkar's Life and Mission, 1951, p. 42.
60. SC AIR 1976, p. 490.
61. Article 15(4).
62. Parliamentary Debates, Vol. XIII, Part II, Government of India, 1951, p. 13.
63. AIR 1967, SC 1012.
64. *Ibid.*, at Para 7-8, pp. 1014-15.
65. AIR, 1968 SC 1379.
66. *Ibid.*, at 1380 Para 6.
67. AIR 1969 SC 1.
68. *Ibid.*, at para 4
69. *Ibid.*, at p. 3 Para 4.
70. *Ibid.*, at p. 2 Para 2.
71. *Ibid.*, at p. 2 Para 3.
72. AIR 1976 SC, p. 490.
73. *Ibid.*, at 505-06 paras 55-56.
74. AIR 1976 SC, p. 490.

75. *Ibid.*, at 491.
76. AIR, 1976, SC, p. 491.
77. *Ibid.*
78. *Ibid.*, at 500 Para 37.
79. *Ibid.*, at 502 Para 45.
80. *Ibid.*, at 492, Paras (124, 125).
81. *Ibid.*, at 498, Para 28.
82. *Ibid.*, at 502 Para 46.
83. AIR 1972, SC 1375.
84. *Ibid.*, at Paras 82, 85, 95.
85. *Ibid.*, at Para 88.
86. *Ibid.*, at Para 97.
87. *Ibid.*, at p. 1400, Para 100.
88. AIR 1981 SC 298.
89. *Ibid.*, at p. 299.
90. Indra Sawhney *v.* Union of India, AIR 1993 477 Paras 57 58, 94A, 292 396, 399-400.
91. 1955 Supp (1) SCC 167 Para 9.
92. 1997 6 SCC 120 Paras 14, 17 & 19.
93. Indra Sawhney *v.* Union of India, AIR 1993 477 Para 95.
94. *Amar Ujala*, Thursday 16 December 2005.
95. 1995 (1) ATJ 410.
96. 1995 SC.
97. 1999 SCC.
98. 1995 [CAT- Ernakulam]
99. O.A. No. 583 decided on 4.8.1999 (CAT—Patna).
100. Malkhan Singh *v.* Union of India, 1997 SCC 315.
101. 1998 SCC 137.
102. *Times of India*, Saturday 6 December 2005.
103. *Times of India*, Thursday, 5 January 2006.
104. Asiad case, 1982 3 SCC 242.
105. Charles Sobraj *v.* Superintendent Central Jail Tihar New Delhi, (2978) 4 SCC at 109.
106. Sunil Batra (II) *v.* Delhi Administration (1980) 3 SCC 488.
107. Bandhua Mukti Morcha *v.* Union of India, AIR 1992 SC 38, p. 49.
108. Munna *v.* State of U.P., 1982, 1 SCC 545.
109. Sheele Barse *v.* State of Maharashtra, 1983 2 SCC 96.
110. Dr. Upendra Baxi *v.* State of U.P., 1983 2 SCC 308.
111. Subhash Kumar *v.* State of Bihar, AIR 1991 SC 420.
112. Article 16(4).

113. AIR, 1968 SC, p. 507.
114. *Ibid.*
115. AIR, 1968 SC, p. 507.
116. *Ibid.*, at Para 5.
117. AIR 1976 SC p. 490.
118. *Ibid.*, at p. 491.
119. *Ibid.*
120. AIR 1995 SC 1648 (Para 9).
121. AIR 1975 SC 2381.
122. *Ibid.*
123. *Ibid.*
124. *Ibid.*
125. AIR 1981 SC 298.
126. *Ibid.*, at p. 299.
127. *Ibid.*
128. AIR 1972 SC 1375 (1395); Rajendran C.A. *v.* Union of India, AIR 1968. SC 507).
129. AIR 1989 SC 48; 1999 7 SCC 120 overruling Post-Graduate Institute of Medical Education and Research *v.* K.L. Narasihan, 1997 6 SCC 283.
130. AIR 1993 SC 477.
131. Articles 14-18.
132. *Ibid.*, at Para 4.
133. *Ibid.*, at Para 8.
134. *Ibid.*, at Para 839.
135. *Ibid.*, at Paras 56, 121(1)(b).
136. *Ibid.*, at Paras 57, 121(2)(a).
137. *Ibid.*, at Paras 292, 366.
138. *Ibid.*, at Para 396.
139. *Ibid.*, at Paras 396, 397.
140. *Ibid.*, at Para 398.
141. *Ibid.*, at Para 399.
142. *Ibid.*, at Paras 58, 400.
143. *Ibid.*, at Para 400.
144. *Ibid.*, at Paras 59, 60, 121(2)(b)(c), 366, 399.
145. *Ibid.*, at Paras 683, 700.
146. *Ibid.*, at Paras 81, 121(3) (1), 577.
147. *Ibid.*, at Paras 80, 82.
148. *Ibid.*
149. *Ibid.*, at Paras 83, 121(3)(b).

150. *Ibid.*, at Para 83(A).
151. *Ibid.*, at Paras 206, 231, 366.
152. *Ibid.*, at Para 412.
153. *Ibid.*, at Para 577.
154. *Ibid.*, at Paras 590, 596, 619, 620, 622, 623.
155. *Ibid.*, at Para 554.
156. *Ibid.*, at Paras 661, 700.
157. *Ibid.*, at Paras 658, 700.
158. *Ibid.*, at Paras 86, 121(3)(d), 450, 451.
159. *Ibid.*, at Para 366.
160. *Ibid.*, at Paras 351, 358.
161. *Ibid.*, at Para 353.
162. *Ibid.*, at Para 662.
163. *Ibid.*, at Paras 700, 694.
164. *Ibid.*, at Para 611.
165. *Ibid.*, at Paras 90, 121(4)(a), 612, 617.
166. *Ibid.*, at Paras 94A, 121(6)(ab), 554, 555, 610, 700.
167. *Ibid.*, at Para 94A.
168. *Ibid.*, at Para 472.
169. *Ibid.*, at Para 366.
170. *Ibid.*, at Paras 302, 306, 3307, 313.
171. Chkradhar Paswan State of Bihar, AIR 1988 SC 959.
172. Union of India *v.* Madhav, 1997 2 SCC 332; Union of India *v.* Brij Lal Thakur, 1997 4 SCC 278; State of Bihar *v.* Bhagashwari Prasad 1995 Suup (1) SCC 432; Suresh Chandra *v.* J.B. Agrawal 1997 5 SCC 363; State of Punjab *v.* G.S. Gill 1997 6 SCC 129; State of Punjab *v.* M.L. Sehgal 1997 6 SCC 777; the court was of the view that decisions in Madhav and Brij Lal Thakur above required reconsideration and a closer scrutiny and referred the matter to be decided by a constitutional Bench. Later in P.G.I.M.E. & R Chandigarh *v.* Faculty Association, 1998 4 SCC 1, the view taken in Madhav and Brij Lal Thakur case were overruled and the decision in Chkradhar case 'no reservation in single directly or by device of rotation of roster points' was approved and P.G.I.M.E. & R. Chandigarh *v.* Faculty Association; 1997 6 SCC 283 was reserved.
173. AIR 1993 SC 477, *Ibid.*, at Para 107.
174. *Ibid.*
175. *Ibid.*
176. *Ibid.*
177. *Ibid.*
178. *Ibid.*, at Paras 466, 467.
179. *Ibid.*, at Paras 604, 607.

180. 1997 AIR SC 2324, Arati Roy Choudharv *v.* Union of India & Ors., 1974 AIR SC 535; and Shri Narayan Chandra Sinha *v.* Union of India & Ors., O.A. No. 139 of 1993 decided on 1.12.1997 (CAT—Guwahati).
181. Suresh Kumar *v.* Union of India & Others, 1995 (CAT—Chandigarh).
182. Methew George *v.* Union of India and Others, 1997 (CAT—New Delhi).
183. National Federation of S.B.I. *v.* Union of India, 1995 3 SCC 532.
184. *Ibid.*, at Paras 95, 96, 121(b)(c).
185. *Ibid.*, at Paras 98, 99, 121(b)(c)(d); Swati Gupta *v.* State of U.P., 1995 2 SCC 560.
186. *Ibid.*, at Para 95.
187. *Ibid.*, at Paras 111, 121(1).
188. *Ibid.*, at Paras 112, 121(f), 336.
189. *Ibid.*, at Para 300.
190. *Ibid.*, at Para 462.
191. *Ibid.*, at Paras 700, 629.
192. *Ibid.*, at Paras 114, 121(9), 455.
193. *Ibid.*, at paras 115, 121(11), 366, 553, 622, 623.
194. *Ibid.*, at Paras 263, 264.
195. *Ibid.*
196. *Ibid.*, at Paras 267, 268.
197. *Ibid.*, at Para 272.
198. E.V. Chinnaiah *v.* State of A.P. (2005) 1 SCC 394.
199. (2005) 1 SCC 394-D.
200. (2005) 1 SCC 394-J.
201. (2005) 1 SCC 394-M.
202. (2005) 1 SCC 394-P.
203. (2005) 1 SCC 394-Q.
204. August 12, 2005, *Hindustan Times*, www.ndtv.com,www.judis.nic.in
205. *Times of India*, Sunday, 23 Oct. 2005, p. 4.
206. *Times of India*, Thursday, 5th Jan. 2006, p. 1.

5

Concept of Creamy Layer in Backward Class Reservation

Preferential treatments given to the Backward Class of citizens in the matter of appointment or posts in Public Services was a controversial issue since the enactment of the Constitution.[1] The provisions for job reservation to SCs and STs are incorporated in the Constitution as a part of the means to abolish the caste based close hierarchical society and to establish an egalitarian society having equal status and opportunity. In the pre independent India since caste was the sole criteria to determine social status and prestige. The members of the downtrodden lower caste/groups therefore were placed in a very disadvantaged position and they were totally excluded from the sphere of public power. So it had become an issue of social justice to adopt some positive measures to uplift these sections of the society. Job reservation for backward classes is justified on the ground that it leads the empowerment of the backward class, groups who had been the subject of repression for centuries.

However, the very purpose of reservation be defeated if the benefit of the reservation is not reached to the real backward classes of the society. So to serve the basic objective of constitutional reservation proper identification of the persons deserving/entitled to get the benefit of reservation is essential. In the post-independence era the Supreme Court of the land had the opportunity to consider the validity of different criteria formulated by various State Governments to find out backward class for the purpose of reservation under Art. 16(4) of the Indian Constitution.[2] In 1992 during examining the validity of the criteria formulated by the *Mandal Commission* to identify backward class of citizens in India, the Supreme Court itself had formulated a concept and criteria in this regard, i.e. *the creamy layer principle.*[3]

Now the principle of *'creamy layer'* has to be critically evaluated under :

(i) judicial approach, and
(ii) Political approach, in the background of its constitutional objective as follows.

PRINCIPLE OF CREAMY LAYER—A JUDICIAL APPROACH

The Concept of 'Creamy Layer' owes for its birth to the apex court of India[4] because Indian Constitution has no room for it, but for the first time the term "creamy layer" introduced by the Sattanathan Commission[5] in 1971 to directe that the "creamy layer" should be excluded from the reservation of civil posts and services granted to the OBCs. The Creamy Layer principle has been laid down by Supreme Court for the exclusion of the advanced sections of the backward class groups for the purpose of reservation and it had caused to the division of the society into *Backward Classes (Consisting of members of Backward Castes excluding creamy layer) and Forward Classes (Consisting of members of Forward Castes + members of Backward Castes coming under creamy layer)*.

The Supreme Court has said that the benefit of reservation should not be given to OBCs children of constitutional functionaries such as the president, judges of the Supreme Court and high courts, employees (class I and class II) of central and state bureaucracies, public sector employees, members of the armed forces and paramilitary personnel above the rank of colonel, lawyers, chartered accountants, docttors, financial and management consultants, engineers, film artists, and authors. OBC children belonging to any family that earns a total gross annual income of Rs. 4.5 lakh[6] belong to the creamy layer and so are also excluded from being categorised as *"socially and educationally backward"* regardless of their social/educational backwardness. Analyzing the approach of Supreme Court towards reservation policy one could find, the Court is very particular that the creamy layer among the backward classes should be excluded for the purpose of reservation.

In the Mandal case the Court formulated these principles after considering almost all relevant aspect viz historical, social, economic, political and developmental. Besides this different methods of judicial pronouncement—like historical, logical and sociological-have been adopted by the Court in formulating this new legal principle, having far reaching social, economic political consequences. The reasoning, given by different panel of adjudicators had provided adequate theoretical foundation to the principle. The political and legal attempts to frustrate the new idea had failed owing to the bold stand taken by the Supreme Court.

In the case of *Indra Sawhney and others* v. *Union of India*[7] petitioner's argument was that some members of designated backward class are highly advanced socially as well as economically and educationally. They constitute forward section of that particular backward class and are as forward as any other forward class member. It was further argued that this upper crust or forward, among backward are lapping up all the benefits of reservation meant for that class without allowing benefits to reach the truly backward members of that class. The petitioner relied *on K.S. Jayasree* v. *State of Kerala*[8] case wherein the Supreme Court had approved the Kerala scheme to keep certain classes out from the reservation benefit by fixing economic ceiling. Case of *State of Kerala* v. *N.M. Thomas,*[9] was also cited where *Krishna Iyer, J.* pointed out one of the dangers of reservation to be that, *"its benefits, by and large, are snatched away by the top creamy layer of the 'Backward Caste' or class keeping away weak and leaving the fortunate layers to consume to the whole cake"*. Therefore, seed of concept of creamy layer has been found in above cases before the *Indra Sawhney case.*

In Indra Sawhney case the first and foremost issue in this respect to be decided was; *whether the philosophy of creamy Layerisation would be limited to OBCs only or would include Scheduled Castes and Scheduled Tribes also,* for whom reservational benefit had been given since long and there have been eyebrow of elitists since long as the issue of reservation on Central Services for OBCs was not in contemplation.

The second issue was; *who were the opponents of giving benefits to all OBCs including their upper crust and was it advisable and realistic outlook to declare the upper crust of OBCs outside the purview of reservation* side by side the vacation of stay order against the union policy?

As to the *first issue Chief Justice Kania and Venkatachaliah, Ahmadi and Jeevan Reddy,* JJ had observed in running way, i.e. this discussion is confined to other Backward Class only and has no relevance in the case of Scheduled Castes and Scheduled Tribes.[10]

Although in *M. Nagraj & others* v. *Union of India & others*[11] *case* with five judges bench it was laid down that concept of creamy layer could be applied in case of SCs and STs also. But Attorney General Milon Banerjee said that here court's view is obiter dicta and it is not part of decision. While in Indra Sawhney case decision was given by nine judges' bench that principle of creamy layer is applicable only on OBCs, whereas in Nagraj case decision is given by five judges bench. And there is another precedent that a similar panel could not overturn a larger bench's verdict.

Recently in *Ashok Kumar Thakur* v. *Union of India*[12] five judges bench laid down that 'creamy layer' principle is one of the parameters to identify backward classes. Therefore, principally, the 'creamy layer' principle cannot be applied to SCs and STs as SCs and STs are separate classes by themselves. Principle of' creamy layer' applicable to OBCs as *Chief Justice K.G. Balakrishnan*[13] stated: "by excluding those who have already attained economic well-being or educational advancement, the special benefits cannot be further extended to them and, if done so, it would be unreasonable, discriminatory or arbitrary resulting in reverse discrimination. But this logic is applied exclusively for OBCs and the logic is not applied for SCs, STs and the unreserved category seats. The criterion is also not applicable to minority institutions. *Chief Justice K.G. Balakrishnan* also said that we are bound by larger bench decision of the Supreme Court in Indra Sawhney case

This observation had been criticized that if the rule of skimming off of upper crust of OBCs is pleaded how it may not be applied to SCs/STs.

India, therefore, has faced a war between legislature vs judiciary whereby the will of the legislature is undermined by the utopian concepts/perception of the supreme court. It is another debate can the judiciary impose any policy upon the government or the legislature. Whether a socially and educationally backward child can be denied the constitutional upliftment by a bench interpreting the constitution for the reason that his/her parents managed to get a combined yearly income of 4.5 lakh is another pandora's box since the "exclusion concept" is used to discriminate within OBCs only.

Mr. K.C. Yadav[14] who challenges the discriminatory use of Creamy Layer formula; said Art. 16(4) takes care of the Backward Classes as a genus of which the Scheduled Castes, Scheduled Tribes and Other backward Classes constitute different species. There is no churning out of the 'creamy layer' from the Schedule Caste and Scheduled Tribes in matter of job reservation. Why should the other Backward Classes be subjected to this discriminatory provision?

Mr. B.K. Roy Burman,[15] one of the members of the Mandal Commission, has also repeated the same charge; "if there is no question of identifying the 'creamy layer' among the Scheduled Castes, Scheduled Tribes, why there should be an effort to do so in relation to the Other Backward Classes".

As to the second issue *except Pandian, J. all the other eight hon'ble justices out of nine* were of the view that reservation to OBCs should be allowed subject immediately to skimming off the creamy layer among them. *Kania C.J. and Venkatachaliah, Ahmadi and Jeevan Reddy, JJ.,* were of the view that creamy layer was ruled for the exclusion, so the criteria must be ability to compete with the forward classes. *Thommen, J.* accepted attainment of certain economic level for exclusion. *Kuldip Singh* accepted means test to skin off the affluent section of the backward classes. *Sahai, J.* found a social purpose in exclusion through proper income, property or status criteria.

While Pandian, J. as dissenting opinion affirmed with the view of *Chinnappa Reddy, J.* when he quoted in *Vasanta Kumar case:*[16]

> "One must, however, enter a caveat to the criticism that the benefits of reservation are often snatched away by the top creamy layer of backward class of caste. That a few of the seats and posts reserved for backward classes are snatched away by the more fortunes among them are not to say that reservation is not necessary. This is bound to happen in a competitive society such as ours. Are not the unreserved seats and posts snatched away, in the same way, by the top creamy layer amongst them on the same principle of merit on which the unreserved seats are taken away by the top layer of the society? How can it be bad if reserved seats and posts are snatched away by the creamy layer of backward classes, if such snatching away of unreserved posts by the top creamy layer society itself is not bad?"

The majority view favoured application of creamy layer but they were not very much sure as to dividing line and wanted to ensure that it should not amount to taken away with one hand what is given by the other. They ruled that the basis of exclusion should not merely be economic one unless economic advancement is so high that it necessarily means social advancement like ownership of a factory.[17]

Jeevan Reddy, J. while delivering the judgment cautioned that line drawn between creamy layer and rest of the class must be a realistic one and income limit should be prescribed as such which may be indicative of social advancement. It should mean and signify social advancement. The Court pointed out certain positions to be *recognized as socially advanced like becoming a member of IAS or IPS or any other All India services.*[18] Exclusion of such advance class was declared to be advantageous to identify the rest of class a truly backward class and thereby would more appropriately serve the purpose and object of Art. 16(4).

Sawant, J. gave his judgment about 'creamy layer' on two grounds: *first,* the natural progress reveals undeniable fact that when society moves at least some individuals and families in the backward classes, however small in number, gain sufficient means to develop their capacities to compete with others in every field. Irrespective of their original birthmark they cannot be called as part of backward classes. To continue reservational benefits to them would violate equality as would amount to treating equals unequally.[19] *Second,* to rank them with the rest of the backward classes would equally violates the right to equality of the rest in those classes, since it would amount to treating unequals equally.[20]

According to him

> ". . . hence, taking out forwards, from among the backward classes is not only permissible but obligatory under the Constitution".[21]

Thommen and Kuldip Singh, JJ., preferred *means test* and pointed out that once a class of citizens is identified on the principles as backward for the purpose of reservation, the "means test" must be strictly and uniformly applied to exclude all those persons in that class reaching above the predetermined economic level. In his view, classes for which reservation is meant are those classes who are totally unable to join mainstream of upward mobility because of their utter helplessness arising from social and educational backwardness and aggravated by economic disability.[22]

Kuldip Singh, J. thought that benefits of special privilege like job reservations were mostly chewed up by richer or more affluent sections of backward classes and the poorer and the really backward sections among them keep on getting poorer and more backward. It is therefore, recommended that *means-test* is imperative to skim-off the affluent sections of the backward classes.[23]

He, for the necessity of Creamy Layer observed;

"the jobs are so very few in comparison to the population

> of the backward classes. It is difficult to give them adequate representation in the State services. It is, therefore, necessary that the benefit of the reservation must reach the poorer and the weaker section of the backward class. Economic ceiling to cut-off the backward class for the purpose of job reservation is necessary to benefit the needy sections of the class. Means test is imperative to skin-off the affluent sections of the backward classes".[24]

Even *S. Ratnavel Pandian, J.*, in dissenting opinion, said that,

> "the office memorandum based on Mandal Commission report does not speak of any "creamy layer test". It is the judiciary which laid down principle of creamy layer to justify reservation for OBCs. He further state that, "there is no dispute that the pseudo-communities who have smuggled into the backward classes should be weeded out from the list of backward class. But he pointed out that the act of weeding out must be done only by the Government on proper verification".[25]

A nine bench of apex court authoritatively came to the conclusion with majority view of B.P. Jeevan Reddy, J. that, 'Creamy Layer' can be, and must be excluded[26] from the said 'classes', and the 'classes' which remains after excluding the 'creamy layers' would more appropriately serve the purpose and object of Art. 16(4). They observed that,

> "The very concept of a class denotes a number of persons having certain common traits which distinguish them from the others. In determining backward class under Art. 16 cls. (4), if the connecting link is the social backwardness, it should broadly be the same in a given class. If some of the members are far too advanced socially (which in the context, necessarily means economically and, may also mean educationally) the connecting thread between them and the remaining class

snaps. They would be misfits in the class. When reservations are making for Backward Class, Creamy layer can be and must be excluded. In fact such exclusion benefits the truly backward. The Supreme Court therefore directed the Government of India to specify the basis of exclusion-where on the basis of income, extent of holding or otherwise-of creamy layer and held that after exclusion of creamy layer reservation is valid.[27]

R.M. Sahai, J., separately observed that,

"While reserving posts for backward classes the departments should make a condition precedent that every candidate must disclose the annual income of the parents beyond which one could not be considered to be backward. What should be that limit can be determined by the appropriated State. Income apart provision should be made that ward of those backward classes of persons who have achieved a particular status in society either political or social or economic or if their parents are in higher services then such individuals should be precluded to avoid monopolization by the services reserved for backward classes by a few. Creamy layer, thus, shall stand eliminated. And once a group or collectivity itself is found to have achieved the Constitutional objective then it should be excluded from the list of backward class. Creamy layer, amongst backward class of citizens must be excluded, by fixation of proper income, property or status criteria".[28]

Regarding the legality of Creamy layer principle *R.M. Sahai, J.* observed that,

"the importance of word "is" in Art. 16(4) should not be lost of. Backwardness and inadequacy should exist on the date the reservation is made. Reservation for a group which was educationally, economically and socially backward before 1950 shall not be valid unless the group continues to be backward today. The group should not have suffered only but it should be found to be suffering with such disabilities. If a class or community ceases to be economically and socially backward or even if it so it is adequately represented then no reservation can be made as it no more continues to be backward even though it may not be adequately represented in services or it may be backward but adequately represented".[29]

It is argued by any stretch of imagination that the government was not aware of some few individuals having both socially and educationally above the general average and entered in the All India Services. Despite the above fact, the Government has accepted the listed groups of SEBCs as annexed to the report and it has not thought it prudent to eliminate those individuals. Therefore, in such circumstances, it is doubtful whether the judicial supremacy can work in the broad area of social policy directing the exclusion of any section of the people from the accepted list of OBCs on the mere ground that they are all "creamy layer" which expression is to be tested with reference to various factors or make suggestions for exclusion of any section of the people who are otherwise entitled for the benefit of reservation in the decision of the Government so long that decision does not suffer any Constitutional infirmity. Therefore, the Supreme Court is not called upon to lay a test or give any guide line as to who are all to be eliminated from the listed groups of the Report, there is no necessity to lay any test much less "creamy layer".[30]

As *S. Ratnavel Pandian, J.*, observed that,

"No section of the SEBCs can be excluded on the ground of creamy layer till the Government takes a decision in this regard on a review on the recommendations of a Commission or a committee to be appointed by the government.[31]

Finally it could be said that there is no disagreement on the principle of 'creamy layer'. Creamy layer amongst backward class of citizens must be excluded by fixation of proper income, property or status criteria. But the task to identify creamy layer is the job of Government by appointing a commission.

As per the direction of Supreme Court *R.N. Prasad committee* was established to identify creamy layer among backward class for the exclusion from the benefit of reservation on February 1993 and this committee submitted its report to the government on 10th March 1993.[32]

In *Ashoke Kumar Thakur v. State of Bihar and U.P case*[33] the Government O.M. dt. 8.9.1993 based on *Ramanandan Committee Report* was approved by the Division Bench of the Supreme Court Consisting of *Kuldip Singh and S. Saghir Ahmad, JJ.* for the exclusion of creamy layer during giving benefit of reservation to the backward classes under section 16(4).

In this case the constitutionality of the criteria for determining 'creamy layer' for the purpose of exclusion from OBCs lay down by the State of Bihar and State of U.P. was challenged. The division bench *declared the creamy layer formula of both the States as invalid for being against the norms indicated by the Hon'ble Supreme Court in Mandal case and R.N. Prasad Committee.*

The creamy layer formulas of two States were like this: The Governor of Bihar promulgated ordinance called *"the Bihar Reservation of vacancies in Posts and Services (for Scheduled Castes, Scheduled Tribes and Other Backward Classes) (Amendment) Ordinance, 1995*. This Ordinance amended the section 4 of Bihar Act 3 of 1992 and after the second proviso, the following proviso was added:

> "Provided also that reservation under cls. (d) shall not apply to the category of Backward Class specified in Scheduled III".

And in the State of Uttar Pradesh, the categories sought to be excluded from the backward classes (creamy layer) are mentioned in *Schedule II read with section 3(b) of the Uttar Pradesh Public Services Reservation of Scheduled Castes and Scheduled Tribes and Other Backward Classes Act, 1994.*

A comparative evaluation of the identification of 'creamy layer' among OBCs by the States of Bihar and U.P. reveals that they had *put some additional conditions for exclusion than what guidelines in Mandal case desired.* The additional requirements put by the two States were that such person should draw a salary more than Rs. 10,000 or more per mensum, the wife and husband be graduate and one of them owing house in urban area. In case of professionals as income of Rs. 10 lakh per mensum was fixed as criterion. It further provided that the wife or husband should at least graduate and the family owns immovable property of the value of at least Rupees 20 lakhs.

Similarly, the criteria regarding traders, industrialists, agriculturists and others was very high e.g. for industrialist it was required that they might have invested Rs. 10 crores for at least 5 years and spouse was at least graduate, for agriculturalists, an income of Rs. 10 lakhs in year from sources other than agriculture and graduation of spouse was essential, for any other person to mention the above categories, the income from all sources required for continuously 3 years was fixed at not less than Rs. 10 lakhs, graduation of spouse and immovable property worth Rs. 20 lakhs.

In this case Supreme Court held that having regard to the observations made in Indra Sawhney-I, the said criteria were ultra vires. *Kuldip Singh, J.* arrived at certain conclusions:

1. The protective discrimination in the shape of job reservations under Art. 16(4) has to be programmed in such a manner that the most deserving section of the backward class is benefited.
2. Means test by which 'creamy layer' is excluded ensures such a result.
3. Due to nature of things there may be disparity among backwards as all cannot be equally backward and therefore some of the members of the class may have individually crossed the barriers of backwardness but while identifying the class they may have come within collectively.
4. It is often seen that comparatively rich persons in the backward class are able to move in the society without being discriminated socially.

5. The members of the backward classes are differentiated into superior and inferior and discrimination which was practiced by the higher class in turn is practiced by the affluent members of the backward class on the poorer members of the same class.
6. The benefits of social privileges like job reservations are mostly chewed up by the richer or more affluent sections of the backward class and the poorer and the really backward sections among them keep on getting poorer and more backward.

Conclusion of *Kuldip Singh, J.* expressed in *Ashoke Kumar Thakur case* are nothing but the echo or reproduction of the dissenting opinion of the learned judge (Pandian) in famous *Mandal Case*. Majority view laid down three conclusion[34] in the said case:

> *first*; Means Test are imperative to skim off the affluent sections of the BCs;
>
> *second*; only the most deserving—the weakest section among the SEBCs should be given the benefit of reservation, and
>
> *third*; identification of the OBCs under Art. 16(4) can be made solely on the basis of economic criterion.

Decision of the *Ashoke Kumar case*[35] is not correlated with the judgment of *Mandal case.*[36] *B.P. Jeevan Reddy, Sawant, JJ.*, observed that the ascent of backwardness does not economic consideration but on social considerations. Identification of the OBCs is to be based on social backwardness whose educational and economic backwardness is on account of social backwardness. This is so, because the purpose of reservation is not to alleviate poverty but to give an adequate share in power.

The court also missed the point that the Court is not competent to issue satisfactory guideline for identification of backward classes. The Government was to be given the upper hand. The direction of the Court itself indicates that the ultimate responsibility/power to identify creamy layer lies with State Government. While allowing the writ petitions and quashing Bihar and U.P. schemes of identification of creamy layer, *Kuldip Singh, J.* directed that the process of identifying backward class cannot be perfected to the extent that every member of the said class is equally backward.

Further he observed,

> "for the identification year 1995-96 the States of Uttar Pradesh and Bihar shall follow the criteria laid down by the Government of India. It will be open to the two States to lay down fresh criteria for the subsequent years in accordance with law."

P.B. Sawant, J. spoke about the 'creamy layer' in the following words:

> "the correct criterion for judging the forwardness of the forward among the backward classes is to measure their capacity not in terms of the capacity of others in their class, but in terms of the capacity of the members of the forward classes, as stated earlier. If they cross the Rubicon of backwardness they should be taken out from the backward classes and should be made disentitled to the provisions meant for the said classes. . . .".[37]

B.P. Jeevan Reddy, J. speaking for the court enunciated, the concept of 'creamy layer' in the following words:

> ". . . In fact such exclusion benefits the truly backward. Difficulty, however, really lies in drawing the line; it should be ensured that it does not result in tacking away with one hand what is given by the other. The basis of the exclusion should not merely be economic, unless, of course, the economic advancement is so high that it necessarily means social advancement".[38]

For example, a member of backward class, (member of carpenter caste), goes to Middle-East and works there as a carpenter. If you take his annual income in rupees, it would be fairly high from the Indian standard. *Is he to be excluded from the backward class? Are his children in India to be deprived of the benefit of Art. 16(4)?* Situation may, however, be different, if he rises so high economically as to become-say a factory owner himself. In such a situation, his social status also rises. He himself would be in a position to provide employment to others. In such a case, his income is merely a measure of his social status. Even otherwise there are several practical difficulties too in imposing an income ceiling. For example, annual income of Rs. 36,000 may not count for much in a city like Bombay, Delhi or Calcutta whereas it may be handsome income in rural India anywhere. The line to be drawn must be realistic one.[39]

Another question would be, should such a line be uniform for the entire country or a given State or should it differ from rural to urban areas and so on. It is supposed that, income from agriculture may be difficult to assess and therefore, *the line may have to be drawn with reference to the extent of holding.* When the income of a person is taken as a measure of his social advancement, the limit to be prescribed should not be such as to result in taking away with one hand what is given with the other. *The income limit must be such as to mean and signify social advancement.* At the same time, it must be recognized that there are certain positions, the occupation of which can be treated as socially advancement without any further enquiry.

For example, if a member of a designated backward class becomes a member of IAS or IPS or any other All India Service, his status in society (social status) rises; he is no longer socially disadvantaged. His children get full opportunity to realize their potential. They are in no way handicapped in the race of life. His salary is also such that he is above want. It is but logical that in such a situation, his children are not given the benefit of the reservation. For by giving them the benefit of reservation, other disadvantaged members of that backward class may be deprived of that benefit. It is then argued that 'one swallow does not make the summer', and that merely because a few members of a caste or class become socially advanced, the class/caste as such do not cease to be backward. *It is pointed out that cls. (4) of Art. 16 aims at group backwardness and not individual backwardness. While we agree that cls. 4 aims at group backwardness, we felt that exclusion of such socially advanced members will make the 'class' a truly backward class and* would more appropriately serve the purpose and object of cls. (4). *This discussion is confined to other backward classes only and has no relevance in the case of Scheduled Castes and Scheduled Tribes...* keeping in mind all these considerations, we direct the Government of India to specify the basis of exclusion—whether on the basis of income, extent of holding or otherwise-of 'creamy layer'".[40]

It is difficult to draw a line where a person belonging to the backward class, ceases to be so and become part of the 'creamy layer'. Although this court brought point briefly by illustrating various stages where a member of a backward class ceases to be backward and starts floating with the 'creamy layer'.[41]

Judges acknowledged that pursuant to the directions by this court in *Mandal case (1992 AIR SCW 3682)* Government of India , Ministry of Personnel, Public Grievances and Pensions (Department of P&T) issued office memorandum dated September 8, 1993 providing for 27% reservation for the Other Backward classes. Para 2(c) of the memorandum excludes the persons/sections mentioned in column 3 of the Scheduled (consisting of creamy layer) to the said memorandum.[42] And this court has no hesitation in approving the rule of exclusion framed by Government of India.[43] *This is vehemently commented that the State Government should follow the Government of India and in down similar criteria for identifying the 'creamy layer'. In this background criteria for identifying the 'creamy layer' laid down by the State of Bihar and Uttar Pradesh has to be examined.*[44]

This court authoritatively lay down that the prosperous part of a backward class called 'creamy layer' has to be excluded from the said class. The backward class under Art. 16(4) means the class which has no element of 'creamy layer' in it. It is mandatory under Art. 16(4) that the State must identify the 'Creamy Layer' in a backward class and thereafter creamy layer are to be excluded and benefits of the Art. 16(4) could only be given to the 'class' which remains after the exclusion of the 'Creamy Layer'.

In II Indra Sawhney v. *Union of India*[45] case validity of *secs. 3, 4 and 6 of Kerala State Backward Classes (Reservation of Appointment or posts in the Services) Act 1995* was challenged as unconstitutional and violative of Arts. 14 and 16 of Indian Constitution, because *sec.* 3 declared that, *"having regard to known facts in existence in the State of Kerala that there are no socially advanced sections in any backward classes who have acquired capacity to compete with forward classes"* and the backward classes in the State were not adequately represented in the services under the State and they would continue to be entitled to reservation under clause (4) of Art. 16 of the Constitution. Sec. 4 provides that existing system of reservation shall continue as per rule made in 1958 and Sec. 6 provides validity to the enforcement of these sections with retrospective effect. This Act was passed on 2.9.95 but was given retrospective effect since 2.10.1992.

Following issues were arises for the consideration of the Court in this case:

1. What is the law declared and what are the directions given in Indra Sawhney case in regard to 'creamy layer' in the context of Arts. 14 and 16?
2. Can the declaration of law in regard to 'creamy layer' in the context of Arts. 14 and 16 in Indra Sawhney and in other rulings be undone by the Kerala Legislature by a reproductive validating law containing a statutory declaration whose effect is to say that no 'creamy layer' exists in the state of Kerala?
3. Are the provisions of Secs. 3, 4 and 6 of the Kerala State of backward classes (Reservation of Appointments or Posts in the Services) Act violative of Arts. 14 and 16 of the Constitution of India?
4. If the provisions of 3, 4 and 6 of the Kerala Act are liable to be struck down, is the report of High level Committee headed by Justice K.J. Joseph to be accepted and are there any valid objections to the report?
5. If Secs. 3, 4 and 6 of the said Kerala Act struck

down, what further directions are to be issued to the State of Kerala?

First of all before considering various issue *Gannadha Rao, J.* said that since Kerala Government failed to implement the directions of *Indra Sawhney-I case*[46] by appointing a commission to identify the creamy layer among the designated backward classes in the State. This court, by its order dated 10.7.1995 held that the State of Kerala was guilty of contempt but gave a further opportunity to the State to purge the contempt and adjourned the matter 11.09.1995. As per the direction of this court a high level committee under the chairmanship of *K.J. Joseph* was appointed to gather the necessary information regarding 'creamy layer' among the backward classes in the State of Kerala. This committee submitted its report to this Court on 4.8.1997.

Regarding *first issue* Supreme Court with view of *Gannadha Rao, D.P. Wadhwa and M.B. Shah, JJ.*, held that although reservation is permissible in favour of backward class of citizens if it is not adequately represented in the services under the State. But the 'caste' only cannot be basis for reservation. Reservation can be for a backward class citizen of a particular caste. Therefore, from that caste, creamy layer and non-backward class of citizens are to be excluded. If the caste to be taken into consideration then for finding out socially and economically backward class, creamy layer of the caste to be eliminated for granting benefit of reservation, because the creamy layer cannot be termed as socially and economically backward.[47] *This question exhaustively dealt with by nine judges in Indra Sawhney case,*[48] *where it has been specifically held that 'only caste' cannot be the basis for reservation.*

For the inclusion of the backward classes, apex court held that care should be taken that the forward castes do not include in the backward castes list and cited observation of *Pandian, J.* in *Indra Sawhney case* that before a conclusion is drawn that a caste is backward or is inadequately represented in the services,

"the existence of circumstances relevant to the formation of the opinion is a *sine qua non*. If the opinion suffers from

> the vice of non-application of mind or formulation of collateral grounds or beyond the scope of the statute, or irrelevant and extraneous material, then the opinion is challengeable."

He further pointed out that, periodic examination of a backward class would lead to its exclusion if it ceases to be socially backward or if it is adequately represented in the services. Once backward, always backward is not acceptable.[49]

In any case, the 'creamy layer' has no place in the reservation system. If creamy layer among backward classes is not excluded, the benefits of reservation will not reach the really backward. Most of the benefits will then be knocked away by the forward castes and the creamy layer. That will leave the truly backward, backward for ever. *Jeevan Reddy, J.* while delivering the majority judgment, *inter alia*; held as under:

> "if the real object is to locate backwardness, and if such backwardness is found in a caste, it can be treated as backward; if it is found in any other group, section or class, they too can be treated as backward. Reservation is not being made under cls. 4 of Art. 16 in favour of a 'caste' but a backward class. Once a caste satisfies the criteria of backwardness, it becomes a backward class for the purposes of Art. 16(4)".[50]

Regarding question relating to 'creamy layer' majority judgment laid emphasis on the relevance of caste and also stated upon a member of the backward class reaching an "advanced social level or status", he would no longer belong to the backward class and would have to be weeded out.

> "After excluding them alone, would the class be compact class. In fat, such exclusion benefits the truly backward".

It is clearly appears from the judgments of the eight judges, viz. *Jeevan Reddy (for himself and three others), Sawant and Sahai,* specifically refer that the persons in higher services like

IAS, IPS and All India services . . . are declared not entitled to be treated as backward. They are to be treated as creamy layer "without further inquiry." Likewise, persons living in sufficient affluence who are able to provide employment to others are to be treated as having reached a higher social status and therefore outside the Backward Class. This judgment also refers to a classification of 'affluent' sections identified by way of income or property holding. It means those persons holding higher levels of agricultural land holdings or getting income from property, beyond a limit have to be excluded from the backward classes. This is a judicial 'declaration', although, 'norms may differ from State to State or from region to region".[51]

The identification of 'creamy layer' in every backward class is in fact based upon horizontal division of every section of the backward class into creamy layer or non-creamy layer. It is also important to notice that such a horizontal division based on such norms will be applicable not only to those presently falling under the norm but the norm or limit so set would also be applicable to those reaching that level in the future. This was the declaration of law made in *Indra Sawhney-I*[52] case in relation to identification and exclusion of 'creamy layer'. The Central and State Governments, under the direction of Indra Sawhney case are obliged to create separate bodies which will identify the creamy layer in the backward classes within a time frame.[53] Issue one decided accordingly.

Regarding validity of Kerala Act *(Issue second and third)* it is held that, the 'creamy layer' in the backward class is to be treated 'on par' with the forward classes and it not entitled to benefits of reservation, it is obvious that if the 'creamy layer' is not excluded, there will be discrimination and violation of Arts. 14 and 16(1) inasmuch as equals (forwards and creamy layer of backward classes) cannot be treated unequally. Again non-exclusion of creamy layer will also be violative of Arts. 14, 16(1) and 16(4) since unequal (the creamy layer) cannot be treated as equals that is to say, equal to the rest of the backward classes. Thus, any executive or legislative action refusing to exclude the creamy layer from the benefits of reservation will be violative of Arts. 14 and 16(1) and also of Art. 16(4).[54]

The question of validation arises in the context of sec. 6 of the Act. It is true that whenever legislative or executive action declared as being violative of the provisions of Part III of the Constitution, it will permissible for the executive or legislature to remove the defect which is the cause for discrimination prospectively. The defect can be removed retrospectively too by legislative action and the previous actions can also be validated. In the context of the law laid down in *Ashoke Thakur & Indra Sawhney case*[55] if the State does not take steps to remove the defect to exclude the 'creamy layer' from the backward classes then the benefits of reservations which are invalidly continued in favour of the 'creamy layer' cannot be declared retrospectively valid merely by a legislative declaration that such creamy layer is absent as done by section 3 (there was no creamy layer in the state of Kerala) and sec. 6 of the Kerala State Backward Classes (Reservation of Appointments or Posts in Services) Act. The creamy layer principle laid down in *Indra Sawhney case*, cannot be ignored as done by Sec. 6 of the said Act. Therefore both the sections are unconstitutional. If under the guise of elimination of the 'creamy layer', the legislature makes a law which is not indeed a true elimination but is seen by the court to be a mere cloak, then the court will necessarily strike down such a law as violative of principle of separation of powers and of Art. 14, 16(1) and Art. 16(4).[56]

Sub-clause (b) of sec. 3 states that since there is no representation of the backward classes in the services of the State of Kerala. This is given as a reason by the State of Kerala for not excluding the creamy layer. For this apex court held that in our view, the Kerala Act has mixed up two different concepts in this sub-clause (b) of s. 3. Art. 16 is an enabling provision which permits the State to provide reservation for backward classes if, in its opinion, such representation is felt necessary and if there is not equate representation.[57] Lack of adequate representation of a particular backward class may be a factor for consideration by the State for providing reservation but it cannot be the sole ground for continuance of the creamy layer in that backward class. *The first step no doubt is the identification of the backward class which is inadequately represented. The second step is elimination of the creamy layer from the backward class.* And this second step cannot be mixed up with the first step nor can it be forgotten.[58]

The mere inadequate representation of a particular backward class in public services flowing as a consequence of exclusion of creamy layer is not legally sufficient to provide or continue reservation to the creamy layer.[59] Reservation even for backward classes can be made only if it will not undermine the efficiency of the administration in the particular department. For all the aforesaid reasons, sub-cls. (b) of sec. 3 does not provide any valid answer for not eliminating the creamy layer and must also be held to be unconstitutional and violative of Arts. 14, 16(1) and 16(4) of the Constitution. Thus sub-clause (a) and (b) of s. 3 are both declared unconstitutional.[60]

Section 4 of the said Act provides for the continuance of reservation for the backward classes as they stood in 1958 ignoring the directives of this court given in the case of Indra Sawhney 1992 for exclusion of 'creamy layer'.

Supreme Court held that continuance of Sec. 4 will amount to ignoring the subsequent, judgment of this court in *Indra Sawhney and Ashoke Kumar case*[61] to the effect that creamy layer is necessarily eliminated. Neither Parliament nor the State legislature can make any law to continue reservation to the creamy layer inasmuch as the said judgment of this court are based on Arts. 14 and 16(1) of the Indian Constitution and no law can obviously be made to override the provisions of Articles 14 and 16(1). Thus for the aforesaid reasons, sec. 4 of the Act along with the non-obstante clause is declared unconstitutional and violative of the judgment of SC and violative of the Arts. 14 16(1) and 16(4) of the Constitution of India.[62] The non-exclusion of creamy layer or the inclusion of forward castes in the list of the backward classes will, therefore, be totally illegal. It is not only violative of Arts. 14 and 16 but it also amounts to violative of basic structure of Indian constitution.[63]

Regarding *issue forth,* it is held that parliament and the legislature cannot transgress the basic feature of the Constitution, namely, the principle of equality enshrined in Art. 14 of which Art. 16(1) is a facet. Whether creamy layer is not excluded or whether forward castes get included in the; list of backward classes, the position will be the same, namely, that there will be a breach not only of Art. 14 but of the basic structure of the Constitution. The non-exclusion of the creamy layer or the inclusion of forward castes in the list of backward classes will therefore be illegal. Such an illegal Act offending the root of the Indian Constitution, cannot be allowed to be perpetuated even the Constitutional amendment. Kerala legislature is therefore, least competent to perpetuate such an illegal discrimination.[64]

In the case of *Nair Service Society* v. *State of Kerala,*[65] the Nair Service Society, challenged the report of Justice K.K. Narendran Commission and its acceptance by the State of Kerala in issuing the impugned notification dated 27.5.2000. Society questioned the validity of the said notification by saying that in the guidelines seven categories of hereditary occupations/calling, which had been excluded from the category of 'creamy layer', have been identified. As regards the income limit in terms of the Joseph Committee Report, (published in 1996) was Rs. 1.5 lakhs; whereas the same according to the Narendran Commission Report, (published in 2000) raised to Rs. 3 lakhs. While in the year 2004 the Central Government fixed the income limit at Rs. 2.5 lakhs. In identifying the backward classes in several categories, i.e. category Nos. I, II, III, V and VA, the exclusion was recorded only on the basis of status and not on the basis of annual income. However, in addition to category No.VI, it was stated that in calculating the annual income, the salary income or income from agriculture would not be taken into account. No reason, however, has been assigned as to why salary income or income from agriculture would not be included for determining the category of 'creamy layer'.

Supreme Court (with bench *of S.B. Sinha & P.P. Naolekar*) said that, at this stage it is necessary to be noticed that by judgment and order dated 13.12.1999[66] in 'Indra Sawhney case -II', this Court, hold the provisions of Sections 3, 4 and 6 of the State Act to be unconstitutional, and accepted the objections to the report of the Joseph Committee, in toto, subject to certain additions of communities and sub-castes. The recommendations made by the Joseph Committee, however, were not implemented forthwith in terms of the directions of this Court. The State, on the other hand, appointed another

Commission headed by Justice K.K. Narendran. The Narendran Commission submitted an interim report and directed the State to implement the report of the Joseph Committee. On 16.2.2000 the State issued fresh guidelines for identifying creamy layer in accordance with the Joseph Committee report. The Commission submitted its final report on 11.4.2000. The order issued by the State on 27.5.2000. The notification issued on dated 12.6.2000 wherein several guidelines were issued, which, *inter alia*, are on the following terms:

> *"The rule of exclusion made mention in the schedule attached to these guidelines will not apply to persons working as artisans or engaged in hereditary occupations, calling and included in Annexure 'B' appended herewith and person/group of persons coming within the definition of the expression "Fishermen Community" in Annexure C appended to these guidelines".*

With the view of *justice Sinha,* apex court observed, that in any view of the matter, when the question of such grave importance has been brought to the notice of this Court, having regard to the principle underlying the purport and object for which the 'creamy layer' was sought to be excluded, this Court cannot shut its eyes and refuse to determine the question.

The concept of identification of 'creamy layer' came up for consideration in *Indra Sawhney-I*[67] and this Court has issued certain directions in this behalf. The State of Kerala did not follow the said direction as a result whereof it was found to be guilty of contempt of this Court. A stern action thereupon was proposed to be taken up against the State of Kerala in view of its contemptuous conduct, as is evident from the order of this Court in *Indra Sawhney vs. Union of India & Ors.*[68] It was in the aforesaid conditions, the legislation passed by the legislature of Kerala was not only struck down during the pendency of the proceedings by this Court, and a Committee was also directed to be constituted. We have noticed hereinbefore that the recommendations of the Joseph Committee were accepted in toto. We have furthermore noticed that the State, without any demur, accepted the recommendations thereof with modification by addition of one caste or sub-caste. It is, therefore, difficult for us to appreciate as to on what basis Narendran Commission was appointed. It is, furthermore, difficult for us to understand as to on what basis, while appointing Narendran Commission, in the terms of reference, the State of Kerala could say that the maximum benefit should be given to a particular section of people.

Keeping in view the legal history, as also the directions made by this Court in a series of judgments referred to hereinbefore, it was obligatory on the part of the Narendran Commission to consider seriously that aspect of the matter. In any event the same could not have been ignored. While fixing the income limit, although a State is entitled to take into consideration the level of literacy, the village income, the rise of living index, the rate of inflation and other relevant factors into consideration, it should not have accepted a report of the Committee which did not proceed scientifically, particularly, having regard to the constitutional scheme as explained by the Court in the judgments referred to hereinbefore. We, therefore, do not find any justification for fixing the income limit at Rs. 3 lakhs.

Equality clauses contained in Arts. 14, 15 and 16 of the Constitution of India may in certain situations constitute the heart and soul of the Constitution of India. When a law is patently arbitrary, such infringement of the equality clause contained in Art. 14 or Art. 16 would be violative of the equality clause of the Constitution. Following the decision of *M. Nagaraj and Ors.* v. *Union of India and Ors.*[69] case where apex court has reaffirmed the importance of the creamy layer principle in the scheme of equality under the constitution, this Court held that the creamy layer principle was on of the important limits on state power under the Equality Clause enshrined under Articles 14 and 16 and any violation or dilution of the same would render the state action invalid. This Court reiterated the limit on state power imposed by the creamy layer rule and the invalidity of any state action in violation of the same. This Court, thus, has categorically laid down the law that determination of creamy layer is a part of the constitutional scheme. The State did not accept even the Narendran Commission report in its entirety. Accordingly, notification dated 27th May, 2000 being merely for notification of general public and the guidelines issued for the concerned officers, it is necessary that the State should amend the guidelines also.

Supreme court finally held, while fixing the income limit, although a State is entitled to take into consideration the level of literacy, the village income, the rise of living index and other relevant factors into consideration, it should not have accepted a report of the Committee which did not proceed scientifically, particularly, having regard to the constitutional scheme. Supreme Court setting aside the report of the Narendran Commission, directed the State to appoint a fresh Commission.

In the case of *Sh. Chander Vijay* v. *Union of India & Others*[70] petitioner[71] filed a petition and seeks a writ of certiorari by quashing notification dated 8.9.1993,[72] 28.9.1993[73] and circular dated 2.2.2001,[74] in which the petitioner is sought to be excluded from the benefit of the OBCs category as part of the "Creamy layer". Petitioner also seeks a writ of mandamus, directing the respondents to issue forthwith OBCs certificate for the year 2002 for the Civil Services Examination, conducted by UPSC.

It is argued that the crux of the controversy is the exclusion of the petitioner under the notification, issued by the Central Government and the State Government, insofar as *they relate to the service category on the ground that the father of the petitioner had retired as a Class I Officer. Petitioner thus formed part of the "creamy layer" and was not entitled to the benefit of the OBCs.*

The Governor of Rajasthan issued an order[75] that 21% of the vacancies in posts and services under the State Government, to be filled through direct recruitment, shall be reserved for the castes and classes included in the list of Backward Classes.[76] But Candidates belonging to Backward Classes recruited on the basis of merit in an open competition on the same standards prescribed for the general candidates shall not be adjusted against the reservation quota of 21%. The aforesaid reservation shall not apply to persons/sections mentioned, as creamy layer, in Column• 3 of the schedule annexed to this notification.

The Schedule annexed with this department's notification[77] specifically mentioned such persons/Categories of persons who will not be entitled (excluded) for the benefit of reservation of Other Backward Classes. With respect to *'Constitutional Posts'* it has been prescribed that the Rule of Exclusion will apply to persons holding Constitutional positions like President of India, . . . and "persons holding Constitutional positions of like nature". In this regard clarification[78] has been sought as to whether Ministers in the State Government would fall under the category of "Persons holding Constitutional positions of like nature" and the rule of exclusion will apply to their sons and daughters. The clarification is made as *Ministers of the State Government are Constitutional functionaries but their tenure being temporary and often transitory so they are not supposed to have shed backwardness in such short periods. Therefore, the Rule of Exclusion will not apply to the sons and daughters of Ministers since their parents do not fall in Category of the Schedule.*

It is also clarified that the *Rule of Exclusion will apply in the case of sons and daughters of the offices enumerated in the "Service Category" even after they retire on superannuation*. Therefore, retirement on superannuation of the specified category of officers has no effect on their offspring, who are once defined as "Creamy Layer."

These clarifications may be brought to thc notice of all concerned and they may be directed to take action accordingly. Judiciary held that the words "is" and "are" in the notifications dated 8.9.1993 and 29.9.1993 are not to be interpreted as being confined to only those persons who were presently holding the posts and are also to include persons who have held such posts mentioned therein. The petitioner is not entitled to the relief sought in the writ petitions. No ground is made out to assail the validity of the impugned notifications. Considering the interpretation given to the words "is" and "are" in the notifications, resort to the circular dated 2.2.2001 was not even necessary. In any case the clarification given in the circular is also in consonance with the interpretation given to the words used in the notification by this Court. Hence challenge to the validity of the circular dated 2.2.2001 also fails. *Manmohan Sarin, J.* held that the writ petitions have no merit and are dismissed.

Regarding constitutional validity of the Creamy Layer concept—it is said that when Indian Constitution does not mentions about the concept of "creamy layer" and nowhere does it prescribe any directive to exclusively discriminate OBCs, the exclusion of creamy layer leads to undermining the constitution itself. Since "socially backward" and "educationally backward" were the key words enshrined after thorough deliberations and the "economic criterion" (cream concept) can never be a criterion in determining reservation policy. Nevertheless, the Supreme Court and its constitutional bench have decided to give sanctity to a concept that they themselves invented during the course of Mandal Commission implementation.

In 2006 when central Government wants to give reservation for OBCs in Central Educational Institutions like IITs, Management (IIMs) and medical institutions (like AIMS) for the implication of The Central Educational Institution (Reservation in Admission) Act, 2006, without exclusion of 'creamy layer section' among the Backward class, it was apposed and challenged in the Apex court of India in *Ashoke Kumar Thakur* v. *Union of India*,[79] government take the plea that concept of creamy layer is applicable only in case of job reservation not in case of reservation in admission in educational institutions. But Supreme Court laid down that it permits reservation for socially and educationally backward classes in the State or State-aided educational institutions subject to the exclusion of the 'creamy" layer from the OBCs. Thus concept is very well applicable to admission in educational institutions also as it is available under Art. 15(5) not under Art. 16(4) as it provides reservation in job. As noticed ealier, determiniation of backward class cannot be exclusively based on caste. Poverty, social backwardness, economic backwardness, all are criteria for determination for determination of backwardness. It has been noticed that among the backward class, a a section of the backward class is a member of the affluent section of society. They do not deserve any sort of reservation for further progress in life.

They are socially and educationally advanced enough to compete for thr general seats along with other candidates.[80]

It is to be understood that 'creamy layer' principle is introduced merely to exclude a section of a particular caste on the ground that they are economically advanced or educationally forward. They are excluded because unless this segment of caste is excluded from that caste group, there cannot be proper identification of backward class. If the 'creamy layer' principle is not applied easily be said that all the castes that have been included among the socially and educationally backward classes have been included exclusively on the basis of caste. Identifacation of SEBC for the purpose of either Arts. 15(4), 15(5) or 16(4) solely on the basis of caste is expressly prohibited by various decisions of this court and it is also against Articles 15(1) and 16(1) of the constitution. To fulfill the conditions and to findout truly what is socilly and educationally backward class, the exclusion of creamy layer is essential.[81]

It may be noted that the 'creamy layer principle' is applied not as a general principle of reservation. It is applied for the purpose of identifying the socially and educationally backward class. One of the main criteria for determining the SEBC is poverty. If that be so, the principle of exclusion of 'creamy layer' is necessary.[82]

Justice pasayat Thakker and Bhandari held that non-exclusion of creamy layer from the list of backward classes will not only breach Art. 14 but also violate the basic structure of the Constitution. Hence, the implied inclusion of the creamy layer among SEBCs/OBCs in Art. 15(5) is severed.[83]

Conclusion; the issue of Creamy layer formula is one which relates to evaluation of compensatory discrimination. Compensatory discrimination policies are argued to entail systematic departure from norms of equality such as merit, evenhandedness and indifference to ascriptive characteristics. Creamy layer formula, therefore, does not amount to taking away by one hand what has been given by the other.

Every scheme of Compensatory discrimination has to be evaluated in terms of costs and benefits. The observation of the *D.A. Desai, J.* in *K.C. Vasanth Kumar* v. *State of Karnataka*[84] case is representative of the case against creamy layer of OBCs, of course his statement about reservation are limited to state of Karnataka where state reservational scheme was in operation and not the national policy of reservation for OBCs.

The learned judge said,

> "Reservation in one or other form has been there for decades. If a survey is made without reference to families in various castes considered to be socially and educationally backward, about the benefits of preferred treatment, it would unmistakably show that the benefit of reservation are snatched away by the top creamy layer of the backward castes. This has to be avoided at any costs".[85]

Desai, J. talked of skimming off from all beneficiaries of reservational justice. Though, he did not allow economic criterion for qualifying for reservational benefits by the SCs/STs as the thousands of years of discrimination or exploitation can not be wiped put in one generation. But even here (in case of SCs/STs) economic criterion is worth applying by refusing preferred treatment to those amongst them who have already benefited by it and improved their position.[86] Thus creamy layer formula ought to have been applied to all the beneficiaries of protective discrimination—SCs/STs/OBCs.

The real issue is: what is main guiding spirit behind the adoption of 'creamy layer formula'. The obvious objects are two-fold—

- First, to ensure (in principle) that the benefit of reservation reaches to really deserving section of OBCs, and
- Second, to cool down impatient anti reservationists and cure their heart-burning against enrichment of affluent section of backwards.

It is argued, will skimming off creamy layer among OBCs ensure the reaching of benefits to non-creamy layer of OBCs? The hard reality is that the desired percentage of reservation for SCs/STs has still not been filled in. In class one services their representation has reached upto 5.68% as against their 22.5% quota and in all class (II, III and IV also) it has reached upto 18.72%. This percentage of reservation is inclusive of the creamy layer. *What will be result if creamy layer is taken away from reservational benefit?* Will not it tender the representation to a poor zero from 5.68% in class I? The same analogy applies with equal force to OBCs (the Supreme Court itself has left SCs/STs unaffected by creamy layer formula). The representation of OBCs with 52% population and 27% reservation of seats had only 4.69% representation to class I till 1980 and 12.55% in all services. If creamy layer is taken away, will the non-creamy layer be able to compete and fill 27% vacancies? Will it not amount to a circuitous deprivation of reservational justice to backward class in collectivity? In mandal case *Pandian, J.* cited that the representation of backward classes is not upto mark and is miserable low. To allow creamy layer to go out of reservational benefit would amount to taking away by one hand what has been given by the other. The only justification for denial to the creamy layer of the reservational benefit is he cooling down of the heart—burning among status quoists.

In Mandal Report it was observed that: "it is certainly true that reservation for OBCs will cause a lot of heart burning to others. But should the mere fact of this heart-burning be allowed to operate as a moral veto against social reform". Thus the 'creamy layer formula' needs a cool and empirical study. It is not easy for anybody to answer the question posed by *Chinnappa Reddy, J.* in *Vasanth Kumar's case*; how can it be bad if reserved seats and posts are snatched away by the creamy layer of backward classes, if such snatching away of unreserved posts by the top creamy layer of society itself is not bad?".[87]

It is submitted that the argument for exclusion of 'creamy layer' on the face of it appears to be attractive and reasonable. No body can dispute that the pseudo (artificial) communities who have smuggled into the backward classes should be weeded out from the list of backward classes but that should be done by the government at opportune time after due empirical study.

CONCEPT OF CREAMY LAYER—
A POLITICAL APPROACH

Framer of the Indian Constitution were intended to abolish the caste based closed society and to create an egalitarian society having equal status and opportunity. Accordingly in the chain of various efforts one step was taken in August 1990 when Central Government issued an Official Memorandum for providing 27% reservation in favour of backward classes in civil services and posts. This O.M. was based on the recommendations of Mandal Commission which identified *3,943 castes* as backward about 52% of the total population. Several writ petitions were filed against this O.M. in the apex Court. Supreme Court issued stay order but in the mean time Central Government issued another modified O.M. on 25th September 1991. It was also challenged. In *Indra Sawhney case*[88] Supreme Court approved O.M. of 1990 as valid but held that it is not applicable on the elite classes which considered as Creamy Layer (socially and educationally advance) among backward class.

All parties welcomed the 27% reservation to socially and educationally backward communities (OBC) But the creamy layer exclusion has varied responses from various political formations. Most political parties are uncomfortable with the rigid criterion for the creamy layer concept although everyone is pleased that 27% quota has got legal sanctity. Mr. Sharad Yadav, JD(U) said that "the net result of job reservation for the Other Backward Classes is that their total representation has declined to less than 5 per cent. A major factor is the "creamy layer" concept, which has become an excuse for keeping the backward castes out. History now repeats itself with the Supreme Court verdict in favour of denying reservation in higher education institutions to the creamy layer among the OBCs, he said. The court tried to take away what Parliament tried to give the OBCs".

As a reaction of this judgment, society led to divided into *Forward class (Castes) and backward class (Castes)*. Indian Constitution while enshrined no provision for creamy layer. The issue of skimming off such groups has been both against SCs/STs and OBCs. *The main issue before us; is it advisable to oust the creamy layer of Backward Class when the reservation scheme is going to be implemented in Central government services as well as in State government services?* In relation to State services also, there has been a strong submission to skim off the forward class among backwards class (ST, SC and OBC). It is expressed that reservation benefits should not be given to those families which had received its benefit and whose children have been brought in higher cultural atmosphere. It is also suggested reservation should not be given to those students whose guardians are income tax payee irrespective of their being SC/ST.

Shri Biju Patnayak, the then Chief Minister of Orissa wrote a letter to the Central Government for fixing the income for awarding reservational benefit in admission and further advised for its application to all SCs/STs and OBCs.

Third Backward Class Commission of Karnataka State also suggested that reservational benefit should not be given to the wards of such people who are employed in Class I or II services, doctors, engineers or income tax and sales tax payees.

CENTRAL GOVERNMENT'S APPROACH FOR REALIZATION OF CREAMY LAYER PRINCIPLE

Supreme Court[89] issued several directions, listed below, to the Government of India, as well as State Governments and the Administration of Union Territories to follow:

(A) The Government of India, State Governments and the Administration of Union Territories, shall constitute a permanent body for entertaining, examining and recommending upon request for inclusion and complain of over-inclusion and under-inclusion in the lists of Other Backward Class of citizens. The *advice tendered* by such body shall ordinarily be *binding upon the government*.

(B) The Government of India shall specify the basis, applying the relevant and requisite socio-economic criteria to exclude socially advanced persons/sections (creamy layer) from the 'Other Backward Class'. The implementation of the impugned O.M.

dated August 13, 1990 shall be subject to exclusion of such socially advanced persons (creamy layer).

In response to the above directions, the Union Government resolved to implement reservation only after identification and exclusion of the 'creamy layer' of OBCs. With a view to search the socio-economic criterion for identification of Creamy Layer the Government of India constituted an Expert Committee.[90] The Expert Committee was constituted under the chairmanship of Sri Ramanandan Prasad with four other members.[91] This committee submitted its report on 10 March 1993. It recognized *a family*-consisting of husband, wife and children, *as a unit* and explained that the brother and sister of an officer falling under creamy layer would not be deprived of reservation and for the purpose of their exclusion the status of their parents would be taken into account.

The rule of exclusion will apply on listed categories, unless exceptions are specifically indicated.[92] Criteria fixed for identification of creamy layer and the rules of exclusion are as listed below :

I. First Criteria is Constitutional Posts: it is said that—

Son(s) and daughter(s) of (a)—President of India; (b)—Vice-President of India; (c)—Judges of the Supreme Court and of the High Courts; (d)—Chairman & Member of UPSC and of the State Public Services Commission; Chief Election Commissioner; Comptroller & Auditor General of India; and the (e)—Persons holding Constitutional positions of like nature are not entitled to get the benefit of reservation.

In this line it is cleared that the Constitutional Posts of Governor, Minister, and Membership of Parliament or State legislatures, is in the very nature of temporary and often transitory. Hence, such persons have not been separately categorized for exclusion as Creamy layer from the benefit of reservation.

II. Second Criteria is Service Class: Group A/Class I Officers of the All India Central and State Services (Direct Recruits)

A. *Rule of Creamy Layer shall apply on the children son(s) and daughter(s): if either of the spouses (parents) is a Class I Officer*

Where both spouses are Class I officers and one of them dies then situation remains unchanged and the rule of exclusion will apply. *However, if both of them die then obviously, the children shall not be denied the benefits of reservation, i.e. the rule of exclusion will not apply to them.* It may be noted if permanent incapacitation occurs which results in putting an officer out of service, then it shall be treated as equivalent to death so far as the application of rule of exclusion to the offspring is concerned. *Hereafter, wherever death has been mentioned it shall include permanent incapacitation as stated above.*

If before the unfortunate event of death or permanent incapacitation of either of or both such spouses occurs, either of the spouses has had the benefit of employment in any international organisation like the UN, IMF, World Bank, etc., for a period of at least five years then exclusion from the benefit of reservation will continued to apply to the offspring.

Provided that the rule of exclusion shall not apply on such sons and daughters :

(a) If their parents, either of whom or both of whom are class-I officers and such parent(s) dies/die or suffer permanent incapacitation.

(b) A lady belonging to OBC category has got married to a class-I officer and may herself like to apply for a job. She will not be disentitled by the rule of exclusion. The reason for saying so is that originally having been a member of SEBCs. She carries with her the attributes of backwardness even after she is married to a Class-I Officer and though she may economically be in a better position, the initial attributes of social backwardness continue to linger on and will not get shaken-off during the short period which will be available to her for getting into any service employment. Therefore, we consider such a person more so because she is a lady (which in our society may be generally regarded as a weaker class) should not be denied the benefit of reservation and rule of exclusion will not apply on such a lady.

B. *Rule of Creamy Layer shall apply on the children of: GROUP B/CLASS II Officers of the Central and State Services (Direct Recruitment)*

(a) If both the spouses are Class II Officers. When only one of the spouses is a Class II Officer rule of creamy layer will not apply, but if a male officer from Class II category gets into Class I category at the age of forty or earlier, the rule of exclusion will apply to his offspring.
Provided that where both spouses are Class II Officers and one of them dies, rule of exclusion will not apply; however, if either of the spouses has had the benefit of employment in any international organisation, as indicated above, for period of not less than five years, then even in the event of death the application of the rule of exclusion will not be taken away. But if both the spouses die, the rule of exclusion will not apply to the offspring even if one of the spouses has had the benefit of employment in an international organisation like UN, IMF, World Bank, etc. for a period of not less than 5 years before their death.

(b) Where the husband is a Class I Officer (Direct Recruit or pre-forty promoted) and the wife is a Class II Officer and the husband dies, the rule of exclusion will not apply on their children. Also when the wife is a Class I Officer (i.e., Direct Recruit or pre-forty promoted) and the husband is a Class II Officer and the wife dies the rule of exclusion will not apply but if the husband dies the rule of exclusion will apply on the principle that one of the parents, namely, the mother continues to be a Class I Officer.

C. *Rule of Creamy Layer shall apply on the children of: Employees in Public Sector Undertakings, etc.*

The criteria enumerated in A & B above in this category will apply mutatis mutandis to officers holding *equivalent or comparable posts* in PSUs, Banks, Insurance Organizations, Universities, etc. and also to equivalent or comparable posts and positions under private employment. The criteria specified in category VI below will apply to the officers in these institutions.

III. Rule of Creamy Layer shall apply on the children of: Armed Forces Including Paramilitary Forces (persons holding civil posts are not included)

The exclusion rule will apply at the level of Colonel and above in the Army and to equivalent posts in the Navy and the Air Forces and the Para Military Forces.

Provided that; if the wife of an Armed Forces Officer is herself in the Armed Forces, i.e. the category under consideration the rule of exclusion will apply only when she herself has reached the rank of Colonel; the service ranks below Colonel of husband and wife shall not be clubbed together; even if the wife of an officer in the Armed Forces is in civil employment, this will not be taken into account for applying in the rule of exclusion unless she falls in the service category under item No. II.

It is noteworthy that no reservation is provided at the stage of recruitment in these services.

IV. Rule of Creamy Layer shall apply on the children of: PROFESSIONAL CLASSES AND THOSE ENGAGED IN TRADE AND INDUSTRY

(a) This will include persons not in service or employment either Government or private, but those who are engaged in profession as a Doctor, Lawyer, Charted Accountant, Income-Tax Consultant, Financial or Management Consultant, Dental

Surgeon, Engineer, Architect, Computer Specialist, Film Professional, Author, playwright, Sports person, Sports professional, Media professional or any other vocations of like status. And the persons engaged in Trade, Business and Industry. All the persons for the purpose of determining whether they fall in the disentitlement category or not, will be governed by the income/wealth criterion as noted in Item No. VI.

(b) Where the husband in a profession and the wife is in a class II or lower grade employment, the income/ wealth test will apply only on the basis of the husband's income. In other words, the wife's employment will not be taken into account. If the wife is in any profession and the husband is in employment in a class II or lower rank post, then the income/wealth criterion will apply only on the basis of the wife's income and the husband's income will not be clubbed with it. The rational is to avoid discouragement of women entering service or professions in a gender discriminatory society such as ours.

V. Rule of Creamy Layer shall apply on the children of: PROPERTY OWNERS like;

A. Regarding Agricultural Land Holdings or Property following observation were made by majority in Indra Sawhney case—[93]

"Further income from agriculture may be difficulty to assess and, therefore, in the case of agriculturists, the line may have to be drawn with reference to the extent of holding. While the income of a person can be taken as a measure of his social advancement, the limit to be prescribed should not be such as to result in taking away with one hand what is given with the other".

Keeping in mind this observation, following criteria on the basis of the extent of land holding is prescribed;

(a) If a person belongs to a family (father, mother and minor children) which owns *only irrigated land and the extent of irrigated land is equal to or more than 65% of the statutory ceiling area. Then the disentitlement will occur.*

It generally happens that a person holds different types of irrigated land. In such a situation, the different types of lands should, on the basis of the conversion formula existing, be brought into a single type of irrigated land as a common denominator and on the basis of such denominator; the above cut-off point of 65% will have to be determined.

(b) In the case of members of a family owning both irrigated and unirrigated land, the exclusion rule will apply where the pre-condition exists that the irrigated area is 40% or more of the statutory ceiling limit for irrigated land. If this precondition of not less than 40% exists, then only the area of unirrigated land will be taken into account. This will be done by converting the unirrigated land on the basis of the conversion formula existing into the irrigated type land. This irrigated type land shall be added to the actual area of irrigated land and if after such clubbing together the total area in terms of irrigated land is 65% or more of the statutory ceiling limit for irrigated land, than the rule of exclusion will apply and disentitled will occur.

(c) The rule of exclusion will not apply if the land holding of a family is exclusively unirrigated.

(d) It is noteworthy that in various States there is no Ceiling Law at all. Under these circumstances the exclusion rule on the basis of land holding will not be applicable there.

B. Regarding PLANTATIONS like coffee, tea, rubber, etc. which are not agricultural holdings, will come under this category. On this category the income/wealth test under Item No. VI will apply. While mango, citrus, apple plantations, etc. are as regarded as agricultural holdings, will be covered by the criterion 'A' above.

VI. Income/Wealth Test

The Committee approved the views of *Pandian and Sawant*,[94] *JJ* it has been clearly emphasized that when a person is placing in the excluded category, it should be unmistakably evident that social backwardness has come to an end. Therefore unless there is social advancement to such a degree as to bring a member of the SEBCs more or less at par with the members of the forward classes, he should not be denied the benefit of reservation. In this connection the following passage of the majority judgement may be usefully quoted:

> "The basis of exclusion should not merely be economic, unless of course the economic advancement is so high that it necessarily means social advancement".[95]

Therefore it is cleared that—

(a) Persons having gross annual income of Rs. 4.5 lakh[96] or above or possessing the wealth above the exemption limit as prescribed in the Wealth Tax Act will be excluded from the benefit of reservation. Only when such level of income or 'wealth' has a consistency for a reasonable period, will it be justified to regard a person as socially advanced on the basis of income. This committee considered a period of three consecutive years to be reasonable period for the purpose of the application of the criteria under consideration.

This income/wealth test also governs categories IV, VB and VC. While for remaining categories, namely, I, II, III and VA specific criteria have been laid down: however, if in these categories, any person, who is entitled to the benefit of reservation, has income from other sources or wealth, which will bring him within the criterion under item no. VI, than he shall be disentitled to reservation, in case his income or his wealth is in excess of cut-off point prescribed under the income/wealth criteria.

(b) Income criterion will stand modified with change in the value of the rupee. The modification exercise may be undertaken every three years but if the situation so demands the interregnum may be less.

(c) This committee excluded certain occupations from the application of 'creamy layer' formula which have been adopted on hereditary basis like pötter, washerman and barber.

(d) Where certificate is required not only of caste but that the candidates is or is not affected by any of the criteria of exclusion, this Committee recommend that Government may make smooth and satisfactory arrangement for the issue of such certificates without delay and without any difficulty.

It suggested for an appropriate single window system needs to be created at State/District level and necessary guidelines to be issued to see that correct certificates are issued promptly, and without harassment to the applicants.

(e) In order to prevent false certifications and to ensure that certificates of caste as well as exclusion/non-exclusion criteria shall be factually correct, innovative arrangement such as transparency through steps like publication in the village/mohalla/Panchayat Raj/offices, etc. may be considered.

The committee also arrived at conclusion that the exclusion of any member of the socially and educationally backward classes should be exception. Before exclusion it should be ascertained that the root of the ill-effect of backwardness has been eradicated and there is no sign of it. The nature of such an exercise itself makes the rule of caution and of erring on the right side inherent. Office Memorandum dated 13th August 1990[97] and 25th September 1991[98] after the judgment of Supreme Court in the *Indra Sawhney case* and the recommendation of the Expert Committee, was modified by inserting rule of creamy rule. The Government of India issued new O.M. on 8.9.93.[99]

APPROACH OF VARIOUS STATE GOVERNMENTS TO APPLY CREAMY LAYER FORMULA

To implement the creamy layer formula in reservation policy most of all the state governments come foreword with clean hands or intention except some states e.g. Bihar, Uttar Pradesh, Kerala, etc., it clears from their political decisions in the form of various ordinance/Act as listed below—

Approach of Bihar Government

The Government of Bihar state promulgated ordinance called *"the Bihar Reservation of Vacancies in Posts and Services (for Scheduled Castes, Scheduled Tribes and Other Backward Classes) (Amendment) Ordinance, 1995* to amend the section 4 of Bihar Act 3 of 1992 and to add after the second proviso, the following proviso:

> *"Provided also that reservation under clause (d) shall not apply to the category of Backward Class specified in Scheduled III".*[100]

Approach of Uttar Pradesh Government

The legislature of Uttar Pradesh Government enacted an Act on 1994 to oust the creamy layer among backward class in the state from the benefit of reservation. However, this Act followed the mandate of Central Government directions but also added some additional provisions. The categories sought to be excluded from the backward classes (creamy layer) are mentioned in *Schedule II* read with *section 3(b) of the Uttar Pradesh Public Services Reservation of Scheduled Castes and Scheduled Tribes and Other Backward Classes Act, 1994.*[101]

A comparative evaluation of the identification of 'creamy layer' among OBCs by the States Government of Bihar and U.P. reveals that they had *put some additional conditions for exclusion* of creamy layer inconsistent with the guidelines given in *Mandal case.*[102] The additional requirements put by the State were that such person should draw a salary more than Rs. 10,000 or more per mensum, the wife and husband be graduates and one of them owing house in urban area. In case of *professionals* as income of Rs. 10 lakh per mensum was fixed as criterion. It further provided that the wife or husband is at least graduates and the family owns immovable property of the value of at least Rupees 20 lakhs.

Similarly, the criteria regarding *traders, industrialists, agriculturists and others* was very high e.g. for industrialist it was required that they might have invested Rs. 10 crores for at least 5 years and spouse was at least graduate, for agriculturalists, an income of Rs. 10 lakhs in year from sources other than agriculture and graduation of spouse was essential, for any other person to mention the above categories, the income from all sources required for continuously 3 years was fixed at not less than Rs. 10 lakhs, graduation of spouse and immovable property worth Rs. 20 lakhs.

These additional provisions were not consistent with the Mandal Commission and Central Act. Although, U.P. government's scheme of identification of creamy layer was quashed by the SC in *Ashok Kumar case*[103] and directed to the State to lay down fresh criteria for the subsequent years in accordance with law. *Although a fresh G.O. has been issued to increase the limit for the exclusion of creamy layer, i.e. if income of a person from salary is more than 3 lakh per annum their offspring shall come under Creamy layer.*

Approach of Kerala Government

The State of Kerala has shown reluctance or unwillingness to adopt the creamy layer formula to oust a section of OBCs from reservation ambit. Because Kerala Government had express its stand to continue the existing system of reservation in Government jobs irrespective of whether or not 'creamy' sections of backward communities have been concerning most of the benefits to the determent of their own downtrodden men. Accordingly, *Backward Class (Reservation of Appointment or Posts in Services under the State), Act, 1995*[104] has been enacted for providing the continuance of the reservation system of 1958 in the State and gave retrospective effect also. At the time of introducing the Bill Kerala Law Minister K.M. Mani said that in piloting the Bill, *"it might be true there is a Creamy Layer among the Backward Class in other States. In Kerala, it is not true."* While CPI(M) hold the view that creamy layer formula should be implemented with sufficient modifications that if there are not enough candidates among the poor in the backward communities, rich in those communities should be allowed to take benefits. But in no circumstances should the benefits meant for the backward classes be transferred to the forward classes-rich poor.

The Central Government which has been committed to the introduction of the creamy layer norm at the National level has been opposing such a move in Kerala. The Supreme Court also, on 11.09.1995[105] expressed its displeasure over the delay in implementation of Mandal verdict's formula by the Kerala Government and moved to start contempt proceeding against the Chief Secretary of the State for non-implementation of creamy layer formula. And accordingly Act held void and unconstitutional. Again in *Nair Service Society* v. *Union of India* case,[106] Supreme Court set aside the recommendation of Narendran Commission as inconsistent with Central Government's guidelines.

Regarding the criteria to determine the creamy layer amongst OBCs O.M. of 8th September, 1993[107] created a lot of bewilderment or confusions. To clarify the confusions Government of India issued, another O.M. on 14th October, 2004[108] to follow by all the States/Union Territories.

In regard to the children of the persons in civil services of the Central and the State Governments, it provides that *such son(s) and daughter(s) shall be treated as falling in creamy layer if their:*

1. (a) parents, both of whom are directly recruited Class-I/Group A officers;
   (b) parents, either of whom is a directly recruited Class 1/Group A officer;
   (c) parents, both of whom are directly recruited Class I/Group A officers, but one of them dies or suffers permanent incapacitation;

(d) parents, either of whom is a directly recruited Class I/Group A officer and such parent dies or suffers permanent incapacitation and before such death or such incapacitation has had the benefit of employment in any International Organisation like UN, IMF, World Bank, etc. for a period of not less than 5 years;

(e) parents, both of whom are directly recruited Class 1/Group A officers and both of them die or suffer permanent incapacitation and before such death or such incapacitation of the both, either of them has had the benefit of employment in any International Organisation like, IMF, World Bank, etc. for a period of not less than 5 years;

(f) parents, both of whom are directly recruited Class II/Group B officers;

(g) parents of whom only the husband is a directly recruited Class II/Group B officer and he gets into Class 1/Group A at the age of 40 or earlier;

(h) parents, both of whom are directly recruited Class II/Group B office and one of them dies or suffers permanent incapacitation and either of them has had the benefit of employment in any International Organisation like UN, IMF, World Bank, etc. for a period of not less than 5 years;

(i) parents of whom the husband is a Class I/Group A officer (direct recruit or pre-forty promoted) and the wife is a directly recruited Class II/Group B officer and the wife dies; or suffers permanent incapacitation; and

(j) parents of whom wife is a Class I/Group A officer (Direct Recruit or pre-forty promoted) and the husband is a directly recruited Class II/Group B officer and the husband dies or suffers permanent incapacitation.

2. The Schedule further provides that *sons and daughters*

of such parents shall not be treated to be falling in creamy layer if their:

(i) parents, either of whom or both of whom are directly recruited Class I/Group A officer(s) and such parent(s) dies/die or suffers/suffer permanent incapacitation;

(ii) parents both of whom are directly recruited Class II/Group B officers and one of them dies or suffers permanent incapacitation;

(iii) parents, both of whom are directly recruited Class II/Group B officers and both of them die or suffer permanent incapacitation, even though either of them has had the benefit of employment in any International Organisation like UN, IMF, World Bank, etc. for a period of not less than 5 years before their death or permanent incapacitation.

3. It is cleared that the criteria prescribed for determining creamy layer status shall apply to the son and daughters of persons holding equivalent posts in PSUs, Bank, Insurance Organizations, Universities, etc. and also holding equivalent posts and positions under private employment. The creamy layer status of the sons and daughters of employees of organizations shall determine on the basis of 'Income/Wealth Test' where assessment of the posts on equivalent basis has not been made. The Income/Wealth Test prescribes that those persons would be treated to fall in creamy layer if their gross annual income is Rs. 4.5[109] lakh or above or possess wealth above the exemption limit (under the Wealth Tax Act) for a period of three consecutive years. But it is provided that 'income from salaries or agricultural land shall not be clubbed.'

4. *During the implementation of the scheme of determination of creamy layer following questions have been raised from time to time* as follows :

(i) Will the sons and daughters of parents either of whom or both of whom are directly recruited Class I/Group A officer(s) and such parent(s) dies/die or suffers/suffer permanent incapacitation after retirement be treated to be excluded from the creamy layer?

(ii) Will the sons and daughters of parents both of whom are directly recruited Class II/Group B officers and one of them dies or suffer permanent incapacitation after retirement be treated to be excluded from the creamy layer?

(iii) Will the sons and daughters of parents both of whom are directly recruited Class II/Group B officers and both of them die or suffer permanent incapacitation after retirement even though either of them has had got the benefit of employment in any International Organisation like UN, IMF, World Bank, etc. for a period of not less than 5 years before their death or permanent incapacitation be treated to be excluded from the purview of creamy layer?

It is clarified with reference to clauses (i), (ii) and (iii) that, the sons and daughters of:

(a) such parents either of whom or both of whom are directly recruited Class I/Group A officers and such parent(s) dies/die or suffers/suffer permanent incapacitation while in service

(b) such parents both of whom are directly recruited Class Il/Group B officers and one of them dies or suffers permanent incapacitation while in service; and

(c) such parents both of whom are directly recruited Class Il/Group B officers and both of them die or suffer permanent incapacitation *while in service*, even though either of them has had the benefit of employment in any International Organization like, IMP, World Bank, etc. for a period of not less than 5 years before their death or permanent incapacitation, *are not treated to be falling in creamy layer.* But if the Parent(s) dies/die or suffers/suffer permanent incapacitation in such cases *after retirement from service,* his/their sons and daughters *would be treated to be falling in creamy layer and would not get the benefit of reservation*

(iv) It is also doubts that will the sons and daughters of parent(s) who retire from the service on the basis of which their sons and daughters fall in creamy layer, continue to fall in creamy layer after retirement of the parent(s)?

It is clarified that sons and daughters of parents who are included in the creamy layer on the basis of service status of their parents shall continue to be treated in creamy layer even if their parents have retired or have died after retirement

When it is asked that,

(v) 'Will the sons and daughters of parents of whom husband is directly recruited as Class III/Group C or Class IV/Group D employee and he gets into Class I/Group A at the age of 40 or earlier be treated to be falling in creamy layer'?

It is answered if the sons and daughters of parents of whom only the husband is a directly recruited Class II/Group B officer who gets into Class I/Group A at the age of 40 or earlier are treated to be falling in creamy layer. But if the father is directly recruited Class III/Group C or Class IV/Group D employee and he gets into Class I/Group A at the age of 40 or earlier, his sons and daughters shall not be treated to be falling in creamy layer.

With reference to question no. (vi), (vii) and (viii) i.e.;

(vi) Will a candidate who himself is a directly recruited Class I/Group A officer or a directly recruited Class II/Group B officer who got into

Class I/Group A at the age of 40 or earlier be treated to be falling in creamy layer on the basis of his service status?

(vii) Will a candidate who himself has gross annual income of Rs. 2.5 lakh or above or possesses wealth above the exemption limit as prescribed in the Wealth Tax Act for a period of three consecutive years be treated to fall in creamy layer?

(viii) The instructions provide that a lady belonging to OBC category has got married to a directly recruited Class I/Group A officer shall not be treated as falling in creamy layer on the basis of her marriage.

Will a man belonging to OBC category, married to a directly recruited Class I/Group A officer be treated as falling in creamy layer on the basis of his marriage?

It is clarified that the creamy layer status of a candidate is determined on the basis of the status of his parents and not on the basis of his own status or income or on the basis of status or income of his/her spouse. Therefore, while determining the creamy layer status of a person the status or the income of the candidate himself or of his/her spouse shall not be taken into account.

Regarding question no. (ix) How will the Income/Wealth Test be apply in case of sons and daughters of parent(s) employed in PSUs, etc. in which equivalent or comparability of posts has not been established *vis-a-vis* posts in the Government?

It is clarified that the creamy layer status of sons and daughters of persons employed in organizations where equivalence of posts *vis-a-vis* posts in Government has not been evaluated, is determined as follows:

Income of the parents from the salaries and from the other sources (other than salaries and agricultural land) is determined separately. If either the income of the parents from the salaries or the income of the parents from other sources

Income of the parents from the salaries and from the other sources (other than salaries and agricultural land) is determined

separately. If either the income of the parents from the salaries and or the income of the parents from the other sources (other than salaries and agricultural land) exceeds the limit of Rs. 4.5 lakh[110] per annum for a period of three years, the sons and daughters of such persons shall be treated to be fall in creamy layer. But the sons and daughters of parents whose income from salaries is less than Rs. 4.5[111] lakh per annum and income from other sources is also less than Rs. 4.5[112] lakh per annum will not be treated as falling in creamy layer even if the sum of the income from salaries and the income from the other sources is more than Rs. 4.5[113] lakh per annum for a period of three consecutive years. It nay be noted that income from agricultural land is not taken into account while applying the Test.

With regard to quarry (x) of para 4, i.e. (x) what is the scope of the explanation 'Income from Salaries or agricultural land shall not be clubbed', given below the Income/Wealth Test?

It is clarified that while applying the Income/Wealth Test to determine creamy layer status of any candidate as given in category-VI of the Schedule to the O.M. income from the salaries and income from the agricultural land shall not be taken into account. It means that if income from salaries of the parents of any candidate is more than Rs. 4.5[114] lakh per annum, income from agricultural land is more than Rs. 4.5[115] lakh per annum; but income from other sources is less than Rs. 4.5[116] lakh per annum, the candidate shall not be treated to be falling in creamy layer on the basis of Income/Wealth Test provided his parent(s) do not possess wealth above the exemption limit as prescribed in the Wealth Tax Act for a period of three consecutive years.

In 2006 parliament has enacted an Act[117] to provide reservation in central educational institutions in favour of OBCs with the inclusion of excluding creamy layer. It was challenged in *Ashok Kumar Thakur* v. *Union of India*[118] in this case Supreme Court upheld that reservation could be applied only with the exclusion of creamy layer.

Above description shows, that governments are not in much enthusiastic to apply creamy layer rulé sincerely and honesty. In the Rajya Sabha on March 16 2004, Prime Minister Atal Behari Vajpayee, Prime Minister conceded that there has been delay in constituting the review committee[119] while the last committee was constituted in 1993. He assured that the Government will soon constitute a review committee to determine the criteria for the creamy layer concept with regard to eligibility for reservations. After Mandal Verdict during last 12 year (i.e. 1993 to till day 2010) only two revision (in 2004, 2008) has been made. By which income limit has been increased up to 4.5 lakh for the exclusion of creamy layer.

In the state of U.P. there is no periodical revision of creamy layer formula or reservation scheme. Nobody bother to check and verify creamy layer certificates. Attitude of political parties is to ignoring implementation of creamy layer because they do not want to loose their vote bank of OBCs. As we know that Mulayam Singh government for the lust of vote bank, convert 16 other backward castes into Scheduled Caste and Scheduled Tribe. Although this order is challenged in Allahabad Court and court stayed its implementation.

At last I could be said that scheme of creamy layer is good but implementation is very poor in almost all the states as well as in central. Nobody came to deal with this scheme with clean hand.

Notes and References

1. K.C. Sunny, Creamy Layer Principle: Its social Relevance and Legal Consequences, ALR 1999, Vols. 23:1 and 2, p. 135.
2. Art. 16(4), Nothing in this article shall prevent the state from making any provision for the reservation of appointment or post of any backward class of citizens which, in the opinion of the State, is not adequately represented in the services under the State.
3. AIR 1993 SC 477.
4. Indra Sawhney *v.* Union of India, AIR 1993 SC 477. Supreme Court tries to define "creamy layer" by quoting an office memorandum of September 8, 1993.
5. N. Sattanathan was chairman of the first Tamil Nadu Backward Classes Commission constituted in 1969 in the regime of DMK Government under M. Karunanidhi. One of it's recommendation was an income limit to prevent the accumulation of reservation benefits by an "upper crust". Although it was first accepted then withdrawn.
6. The income ceiling for creamy layer rose from 2.5 lakh to 4.5 lakh in October 2008 by O.M. of 10 October 2008.

7. Indra Sawhney *v.* Union of India, AIR 1993 SC 477.
8. 1979, 3 SCC 730.
9. AIR 1976 SC 490.
10. Mandal Case, Para 792.
11. (2006) 8 SCC 212.
12. (2008) 6 SCC 1.
13. First Chief Justice of India belongs to Scheduled Caste.
14. K.C. Yadav, Flaws in the Creamy Layer Concept, *The Times of India,* 7 October 1993, p. 10.
15. *The Times of India,* March 12, 1993, p. 3.
16. AIR 1985 SC 1495.
17. Mandal Case, p. 428 (Para 792).
18. *Ibid.*, p. 429.
19. Mandal Case, p. 257 (Para 520).
20. *Ibid.*
21. *Ibid.*
22. *Ibid.*, p. 159 (Para 295).
23. *Ibid.*, p. 196.
24. *Ibid.* at Para 611.
25. *Ibid.*, p. 128.
26. *Ibid.* at p. 586, Para 121(3)(d).
27. *Ibid.* at Para 86, 121(3)(d), 450, 451.
28. *Ibid.* at Paras 700, 694.
29. *Ibid.* at Para 662.
30. *Ibid.* at Paras 351, 358.
31. *Ibid.* at Para 121(3)(d), 450, 451, 366.
32. Annexure enclosed.
33. AIR, 1996 SC 75, p. 421.
34. Mandal case, Paras 385, 386.
35. AIR, 1996 SC 75, p. 421
36. AIR 1993 SC 477.
37. AIR, 1996 SC 75, at Para 5.
38. *Ibid.*
39. *Ibid.*
40. *Ibid.* at pp. 77, 78-82.
41. *Ibid.* at Para 7.
42. *Ibid.* at Para 8
43. *Ibid.* at Para 9.
44. *Ibid.* at Paras 10-11.
45. AIR 2000, SC, 498.
46. AIR 1993 SC 477.

47. *Ibid.* at Para 8.
48. AIR 1993 SC 477.
49. AIR 1992 SCC 174.
50. AIR 2000 SC p. 505, Para 10.
51. *Ibid.* at Paras 22-23.
52. 1992 AIR SCW 3682: AIR 1993 SC 477: 1993 Lab IC 129) and in Ashok Kumar Thakur (1995 5 SCC 403:1995 AIR SCW3731.
53. *Ibid.* at Para 25.
54. *Ibid.* at Para 27.
55. AIR 1996 SC 75, p. 421, AIR 2000 SC 498.
56. *Ibid.* at Paras 28-29.
57. Ajit Singh II *v.* State of Punjab 1999 7 SCC 209.
58. *Ibid.* at Para 45.
59. *Ibid.* at Paras 49 and 54.
60. *Ibid.* at p. 516, Paras 55, 56.
61. AIR 1996 SC 75, p. 421, AIR 2000, SC 498.
62. *Ibid.* at Paras 60-61.
63. *Ibid.* at Paras 66-67.
64. *Ibid.* at Paras 66, 67.
65. 2007 (4) SCC 1,
66. AIR 2000 SC 498
67. AIR SC 1993 477
68. 2006 (8) SCC 212.
69. *Ibid.*
70. W.P. (C). No. 1085/2003, High Court of Delhi decided on July 6, 2004 on subject of Reservation for OBC: Creamy Layer.
71. Petitioner appeared and qualified for the Central Civil Service Examination 2002, Petitioner being a 'Jat' by caste and a resident of Rajasthan had applied for issuance of the Other Backward Class Certificate (OBC) Category. This certificate had been denied. Petitioner qualified even in the general category with a rank of 127. Petitioner's case is that he is entitled to the OBC Certificate and upon the same being granted, his ranking would go up and he would get a better posting.
72. See Annexure A.
73. See Annexure B.
74. See Annexure C.
75. Notification dated 28.9.1993.
76. As notified vide Social Welfare Department Notification No.F.11 (125) R&P/SWD/46631, dated 27th August, 1993, published in Rajasthan Gazette, Extra-ordinary dated Ist September, 1993.
77. No. F.9(8) DOP/A-V/90 dated 28.9.1993.

78. Circular dated 2.2.2001.
79. (2008) 6 SCC 1.
80. *Ibid.*, (Balakrishnan, C.J. Paras 165 and 168).
81. *Ibid.*, (Balakrishnan, C.J. Paras 170, 171, 176, 226 and 234).
82. *Ibid.*, (Balakrishnan, C.J. Paras 170 and 171).
83. Shortnote Q. of (2008) 6 SCC 1, Ashok Kumar Thakur *v.* Union of India.
84. AIR 1985 SC 1495.
85. *Ibid.* at p. 1506 (Para 28).
86. *Ibid.* at p. 1507 (Para 31).
87. AIR 1985 SC 1495 at p. 1525 (Para 72).
88. AIR 1993 SC 477.
89. *Ibid.*
90. Ram Nandan Committee 22 February 1993, OM 12011/16/93-BCC(C), Govt. of India, Ministry of Welfare, N. Delhi.
91. See Appendix 8.
92. Report of Ram Nandan Committee 1993 at pp. 3-9.
93. AIR 1993 SC 477.
94. *Ibid.*
95. *Ibid.* at Para 809.
96. Initially it was 1 lakh, than in 2005 it was raised from 1 lakh to 205 lakh than in Oct. 2008 it is raised to 405 Lakh.
97. See Appendix 2.
98. See Appendix 3.
99. See appendix Notification No. 12011/10/93-BCC (c), Government of India, ministry of Welfare, New Delhi dated 22 Feb. 1993.
100. Scheduled III : 1. The son or daughter of the president of India, the Vice-President of India, the Chief Justice and Judges of the Supreme Court of India, the Chief Justice and Judges of the High Courts, the chairman and Members of the Union Public Service Commission and Chief Election Commissioner; 2. The Son or daughter of such officers who has been directly recruited in class I services of the Government or an undertaking or an institution fully or partially financed by them; and (a) whose income from salary is rupees ten thousand or more per mensum, and (b) whose wife or husband, as the case may be, is at least a graduate, and (c) who or his wife or her husband, as the case may be, owns a house in an urban area, and (d) whose mother or father has also been directly recruited to class I services. 3. The son or daughter of such person engaged as doctor, advocate, chartered accountant, tax consultant, financial consultant, management, architect or other professionals, and (a) whose average income from all sources for three consecutive financial years is not less than rupees ten lakh per annum; and (b) whose wife or husband, as the case may be, is at least a

graduate; and (c) whose family owns immovable property at least of rupees twenty lakhs. 4. The sons or daughter of such person engaged in trade or commerce, and (a) whose average income from all sources for three consecutive financial years is not less than rupees ten lakh per annum; and (b) whose wife or husband, as the case may be, is at least a graduate; and (c) whose family owns immovable property at least of rupees twenty lakhs. 5. The son or daughter of such industrialist—(a) whose level of investment in running or units is more than rupees ten crores, and (b) such unit or units are engaged in commercial production for at least five years; and (c) his wife or husband, as the case may be, is at least a graduate. 6. The son or daughter of such agricultural landholder—(a) whose average income from all sources other than agriculture for three consecutive financial years is not less than ten lakhs per annum; and (b) whose wife or husband, as the case may be, is at least a graduate; and (c) who or his wife or her husband, as the case may be, owns house at least of rupees twenty lakh in an urban area. 7. The son or daughter of person, other than the persons specified in serial Nos. 1 to 6 of this scheduled—(a) whose main source of income is other than animal husbandry, fisheries, poultry, weaving, craftsmanship, handicraft and artisanship; and (b) whose average income from all sources for three consecutive financial years is not less than ten lakhs per annum; and (c) whose wife or husband, as the case may be, is at least a graduate; and (d) whose family owns immovable property at least of rupees twenty lakhs. 8. If a person included in serial Nos. 1 to 7 of this scheduled performs inter-castes marriage with a backward class person other than serial nos. 1 to 7 of this scheduled, his/her son or daughter shall not be excluded.

101. Schedule II, Section 3(b) 1. Sons and daughters of—(a) IAS, IFS, IPS, Indian Forest services & other general services (direct or promotee) officers; (b) U.P. civil services, U.P. Police service, State Service. (Direct recruit) officers; (c) Group A/Class I Officers of any Department or Ministry of Government of India or educational research or other institutions (no. 1 included in above (a); (d) Group A/Class I Officers of any Department or Institution of State Government (No. 1 included in (b) above); (e) Officer of defence forces or Para military forces not below the rank of colonel or equivalent—*shall fall under creamy layer if,* (i) Income from salary of such member of services is Rs. 10,000 or above per mensum; (ii) Spouse is at least graduates; (iii) He or his spouse owns a house in urban area. 2. Sons and daughters of—Persons engaged in profession as a doctor, surgeon, engineer, lawyer, architect, chartered accountant, media and information professional, management and other consultant, film artist and other film professional, running educational institution or coaching institute or engaged in the business as a share broker or in entertainment

business—*shall be treated under Creamy layer if,* (i) His average income from all sources should not be less than Rs. 10 lakh per year for 3 consecutive financial years; (ii) Spouse is at least graduates; (iii) His family property (immovable) should be worth Rs. 20 lakhs. 3. Sons and daughters of—businessman; and 4. Sons and daughters of—industrialist; *shall be treated as Creamy layer if,* (i) Whose level of investment in running units is over Rs. 10 crores and such units are engaged in production for at least 5 years; (ii) Spouse is at least graduates. 5. Sons and daughter of—a person whose holding is within limit fixed under the U.P. imposition of ceiling and Land Holding Act, 1960; and 6. Sons and daughters of—any other person not mentioned in aforementioned categories-come *under Creamy Layer if,* (i) whose income from all sources for 3 consecutive financial years is not less than Rs. 10 lakh per annum; (ii) Spouse is at least graduates; (iii) His family property (immovable) should be worth Rs. 20 lakhs.

102. AIR 1993 SC 477.
103. AIR 1996 SC 75.
104. Krishna Kumar, creamy prospects, *Frontline,* Oct. 6, 1995.
105. II Indra Sawhney Case, AIR 2000 SC 477.
106. 2007 (4) SCC 1, The Judgment was delivered by hon'ble Justice S.B. Sinha.
107. O.M. No. 36012/22/93-SCT.
108. See Appendix—O.M. No. 36033/5/2004-Estt. (Res), Government of India, Ministry of Personnel, Public Grievances & Pensions, Department of Personnel and Training, 14 Oct. 2004.
109. Raised from 205 lakh to 4.5 in Oct. 2008.
110. *Ibid.*
111. *Ibid.*
112. *Ibid.*
113. *Ibid.*
114. *Ibid.*
115. *Ibid.*
116. *Ibid.*
117. The Central Education Institutions (Reservation in Admission) Act, 2006.
118. (2008) 8 SCC1.
119. In Mandal verdict it is directed to central as well as state government to review its scheme of creamy layer after every three year.

APPENDIX A

NOTIFICATION DATED 8.9.1993

Subject: Reservation for Other Backward Classes in Civil Posts and Services under the Government of India—Regarding:

1. The undersigned is directed to refer to this Department's O.M. No. 36012/31/90. Estt. (SCT), dated the 13th August, 1990 and 25th September, 1991 regarding reservation for Socially and Educationally Backward Classes in Civil Posts and Services under the Government of India and to say that following the Supreme Court judgment in the *Indira Sawhney and others* v. *Union of India and others case* the Government of India appointed an Expert Committee to recommend the criteria for exclusion of the socially advanced persons/sections from the benefits of reservations for Other Backward Classes in Civil posts and services under the Government of India.
2. Consequent to the consideration of the Expert Committee's recommendations, this Department's Office memorandum No. 36012/31/90, Estt. (SCT) dated 13.8.90 referred to in Para (1) above is hereby modified to provide as follows:
   (a) 27% (twenty seven per cent) of the vacancies in civil posts and services under the Government of India, to be filled through recruitment, shall be reserved for the other Backward Classes. Detailed instructions relating to the procedure to be followed for enforcing reservation will be issued separately.
   (b) Candidates belonging to OBCs recruited on the basis of merit in an open competition on the same standards prescribed for the general candidates shall not be adjusted against the reservation quota of 27%.

(c) (i) The aforesaid reservation shall not apply to persons/sections mentioned in column 3 of the Schedule to this office memorandum.

Column 3 of the Schedule—"II Service Category"

A. Group A/Class I officers of the All India Central and State Services (Direct Recruits):

Rule of exclusion will apply on those son(s) and daughter(s) of:

(a) Parents, both of whom are Class I officers;
(b) Parents, either of whom is a Class I officer;
(c) Parents, both of whom are Class I Officers, but one of them dies or suffers permanent incapacitation;
(d) Parents, either of whom is a Class I officer and such parent dies or suffers permanent incapacitation and before such death or such incapacitation has had the benefit of employment in any International Organisation like UN, IMF, World Bank, etc., for a period of not less than 5 years;
(e) Parents, both of whom are Class-I officers die or suffer permanent incapacitation and before such death or such incapacitation of the both, either of them has had the benefit of employment in any International Organisation like UN, IMF, World Bank, etc., for a period of not less than 5 years.

Provided that the rule of exclusion shall not apply in the following cases:

(a) Sons and daughters of parents either of whom or both of whom are Class-I Officers and such parent(s) dies/die or suffer permanent incapacitation.
(b) A lady belonging to OBC Category has got married to a Class-I officer, and may herself like to apply for a job.

APPENDIX—B

NOTIFICATION OF RAJASTHAN GOVERNOR DATED 28.9.1993

The Governor is hereby pleased to order that 21% (Twenty-one per cent) of the vacancies in posts and services under the State Government, to be filled through direct recruitment; shall be reserved for the castes and classes included in the list of Backward Classes as notified vide Social Welfare Department Notification No. F.11 (125) R&P/SWD/ 46631, dated 27th August, 1993, published in Rajasthan Gazette, Extra-ordinary dated Ist September, 1993.

These reservations will be subject to the following conditions:

(a) Candidates belonging to Backward Classes recruited on the basis of merit in an open competition on the same standards prescribed for the general candidates shall not be adjusted against the reservation quota of 21%. Detailed instructions relating to the procedure to be followed for enforcing reservation will be issued separately.

(b) (i) The aforesaid reservation shall not apply to persons/sections mentioned in Column 3 of the schedule annexed to this notification.

(ii) The rule of exclusion will not apply to persons working as artisans or engaged in hereditary occupations and callings. A list of such occupations and callings will be issued separately.

"II Service Category"

A. Group A/Class I officers of the All India Central and State Services (Direct Recruits).

Son(s) and daughter(s) of: (a) Parents, both of whom are Class I officers; (b) Parents, either of whom is a Class I officer; (c) Parents, both of whom are Class I

Officers, but one of them dies or suffers permanent incapacitation;

(d) Parents, either of whom is a Class I officer and such parent dies or suffers permanent incapacitation and before such death or such incapacitation has had the benefit of employment in any International Organisation like UN, IMF, World Bank, etc., for a period of not less than 5 years;

(e) Parents, both of whom are class I officers die or suffer permanent incapacitation and before such death or such incapacitation of the both, either of them has had the benefit of employment in any International Organisation like UN, IMF, World Bank, etc., for a period of not less than 5 years.

Provided that the rule of exclusion shall not apply in the following cases:

(a) Sons and daughters of parents either of whom or both of whom are Class-I Officers and such parent(s) dies/die or suffer permanent incapacitation.

(b) A lady belonging to OBC Category has got married to a Class-I officer, and may herself like to apply for a job.

6

Effect of Backward Class Reservation

Indian Constitution is too extensive about prefential treatment to the down-trodden, underprivileged and depressed classes. These provisions manifest a national urge to bring revolution by wiping out the caste prejudice from the Indian soil. The backward classes in India were totally educationally and socially depressed, economically dependent, politically marginalized and culturally deprived and starved.

Founding fathers of Indian Constitution duly recognized this tragic situation of the backward communities and therefore incorporate the principle of *'preferential treatment'* in the form of the reservation policy. The two important components of reservation; i.e. reservation in government appointments and in education are conceived *as long-term measures*[1] while reservation in parliament and state assembly are conceived *as short-term measure*. Thus the function of reservation policy is to mitigate the centuries old all-pervasive injustices inflicted upon the backward communities and to enable them to contribute in the process of development and social change or to minimize the social and economic disparities between the disadvantaged groups' vis-à-vis upper classes and to build an egalitarian social order. Since acceptance of the reservation policy is equivalent to accept the fact that the benefits of the economic growth would not automatically 'trickle-down' to the weaker sections of the society and still less to the socio-educationally disadvantaged groups. This made positive discrimination in their favour by the State as historical necessity. These provisions therefore, aim at improving their socio-economic conditions and integrating them with mainstream.

Effect of reservation provisions could be considered under the various heads, i.e. *review of the reservation policy as a whole; Implementation of the policy; dedication of the officers; Punishment to erring officials.*

Reservation to SCs, STs and OBCs, in case of direct recruitment, is available in all groups of posts. When direct recruitment is made on all India basis by open competition, reservation for SCs, STs and OBCs is respectively 15, 7.5 and 27 per cent; and when direct recruitment is made on all India basis otherwise than by open competition it is 16.66, 7.5 and 25.84 per cent respectively. In case of direct recruitment to Groups 'C' and 'D' posts normally attracting candidates from a locality or a region, percentage of reservation for SCs and STs is generally fixed in proportion to the population of SCs and STs in the respective States/UTs and reservation for OBCs in such cases is so fixed that it is not more than 27 per cent and total reservation for SCs, STs and OBCs does not exceed the limit of 50 per cent.[2]

Reservation in promotion by non-selection method is available to SCs and STs in all groups of services at the rate of 15 per cent and 7.5 per cent respectively. In case of promotion by selection method, SCs and STs get the benefit of reservation upto the lowest rung of Group 'A' and quantum of reservation for them in such case is the same as in the case of promotion by non-selection. In case of promotion, there is no provision of reservation for OBCs.[3]

Various relaxations and concessions are given to SC and ST candidates so as to improve their representation in Services. For example they get relaxation in the upper age limit, unlimited number of chances within the relaxed age limit prescribed for appearing in the competitive examinations, exemption from payment of examination fee and relaxation in standards of suitability. Likewise, the OBC candidates get concessions like relaxation in the upper age limit upto three years, relaxation in number of chances upto seven within the relaxed age limit for appearing in the Civil Services Examination, etc. The SC/ST/OBC candidates appointed on their own merit are adjusted against unreserved vacancies. To ensure that posts reserved for SCs, STs and OBCs are filled by candidates belonging to these categories of persons only, there is a ban on de-reservation of vacancies in case of direct recruitment.[4]

Over the period reservation has helped in increasing the representation of SCs and STs in Services of the Government of India. As per available information they were only 13.17 and 2.25 per cent respectively in services as on January 1, 1965 while their representation has increased to 16.75 and 6.75 per cent as on January 1, 2006[5]. Representation of OBCs in services is still quite low because reservation for them started only in 1993. It is important to note that the information about OBCs does not appear to include such members of Other Backward Communities who were appointed prior to introduction of reservation for them or who fall within the creamy layer. It is expected that as a result of introduction of reservation, their representation in services would increase in due course of time. Representation of SCs, STs and OBCs in the Central Government Services as on January 1, 2006 is given in the statement at Table 1.[6]

Almost all the vacancies reserved for SCs, STs and OBCs in the All India Services and other Central Services to which recruitment is made through the Civil Services Examination have been filled by the candidates of respective categories in the recent years. Vacancies reserved and filled in Indian Administrative Service, Indian Foreign Service and Indian Police Service in the year of Examination 2008 are given in Table 2.[7]

Quantum of reservation for the SCs, STs and OBCs in any grade/cadre is determined on the basis of number of posts in the grade/cadre. However, in small cadres having less than 14

TABLE 1

Representation of SCs, STs and OBCs in the Central Government Services as on January 1, 2008

Group	*Total number of employees*	*SCs*	*%*	*STs*	*%*	*OBCs*	*%*
A	91881	11446	12.5	4419	4.8	5031	5.5
B	137272	20481	14.9	7900	5.8	5420	3.9
C	1810141	284925	15.7	127074	7.0	145819	8.1
D (Excluding Sweepers)	696891	134907	19.4	48133	6.9	34528	5.0
Sweepers	75901	39014	51.4	4576	6.0	2430	3.2
Total (Excluding Sweepers)	2736185	451759	16.51	187526	6.85	90798	6.97
Total (Including Sweepers)	2812086	490773	17.45	192102	6.83	193228	6.87

Note : It does not include information in respect of Six Ministries/ Departments.

Source : Annual Report (2009-10) of Ministry of Personnel, Public Grievances and Pensions, p. 64.

posts, where it is not possible to give reservation to all the three categories on the basis of this principle, reservation is provided by rotation by way of L-Shaped 14-Point rosters.[8] While determining reservation, it is ensured that total number of reserved posts for SCs, STs and OBCs in any cadre does not exceed 50 per cent of the total number of posts in the cadre. At the same time, total number of vacancies earmarked reserved in a year in any cadre should not be more than 50 per cent of the total vacancies of the year. However, the backlog reserved vacancies are treated as a separate and distinct group, on which limit of 50 per cent does not apply.[9]

In each Ministry/Department, the Deputy Secretary in-charge of administration or any other officer is appointed to act as Liaison Officer in respect of matters relating to the representation of Scheduled Castes and Scheduled Tribes in all establishments and Services under the administrative control of the Ministry/Department. He is, *inter alia*, responsible for

TABLE 2

Vacancies Earmarked Reserved and Filled in Indian Administrative Service, Indian Foreign Service and Indian Police Service on the basis of Civil Services Examination, 2008

Services	*Unreserved*		*Scheduled Castes*		*Scheduled Tribes Backward Classes*		*Other*	
	Vacancies earmarked unreserved	*Vacancies filled as unreserved*	*Vacancies earmarked reserved for SCs*	*Vacancies filled by SCs by reservation*	*Vacancies earmarked reserved for STs*	*Vacancies filled by STs by reservation*	*Vacancies earmarked reserved for OBCs*	*Vacancies filled by OBCs by reservation*
(1)	(2)	(3)	(4)	(5)	(6)	(7)	(8)	(9)
IAS	60	60	17	17	10	10	33	33
IES	13	13	4	4	1	1	8	8
IPS	65	65	20	20	9	9	36	36

Source : Annual Report (2009-10) of Ministry of Personnel, Public Grievances and Pensions, p. 65.

ensuring due compliance of the orders and instructions pertaining to the reservation of vacancies in favour of SCs and STs and other benefits admissible to them.. On March 6, 1997 orders were issued to appoint separate Liaison Officers in each Ministry/Department for looking into the matters concerning reservation for Other Backward Classes.[10]

In order to protect the interests of SC/ST/OBC communities and to ensure that the posts reserved for them are filled up only by candidates belonging to these categories, it has been decided that where sufficient number of candidates belonging to these categories are not available the vacancies would not be filled. Such vacancies are carried forward to the subsequent recruitment year as backlog reserved vacancies. Some reserved vacancies of SCs and STs in promotion are also not filled and carried forward as backlog vacancies. A Special Recruitment Drive was launched in 2004 to fill up all the backlog reserved vacancies of SCs and STs, both in direct recruitment quota and promotion quota. More than 60,000 backlog vacancies were filled up during the Drive.[11] A Special Recruitment Drive to fill up the backlog reserved vacancies of OBCs could not be launched in 2004 because there was no provision of treating their backlog reserved vacancies at that time and a limit of 50 per cent reservation was applied to such vacancies. The Government in July, 2008 took a decision to treat the backlog reserved vacancies of OBCs as a separate and distinct group on which the ceiling of 50 per cent would not apply. After this the Government has launched a fresh Special Recruitment Drive in November, 2008 to fill up the backlog reserved vacancies of SCs, STs and OBCs.[12]

Wherever a Selection Committee/Board exists or has to be constituted for making recruitment to 10 or more vacancies in Group 'C' or Group 'D' Posts/Services, it is mandatory to have one member belonging to SC/ST/OBC and in such Committees/Boards.[13]

After review the reservation policy effect of reservation, further, could be studied as—

(a) Reservation Policy and Most Backward Class,
(b) Reservation Policy and Forward Classes, and
(c) Reservation Policy and Society.

RESERVATION POLICY AND MOST BACKWARD CLASS

"Now the bid by the deprived sections is not for mere jobs or any other benefit of powers but to operate the levers of power itself."

(V.P. Singh's Lecture at Harvard)

In India since independence (1947) reservation for SC and ST is applicable in government services. Earlier 12.5% seats for SC and 5% seats for ST candidates were reserved in the all India competitive examination, this percentage was increased in 1970 up to 15% and 7.5% respectively. But for Other Backward Classes (OBCs) the Central Government had not provided any reservation in government employment or in education before 1993. Although in some States especially in South India OBCs alongwith SCs and STs were enjoying reservation facilities in government's services as well as in admission in educational institution. However, percentage of reservation was uneven state to state.

If we review reservation policy, it raises two points; upto what extent the deprived communities in general and particular had taken advantage of the legal provisions and improved their condition and what are its overall consequences carried on to the deprived communities, forward class as well as on the whole society; How did the dominant stratum of society (upper class) react to these provisions.

In the first decade, this policy couldn't be prove successful to improve the position of the backward classes substantially because in order to secure qualifying examinations for which at least eleven years of education was needed. Moreover, State Governments failed to carry on proper implement of reservations policy in government jobs. We noticed that maximum posts filled by Scheduled Castes and Scheduled Tribes are only in Class III and Class IV services while posts in Class II and I services reserved for SC and ST remained unfilled. Several reasons are found responsible for low profile of recruitment of backward class candidates e.g.: (1) large number of posts and some departments were effectively kept outside the scope of

Panchayat has been proved fruitful to Scheduled Castes/ Scheduled Tribes categories. This political safeguard, however, is not available to the candidates of OBCs.[15] Political leaders belonging to backward class secured good legislative positions. However, it is alleged that representation of these backward classes are not significantly increased in Parliament and State Assemblies; even than it can't be denied that Schedule Castes/ Tribes political leaders, whose number are assured, have been co-opted easily by the national parties. Now they also have opportunity to access the supreme political power in policy-making decision concerning advancement of their castes and communities. Without reservation in legislature it was almost impossible for a person of backward community to be elected in the given power structure.[16] There are various examples—*K.R. Narayan, Suraj Bhan, Mayavati, Maya Kumar, Ram Vilas Paswan, etc.* Due to the provision of reserved constituency they become empower politically. Government is trying to give political reservation to OBCs also in Panchayat level. It can be evident from new declaration of Mulayam Singh Government (U.P.) when he declared 16 caste of other Backward Class as Scheduled Caste just before the Panchyat election in U.P.[17]

This reservation in jobs, education and in legislature (SC/ ST) for backward class is in operation since over 58 years yet, majority of the people among backward class opted for the continuation of this policy till the backward classes come equal to upper classes, both socially and economically and reaches one and every family among the rural poor. Some persons said, *"Reservation should continue till complete transformation of the entire community is brought about"*.[18]

As a negative aspect Reservation did not help generally in improving the overall condition of the deprived communities, i.e., the Scheduled Castes, Scheduled Tribes. They still leg behind the upper and middle castes in educational and economic spheres. Only a tiny number have succeeded in acquiring the benefits of reservation. The fortunate among the deprived communities are those who have property or marketable skills which enable them to acquire secondary or higher education. Our educational system caters to the needs of a small section of society which belongs to a privileged status. It consigns the bulk of the children belonging to the poor to be dropouts and failures. Hence as evidence shows that despite scholarships and other facilities only very few students of the deprived communities could clear high school and college education.[19]

RESERVATION POLICY AND FORWARD CLASSES

"The higher castes feel that the advancement and participation of the lower communities will lower their position socially and po1itically".

(I.P. Desai, Caste, Conflict and Reservation Centre for Social Studies)

Reservation for backward classes had multiple effects. One of the immediate effects is that the dominant castes had loosed their control over the backward class. Forward classes however seem angered with the policy of reservation because it picks up undeserving candidates at the cost of meritorious candidates who, although eligible, find themselves excluded from the list of successful candidates because a percentage of jobs going to reserved category. This anger has been vented in the shape of agitations and anti-reservation stirs taking place from time to time.

Due to reservation in employment as well as in education, the upper and middle castes, have increasingly felt endangered as Scheduled Castes, Scheduled Tribes and OBCs have started taking advantage of reservation in greater numbers. The dominant castes have started opposing reservation on various grounds. The conflict between the upper castes and lower castes has come to the surface, i.e. in the High Court and Supreme Court. Majority of the cases are related to criteria and extent of reservation, departmental promotions and admission to professional courses.

Due to political safeguard (reservation) to backward classes (SC/ST) apparently reduced the monopoly of political power of the traditional dominant groups. They have been compelled to part with a few parliamentary or legislative seats to Scheduled Castes and Scheduled Tribes individuals. Consequently, as their chance for contesting from their constituency, which declared to have been as reserved, are finished. Due to reserved political constituency, political ambitions among forward classes of that particular constituency are extinguishing.

Among forward society hatredness towards backward classes is ever-increasing day-by-day. Therefore they are under frustration and its cause is reservation in service and education. A positive effect of reservation on the forward class is: they think that if they want to exist themselves and to remain their dominating position, they have to work hard and consequently potentiality of their intelligentsia is increasing step-by-step.

RESERVATION POLICY AND SOCIETY

In the society it is found that more than 80% among backward classes are in favour of reservation. In my viewpoint three important reasons are stand out in favour of reservation. These are: reservation prevents injustice in services and in admissions; reservation promote social mobility; and reservation guarantees the minimum slice.

Opinion on 'Reservation prevents injustice in admission and in service' is endorsed by a vast majority. It means reservation policy could be an apparatus for promoting social mobility. Social mobility means that with all limitations, the reservation policy is bound to promote mobility among backward classes. It is panorama of changes in the socio-economic condition, together with higher status that really inspires high hopes and aspirations. A majority of the backward class repose faith in statement. "Reservation guarantees minimum share." Those who raise the issue of minimum share in administration, also feel that reservation is just a drop in the ocean of administration it cannot be a solution to all the ills of the backward classes. Even then without this policy, this minimum share would be a dream. Therefore, it could be said that without reservation the backward classes would not have got what is only a resemblance of justice.

Reservations had certainly helped, at least to a very small number of backward classes, in acquiring political and administrative positions. A small stratum has become middle class, getting disassociated from their traditional castes ties in day-to-day relationships because of their imitation of the lifestyle and values of the established middle class. Consequently, the composition of middle class has been widened to some extent during the last five decades, because low castes including Scheduled Castes, Scheduled Tribes and OBCs have entered in it.

Due to reservation economic differentiations among the society members have become sharp, which have initiated the process of disintegration of these deprived groups. Society is dividing into forward class, most backward class and backward classes regarding matters of admission in educational institutions and opportunity of employment in government services. A sharp gape in the society between different backward classes is increasing. However, the privileged strata of the deprived communities have not yet integrated in the middle class dominated by upper and middle castes. It is also found that upto some extent reservation have throttled the growth of militancy among the deprived groups. On the other hand, the tensions between the traditionally upper and middle castes and lower castes have come to the surface. This is inevitable because those who dominate in political and economic spheres would not like to share the benefits whereas the deprived groups are bound to assert their rights. It is said that *Old Chaturverna system (Brahmin, Kshatriya, Vaishya and Shudra) still remain although it changed its clothes and exist, due to reservation, in new form SC, ST, OBC, and GEN; like old wine in new bottle.*

It is often argued that reservation on caste basis is responsible for the ugly face of casteism and that invokes caste feelings and strengthens caste consciousness in the society which is antithetical to secularism. This view ascribes that casteism was not strong before the introduction of reservation, although untouchability was prevalent in ugly form. It also assumes that the members of upper middle castes are benevolent, tolerant and secular. They oppose reservation because it strengthens casteism and hampers the process of secularization. It is also argued that although reservation provides social justice to the deprived class, it demands a heavy cost by penetrating efficiency and merit. It is often said that the present day inefficiency in the administration is due to reservation as less qualified persons are recruited for the position.

Certain negative consequences result from the reservation policy. These negative fallouts affect the social relationships and interactions within the backward classes themselves. Generally, it is felt that there is a certain amount of homogeneity among the backward classes. This common factor acts as the binding force. But reservation policy leads to disturb this existing equilibrium among this deprived class and results in emergence of alienation or a new class. Emergence of a new class would suggest itself vertical social mobility which brings a better and assured social status to one group as against the other. And these people who attain such a social status have a tendency of asserting their superiority and in course of time they identify themselves with the higher classes. In other words, they are likely—to lose their identity and commitment to their own people. It is a settled opinion that reservation definitely results in alienation. This is inevitable and unavoidable product of the process of reservation. While the castes Hindus hold the view that because of alienation the reservation facility does not help the Backward Classes in masses, there are other social groups who hold the view that they do not want reservation to be scrapped just because of this.

Reservation has affected efficiency of administration also. It clearly shows from the evidence that maximum government sectors are running in deficit. Due to continue loss or deficit in these sectors, government decided to open these sectors for disinvestment or privatization. While private sectors in maximum are running in profit. Same situation could be seen in government educational institutions.

But at last I want to say that whatever may be the shortcomings and oppositions, or behind the screen scheming that go against Reservations, the Reservations had served well, the Nation and the Indian Society. Reservations are really and truly proved beneficial not only to the people concerned like the SCs & STs and OBCs, but also to the whole Nation and the Society for the overall and just development. *Survey find out that dosage of the reservational medicine could not reach to all the deprived, needy and deserving candidates and reaped fruits of reservation policy are like cumin in the mouth of Camel, therefore, better implementation of reservation policy is still required.*

Notes and References

1. Sanjay Paswan and Paramanshi Jaideva, Vol. (1) Pub. Kalpaz, Encyclopedia of Dalits in India: Reservation, p. 186.
2. Annual Report (2009-10) of Ministry of Personnel, Public Grievances and Pensions, pp. 56-57.
3. *Ibid.*, at p. 57.
4. *Ibid.*
5. *Ibid.*, at p. 58.
6. *Ibid.*, at p. 58.
7. *Ibid.*, at p. 58.
8. Prescribed by Department of Personnel and Training Office Memorandum No. 36012/2/96-Estt. (Res.) dated July 2, 1997.
9. *Ibid.*, at p. 59.
10. *Ibid.*
11. *Ibid.*, at p. 60.
12. *Ibid.*
13. Annual Report (2009-10) of Ministry of Personnel, Public Grievances and Pensions, pp. 60-61.
14. Sanjay Paswan and Paramanshi Jaideva, Vol. (1) Pub. Kalpaz, Encyclopedia of Dalits in India: Reservation, pp. 155-56.
15. Articles 330 and 332.
16. Sanjay Paswan and Paramanshi Jaideva, Vol. (1), Pub. Kalpaz, Encyclopedia of Dalits in India: Reservation, p. 185.
17. *Amar Ujala*, 6 October 2005, p. 1.
18. Sanjay Paswan and Paramanshi Jaideva, Vol. (1), Pub. Kalpaz, Encyclopedia of Dalits in India: Reservation, p. 152.
19. *Ibid.*, at pp. 151-52.

7

Conclusion and Suggestions

CONCLUSION

After above detailed dialogue evidences established that history of Backward Class in India is divided mainly into three periods, i.e. Ancient, Medieval and Modern. Ancient history of backward class has roofed their social status and caste system existed during Indus valley civilization to post-Gupta period while medieval history of backward class has covered that caste system or social status which prevailed during post Gupta period to the late regime of Mughal empire and modern history of backward class enclosed those social conditions prevailed in post-Mughal period (British Regime) to till date.

In all the religious and literary text of ancient period, i.e. Vedas, Upanishads, Purans, Dharmashastra, Ramayana, Mahabharata, Baudh, Jains literature and Manusmriti, etc., indian society had represented as unequal society. These literatures are evident that after the arrival of Aryans in India, society stratified into *four Varnas—Brahmins, Kshatriya, Vaishya and Ṣhudra*. Most of the local and original inhabitants who were defeated by the Aryans were known as Dasyu, later on as Shudra Varna. Shudras were *not given any right to property, sacrifice, education and choice of occupation*. They were representing as *subjugation to dominant class*. All the religious laws were made as detrimental to the interest of Shudras. Society was totally class based not caste-based. But in the latter part of ancient time *fifth class* was come into existences which were called as *Chandalas*, etc.

In the medieval period, society had grown up as caste ridden society. After the invasion of muslim rulers in India condition of Shudras or other lower class or caste (latter called them as backward class, deprived class or depressed class) was very pitiable and unfortunate. Still they were having no right at all. *They were living on the mercy of others and their social economic status was too stumpy or we could say that they were having no status in the society*. In addition to this, more and more restrictions were imposed to deprive them from all dignity of life. But with the change of the time several things were changed. Religious movements such as Vaishnavism and Saivism questioned the legitimacy accorded to social inequality. The *Bhakti movement as religious reforms initiated by Kabir and Raidas had present a saintly tradition of India in which lower castes have been treated with respect*.

In modern period the *social reformist movements* launched for them by Brahma Samaj, Arya Samaj and Ram Krishna Mission, all have generated the idea of equality of men. In pre-independence period *Gandhi and Ambedkar adopted the cause of backward classes*. Gandhi's crusade for common brotherhood on behalf of untouchables gave a great impetus to Hindu reformism. Ambedkar took birth in the form of God for down-trodden people. Term Scheduled Tribes, Scheduled Caste and Backward Classes for these deprived people have originated only in modern time. Term Scheduled Tribes includes such races or tribes who lived in hilly and remote area, while term 'Schedule Castes' include 'Depressed Classes', i.e. such sub-castes corresponding to the classes of person formerly known as the depressed classes or fifth class (as used in the Government of India Act, 1935). While term Other Backward Classes has been given to occupational, peasantry and fourth class of the society in the 20th century only.

Thus the question *'who are Backward Classes'* is answered after a long debate, by including all Scheduled Castes,

Scheduled Tribes, Untouchables, Depressed, Harijans, Out-Castes and Other Backward Classes. At present, the term 'backward Classes' denotes three different categories of castes such as Scheduled Castes (SCs), Scheduled Tribes (STs) and Other Backward Classes (OBCs).

Founder of Indian Constitution were intended to establish egalitarian, i.e. casteless and classless society. To uplift the down-trodden people and to provide them equality of status and opportunity in employment, provisions of reservation in education and employment were made. In the beginning reservation was given to Scheduled Castes and Scheduled Tribes only. Although voices were raised from time to time in substantial number by members of Parliament to give reservation to Other Backward Classes also specially in southern and northern states of India.

After considering their voice, first backward class commission (Kaka Kalelkar) was appointed in January 1953 to identify and investigate socially and educationally backward class. Recommendations of this Commission were based on the caste criteria and it listed *2,399 castes as socially and educationally backward* and recommended for reservation to certain castes who were engaged in some traditional occupation or most backward. The chief merit of this commission may be viewed as its recommendation divided backward classes into most backward and backward. Out of 2,399 castes (identified as backward castes) 837 castes were treated as most backward and remaining 1562 castes were declared to be backward castes. But finally Chairman of this backward class commission extracted from its report or recommendation and criticized that the reservation on the basis of caste would not be in the interest of the society and the country. Therefore, report of this commission could not be enforced.

After 25 year, Second Backward Class Commission (Mandal Commission) presents some improvement upon Kaka Kalelkar Commission. In 1979 this commission was appointed to determine the criteria for socially and educationally backward classes and to make provisions for the reservation in favour of such backward classes of citizens who are not adequately represented in the public services. To identifying a specific caste/class as 'backward' commission used three indicators: social, educational, and economic. In all three indicators there were eleven indicators. Among all eleven indicators the social indicators were given a weightage of three points, the educational indicators two points, and the economic indicators were accorded one point. Thus, the castes which secured the score of 50%, i.e. eleven points or above, was listed as 'backward'. At last commission identified 3743 castes or 52% population of total population as backward, which are termed as other backward class and it make recommendation to give them 27% reservation in the service and employment in addition to Scheduled Caste and Scheduled Tribe.

Report of Mandal Commission faces severe criticism from several quarters on various scores. It is criticized that:

(i) the criteria used for defining or identify the other backward castes/classes were unreliable, whimsical and politically motivated. It was not based on a rigorous scientific method. The eleven indicators adopted to determine social, educational and economic backwardness of caste/classes, do not largely satisfy the characteristics of good indicator. For example, the social indicator pertaining to the criterion of early marriage is not wedded to any particular caste or class. It is an age-old social evil prevalent in all castes or classes in general. Hence, it should not have been taken as an indicator to distinguish the castes or classes. Similarly, a person was to be treated as 'educationally backward' if neither his father nor his grandfather had studied beyond the primary level. He was to be treated as 'socially backward' if (in the case of Hindu) he did not belong to any of the three twice-born (dvij) varnas, that is, he was neither a Brahmin, nor a Kshatriya, nor a Vaishya, and/or (in the case of a non-Hindu), he was converted from those Hindu communities which have been defined as socially backward, or his parental income was below the prevalent poverty-line, that is, Rs. 71 per head per month. Were these elaborate inquiries really made? The evidences do not indicate this.

(ii) It is also criticized that commission had used very old census data for making population projections on the basis of an assumed constant rate of population growth. The population projection of the categorization of castes was based on the use of the 1931 census data. At that time, the social, economic and demographic map of India was totally different. 'Caste' was identified on the basis of its traditional occupation. After 1931, the listing of caste was discontinued in census operations, and many changes have taken place between 1931 and 1990 by the rapid increase in industrialization, urbanization, educational growth, migration and mobility. As such, the old census basis adopted in 1980 by the Mandal Commission gives a totally vague picture of the criteria adopted. Land reforms made since independence have appreciably altered the social and educational status of various castes and made them a significant part of the rural elite. The Yadavas and the Kurmis in Bihar and Uttar Pradesh are the best example. The Gujjars, the Koeris and the Lodhis, etc. have also become owner cultivators in some States.

It is also criticized that the commission had not taken into account following changes in assuming the population of the OBCs in 1980 to be 52 percent of the total. The urban population had increased from 12 per cent (in 1931) to about 24 per cent in 1984. In urban areas, the level of income and occupation influences social status to a greater extent than position in the traditional caste hierarchy.

Report of the Mandal Commission was kept lying in the limbo for ten years and it was not updated before the acceptance of its implementation by the Government. When any report is dug out after such a long time, it should be updated and examined in terms of the altered needs and its lacunae, and evaluated in terms of its effects of acceptance. The government who announced the acceptance of the Mandal

Commission's report never bothered to go through this process, with the result that with its lacunae, it led to violence and agitations.

Though great pains were taken to define 'caste', but no definition of 'class' was provided, and in sociologically speaking, caste and class are two distinct categories. Hence, the Mandal Commission's report at best located 'other backward castes' and not 'other backward classes' as required.

One of the basic flaws of the reservation policy is that it does not take into account economic backwardness as a criterion. There is no guarantee that the beneficiaries of new policy will unnecessarily be poor. This calls for a suggestion to bar those who had availed benefit of reservation, from receiving benefit again in the larger interests of the communities concerned. *Besides cast/class criteria economic criteria should also take into account for granting Reservation.*

Since the aim of the framer of Indian constitution was to make casteless and egalitarian society and to endow with dignity to every individual. There can be no dignity without equality of status and opportunity. The absence of equal opportunities in any walk of social life is considered as denial of equal status and equal participation in the business of society. They (founding fathers) therefore wanted to minimize inequalities in the society and to provide opportunities not only among individuals but also to groups of people so that they may secure adequate means of livelihood and their education and economic interests could be protected. Articles 14, 15, 16, 17, 18, 23, 24, 38, 39, 39A, 41, 46, 330, 332, 334, 335, 338, 339, 340 and 341 are mentioned in the Constitution of India to protect them from social injustice and exploitation.

To fulfil the aim of Indian Constitution (casteless and classless society), prefential treatment are given under Articles 15(4), 15(5) and 16(4) for the upliftment and advancement of backward classes and to give them reservation in the education and employment. Articles 15(4), 15(5) and 16(4) enable the State to act positively in the direction of uplifting the weaker elements in the society by making a reasonable classification. These articles classify that during making a classification which shows favoured treatment to the backward class, the

State might use the forbidden criteria because any real classification will have to take into account the inequalities based on the abuse of caste, religion, race, etc.

Initially reservation was given to those communities who belong to Shudra Varna, located below the three upper castes (Brahmans, Kshatriyas and Vaishyas) and considered as outcastes (Panchamas) which are referred as Scheduled Caste and Scheduled Tribes in the Constitution. This Act of government was not much opposed by anybody and rather welcomed as a goodwill gesture to their brothers who had suffered discrimination since centuries. Later, in 1993 reservation for OBCs also is provided and Supreme Court upheld on the ground that there are various peasantry and occupational castes or classes which are backward socially and educationally, their advancement require reservation in services and education.

Articles 15(4), 15(5) and 16(4) indicates only one of the means to achieve equality of opportunity namely by the means of reservation in education and appointments or post in favour of underrepresented backward classes of citizens. But there are certain other measures like relaxation in age, relaxation in fees and special training and coaching programmes, usually accompany reservations. These concession and facilities are upheld under the general doctrine of classification under Articles 14 or 16(1) on the clues supplied both by Articles 16(4) and 46.

Anti-reservationists criticized that Art. 15(4) does not provide any reservation in educational institute expressly. If we interpret the words used in Art. 15(4), it is found that the *state is authorized to make special provisions for the educational and social advancement of backward classes or SC and ST. Phrase 'educational advancement' does not mean reservation*. It is the executive or judiciary who interpreted this phrase in such manner and used reservation in education as apparatus for educational advancement. Although Art. 16(4) clearly mention for reservation only in the appointments or posts in favour of any backward classes of citizens not in educational institution. It should be remember that in many cases judiciary decided that right to reservation is an enabling provision therefore it is not a fundamental right.

It is also criticized that arrangement of reservation was made only for temporarily phase not as permanent arrangement. That time it was thought as soon as deprived or underprivileged backward class come on track of advancement with the upper segment of society reservation shall bring to an end in both (education or in employment). But even after completing 63 years of independence of the country the political leader of this country use dosages of reservation for political purpose as vote bank not to cure evil. Since 52% population of India is backward and 23% population belong to SC and ST, if they become annoyed with a particular political party that party will loose their 100% vote bank, which are secured in the shape of backward community. Therefore all the parties try to remain this reservation; even they are interested to extend it in other way in the name of social justice. For example—Mulayam Singh (Chief Minister) government in Uttar Pradesh is called party of Yadavas or a backward class community. He always did act in his government for the pleasure of backward class community and minorities in the name of social justice so that their vote banks remain safe with particular party. Recently Chief Minister of UP, (Mulayam Singh) made a declaration just before Panchyat election in U.P. that 16 other backward castes shall include in the list of Scheduled Caste and 1 other backward class shall include in Scheduled Tribe to give political reservation to these backward class community. He did it to benefited them by another way because political reservation is not provided to other backward class.

Another example to lust these backward classes, a new Act has been enacted by Central Government to give reservation not only in unaided educational institutions even in all professional educational institutions. For this new clause 15(5) has been incorporated in the Indian Constitution.

For political upliftment of these downtrodden people, reservation of seats in the Lok Sabha and State Assembly are provided to SCs and STs under Articles 330 and 332. Initially the framers of the Indian Constitution stipulated a period of 20 years for political reservation to the Scheduled Castes and Scheduled Tribes. But the government has enhanced the time periodically by 10 years every time and the provisions are still in operational form. It is mockery of our so called good governance of Indian government. It is criticized with the argument that when reservation could be given to socially and educationally backward classes in education and employment like SCs and STs why not in political area.

To protect the right of backward classes' apex court of this land come ahead as a liberator, protector and harbinger. In various cases judiciary decided that although reservation is provided only to the backward class not to caste but if all the member belonging to a particular caste or community are backward, it shall be designated as a backward class and there would have no problem in granting reservation or those who are not adequately represented in the services of the State. Thus, if after collecting the necessary data it is found that the caste as a whole is socially and educationally backward the reservation made for such persons will have to be upheld notwithstanding the fact that a few individuals in that group may be both socially and educationally advance above the general average.

Judiciary also authorized the state to adopt a system of reservation by making a proper classification to promote the educational and economic interest of the weaker sections and reservation in educational institutions and it is upheld valid under Art. 46 on the ground that it must be taken as an exception to Article 29(2). But the classification of backward classes into backward and more backward is not permissible. It is not so warranted. Article 15(4) required both social and educational backwardness and not either social or educational.

The judiciary upheld Concept of Compensatory discrimination valid if it is based on social, economic, or educational backwardness of certain groups, it means discrimination in favour of certain groups marked out by multiple criteria of backwardness such as caste, poverty, occupation and so on is valid. Judiciary further held that the criterion for determining the backwardness must be similar to the backwardness from which the Scheduled Castes and Scheduled tribes suffer. Judiciary treated Art. 16(4) as a means to bring social justice and acts as proviso of Art. 16(1) and (2) in the interest of downtrodden or backward classes. However in subsequent case it is not considered as proviso.

The boundary or limit of reservation upto 50% has been fixed by the apex court in several cases but it further held that in exceptional cases it could be extended. Although this decision is repeated in several cases but by taking benefit of this proviso, States have tried to cross the limit of 50% in the name of social justice and welfare of downtrodden weaker and minority. As done by state of Tamilnadu and Rajasthan. *As recently done by Andhra Pradesh Government and HRD Ministry to give reservation in Aligarh Muslim University on the name of religion* and it also crossed the limit of 50 percent.

When the Central Government announced its decision to implement the Mandal Report, major political parties gave implicit or overt support to the report with the stipulation that *it should be based on economic need rather than on caste.* The case of implementing Mandal Commission's report was, however, taken to the Supreme Court, who in its historic judgment (*Indra Sawhney–I case*) on November 15, 1992 endorsed job reservation formula and upheld the union government's decision to reserve 27 per cent government job for all the backward castes (3743) which are scheduled in the Other Backward Class list but struck down Central Government's decision to reserve 10 percent of the vacancies in government civil posts and services for economically backward sections of the people who are not covered by any of the existing schemes of reservation.

The salient features of the Supreme Court verdict were as following: (i) Caste has been accepted as a basis for identifying the beneficiaries of reservations; (ii) The upper limit of reservations has been fixed at 50 per cent although in exceptional case it could be extended; (iii) 'Creamy layer' among backward class has to be excluded from the benefit of reservation; (iv) Reservation in certain technical posts is not advisable; (v) There can be no reservations in promotions; (vi) The Union Government shall specify the socio-economic criteria to exclude socially advanced persons among the backward classes; (vii) Permanent commissions should be set up by the union and state governments to examine complaints of over-inclusion and under-inclusion and requests for inclusion in the list of backward classes. Apex court therefore upheld the Report of Mandal Commission (1980) to implement in the year of 1993 without updating. Due to the politics of vote Bank Central Government decided to give benefit of reservation to all identified backward castes (3743).

By giving this verdict the Supreme Court has opened the floodgates of contending claims and litigation; it has also overruled government's attempts to innovate upon the Mandal formula. Here some question arises in my mind about the role of Judiciary. Is judiciary competent to direct the Government to make amendment in the Constitution? Whether is judiciary having jurisdiction to decide the item which is not mention in the Indian Constitution. Indian Constitution provided reservation on the basis of Class only, could judiciary interpret differently?, Can judiciary work as policy-maker?

Recent decision of Hon'ble R.C. Lohati chief justice of Supreme Court is appreciable when it shouted on the government and ordered to stop dirty politics. It said that reservation provisions could not be applicable in private educational institutions and private sectors unless and until there is express law for this. Government has to first amend constitution and then to enact law to apply reservation provision in private or unaided sector or educational institution, without this there is no scope to apply reservation provision in these sector. To nullify this decision Government has taken effort to amend Indian constitution to give way for reservation in private educational institution [by inserting Art. 15(5)] in favour of backward classes of citizens. After amending Indian constitution central government brought a law to provide reservation in favour of OBCs with the inclusion of creamy layer, in the central educational institutions. Validity of Article 15(5) and the central educational institutions (reservation in admission) Act, 2006 was challenged in *Ashok Kumar Thakur* v. *Union of India,* in which Supreme court upheld the validly of Article 15(5) upto the extent of its application in aided educational institutions although question regarding unaided educational institution is left to be decide in later appropriate case. Regarding the validly of the central educational institutions (Reservation in Admission) Act, 2006 Supreme Court upheld the reservation but with the exclusion of creamy layer only.

In another significant judgement Allahabad High Court ruled that if a candidate from the reserved category applies for an appointment in the general category, he cannot apply for the reserved category and *vice versa*. The court further said that any other interpretation of UP SC/ST and OBC Reservation Act, 1994, will not only disturb the balance of the extent of reservation provided under the Act, but will also upset interest of other claimants of the society—namely the general category.

It is surprising that when reservation on economic basis is demanded, the political parties refused it to accept by saying that it can not be possible because there is no provision in the Indian constitution for it. Really it is ridicule that for providing reservation to the backward classes, Scheduled Castes and Scheduled Tribes, Constitution could amend in the name of social justice, for providing reservation to SC/ST in promotion, constitution could amend in the name of social justice, constitution could amend to continue reservation for them even after the expiry of time period in the name of social justice, now again constitution is amended for providing reservation in private and all professional educational institutions in the name of social justice and welfare of these classes. But constitution could not amend for giving reservation to other economic weaker sections of the society who are not covered under any reservational provision. I think in their opinion other economic weaker are not part of the society perhaps they live in haven, they are not needy because they belong to forward class, therefore, reservation should not be given to them. It is really sad to say that above attitude of government or political parties is discriminatory towards general section of the society. I agreed with the concept of social justice, you do for the welfare of them but you should not snatch from the others.

Laying down of *Creamy layer principle* in *Indra Sawhney Case* (1992 SCC) is an intelligent and wise work of the judiciary. It says that if any creamy layer exists among backward class, benefit of reservation should not be given to the persons belonging to creamy layer. *It defines creamy layer principle as if any person among backward class, socially and educationally forward or constitute elite class, he/she shall not be entitled for the benefit of reservation.* Thus Creamy Layer principle provides for the exclusion of the advanced sections of the backward caste groups for the purpose of reservation and it had caused to the division of the society into Backward Classes (Consisting of members of Backward Castes excluding creamy layer) and Forward Classes (Consisting of members of Forward Castes + members of Backward Castes coming under creamy layer). But it is doubtful that, will skimming off of creamy layer of OBCs ensure the reaching of benefits to non-creamy layer of OBCs. The real issue in my mind is two-fold—first, to ensure the benefit of reservation to really deserving section of OBCs, and second, to cool down impatient anti-reservationists and cure their heart-burning against enrichment of affluent section of backwards.

Here again doubt arises that: (i) Is the judiciary have power to lay down such a principle which has no room in the Indian Constitution; (ii) if concept of creamy layer is applicable on elite person of backward class why could not be applicable on elite class of SCs and STs.

Judiciary directed the Central Government as well as State Government to appoint a permanent backward commission and a committee to deduct or listed creamy layers among backward class. In preparing the lists of creamy layer categories State Governments have to be guided with the list of Central Government. As per the directions of hon'ble Supreme Court, central government has appointed a committee under the chairmanship of R.N. Prasad to find out those who come under creamy layer. This committee prepared an elaborate list of the persons/Categories of persons who will not be entitled (excluded) for the benefit of reservation of Other Backward Classes.

This committee listed all constitutional post, salaried person, business class person, industrialist, agriculturist and other property owners but does not include political persons. The entire political lobby (ministers including chief minister and other M.P. and MLA) are excluded from the list of creamy layer. It is said that these persons are civil servant and elected for temporarily period. Besides it they get very nominal in salary, therefore they should be excluded from the list of creamy layer. But in practical we all know that these entire political persons get a lot in other way. Once a person become

M.P. or M.L.A. or minister he/she earn such amount within a short period which could be used for at least three generation.

In Indra Sawhney case Supreme Court also directed the government to review the scheme of Creamy layer after expiry of every three year and to review the functioning of backward class commission and implementation of reservation policy after 20 year. But it is very heart-breaking that there is no regular review of creamy layer policy even after completing 13 year. Only two revisions have been made in 2004 and in 2008. Here it is to be noticed that Chairman of the National Backward Class Commission urged to call the meeting up to review the scheme of creamy layer in time (as per rule it has to be revise after every three years) but government is not serious about this. National Backward Class Commission can suggest only, it has no power except inclusion of backward class/and exclusion of caste.

Likewise in the State of Uttar Pradesh, Mr. Chairman of State Backward Class Commission recommended State Government several times to revise the scheme of creamy layer, but the Government is sleeping and not interested what the commission can do? It can only recommend the Government. The Government thinks that *Chal raha hai jaisa chalane do. Need not to worry.* Although it is very fascinating to know that limit of income for the exclusion from the list of creamy layer is raised just because of dirty politics.

When one see the effect of reservation on backward classes it appears *prima-facie* from their educational, social, economic status. A good effect of reservation also reflects from their political and cultural achievement also. Although it is also found that benefits of reservation are not successfully reaching to those backward class who are really needy and most deserving candidates even than it proved fruitful to the backward classes or weaker sections of society. It is found that a large number of backward classes feel encouraged by the policy of reservation. It is said that nine backward classes out of ten have entered into services or education through the policy of reservation. It is very exciting to note that those who got entry into government services have come up the social hierarchy. Their standard of living has gone up. Their views and attitude towards living and socializing as also towards problems of the society have changed for the better. These entire things apparent the fact that a sea-changes has been brought in the lives of the downtrodden by the reservation.

A negative effect of reservation on the backward class is found from the fact that these classes have become used to grasp benefit of reservation; therefore they wanted to remain backward. They think that they would get reservation at any cost even if they do less work or possess less intelligentsia. Due to this feeling they want to remain backward. They do not want to become more competent or knowledgeable educationally and culturally even in the age of cut-throat competition. They therefore demanded reservation forever not for limited period. One can see the adverse effect of the reservation in the efficiency of government sector or in government educational institutions. These government sectors are running in loss. Government educational institutions are not capable to product intelligentsia in number due to bogus implementation of reservation policy. *That's why government planned to disinvestments in these sectors and to implement this reservation policy in private sector also.*

Effect of 27% reservation to OBCs on the society seems in this way that society is divided into several parts. Person belonging to OBCs are not having good/healthy feelings about Scheduled Castes and Scheduled Tribes category. They treated them as their rivals/competitor because candidate of SC/ST/OBCs gets reservation according to the proportion of their population. *Thus main effect of reservation policy is that Indian society is clearly divided into four parts, i.e. SC/ST/OBCs/General. In a healthy opinion it is not a good sign on the line of building an egalitarian society as aimed by framers of Indian Constitution.*

On the other hand due to 50% reservation in services and educational institution forwards class become more and more intelligent and competent because they are having no other option then to do hard work and have intelligentsia to get employment when job opportunities are less in comparison to requirement. In the age of globalisation and privatization when government job are becoming lesser day-by-day they could exist or get job only on the basis of intelligentsia and hard work.

Another effect is also seems to be appears from the attitude and thinking of forward class which one feet is that due to politics of vote bank they start thinking to give birth more and more children especially in rural area. They say since their population is less in comparison to backward class so they should increase their population. This dirtily politics is functioning only on cast basis and divides whole society into backward caste and forward caste and when forward class realized that their population is only 15% (as per mandal report) they feel it they are in minority in number therefore they become raring to go to increase the participation of their population in politics.

SUGGESTIONS

After reviewing various dimensions of reservation policy of the government protected under Arts. 15(4), 15(5) and Art. 16(4), several shortcomings of reservation policy brought into the notice. To remove them and to achieve set goal of reservation policy, my humble suggestions are as follows:

A. Suggestion to Adopt Old Approach

1. *Census on the Basis of Caste: First of all it is suggested that now Government of India should start Census on cast-basis, as was done before 1931 in British India.*
   It is necessary to collect the accurate figure of different caste or community. The argument that census on cast basis will increase casteism is just a fear of our mind. When data of Scheduled Caste and Scheduled Tribe population could be collected in census on cast basis why could data of backward class population not be collected on cast basis? Another argument in this favour is that when reservation is granted on cast basis why census could not be made on cast basis.
2. *Roster System should Apply Effectively, where Seats or Vacancies are less in Number.*
   There are two pattern of Roster; (i) the post-wise reservation, and (ii) total or cadre-wise reservation.

There is one fatal demerit in post to post reservation as administrative office can play well calculated mischief by reserving a particular post for the backward class candidates where such candidates are not available at all. The cadre-wise reservation may face problem if common selection committee is not ensured. *My suggestion is that any roster should apply in such a way that reservational posts should not lose.*

3. Exchange of quota should prefer instead of deservation of posts, whenever filling of the post by successive three efforts and after the permission of the departmental authorities is not reasonably possible. Even between different reservational categories situation, exchange of quota should prefer instead of dereservation that is to say that if a post reserved for ST remains unfilled, later it should be filled by SC and if SC's post remains unfilled, it should filled by OBCs.

B. Suggestion for Some Constitutional Amendments

4. *A constitutional amendment is required to clear the ambiguity of term 'backward classes'.*

   Art. 15(4) has used expression 'socially and educationally backward classes of the citizens' or 'Scheduled Caste and Scheduled Tribe'. While Art. 16(4) mentions the expression 'backward class of citizens'. Art. 46 mentions 'other weaker sections of people' or 'SC and ST' term. While Art. 335 uses 'SC and ST' word only. Several times these expressions make confusion because women, children, and persons living below poverty line are also categorized as backward and weaker sections. Judiciary also interpreted all the expression (SC, ST, and socially and educationally backward class of citizens, backward class and weaker section) in the similar sense as backward. Therefore, to remove this ambiguity an amendment for clarity should make.

5. *Reservation at promotional stages*: should not be given to anybody because it can create inefficiency in administration as well as in candidate also. If reservation is necessary to SC/ST at promotional stages in the name of social justice, percentage of reservation should very low and it should be given to OBCs also. Behind this argument is that when Clause 4A of Art. 16(4) by Constitutional (Seventy-seventh Amendment) Act, 1995, has been inserted to nullify the effect of Mandal case on the point of promotion in relation to SCs/STs. There is no reason why it should not be applicable to OBCs and why have they been left out from this scheme. OBCs are also under represented in upper posts. Thus suggestion is that clause (4A) of Article 16 should suitably be amended to include OBCs in addition to SCs/STs, not having adequate representation in the services.
6. Regarding political safeguard or reservation to backward class (SC/ST) under Art. 320. It is often complained that the political parties and the Government in power wanted to sustained the reservations, just for the sake of getting the votes of the backward classes (SCs STs & OBCs) and to preserve them as their Party's solid Vote Banks. Therefore, suggestion is; it is the right time to abolish such type of reservation by constitutional amendment. Because due to this reservation politics is becoming dirty day-by-day. *Due to reserved constituency efficient candidate are not coming in politics also.* Even then if there is any necessity to continue such type of reservation, it should be given strictly only to those backward classes who are having no representation at all in Lok Sabha or States Assemble through filtering mechanism.
7. Another Constitutional amendment is suggested in Article 335 to consider claims of OBCs also in the services and posts in addition to SC and ST, because reservation is provided to only those OBCs whose backwardness is similar to backwardness of SC/ST.

C. Suggestion to Review the Scheme/Policy

8. An amazing vigilant approach is required for in classification of 'creamy layer'. i.e., consistency of creamy layer classification and scattering of cream should be the shaping factor. For the exclusion of creamylayer, in my opinion persons in Class II service and all income tax payers should be considered as Creamy layer. All politicians should also include in creamy layer list. Besides it is *strongly recommended that the concept of creamy layer should apply on elite class of Scheduled Caste and Scheduled Tribe also. It is also suggested that scheme of Creamy layer should properly be review scientifically and in time as prescribed (after every three year).*
   Regarding this one thing I would like to say that issue of 'creamy layer' among OBCs is not as effortless as it has been taken by majority decisions in Mandal Case. When Indian Constitution does not contain a single word about it, it is really very tricky to classify and trace out creamy layer among backward class; it is left on the Committee's decision. And report of Justice R.N. Prasad Committee couldn't be said satisfactory because it submitted its report within 17 days after its constitution. Observations of this Committee need to be verified and tested. This couldn't be prepared on hazy conclusion sitting in ivory towers. There must be some solid empirical grounds with Brandeis Brief for listing of creamy layer.
9. *Regular revision of whole Reservation Policy*: It should be mandatory for Central Government as well for State Government to review, assess and to make change from time to time, in both—the long term and short-term policy to evolve better schemes and programmes for upliftment of downtrodden people.

D. Suggestion to take Strict or Penal Actions

10. The skirt of reservation should not exceed from 50%

at any cost, it is a conventional interpretation of equalitarian justice with balance between reservational posts and general pool. On violating this norm strict or penal action should be taken against disobedient authorities.

11. No reservation on the ground of minority or religion: Reservation on the basis of minority and religion should strictly be prohibited. If any attempt is taken by an authority or State Government, not only strict action but penal action should be taken against because reservation on minority basis will increase conversion of religion which could not be consider a healthy practice in the line building casteless or egalitarian Indian society. It is an appreciable decision of Hon'ble Supreme Court by which decision of Aligarh Muslim University administration and decision of A.P. Government regarding reservation on religion basis was struck down. Besides this, it ordered to close down minority status of Aligarh Muslim University
12. It is strongly recommended that criteria for reservation should be economic also because there are many people or class other than backward classes who are living under very mercy able conditions.
13. *Stern action for false certification*: Benefit of reservation on production of false certificates is although punishable offence even than it is in practice in excess. Therefore, it suggested to take stern action against such candidates as well as against issuing authority because due to this practice most deserving candidate remains unaffected.
14. *Penal provisions for non-implementing the reservation policy*: It is condemned that even after completing 58 years of independence and working of the Constitution the condition of the backward classes have not been improved. This is partly because of the lethargic attitude of the officers who are in charge of the programme in not implementing them properly and partly due to the absence of proper

check or rider on the dealing authority. It is, therefore, suggested that the provisions of Reservation Act of Central Government as well as State Government should implement with heartedly, honestly, morally fairly and in full proficiently. It should not only be formal law written in black and white without an intention to be implemented.

For the better implementation of reservation policy on other suggestion is that the accountability of the officers should be fixed. State should punish such officers who failed to implement these schemes for the benefit of backward class and to exclude all 'creamy layers' among backward class from the skirt of reservation benefit with untainted hands. As no penal clause at Central level or state level for non-implementing the reservation provisions has been enacted till yet. Therefore, it is right time for the Central Government as well as for the State Government to enact penal provisions for non-implementing the reservation policy.

E. Other Suggestions

15. *Regarding reservation in higher education and services*: It is suggested that instead of reservation other measures should provide for i.e.—Incentives and Financial Assistances to individual backward class, wanting to pursue higher studies, particularly Post Graduate Studies in Professional Spheres like Architecture, Engineering, Medicine, Management, Law, etc., and take up Advanced Courses like M.Phil, Ph.D. and Post-Doctoral Studies. It could be justified on the ground that the representation of backward class (especially ST) is very low in this area. We found exceptional strength of ST candidate in legal profession or in medical profession and very rare Ph.D. of ST researcher in law. If we want to increase their percentage, reservation in terms of financial support in Higher education is desirable.

16. *It is strongly recommended, now time has come to restrict the reservation strictly upto only one generation*. Because reservational benefit is such a drug the extensive use of which shall be prove harmful to the particular class or community and to the society also.
17. *Reservation is advocated in private sector or undertaking also*: In the age of liberalisation, privatization and globalisation Government job opportunities are shrinking sharply and abruptly for the public. In this scenario what we need more urgently now, is liberation of the people of down-trodden or we could say backward classes. The proposal of reservation in private sectors given by Dr. Man Mohan Singh (Hon'ble PM of India) could be justified only on one point, when Government sector are coming to vanish day-by-day, and privatization are ever-increasing, social welfare concept has been shifted from Government to private sector, and therefore it is their duty to apply reservation policy. In this regard my suggestion is in three tires:

    (i) percentage of reservation should reduce;
    (ii) Policy of minimum qualification as applicable on general class should apply on backward classes also in the same manner in appointment. It is necessary to maintain the efficiency of administration; and
    (iii) Reservation benefit should be given only for one generation in a particular family.

18. *Cultural advancement*: Besides social and educational advancement cultural advancement of all the backward class of citizens is also required. It is said that these classes have no its own culture and literature. Therefore, it is suggested that government should initiate some programme for their cultural and literature advancement.
19. *Change in physiology*: Last but not the least suggestion is that a change in mind set is required. Often voices come from the backward class, "we want no

reservation, we want change attitude, (removal of untouchability) with peace from the side of forward class. To remove the feeling of casteism I would like to recommend that, title or surname like thrivedi, Sharma, Chandra, etc. after the name should not use. In any application.provision to mention category or surname should abolish. It is necessary to eliminate the caste feeling. The question arises as how to tackle such a deeply entrenched cultural divide? Governments' action alone cannot do so. *What is needed is that reservations within our hearts must finally go.* The need of governmental reservations will then vanish.

At last I would like to say that no doubt, reservation policy has brought a new good morning for the thousand years oppressed class, but to a vast number of potential beneficiaries, it is yet to effect realization. This may perhaps be due to some slackness in its execution. It is also due to lack of awareness among those for whom the policy is intended that its benefits are yet to trickle down. Nevertheless, it has positively prominent expectations and with passage of time, it is going to resolve the inequalities. There is still a long way to go and the policy should be sustained for quite some time before it is withdrawn. The practice of a honey tongue and a heart of gall cannot succeed therefore stern work, then, will have to be done in order to achieve the set targets with clean and clear heart.

APPENDIX 1

DEFINITION AND IDENTIFICATION OF AN SC/ST/ OBCs PERSONS

(i) A person shall be deemed to be a member of SC/ST if he belongs to a Caste or Tribe declared as SC/ST for the area, of which he is a resident, by an order issued under Articles 341/342 of the Constitution of India.

(ii) No person who professes a religion other than the Hindu, Sikh or Buddhist religion shall be deemed to be a member of the SC, ST Person can profess any religion.

(iii) A children born to SC/ST parents and residing in the area will automatically belong to SC/ST.

(iv) If a SC/ST person migrates within the State concerned, he will continue to belong to SC/ST.

(v) If an SC/ST person migrates outside the State, he will be a SC/ST only w.r.t. the State to which he originally belonged and not w.r.t. State he has migrated to.

(vi) A non-SC/ST person will not be deemed to belong to SC/ST simply because he has married an SC/ST.[1]

(vii) An SC/ST person would continue to be an SC/ST person even after marriage to a non SC/ST person.

(viii) If a SC person gets converted to a religion other than Hindu, Sikh or Buddhist, he will no longer belong to SC. But if he/his desendants get reconverted to Hindu/Sikh or Buddhist he will be an SC if only he is accepted by the particular Caste as one among them.

(ix) A person duly adopted by an SC in accordance with law, customs and usage prevalent for long period, will belong to SC.[2]

(x) Children born to parents, one being SC another being non-SC, is not automatically entitled to SC status. Generally, if only the child accepted by the persons of the Caste as belonging to their community and has been brought up in that community, the child will belong to SC.[3]

(xi) For claiming as belonging to SC/ST, the permanent place of residence of the person at the time of presidential orders declaring his Caste/Tribe as Scheduled has to be taken into consideration.[4]

For the identification of SC/ST/OBC various case are decided by the Hon'ble Supreme Court:

(1) On reconversion to Hinduism, a person can once again become a member of the caste in which he was horn and to which he belonged before conversion to another religion, if the members of the caste accept him as a member. When a person is reconverted to Hinduism, the social and economic disabilities once again revive and become attached to him because these are disabilities inflicted by Hinduism.[5]

(2) The Scheduled Castes/Scheduled Tribes are to be treated as such for getting the benefits of reservation in employment only in the State/Union Territory where they are so declared and not elsewhere.[6]

(3) Where a SC or ST in relation to State 'A' migrates to State 'B' where a Caste or Tribe with the same nomenclature is specified for the purpose of the Constitution to be a SC/ST in relation to that State 'B', that person will not be entitled to claim the privileges and benefits admissible to persons belonging to SC/ST in State 'B'.[7]

(4) A person born in a forward caste family cannot be declared to be entitled to the benefits of a SC on the basis of her marriage to a person belonging to SC.[8]

(5) By marriage, a change of community of a person does not take place and such a person would not be eligible for the purpose of reservation. A person cannot become a member of the backward community by choice.[9]

(6) An SC employee, though in possession of a caste certificate, may still be required to prove that he belongs to the SC specified in the Presidential Notification in relation to the State to which he belongs and was born.[10]

(7) It is a settled law that the personal law by which a person is governed follows him wherever he goes, until and unless he voluntarily changes his religion.[11]

(8) The Scheduled Tribes Order must be read as ii is. It is not even permissible to say that a tribe, sub-tribe, part of or group of any Tribe or Tribal community is synonymous to the one mentioned in the Scheduled Tribes Order if they are not so specifically mentioned in it.[12]

(9) For appointment under Central Government for the reserved posts, there is no restriction with regard to origin or migration from one state to another. Any person with a valid caste certificate issued by any State/UT and staying in any place can apply against reserved posts in Central Government.[13]

NOES AND REFERENCES

1. Refer to Valasamma Paul *v.* Rani George & others, 1995 (2) .SLJ (Kerala) 81 and State of Tripura & others *v.* Smt. Namita Majumdar (Barman) 1998 SCC (L&S) 526.
2. Answer to a Parliament Question.
3. *Ibid.*
4. *Ibid.*
5. CM. Arwnugham *v.* S. Rajagopal, AIR 1976 SC 939 and A. Paul Raj *v.* Union of India and Others, GA. No. 982 of 1991 decided on 16.9.1993 (CAT, Madras).
6. D.S. Bansu *v.* Union of India & Others, O.A. No. 466 of 1992 on 8.1.1993 (CAT—Ahmedabad).
7. Sivachaninugavelon and Others *v.* Union of India & Others, O.A. Nos. 199 and 214 of 1996 decided on 5.11.1996 (CAT—Madras).

8. State of Tripura & Others *v.* Smt. Namita Majumdar (Barrman) 1998 SCC (L&S) 526.
9. Valasamma Paul *v.* Rani George & Others, 1995 (2) SLJ (Kerala) 81 and Smt. Rani Koch *v.* Union of India & another, O.A. No. 31(G) of 1990 on 18.9.1995 (CAT—Guwahati).
10. G. Sundaresan *v.* Union of India & another, SLP (C) No. 12376 of 1995, decided on 12.7.1995 (SC).
11. Phanindra Mohan Mandal *v.* Union of India 1991 (17) ATC 127 (Calcutta).
12. State of Maharashtra *v.* Milind and Others, 2001 SCC (L&S) 117.
13. Narender *v.* UT of Chandigarh & another, OA No. 203/HR1 2002, Chandigarh, 29.1.2003.

APPENDIX 2

NO. 36012/31/90-ESTT. (SCT) GOVERNMENT OF INDIA, MINISTRY OF PERSONAL, PUBLIC GRIEVANCES AND PENSIONS DOPT DT. 13.8.1990

OFFICE MEMORANDUM

Subject: Recommendation of the Second Backward Classes Commission (Mandal Report)—Reservation for Socially and Educationally Backward Classes in services under the Government of India.

In a multiple undulating society like ours, early achievement of the objective of social justice as enshrined in the Constitution is a must. Second Backward Classes Commission called the Mandal Commission was established by the then Government with this purpose in view, which submitted its report to the Government of India on 31.12.1980.

Government have carefully considered the report and the recommendations of the Commission in the present context regarding the benefits to be the socially and educationally backward classes as opined by the Commission and are of the clear view that at the outset certain weightage has to be provided to such classes in the services of the Union and their Public undertakings. Accordingly orders issued as follows:

(i) 27% of the vacancies in civil posts and services under the Government of India reserved for SEBCS.

(ii) The aforesaid reservation shall apply to vacancies to be filled by direct recruitment. Detailed instructions relating to the producer to be followed for enforcing reservation will be issued separately.

(iii) Candidates belonging to SEBS recruited for the

general candidates shall not be adjusted against the reservation quota of 27%.

(iv) The SEBC would compromise in the first phase the castes and communities which are common to both the list in the report of the mandal Commission and the State Government's lists. A list of such castes/ communities is being issued separately.

(v) The aforesaid reservation shall take effect from 7.8.1990. However, this will not apply to vacancies where the recruitment process has already been initiated prior to the issue of these orders.

3. Similar instructions in respect of public sector undertakings and financial institutions including public sector banks will be issued by the Department of Public Enterprises and Ministry of Finance respectively.

Joint Secretary to the Government of India

APPENDIX 3

TEXT OF DOP&T, O.M. NO. 36012/31/90-ESTT. (SCT), DT. 25.9.1991

RESERVATION FOR SOCIALLY AND EDUCATIONALLY BACKWARD CLASSES IN SERVICES UNDER THE GOVERNMENT OF INDIA, MODIFICATION

The undersigned is directed to invite the attention to O.M. of even number dated the 13th August, 1990, on the above mentioned subject and to say that in order to enable the poorer sections of the SEBCs to receive the benefits of reservation on a preferential basis and to provide reservation for other economically backward sections of the people not covered by any of the existing schemes of reservation, Government have decided to amend the said Memorandum with immediate effect as follows:

- (i) Within the 27% of the vacancies in civil posts and services under the Government of India reserved for SEBCs, preference shall be given to candidates belonging to the poorer sections of the SEBCs. In case sufficient numbers of such candidates are not available, unfilled vacancies shall be tilled by the other SEBC candidates.
- (ii) 10% of the vacancies in civil posts and services under the Government of India shall be reserved for other economically backward sections of the people who are not covered by any of the existing schemes of reservations.
- (iii) The criteria for determining the Poorer sections of the SEBCs or the other economically backward

sections of the people who are not covered by any of the existing schemes of reservations are being issued separately.

The O.M. No. of even number dated the 13th August, 1990, shall be deemed to have been amended to the extent specified above.

APPENDIX 4

TEXT OF DOP&T, O.M. NO. 36012/2/93-ESTT. (SCT), DT. 2.2.1993

SUPREME COURT JUDGMENT OF 16.11.92 RELATING TO RESERVATIONS FOR SOCIALLY AND EDUCATIONALLY BACKWARD CLASSES (SEBCS) ETC.

The undersigned is directed to say that the Supreme Court delivered its judgment on 16.11.92 in writ petition filed by Smt. Indira Sawhney and others against this Department's O.M. dated 13.8.90 and 25.9.91 providing for reservation in civil posts and services under the Government of India in favour of SEBC and other economically weaker Sections. In this Judgment the Supreme Court has directed all concerned authorities, High Courts and Central/State Administrative Tribunals that any petition or proceedings questioning the validity, operation or implementation of the two impugned memorandum or any grounds whatsoever, shall be filed or instituted ONLY before the Supreme Court and not before any High Court or other Court or Tribunal.

This is brought to the notice of all Ministries/ Departments of the Govt. of India.

APPENDIX 5

NO. 36012/22/93-ESTT. (SCT), GOVERNMENT OF INDIA, MINISTRY OF PERSONAL, PUBLIC GRIEVANCES AND PENSIONS DOPT-OFFICE MEMORANDUM

Subject: Reservation for other Backward Classes in Civil Posts and services under the Government of India-Regarding.

The undersigned is directed to refer to this Department's O.M. No. 36012/31/90-Estt. (SCT), dated the 13 August, 1990 and 25th September, 1991 regarding reservation for Socially and Educationally Backward Classes in civil posts services under the Government of India and to say that following the Supreme Court Judgment in the *Indra Sawhney and others* v. *Union of India and others case* (writ petition no. 930 of 1990) the Government of India appointed an expert Committee to recommend the criteria for exclusion of the socially advanced persons/sections from the benefits of reservations for Other Backward Classes in civil posts and services under the Government of India.

2. Consequent to the consideration of the Expert Committee's recommendations this Department Office Memorandum No. 36012/31/90-Estt. (SCT), dated 13.8.90 referred in Para (1) above is hereby modified to provide as follows:

(a) 27% of the vacancies in civil posts and services under the Government of India, to be filled through direct recruitment, shall be reserved for other backward classes. Detailed instructions relating to the producer to be followed for enforcing reservation will be issued separately.

(b) Candidates belonging to OBCs recruited on the basis of merit is an open competition on the same standards prescribed for the general candidates shall not be adjusted against the reservation quota of 27%.

(c) (i) The aforesaid reservation shall not apply to persons/sections mentioned in column 3 of the scheduled to this office memorandum.

(ii) The rule of exclusion will not apply to persons working as artisans or engaged in hereditary occupations, callings. A list of such occupations, calling will be issued separately by the Ministry of welfare.

(d) The OBCs for the purpose of the aforesaid reservation would comprise, in the first phase, the castes and the state Governments lists. A list of such castes and communities is being issued separately by the Ministry of welfare.

(e) The aforesaid reservation shall take immediate effect. However, this will not apply to vacancies where the recruitment process has already been initiated prior to the issue of this order.

3. Similar instructions in respect of public sector undertakings and financial institutions including public sector banks will be issued by the department of Public Enterprises and by the Ministry of Finance respectively effective from the date of this Office Memorandum.

(SMT. SARITA PRASAD)
Joint Secretary of the Government of India

APPENDIX 6

TEXT OF DOP&T O.M. NO. 36120/22/93-ESTT. (SCT), DATED 30.12.1993

UNFILLED VACANCIES OF OBCs SHOULD NOT BE DERESERVED BUT CARRIED FORWARD

The undersigned is directed to say that the question of deservation and carry forward to fulfilled posts reserved for Other Backward Classes has been examined by the Government. It has since been decided that the Posts Reserved for Other Backward Classes which remain unfilled should not be deserved but should be carried forward as such for a period of three years or till posts are filled by OBC candidates, which ever is earlier.

APPENDIX 7

Guidelines for Consideration of Requests for Inclusion and Complaints of under-Inclusion in the Central List of Other Backward Classes.*

The Commission, after studying the criteria/indicators framed by the Mandal Commission and the Commissions set up in the past by different State Governments and other relevant materials, formulated the following guidelines for considering requests for inclusion in the list of Other Backward Classes:

A. Social

1. Castes and communities generally considered as socially backward.
2. (a) Castes and communities, which mainly depend on agricultural and/or other manual labour for their livelihood and are lacking any significant resource base.
   (b) Castes and communities, which, for their livelihood, mainly depend on agricultural and/or other manual labour for wage and are lacking any significant resource base.
   (c) Castes and communities, the women of which, as a general practice, are for their/family's livelihood, engaged in agricultural and/or other manual labour, for wage.
   (d) Castes and communities, the children of which, as a general practice, are, for family's livelihood or for supplementing family's low income,

*MGIPF-385 M/O Welfare/94.

mainly engaged in agricultural and/or manual labour.

(e) Castes and communities, which in terms of the caste system, are identified with traditional crafts or traditional or hereditary occupations considered to be lowly or undignified.

(f) Castes and communities, which in terms of the caste system, are identified with traditional or hereditary occupations considered to be 'unclean' or stigmatized.

(g) Nomadic and semi-nomadic castes and communities.

(h) Denotified or Vimukta Jati castes and communities.

Explanation: This term refers to castes/communities which had been categorized as Criminal Tribes under the Criminal Tribes Act, 1924, passed by the Indian Legislature and repealed by the Criminal Tribes (Repeal) Act, 1952 and subsequently referred to as Denotified or Vimukta Jatis.

3. Castes and communities, having no representation or poor representation in the State Legislative Assembly and/or district-level Panchayat Raj institutions during the ten years preceding the date of the application.

   Explanation: This is only intended to measure, as an indicator, the presence of a caste or community in these bodies. The term 'poor representation' may be taken to refer to a caste or community whose presence in the body is less than 25% of its proportion in the population.

B. Educational

1. Castes and communities whose literacy rate is at least 8% less than the State or district average.
2. Castes and communities of which the proportion of matriculates is at least 20% less than the State or district average.
3. Castes and communities, of which the proportion of

graduates is at least 20% less than the State or district average.

C. Economic

1. Castes and communities, a significant proportion of whose members reside only in Kaccha houses.
2. Castes and communities, the share of whose members in number of cases and in extent of agricultural lands surrendered under the Agricultural Land Ceiling Act of the State, is nil or significantly low.
3. Castes and communities, the share of whose members in State Government posts and services of Groups A & B/Classes I & II, is not equal to the population—equivalent proportion of the caste/community.

Illustration

Population-equivalent proportion

- Population of a State 10,000,000
- Population of the caste/community under consideration in the State 1,00,000
- Proportion of the population of the caste/community under consideration to the total population of the State 10%
- Number of posts in Class-I in the State 1,000
- Therefore, population equivalent proportion of Class-I posts in the State in respect of the caste/community under consideration 100

Explanation 1 : In the case illustrated above, if members belonging to the caste/community under consideration hold 100 Class-1 posts or more, its share is equal to or more than its population-equivalent proportion.

In that case that caste/community will not be considered to have fulfilled this indicator of backwardness.

In the case illustrated above, if the members of the caste/ community under consideration have 99 Class-1 posts or less, its share is less than its population-equivalent proportion and will, therefore, be considered to have fulfilled this criterion of backwardness.

Explanation 2: This guideline is only an indicator to assess backwardness or its absence and has no relation to the condition of inadequacy under Article 16(4).

Explanation 3: The population-equivalent proportion of posts may be composed of posts secured through merit only or through reservation only or through both—figure needs to be furnished separately for posts secured through merit/posts secured through both—figure needs to be furnished separately for posts secured through merit/posts secured through reservation.

D. In addition to the above, arising from Article 16(4) the following condition has also to be fulfilled:

> Castes and communities, which are not/are inadequately posts and services of Groups A & B. Each Group/Class should be taken separately.

PROCEDURAL CLARIFICATION ON GUIDELINES

1. The above social, educational and economic guideline for consideration of requests for inclusion in the list of Other Backward Classes are intended to aid the Bench/Commission to identify Castes and Communities which deserve to be included in the list of OBC in terms of the National Commission for Backward Classes Act and not to fetter due exercise of discretion by it.

2. The term 'local', wherever used, is intended to mean State level or intra-State regional level or district level, as appropriate, in the light of the demographic distribution of the caste/community concerned.

However, wherever the Bench/Commission has adequate reasons, the sub-district level positions may be taken into account.

In some guidelines State or local, or State or district have been given as alternatives. In such instances the appropriate alternative may be chosen depending on the circumstances such as demographic distribution, ready availability of data etc.

3. Some of the guidelines are capable of quantification but data are not available in every State. In respect of States, where such data are readily available (e.g. specific percentage figures), the Bench/Commission may examine the cases before it in terms of such quantifiable data and their own observations as well and other relevant materials that may be available to it. In respect of States where such quantifiable data are not available, the Bench/Commission may consider castes/ communities on the basis of their own observations and other relevant materials that may be available to it.

4. Under each of the categories A, B & C, of guidelines, there are 3 or 4 guidelines. They are not necessarily cumulative. Cumulative data would no doubt be advantageous. But where data-base does not readily permit, each caste or community may be considered in terms of such of the guidelines, under each of the categories A, B & C as are practicable.

5. Regarding the condition at D, till information regarding the position of each caste in the Government of India's services becomes readily available, it may be presumed that this factor is fulfilled by a caste/community/sub-caste/synonym/sub-entry, in case it is found that it fulfils tot the guideline in C 3.

6. Wherever a caste or community fulfils the guidelines 2(e) or (1) or (g) or (h), the Bench/Commission may take it as adequate evidence of backwardness. In such cases, the Bench shall take into account such other data/information that may be made available to it or comes to its notice, and it may make such further inquiry as it deem proper and necessary.

Having done so and being satisfied that there are no sufficient grounds to take a contrary view with regarding the backwardness of the caste or community making the request, the Bench may, after examining the matter of inadequacy of representation as indicated in D, proceed to with formulate its findings.

7. Occupations mentioned at guideline 2(e) and 2(f) may include traditional artisanal crafts; fishing, hunting, bird-snaring; agricultural labour on the lands of others; earth work, stone-breaking, salt-manufacturing, lime-burning; toddy-

tapping; animal-rearing; butchery; hair-cutting; washing of clothes; ferrying by boat; safai (i.e. scavenging"); knife grinding, grain roasting; entertaining through song and dance, acrobatics jugglery, snake-charming, acting; begging or mendicancy.

Explanation: This refers only to castes or communities which traditionally depended on begging or mendicancy in the past, i.e. until it was prohibited by law. The Bench/Commission may take into account any other occupation which may be similar to these occupations.

8. In respect of any case of request, found to be one of apparent clerical error, or factual mistakes at the stage of preparation of the common lists and if there is no contrary view expressed and data furnished before or otherwise available to/in the notice of the bench/Commission such castes/communities may be included and findings/advice formulated to that effect.

9. In case of synonyms/sub-castes/different names of the same caste or community/local variants of the same caste or community, if and after it is established that, they are, in fact, such synonyms/sub-castes/different names of the same caste/local variants, etc. and if there are no contrary views expressed and data furnished before or otherwise available to/in the notice of the Bench/Commission and the Bench/Commission does not find any ground to take a contrary view, such synonyms/sub-castes/different names of the same caste/local variants of the same caste, such cases may be included, and findings/advice formulated to that effect.

10. In all cases, publicity regarding the date and venue of the sitting of the Commission's bench and the castes/communities, etc. to which the sitting pertains may be made through mass media and all those who have any views to express or data to furnish to the bench may be invited to do so, in addition to addressing the State Governments and applicants to furnish all material and data in their possession.

11. These guidelines of identification and procedure will be applicable to all categories of States/UTs and all categories of castes/communities whether included in the State list but in the Mandal List or included in the Mandal list but not in the State list, or included in neither.

APPENDIX 8

JUSTICE RAM NANDAN PRASAD EXPERT COMMITTEE ON FORMER JUDGE SOCIALLY AND EDUCATIONALLY BACKWARD CLASSES

Patna High Court
CHAIRMAN
New Delhi-110001 Dated 10th March, 1993

Dear Hon'ble Minister,

I have the privilege of presenting the Report of the Expert Committee constituted under Resolution No 120I1/16/93-BCC(C) dated 22nd February, 1993 of the Ministry of Welfare Government of India. I and the other Member of the Committee, Dr. M.L. Sahare, Shri P.S. Krishnan and Shri R.J. Majithia, assumed charge on 23rd February, 1993 and from day one, we got down to serious work as all of us were fully conscious that the Report has to be completed and presented by the 10th March, 1993.

2. Needless to say, all of us had to work very hard to complete the Report and in this difficult and daunting task, we received full cooperation from you as well as all the officers and staff of the Ministry of Welfare. We justifiably feel happy that we have completed the work within the targeted time.

3. We hope that our labour will serve the purpose and our Report will enable the Government to commence Implementation of the policy of reservation for Socially and Educationally Backward Classes at the earliest fulfilling the detractions of the Supreme Court.

With regards,

Yours Sincerely
Sd/-
(RAM NANDAN PRASAD)

NO. 12011/16/93-BCC(C),GOVERNMENT OF INDIA MINISTRY OF WELFARE, NEW DELHI, THE 22ND FEBRUARY, 1993 RESOLUTION

The Supreme Court in its Majority Judgement in Writ Petition (Civil) No. 930 of 1990, *Indra Sawhney and Others,* etc. v. *Union of India and Others,* etc. delivered on 16th November. 1992 has, *inter alia,* directed that "within four months from today the Government of India shall specify the basis applying the relevant and requisite socio-economic criteria to exclude socially advanced persons/sections ('creamy layer') from 'Other Backward Classes' and further that the implementation of the impugned O.M. dated 13th August, 1990 shall be subject to exclusion of such socially advanced persons ('creamy layer')".

2. Having regard to the fact that a lot of specialized inputs would be needed to determine the bases viz., Scio-economic criteria for identification of the 'creamy layer', it has been decided to set-up an Expert Committee consisting of:

1. Justice Ram Nandan Prasad (Retd.), High Court Patna — Chairman
2. Shri M.L. Sahare (Social Scientist), Former Chairman, UPSC. — Member
3. Shri P.S. Krishnan, Former Secretary (Welfare) Govt. of India — Member
4. Shri R.J. Majithia, former Chairman Revenue Board, Govt. of Rajasthan, Secretary to make recommendations to the Govt. of India, in regard to the said socio-economic criteria. The Committee will also give recommendations on such other matters relating to the implementation of the Judgement of the Supreme Court, as the Government of India may consider necessary.

3. The Headquarters of the Committee will be located at Delhi.

4. The Committee will devise its own procedures in the discharge of its functions. All the Ministries and Departments

of the Government of India will furnish such information and documents and provide such assistance as may be required by the Committee. It is hoped that the State Governments and Union Territory Administrations and others concerned will extend their fullest cooperation and assistance to the Committee.

5. The Committee shall submit its Report on the socio-economic criteria for exclusion of the 'creamy layer' from Other Backward Classes latest by 10th March, 1993.

Sd/-
(M.S. PANDIT) Jt. Secy. (M & BC)

ORDERED that a copy of the resolution be communicated to all Ministries/Departments of the Government of India/ State Governments and U.T. Administrations. ORDERED also that the resolution be published in the Gazette of India for general information.

Sd/-
(M.S. PANDIT) Jt. Secy. (M & BC)

Report of the Expert Committee for specifying the criteria for identification of socially advanced persons among the socially and educationally backward classes.

The 9-Member Constitution Bench of the Supreme Court of India delivered its historic Judgement in the Reservation case relating to Socially and Educationally Backward Classes (*Indra Sawhney and Other* v. *the Union of India and Others*) on the 16th of November, 1992. The case arose out of several writ petitions filed to challenge the Office Memorandum dated 13th August, 1990 and the office Memorandum dated 25th September, 1991 issued by the Government of India for implementing, according to the respective modes prescribed in the two office Memoranda, the recommendations for reservation for Socially and Educationally Backward Classes (SEBCs) in public employment, made by the Second Backward Class Commission appointed under Article 340 of the Constitution, popularly known as the Mandal Commission.

2. The Supreme Court while upholding by majority the basic principle of reservation for the SEBCs have at the same time, directed that the socially advanced persons of (lie SEBCs category ought not to be give benefit of reservation. In order to carry out this directive and specifying and determining as to who from amongst the SEBCs would be liable to be excluded from the benefit of reservation, the Government has appointed the Expert Committee as per Resolution No. 1201 1/16/93-BCC(C), dated (the 22nd February, 1993 of the Ministry of Welfare, Government of India. The Court has also directed that the reservation shall not become operative till the criteria to exclude the socially advanced persons are ascertained and specified.

3. Four Hon'ble Judges who were members of the Special Bench, namely, the then Hon'ble Chief Justice Shri M.N. Venkatachaliah (now Chief Justice), Hon'ble Justice A.M. Ahmadi and Hon'ble Justice B.P. Jeevan Reddy, delivered a common Judgement written out by Hon'ble Justice B.P. Jeevan Reddy and this is known as the majority Judgement and we shall refer to it as such in our report. Hon'ble Justice S.R. Pandian and Hon'ble Justice P.B. Sawant have, no doubt, written out separate judgments of their own, but they have in substance supported most of the conclusions of the majority judgment and we will refer to the judgments of these two Hon'ble Judges by their respective names. The dissenting judgments separately written out by Hon'ble Justice T.K. Thommen, Hon'ble Justice Kuldip Singh and Hon'ble Justice R.M. Sahai have a common operative order and this is known as the dissenting judgment and we shall refer, if need be, to the same in the above terminology When we refer to the ratio decidendi of the entire judgment we will be referring to it as the Judgement of the Court.

4. It is necessary to bear in mind that the Court has accepted the principle of reservation on the reasoning that the SEBCs on account of their social and educational backwardness are truly in need of reservation. In other words, the dominant consideration for upholding the reservation is the social and educational backwardness and not the income test, although in actual life it mostly happens that economic backwardness is a natural consequence of the social and

educational backwardness. It logically follows, therefore, that for determining who from amongst the SEBCs shall be denied the benefit of reservation, the basics again would be the social and educational factors and only when the advancement in this regard is such as to put that person at par with the forward classes that he may be placed in the excluded category. In the majority judgment, it has been observed that only when a person's social and educational advancement is such that it totally snaps the connecting link of backwardness between him and other members of his community, he can then be said to be a misfit in his own class and so ought to be taken out from there and placed in the "Creamy Layer" category. The following passage in the judgment of Hon'ble Justice Sawant (paragraph 522, Judgments Today, Vol. VI, No. 9, 30th November, 1992) elaborates the point more succinctly:

> "The correct criterion for judging the forwardness of the forwards among the Backward Classes is to measure their capacity not in terms of the capacity of others in their class, but in terms of the capacity of the members of the Forward Classes, as stated earlier. If they cross the Rubicon of backwardness, they should be taken out from the Backward Classes and should be made disentitled to the provisions meant for the said classes".

Hence while determining the criteria of exclusion we have kept in mind the guiding principle laid down by the Hon'ble Court as mentioned above, However, if economic betterment flows from social and educational advancement, then this also has to be taken note of.

5. Before specification of the actual determinants is taken up, it will be useful, may necessary, to indicate and explain what exactly the term 'Creamy Layer' or the Rule of Exclusion in actual application would imply. When a person has been able to shed off the attributes of social and educational backwardness an has secured employment or has engaged himself in some trade/profession of high status, as categorized by us below, lie, at that stage is normally no longer in need of reservation for himself. For example, if a person gets

appointed as a Class I Officer either on open competition basis or reservation basis, the question of excluding him on the ground that he forms part of the 'Creamy Layer' does not at all arise. But since he himself has come into the socially advanced category, he will be in a position to provide the means, the equipment and the opportunities which are necessary for the uplift of his offspring from the level of social and educational backwardness. As such, the question of applying the Rule of Exclusion will arise only in the case of his offspring. In the present social set-up, when the joint family system, particularly among the upper strata of society, has been breaking up, we are regarding the family to constitute husband, wife and children and on that basis applying the exclusion principle. In other words, even if a person, says Mr. "X", has become a Class I Officer, this will not deprive his brother and sister of the benefit of reservation on the basis that Mr. "X" has become a Class I Officer. The question as to whether the brother or sister of Mr. "X" will or will not get the benefit of reservation shall depend upon the status of their parents.

6. Now we proceed to indicate and define the criteria for application of the Rule of Exclusion. The rise in social and educational status may result from different kinds of positions and placements in life and we shall deal with them one by one as noted below. To the categories listed below, the Rule of Exclusion will apply unless exceptions are specifically indicated.

I. Constitutional Posts

7. President, Vice-President, Judges of the Supreme Court and High Courts, Chairman/Members of the Union Public Service Commission and State Public Service Commissions, Chief Election Commissioner, Comptroller and Auditor General of India and persons holding Constitutional positions of like nature.

The Constitutional posts of Governor, Minister and Membership of Legislatures are, in the very nature of things, temporary and often transitory. Further, in most cases such persons would be covered in one or the other categories which have been enumerated in this report. Hence, such persons have not been separately categorized.

II. Service Category

A. Group A/Class I Officers of the All India, Central and State Services (Direct Recruits)

8. If either of the spouses is a Class I Officer rule of exclusion will apply Where both spouses the Class I Officers and one of them dies the situation remains unchanged and the rule of exclusion will apply. However, if both of them die then obviously, the offspring are not only left to suffer mental agony and hardships in different ways but they are also denied the benefits and status resulting from the posts of their parents, and due to this disadvantage thrust upon them, the children shall not he denied the benefits of reservation, i.e. the rule of exclusion will not apply to them. It may be noted that if permanent incapacitation occurs which results in putting an officer out of service, then it shall be tried as equivalent to death so far as the application of rule of exclusion to the offspring is concerned. Hereafter, wherever death has been mentioned it shall include permanent incapacitation as stated above.

To the unfortunate situation of death or permanent incapacitation of the only spouse who is in the category of service, or of both spouses who are in this category of service, an exception has to be recorded. If before the unfortunate event of death of either of or both such spouses occurs. either of spouses has had the benefit of employment in any international organisation like the UN, IMF, World Bank, etc., for a period of not less than five years then exclusion from the Benefit of reservation will continued to apply to the offspring.

9. It sometimes may happen that a lady who has got married to a Class I officer may herself like to apply for a job. If she belongs to SEBC category, she will not be disentitled by the rule of exclusion. The reason for saying so is that originally having been a member of SEBC; she carries with here the attributes of backwardness even after she is married to a Class I Officer and though she may economically be in a better position. The initial attributes of social backwardness continue to linger on and will not shaken-off during the short period (in view of the ago limit) which will be available to her for getting into any service employment. Therefore, we consider that such

a person; more so because she is a lady (which in our society may be generally regarded as a weaker class) should not be denied the benefit of reservation. Therefore, to such a lady rule of exclusion will not apply.

B. Group B/Class H—Central Services and State Services (Direct Recruitment)

10. If both spouses are Class II Officers then rule of exclusion will apply to their offspring. If only one of the spouses is a Class II Officer it will not apply, but if a male officer from Class II category gets into Class I category at the age of forty or earlier, then the rule of exclusion will apply to his offspring. Where both spouses are Class II officers and none of them dies, it is better to let the children have the benefit of reservation which means rule of exclusion will not apply; however, if either of the spouses has had the benefit of employment in any international organisation, as indicated above, for a period of not less than five years, then even in the event of death the application of the rule of exclusion will not be taken away. But if by great misfortune both the spouses die, then the rule of exclusion will not apply to the off-spring even if one of the spouses has had the benefit of employment in an international organisation.

Where the husband is a Class I Officer (Direct Recruit or pre-forty promoted) and the wife is a Class II Officer and the husband dies, the rule of exclusion will not apply. Also when the wife is dies Officer (i.e., Direct Recruit or pre-forty promoted) and the husband is a Class II Officer and dies the rule of exclusion will not apply but if the husband dies the rule of exclusion will apply on the principle that one of the parents, namely, the mother continues to be a Class I Officer.

C. Employment in Public Sector Undertakings etc.

12. The service category is not confined to employment under the Government only, whether at the Union or at the State level. The criteria enumerated above will apply *mutatis mutandis* to officers holding equivalent or comparable posts in public sector undertakings, banks, insurance organizations, universities, etc. and also to equivalent or comparable posts and positions under private employment.

13. The evaluation of the posts on equivalent or comparable basis is bound to take some time. In order that this may not become a ground for postponing the implementation of reservation in respect of persons under this category, it is made clear that so long as the evaluation process is not completed and made operative, the income/wealth test under item VI will govern the persons under this category. In other words, even during the interim period, the employees under this category will get the benefit of reservation, and if any exclusion is to be made it shall be on the basis of the criterion under item VI.

III. Armed Forces Including Para Military Forces (this will not include persons holding civil posts)

14. The exclusion rule will apply at the level of Colonel and above in the Army and to posts in the Navy and the Air Force and the Para Military Forces. If the wife of an Armed Forces officer is herself in the Armed Forces (i.e., the category under consideration) the rule of exclusion will apply only when she herself has reached the rank of Colonel: the service ranks below Colonel of husband and wife shall not be clubbed together. Even if the wife of an officer in the Armed Forces is in civil employment, this will not be taken into account for applying the rule of exclusion, unless she falls in the service category under Item No. 11 in which case the criteria and conditions enumerated therein will apply to her independently. In making these recommendations, we have borne in mind the peculiar nature of the service and hardships faced by the members of the Armed Forces and the Para Military Forces. It has also to be remembered that there is no reservation in recruitment to the Armed Forces, which means that a person at the stage of recruitment in these services is denied the benefit of reservation even though he may otherwise be entitled to it

IV. Professional Class and those Engaged in Trade, Business and Industry

15. This will include persons not in service employment either Government or private, but those who are engaged in professions as a doctor, lawyer, chartered accountant, income-tax consultant, financial or management consultant, dental

surgeon, engineer, architect, computer specialist, film artiste and other film professional, author, playwright, sports person, sports professional, media professional, or any other vocations of like status. All these persons for the purpose of determining whether they will fall in the disentitlement category or not will be governed by the income/wealth criterion as noted in Item No VI. Likewise persons engaged in trade, business and industry will be governed by the income/wealth criterion.

16. In a situation where the husband is in some profession and the wife is in a Class II or lower grade employment, the income/wealth test will apply only on the basis of the husband's income: in other words, the wife's employment will not be taken into account. If the wife is in any profession and the husband is in employment in a Class II or a lower rank post, then the income/wealth criterion will apply only on the basis of the wife's income and the husband's income will not be clubbed with it. The rationale is to avoid discouragement of women entering service or professions in a gender discriminating society such as ours.

V. Property Owners

A. *Agricultural Land Holdings*

17. It may not only be difficult but hazardous to prescribe any criteria on the basis of income from agricultural land holdings and this is borne out by the following observations in paragraph 809 of the majority judgment (Judgments Today)—

> "Further, income from agriculture may be difficult to access and, therefore, in the case of agriculturists, the line may have to be drawn with reference to the extent of holding. While the income of a person can be taken as a measure of his social advancement, the limit to be prescribed should not be such is to result in taking away with one hand what is given with the other."

So we proceed to indicate the criteria on the basis of the extent of land holding.

18. If a person belongs to a family (father, mother and minor children) which owns only irrigated land and the extent

of irrigated land is equal to or more than 65% of the statutory ceiling area, then the disentitlement will occur. It generally happens that a person holds different types of irrigated land. In such a situation, the different types of lands should, on the basis of the conversion formula existing, he brought into a single type of irrigated land as a common denominator and on the basis of such denominator, the above cut-off point of 65% will have to be determined.

19. The rule of exclusion will not disentitle persons belonging to families owning only unirrigated land irrespective of the area of such land. This is on account of the constraints imposed on and implicit in unirrigated cultivation.

20. In the case of members of a family owning both irrigated and unirrigated land, the exclusion rule will apply where the pre-condition exists that the irrigated area (having been brought to a single type under a common denominator) is 40% or more of the statutory ceiling limit for irrigated land (this being calculated by excluding the unirrigated portion). If this pre-condition of not less than 40% exists, then only the area of unirrigated land will be taken into account. This will be done by converting the unirrigated land on the basis of the conversion formula existing into the irrigated type. The irrigated area so computed from unirrigated land shall be added to the actual area of irrigated land, and if after such clubbing together the total area in terms of irrigated land is 65% or more of the statutory ceiling limit for irrigated land, then the rule of exclusion will apply and disentitlement will occur.

21. On the basis of data supplied to us find that there is no Ceiling Law in the States of Nagaland, Mizoram, Meghalaya, and Arunachal Pradesh and Goa and in the Union Territories of Andaman & Nicobar Islands, Lkshadweep, Daman & Diu. Apparently this is on account of the peculiar situation prevailing in these areas including topography, climatic conditions, etc. Under the circumstances the exclusion rule on the basis of land holding will not be applicable here. However, if at a future date Ceiling Law is enacted for any of such States or Union Territories, it would then have to be considered and determined lithe rule of exclusion on the basis

of land holding criterion will be made applicable or not and if so, in what manner.

B. Plantations

22. The plantations like coffee, tea, rubber, etc. which are not regarded as agricultural holding will come under this category. Since they are not regarded as agricultural holdings, they are not covered by ceiling laws. Therefore, the criterion at "A" above cannot apply to them and there is no alternative but to apply the criterion of income/wealth under Item No. VI.

23. From the data supplied to us, it appears that mango, citrus, apple plantations, etc., are regarded as agricultural holdings and they will be covered by the criterion at 'A' above.

C. Vacant Land and/or Buildings in Urban Areas or Urban Agglomeration

24. To identify those who come under this category the criterion of income/wealth under Item No. VI will apply. When we refer to a building it is made clear that the building may be used for residential, industrial or commercial purposes and the like, or two or more such purposes.

VI. Income/Wealth Test

25. This criterion is on the basis of income or wealth. We are conscious of the fact that in the majority Judgement and the judgments of Pandian and Sawant, JJ. it has been clearly emphasized that when placing a person in the excluded category, it should be unmistakably evident that social backwardness has come to an end. Their Lordships have emphasized that unless there is social advancement to such a degree as to bring a member of the SEBC more or less at par with the members of the forward classes, he should not be denied the benefit of reservation.

26. Since the people of this country are engaged in innumerable types of vocations and callings, it is simply not possible to assess the degree of social backwardness or advancement by specifying each one of such vocations for callings and under these circumstances, we have to take recourse to the only discernible criterion available, namely the

criterion of income or wealth. As such, this category may be said to be the residuary category. However, while prescribing the limit for this category, it has been kept in view that improvement in economic condition is so marked as to necessarily imply social advancement. Thus, here the rise in social status is presumption-based indicating that it has followed necessarily from the economic betterment. This aspect of treating social advancement on the basis of presumption has been kept in mind in prescribing the limit of gross income. In this connection, the following passage occurring in paragraph 809 of the majority judgment may be usefully quoted:

> "The basis of exclusion should not merely be economic, unless of course the economic advancement is so high that it necessarily means social advancement."
> (Vide *Judgement Today,* Vol. VI, No. 9, Nov. 30. 1992)

Hence, persons having gross annual income of Rs. 1 lakh or above or possessing wealth above the exemption limit as prescribed in the Wealth Tax Act will he excluded from the benefit of reservation. Only when such level of income or wealth has a consistency for a reasonable period will it be justifiable to regard a poison as socially advanced on the basis of income. We consider a period of three consecutive years to be a reasonable Period for the purpose of the application of the criteria under consideration.

21. In addition to the above, we have to say that the income/wealth test governs categories IV, VB and VC as stated earlier. For the remaining categories namely, II, III and VA specific criteria have been laid down: however, if in these categories, any person, who is not disentitled to the benefit of reservation will bring him within the criterion under Item No. VI, then he shall be disentitled to reservation, in case his income—without clubbing his income from salaries or agricultural land—or his wealth is in excess of cut-off point prescribed under the income/wealth criteria.

28. Since the rupee value is bound to undergo change the income criterion in terms of the rupee as stated above will accordingly stand modified with change in the value. The

modification exercise may, normally speaking, be undertaken every three years but if the situation so demands the interregnum may be less.

29. Persons working as artisans or engaged in the hereditary occupations, callings etc. like potters, washermen, barbers, etc. are exempted from application of the rule of exclusion.

30. The Supreme Court Judgement indicates that classifying the socially and educationally backward classes into two or more categories (backward, more backward, most backward and if necessary, further sub-categorization) is not only desirable but perhaps actually necessary. As and when such categorization is done we feel that for those fall in the two lowest strata at the bottom, i.e., the strata having the maximum backwardness, the application of the rule of exclusion may be kept in abeyance on the reasoning that the process of "creamy layer" formation will take more time in their case. While doing so the Government may examine its legal permissibility in terms of the Supreme Court Judgement.

31. We are aware of the strain imposed on candidates who seek certificates of caste, etc. The strain for them and the existing administrative machinery will be all the more where certification is required not only of caste but that the candidate is or is not affected by any of the criteria of exclusion. In order that SEBC candidates are not put to any harassment in this regard. We recommend that Government may make smooth and satisfactory arrangements for the issue of such certificates without delay and without any difficulty. Government has created a single window system for entrepreneurs applying for certificates and facilities for setting up new industries. Similarly, an appropriate single window system needs to be created at State/District level and necessary guidelines to be issued to see that correct certificates are issued promptly, and without harassment to the applicants.

32. We are also aware of the fact that in some cases false certificates of caste are issued to candidates who do not belong to the reserved categories. In order to prevent this and to ensure that certificates of caste as well as exclusion/non-exclusion criteria are factually corrected innovative arrangements such as transparency through steps like

Publication in the village/mohalla/panchayat Raj offices, etc., may be considered.

CONCLUSION

33. In specifying the determinists and prescribing the different formulation therein, we have adopted a pragmatic approach and we have considered it prudent as well as desirable to err on the right side. In other words, where it appeared while defining the criteria that a more strict formulation possible effect of excluding more than it ought to, we have chosen not to adopt such a course. And for this approach of ours we find support from in observations in different Judgments of the special Bench as well as from sources.

34. Reservation has been adopted as a remedy for curing the historical discrimination and its continuing ill-effects in public employment. That being the object in view, the denial of reservation to any member of a socially and educationally backward class is, and has to be, treated as an exception. In identifying such an exception, i.e., applying the rule of exclusion, it has to be ensured that the ill-effects have been fully and finally eliminated and no grey zone is discernible. The nature of such an exercise itself masks the rule of caution inherent

35. Hon'ble Mr. Justice Pandian does not subscribe to the "creamy layer" theory. Dealing with the oft-repeated criticism that the reserved posts are lapped up by the socially advanced ("creamy layer") among the socially and educationally backward classes. Pandian, J. has quoted with approval the observation of *Chinnappa Reddy, J. in the case of Vasanta Kumar.* The relevant passage is given below—

> ". . . that a few of the seats and posts reserved for backward classes are snatched away by the more fortunate among them is not to say that reservation is not necessary. This is bound to happen in a competitive society such as ours. Are not the unreserved seats and posts snatched away, in the same way, by the top creamy layers amongst them on the same principle of merit on

which the non-reserved seats are taken away by the top layers of society? How can it be bad if reserved seats and posts are snatched away by the creamy layer of backward classes if such snatching away unreserved posts by the top creamy layer of society itself is not bad?"

Pandian, J. says : "The above observation, in my view, is an apt reply to such a criticism with which I am in full agreement." (Paragraph, 229 and 230, *Judgments Today*)

36. Another passage from the judgment of Hon'ble Mr. Justice, Pandian in justifies the rule of caution and of erring on the right side adopted by us. The passage is as below:

> "It is after 42 years since the advent of our Constitution, the Government is taking the first step to implement this scheme of reservation for OBCs under Article 16(4). In fact, some of the States have not even introduced policy of reservation in the matters of public employment in favour of OBCs". (Paragraph 225, *Judgments Today*)

37. In the above context would it not be proper, nay desirable to let there be acceleration and let some distance be covered before we apply the brakes?

38. What the Supreme Court has directed is identification of the 'creamy layer". This obviously means that we have not to take note of sprinklings of cream or the mere appearance of cream at the surface. Only when the "creamy layer" is substantial and stable, formed after crossing the Rubicon of social backwardness, then and then alone can it be made the basis for disentitlement. In such a situation, can it be said that adopting a rule of caution and cringe on the right side is not justified! Apprehension has been expressed, and rightly, that applying the rule if exclusion on the ground of social advancement may be counter-productive, inasmuch as by excluding those who have become capable of facing the fierce competition for appointment in the services what will remain are those of the socially backward who are simply not equipped and ready to face the competition and this will have

the effect of many of the reserved seats being left vacant. The well-known writer and columnist. Mr. S. Sahay is one among many who have expressed such an apprehension. In an article entitled "A Moment of Truth" published in the *Hindustan Times*, Patna Edition dated 26-1 1-1992; this is what he has to say :

> ". . . Approval in principle of the concept of backward and more backward is rational and so is the exclusion of the creamy layer. However, the consequences in the immediate future of the exclusion of the creamy layer, even though desirable and necessary are not going to be happy.......The poor remain both poor and uneducated. Count the cost of education today and realize for yourself whether the boy or girl from the chaupal has ever the chance of getting a higher appointment under the Central Government. Even now the reserved Jobs for the Scheduled Castes and Tribes are not fully filled. Would the lot of the OBCs be any better, especially after excluding the creamy layer?"

39. We can cite many more such quotations and also give more reasons in support of the approach which we have adopted, but in our opinion what we have said above is sufficient to highlight the point under consideration.

40. We are happy to say that all the Members of this Expert Committee have worked day and night in a spirit of cooperation and understanding with each other. There has been free and frank exchange of views on almost every point dealt with in this Report and thereafter the Committee has arrived at a Consensus on the basis of which the criteria have been laid down.

41. For its deliberations, the Committee had to gather and examine a large volume of literature and documents including the judgment under consideration (*Indra Sawhney & Others*), various other related Judgement on the subjects, report of the Mandal Commission, report of the Chinnappa Reddy Commission, reports of the various State Commissions on OBCs/SEBCs. We have had also to look into large amount of data furnished by the Ministry of Welfare itself or by other

Ministries/Departments through the Ministry of Welfare which had relevance to or threw light on the points under consideration.

42. It is not out of place to mention that formulation of the criteria for ascertainment of the socially advanced among the SEBC (termed Creamy Layer by the Supreme Court) in the manner it required to be done for practical application, is unique in the sense that to our knowledge, such an exercise has been taken up in this country for the first time. Though we find that in the Report of the Third Backward Classes Commission for Karnataka, 1990, there is mention at page 174, Vol. I, of categories among socially and educationally backward classes who should not be entitled to reservation, but we have undertaken an elaborate exercise to make the formulations as far-reaching and comprehensive as possible. Of course, it may be desirable, perhaps even necessary at a future date, to give a second look to the criteria evolved by us and make suitable changes on the basis of experience of implementation and other relevant factors.

43. 'We are happy to place on record our gratitude for the unstinted cooperation extended to the Committee in the discharge of its work by the Hon'ble Minister of Welfare, Government of India, Shri Sitaram Kesari and by the Secretary and all other officers and stair of the Ministry of Welfare, and it is because of this, we have been able to complete this difficult task within the allotted short time.

APPENDIX 9

TEXT OF DOP&T O.M. NO. 36012/22/93-ESTT. (SCT), DT. 22.10.1993

RESERVATION FOR OTHER BACKWARD CLASSES IN CIVIL POSTS AND SERVICES UNDER THE GOVERNMENT CEILING OF 50% AND REVISED ROSTERS

The undersigned is directed to refer to this O.M. of even number dated the 8th September, 1993 on the above subject and to say that in accordance with the Supreme Court Judgement in the *Indira Sawhney case,* the reservations contemplated in clause 4 of Article 16 should not exceed 50%. For the purpose of applying the rule of 50%, an year should be taken as the unit and not the entire strength of the cadre, service or the unit as the case may be. This Position would also apply in the case of carry forward vacancies. Therefore, the ministry/departments are requested to ensure that the reservations provided to SC/ST/OBCs put together do not exceed 50% of vacancies arising in a year.

2. In the light of the reservations provided to other backward classes it is necessary to revise the existing reservation rosters. In respect of direct recruitment on All India basis by open competition where there is a reservation for 15% for SC and 7.5 for ST, the existing 40% point roster has been revised into a 200 point roster. The revised roster will come into effect immediately. Vacancies filled on or after 8.9.1993 should be shown in the new roster. The old roster shall be deemed to have been closed from this date. The reservations which had to be carried forward in the previous roster shall now be carried forward to the new roster.

3. There is no change in the existing reservation rosters in so far as promotion is concerned, as there is no reservation for OBCs in promotion.

4. No other relaxation concession is admissible to OBCs. There is no provision for any relaxed standard to be applied in the case of OBCs.

5. In Para 2(d) of this Department's O.M. of even number dated 8th September 1993, it has been stated that a list of castes and communities for the purpose of the reservation for OBCs is to be issued separately by the Ministry of Welfare. The Ministry of Welfare have since notified the said list vide their Resolution No. 1201/68/93-BCC(C) dated 10th September, 1993 published in the Gazette of India Extraordinary Part I Section, dated 13th September 1993. For the purpose of verification of the castes/communities the certificate from the following authorities only will be accepted:

(a) District Magistrate/Additional District Magistrate/ Collector/Deputy Collector/Commissioner/ Additional Deputy Commissioner/Ist Class Stipendiary Magistrate/Sub-Divisional Magistrate/ Taluka Magistrate/Executive Magistrate/Extra Assistant Commissioner (not below the rank of 1st Class Stipendiary Magistrate).
(b) Chief Presidency Magistrate/Additional Chief Presidency Magistrate/President Magistrate.
(c) Revenue Officer not below the rank of Tehsildar; and
(d) Sub-Divisional Officer of the area where the candidate and/or his family resides.

Not reproduced for revised post-based rosters, now refer to Chapter 'Rosters for Reservation'.

APPENDIX 10

No.-13/34/90-(2)/Karmic-1/1994

Subject : *Roster for Implementing Reservation in Promotion*

Sir,

It is directed to bring your kind attention on Government Order no. 13/34/90 (1)-1/1994, dated 10 October 1994, which permit 21% reservation to Scheduled Castes and 2% reservation to Scheduled Tribes in promotion.

2. By cancelling old Roster following new Roster system has been prepared to confirm above reservation in promotion:

1. Scheduled Caste;
2. Unreserved;
3. Unreserved;
4. Unreserved;
5. Unreserved;
6. Scheduled Caste;
7. Unreserved;
8. Unreserved;
9. Unreserved
10. Unreserved
11. Scheduled Caste;
12. Unreserved;
13. Unreserved;
14. Unreserved;
15. Unreserved;
16. Scheduled Caste;
17. Unreserved;
18. Unreserved;
19. Unreserved;
20. Unreserved;
21. Scheduled Caste;
22. Unreserved;
23. Unreserved;
24. Unreserved;
25. Unreserved;
26. Scheduled Caste;
27. Unreserved;
28. Unreserved;
29. Unreserved;
30. Unreserved;
31. Scheduled Caste;
32. Unreserved;
33. Unreserved;
34. Unreserved;
35. Unreserved;
36. Scheduled Caste;
37. Unreserved;
38. Unreserved;

39. Unreserved;
40. Unreserved;
41. Scheduled Caste;
42. Unreserved;
43. Unreserved;
44. Unreserved;
45. Unreserved;
46. Scheduled Caste;
47. Unreserved;
48. Unreserved;
49. Scheduled Caste;
50. Unreserved;
51. Scheduled Caste;
52. Unreserved;
53. Unreserved;
54. Unreserved;
55. Unreserved;
56. Scheduled Caste;
57. Unreserved;
58. Unreserved;
59. Unreserved;
60. Unreserved;
61. Scheduled Caste;
62. Unreserved;
63. Unreserved;
64. Unreserved;
65. Unreserved;
66. Scheduled Caste;
67. Unreserved;
68. Unreserved;
69. Unreserved;
70. Unreserved;
71. Scheduled Caste;
72. Unreserved;
73. Unreserved;
74. Unreserved;
75. Unreserved;
76. Unreserved;
77. Unreserved;
78. Unreserved;
79. Unreserved;
80. Unreserved;
81. Scheduled Caste;
82. Unreserved;
83. Unreserved;
84. Unreserved;
85. Unreserved;
86. Scheduled Caste;
87. Unreserved;
88. Unreserved;
89. Unreserved;
90. Scheduled Caste;
91. Unreserved;
92. Unreserved;
93. Unreserved;
94. Unreserved;
95. Scheduled Caste;
96. Unreserved;
97. Scheduled Caste;
98. Unreserved;
99. Scheduled Caste.

3. It is requested that above roster shall apply accordingly in promotion.

APPENDIX 11

क्रम सं– 757 रजि.सं.एल.डब्ल्यू./एम.वा/एम.वा/–11

सरकारी गजट, उत्तर प्रदेश

उत्तर प्रदेशीय सरकार द्वारा प्रकाशित

असाधारण विधायी परिशिष्ट

भाग–4, खण्ड (ख)

(परिनिति आदेश)

लखनऊ, शुक्रवार, 8 दिसम्बर 1995

अग्रहायण 17,1917 शक सम्बत्

उत्तर प्रदेश सरकार

कार्मिक अनुभाग–2

संख्या 22/16–92–का–1995

लखनऊ, 8 दिसम्बर, 1995

अधिसूचना

प्रकीर्ण

पं.मा.–2525

रिट याचिका सं. 631/04 अशोक कुमार ठाकुर बनाम बिहार राज्य और अन्य में दिनांक 04 सितम्बर, 1995 को माननीय उच्चतम न्यायालय ने उ.प्र. लोक सेवा (अनुसूचित जातियों/अनुसूचित अजन–जातियों और अन्य पिछडा वर्गों के लिये आरक्षण) अधिनियम, 1994 (उ.प्र. अधिनियम संख्या 4, सन् 1994) की अनुसूची–2 की निरस्त कर दिया है और यह निर्देश दिए हैं, कि उ.प्र. राज्य में 1995–96 के शैक्षणिक सत्र में केन्द्र सरकार के मेमोरेण्डम दिनांक 08 सितम्बर, 1993 में निर्धारित क्रीमिलेयर का अनुसरण किया जाएगा।

अतएव उ.प्र. लोक सेवा (अनुसूचित जातियों, अनुसूचित जनजातियों और अन्य पिछड़ा वर्गों के लिये आरक्षण) अधिनियम, 1994 (उ.प्र. अधिनियम संख्या 4, सन् 1994) की धारा 13 के अधीन शक्ति का प्रयोग करके, राज्यपाल उपर्युक्त अधिनियम की अनुसूची दो को निम्नवत् संशोधित करते हैं ओर यह भी निर्देश देते हैं कि यह अनुसूची जो केन्द्र सरकार के मेमोरेण्डम दिनांक 08 सितम्बर, 1993, जैसा कि उत्तर प्रदेश राज्य की स्थिति में लागू हो सके, शिक्षण संस्थाओं के शैक्षणिक सत्र 1995–96 के प्रवेश में भी लागू समझी जाएगी।

उत्तर प्रदेश असाधारण बजट, 8 दिसम्बर 1995
संशोधन

उपर्युक्त अधिनियम की अनुसूची दो के स्थान पर निम्नलिखित अनुसूची दो रख दी जाएगी, अर्थात

अनुसूची–दो
(धारा 3(1) देखिए)

एक – संवैधानिक पद

निम्नलिखित के पुत्र या पुत्री

(क) भारत के राष्ट्रपति,
(ख) भारत के उपराष्ट्रपति,
(ग) उच्चतम न्यायालय और उच्च न्यायालयों के न्यायाधीश
(घ) संघ लोग सेवा आयोग और राज्य लोक सेवा आयोगों के अध्यक्ष और सदस्य, मुख्य निर्वाचन आयुक्त, भारत के नियंत्रक और महालेखा परीक्षक
(ड) इसी प्रकार के संवैधानिक पदों पर आसीन व्यक्ति ।

दो–सेवा श्रेणी

(क) अखिल भारतीय केन्द्रीय और राज्य सेवाओं (सीधी भर्ती) के समूह क/श्रेणी एक अधिकारी

निम्नलिखित के पुत्र या पुत्री –

(क) जिनके माता पिता दोनों समूह क/श्रेणी एक के अधिकारी हों,

(ख) जिनके माता पिता में से कोई भी समूह क/श्रेणी एक का अधिकारी हो,

(ग) जिनके माता पिता दोनों समूह क/श्रेणी एक के अधिकारी हों किन्तु उनमें से किसी एक की मृत्यु हो जाये या वह स्थायी अक्षमता से ग्रसित हो जाय,

(घ) जिनके माता पिता में से कोई भी समूह क/श्रेणी एक का अधिकारी हो और ऐसे माता पिता की मृत्यु हो जाय या वह स्थाई अक्षमता से ग्रसित हो जाए और ऐसी मृत्यु या अक्षमता के पूर्व उसे किसी अन्तर्राष्ट्रीय संगठन जैसे संयुक्त राष्ट्र, अन्तर्राष्ट्रीय मुद्रा कोष, विश्व बैंक आदि में पांच वर्ष से अन्यून अवधि के लिये नियोजन का भाग प्राप्त हुआ हो, और

(ड) जिनके माता पिता दोनों समूह क/श्रेणी एक के अधिकारी हों और ऐसे माता पिता दोनों को मृत्यु हो जाये या वे स्थायी अक्षमता से ग्रसित हो जाए और दोनों की ऐसी मृत्यु का अक्षमता के पूर्व उनमें से किसी एक को किसी अन्तर्राष्ट्रीय संगठन जैसे संयुक्त राष्ट्र, अन्तर्राष्ट्रीय मुद्रा कोष, विश्व बैंक आदि में पांच वर्ष से अन्यून अवधि के लिये नियोजन का लाभ प्राप्त हुआ हो,

(ख) केन्द्रीय और राज्य सेवाएं (सीधी भर्ती) समूह ख/श्रेणी दो के अधिकारी।

निम्नलिखित के पुत्र या पुत्री

(क) जिनके माता पिता दोनों समूह ख/श्रेणी दो के अधिकारी हों,

(ख) जिनके माता पिता में से केवल पिता समूह ख/श्रेणी दो का अधिकारी हो और वह चालीस वर्ष या इसके पूर्व की आयु में समूह क/श्रेणी एक आ में जाय,

(ग) जिनके माता पिता दोनों समूह क/श्रेणी बी के अधिकारी हो ओर उनमें से एक की मृत्यु हो जाय या वह स्थायी अक्षमता से ग्रसित हो जाये और उनमें से किसी एक की ऐसी मृत्यु या स्थायी अक्षमता के पूर्व किसी अन्तर्राष्ट्रीय संगठन में से संयुक्त राष्ट्र, अन्तर्राष्ट्रीय मुद्रा कोश, विश्व बैंक आदि में पांच वर्ष से अन्यून अवधि के लिये नियोजन का लाभ प्राप्त हुआ हो।

(घ) जिनके माता – पिता में से पिता समूह क/श्रेणी का (सीधी भर्ती) या चालीस वर्ष के पूर्व पदोन्नति अधिकारी हो और माता समूह ख/श्रेणी का अधिकारी हो ओर माता की मृत्यु हो जाय या वह स्थायी अक्षमता से ग्रसित हो जाये और

(ड) जिनके माता पिता में से माता समूह क/श्रेणी एक की (सीधी भर्ती) या चालीस वर्ष के पूर्व पदोन्नति अधिकारी हो और पिता समूह ख/श्रेणी दो का अधिकारी हो और पिता की मृत्यु हो जाये या वह स्थाई रूप से ग्रसित हो जाये।

स्पष्टीकरण – इस श्रेणी के प्रयोजनों के लिये यह स्पष्ट किया जाता है कि पद, ''स्थायी अक्षमता का'' तात्पर्य ऐसी अक्षमता से है जिसके कारण कोई अधिकारी सेवा से बाहर हो जाय।

(ग) सार्वजनिक क्षेत्र के उपक्रमों के कर्मचारी

ऊपर उप श्रेणी (क) और (ख) में विनिर्दिष्ट मानदण्ड यथावश्यक परिवर्तन सहित उन अधिकारियों पर लागू होंगे जो सार्वजनिक क्षेत्र के उपकमों, बैंकों, बीमा, संगठनों, विश्वविद्यालयों आदि में समकक्ष या तुलनीय पदों पर और निजी नियोजन के अधीन भी समकक्ष या तुलनीय पदों और स्थानों पर हों, इन संस्थाओं में समक्षक या आधार पर पदों के मूल्यांकन के लम्बित रहते नीचे श्रेणी में विनिर्दिष्ट मानदण्ड, इन संस्थाओं के अधिकारों पर लागू होगा।

अर्द्धसैनिक बलों को सम्मिलित करते हुये सशस्त्र बल (सिविल पदों की धारण करने वाले व्यक्ति सम्मिलित है।)

ऐसे माता पिता जिनमें से कोई एक या दोनों सेवा में कर्नल और उसके ऊपर के पद पर हो या नौ सेना, वायु सेना और अर्द्ध सैनिक बलों या उसके समकक्ष पदों पर हों, के पुत्र या पुत्री।

स्पष्टीकरण – इस श्रेणी के प्रयोजनों के लिये पिता और माता के कर्नल से नीचे के सेवा पदों को एक साथ छोडा नहीं जाएगा।

व्यावसायिक वर्ग और व्यापार धन्धे और उद्योग में श्रेणी ख में विनिर्दिष्ट मानदण्ड निम्नलिखित पर लागू होंगे।

(क) डाक्टर, वकील, चार्टेड एकाउण्टेन्ट, आयकर परामर्शदाता, दन्त चिकित्सक, अभियन्ता, वास्तुविद, फिल्म कलाकार और अन्य फिल्म व्यवसायी, लेखक, नाटककार, खिलाडी, खेलकूद, व्यवसायी, मीडिया व्यवसायी या इस प्रकार के किसी अन्य व्यवसाय में लगे व्यक्ति, और

(घ) धन्धे, व्यापार और उद्योग में लगे व्यक्ति

स्पष्टीकरण – (एक) जहां पिता किसी व्यवसाय में हो और माता समूह ख/श्रेणी दो या निम्न श्रेणी क नियोजन में हो, वहां नीचे श्रेणी छः में विनिर्दिष्ट मापदण्ड केवल पिता की आय के आधार पर लागू होगा और माता की आय इसके साथ नहीं जोडी जाएगी।

(दो) जहां माता किसी व्यवसाय में हो और पिता समूह ख/श्रेणी दो या निम्न श्रेणी के नियोजन में हो, तो नीचे श्रेणी छः में विनिर्दिष्ट मानदण्ड केवल माता की आय के आधार पर लागू होगा और पिता की आय उसके साथ नहीं जोडी जाएगी।

सम्पत्ति स्वामी

(क) कृषि भूमि जोत

ऐसे माता पिता जिसमें से कोई एक अपने परिवार के साथ जिसमें वह स्वयं उसकी पत्नी/पति और नाबालिग वे सम्मिलित हैं, निम्नलिखित भूमि का स्वामी हो, के पुत्र या पुत्री –

(क) केवल सिंचित भूमि जो कानूनी (अधिकतम जोत सीमा के पच्चासी प्रतिशत बराबर या उससे अधिक हो, या

(ख) सिंचित और असिंचित दोनों प्रकार की भूमि हो, जहां सिंचित भूमि (जो किसी सामान्य डिनोमिनेटर के अधीन किसी एक प्रकार में लायी गई हो) सिंचित भूमि की साविधिक कानूनी अधिकतम जोत सीमा के चालीस प्रतिशत से अधिक है, वहां असिंचित भूमि विद्यमान परिवर्तन फार्मूला के आधार पर सिंचित भूमि में परिवर्तित कर दी जाएगी और इस प्रकार संगणित सिंचित क्षेत्र को 'सिंचित भूमि के वास्तविक क्षेत्र के साथ जोड दिया जाएगा और इस प्रकार आई सिंचित भूमि के अनुसार कुल क्षेत्र सिंचित भूमि के लिये कानूनी अधिकतम जो सीमा के अस्सी प्रतिशत के बराबर या अधिक हो।

स्पष्टीकरण – पद ''कानूनी अधिकतम जोत सीमा'' और ''परिवर्तन फार्मूला'' का अर्थ उस क्षेत्र या अधिकतम कृषि जोत सीमा से सम्बन्धित विधि के अनुसार लगाया जाएगा। जिसमें प्रश्नगत भूमि स्थित हो।

(ख) पौधा रोपण

(एक) काफी, चाय, रबर आदि

नीचे श्रेणी छः में विनिर्दिष्ट मानदण्ड लागू होगा,

(दो) आम, निबूवंश, सेब आदि

ऐसे पौधारोण की भूमि कृषि भूमि जोत समझी जाएगी और ऊपर उप श्रेणी (क) के अधीन विनिर्दिष्ट मानदण्ड लागू होगा।

(ग) शहरी क्षेत्रों या शहरी समूहों में खाली भूमि या भवन

नीचे श्रेणी छः में विनिर्दिष्ट मानदण्ड लागू होगा।

स्पष्टीकरण – इस उप श्रेणी के प्रयोजन के लिये यह स्पष्ट किया जाता है कि भवन का प्रयोग आवासीय, वाणिज्यिक या औद्योगिक प्रयोजनों या इस प्रकार के दो या अधिक प्रयोजनों के लिये किया जा सकता है।

आय या सम्पत्ति मापदण्ड

निम्नलिखित के पुत्र या पुत्री

(क) ऐसे व्यक्ति जिनकी निरन्तर तीन वर्ष की अवधि के लिये सकल वार्षिक आय एक लाख या इससे अधिक हो या जिसके पासधनकर अधिनियम, 1957 में मय/विहित छूट सीमा से सम्पत्ति हो।

(ख) श्रेणी एक, दो, तीन या पांच (क) में विर्निदिष्ट व्यक्ति जो आरक्षण के लाभ किन्तु जिनकी अन्य स्रोतों से आय इतनी हो जो उन्हें ऊपर उप श्रेणी (क) में विर्निदिष्ट मापदण्ड के भीतर लाती हो।

स्पष्टीकरण–इस श्रेणी के प्रयोजनों के लिये यह स्पष्ट किया जाता है कि–

(एक) वेतन या कृषि भूमि से आय को मिलाया नहीं जाएगा

(दो) उपरोक्तानुसार प्रत्येक तीन वर्ष में जिसके मूल्य परिवर्तन कोध्यान में रखता रूपान्तरित किया जाएगा। परन्तु यदि स्थिति का ऐसी मांग हो तो इसका अन्तराल कम हो सकता है।

आज्ञा से

कालिका प्रसाद,

सचिव।

संख्या 22/16/92–टी.सी.–।।।/का–2/2002

प्रेषक,

राजेन्द्र भौनवाल,

प्रमुख सचिव,

उत्तर प्रदेश शासन।

सेवा में,

1–समस्त प्रमुख सचिव/सचिव, उ.प्र. शासन।

2–समस्त विधागाध्यक्ष/प्रमुख कार्यालयाध्यक्ष, उ.प्र.।

3–समस्त मण्डलायुक्त/जिलाधिकारी, उ.प्र.।

लखनऊ, दिनांक 22 अक्टूबर, 2002

कार्मिक अनुभाग –2

विषय : राज्याधीन सेवाओं में आरक्षण हेतु जाति प्रमाण पत्र।

महोदय,

राज्याधीन लोक सेवाओं एवं पदों में सीधी भर्ती के प्रक्रम पर आरक्षित वर्गों को आरक्षण का लाभ देने के लिये उत्तर प्रदेश लोक सेवा (अनुसूचित जातियों, अनुसूचित जनजातियों और अन्य पिछड़ा वर्गों के लिये आरक्षण) अधिनियम, 1994, जैसा कि उ.प्र. अधिनियम संख्या 21 सन् 2001 एवं उ.प्र. अधिनियम संख्या 1 सन् 2002 द्वारा संशोधित किया गया है, प्रवृत्त है।

2–उ.प्र. लोक सेवा (अनुसूचित जातियों, अनुसूचित जनजातियों और अन्य पिछडा वर्गों के लिये आरक्षण) (संशोधन) अधिनियम, 2002 (अधिनियम संख्या 1 सन् 2002) दिनांक 15.09.2001 से प्रभावी है, जिसके द्वारा उ.प्र. लोक सेवा (अनुसूचित जातियों, अनुसूचित जनजातियों और अन्ये पिछड़ा वर्गों के लिये आरक्षण) (संशोधन) अधिनियम, 2001 (उ.प्र. अधिनियम संख्या 21 सन् 2001) को संशोधित किया जा चुका है। अतएव, इसके अधीन जाति प्रमाण–पात्र के सम्बन्ध में जारी किया गया शासनादेश संख्या 22/16/92–टी.सी.–।।।/का–2/2001 दिनांक 10.10.2001 एवं समसंख्यक शासनादेश दिनांक 10.12.2001 तथा इसके साथ संलग्न

निर्धारित प्रपत्र एवं शासनादेश सं. 22/16/92–टी.सी.–।।।/का–2/2002 दिनांक 03 जुलाई 2002 एतद् द्वारा निरस्त किये जाते हैं।

3–मुझे यह कहने का निदेश हुआ है कि अनुसूचित जातियों, अनुसूचित जनजातियों तथा अन्य पिछडा वर्गों के लिये एतदद्वारा संलग्न प्रारूप में जाति प्रमाण–पत्र जारी किए जाएं। शासनादेश संख्या 22/16/92/का–2/1996 दिनांक 5–1–1996, जिसके द्वारा जाति प्रमाण पत्र निर्गत किये जाने की प्रक्रिया निर्धारित की गई है, के अनुसार सक्षम प्राधिकारी द्वार संलग्न प्रारूप में जाति प्रमाण–पत्र, आरक्षण का लाभ पाने के लिये, जारी करना सुनिश्चित किया जाए।

4–नागरिकों के अन्य पिछडा वर्गों के व्यक्तियों को पूर्वोक्त जाति प्रमाण–पत्र निर्गत करने से पूर्व यह बातध्यान में रखी जायेगी कि पूर्वोक्त आरक्षण अधिनियम की यथा संशोधितधारा–3(1) के प्रथम परन्तुक के उपबन्ध के अनुसार, अनुसूची–दो में विर्निदिष्ट नागरिकों के अन्य पिछड़ा वर्गों की श्रेणी को आरक्षण अनुमन्य नहीं है। पूर्वोक्त आरक्षण संशोधन अधिनियम, 2001 द्वारा प्रतिस्थापति की गई अनुसूची–दो, जिसमें पूर्वोक्त आरक्षण संशोधन अधिनियम–2002 द्वारा कतिपय संशोधन किये गये हैं, प्रवृत्त है। यथा संशोधित अनुसूची दो के अनुच्छेद छः के प्रावधान के अनुसार अन्य पिछड़ा वर्गों के ऐसे व्यक्तियों के पुत्र या पुत्री को आरक्षण का लाभ अनुमन्य नहीं होगा, जिनकी निरन्तर तीन वर्ष की अवधि के लिये सकल वार्षिक आय तीन लाख रूपये या इससे अधिक हो या जिसके पासधनकर अधिनियम, 1957 में यथा विहित छूट सीमा से अधिक सम्पत्ति हो।

भवदीय,

राजेन्द्र भौनवाल
प्रमुख सचिव

APPENDIX 12

OFFICIAL GAZETTE UTTAR PRADESH

Published by U.P. Government
Not Ordinary
Legislative Appendix
Part-1, Section (A)
U.P. Act
Lucknow Saturday 31 August, 2002
Notification
No. 1576(2)/XVII-V-1-1(KA)/11-2002

The Governor of U.P. is pleased to give consent on 29 August 2002 on the Uttar Pradesh Public Services (Reservation for Scheduled Castes, Scheduled Tribes and Other Backward Classes) (Amendment) Act, 2002 enacted by UP legislature under Article 200 of Indian Constitution.

The Uttar Pradesh Public Services (Reservation for Scheduled Castes, Scheduled Tribes and Other Backward Classes) (Amendment) Act, 2002

(U.P. Act No. 1 of 2002)

An Act

Further to amend the Uttar Pradesh Public Services (Reservation for Scheduled Castes, Scheduled Tribes and 0ther Backward Classes) Act, 1994.

It is HEREBY enacted in the Fifty-third Year of the Republic of India as follows:

1. (1) This Act may be called the Uttar Pradesh public Services (Reservation follows: for Scheduled Castes, Scheduled Tribes and other Backward Classes) (Amendment), Act, 2002.

   (2) Section 2. sub-section (1) of section 3 of the principal Act, except the second proviso thereto, as substituted by clause *(a)* of section *3*, sub-clause (1) of clause *(b)* of section 3, section 4, section 5 and section 6 shall be deemed to have come into force on September I5, 2001; the remaining provisions of clause *(a)* sub-clause (ii) of clause *(b)* and clause *(c)* of section *3* shall be deemed to have come into force on June 25, 2002, and the remaining provisions shall come into force at once.

2. In section 2 of the Uttar Pradesh Public Services (Reservation for Scheduled Castes, Scheduled Tribes and other Backward Classes) Act, 1994 hereinafter *referred* to as the principal Act:

   (a) for clause *(b)* the following clause shall be *substituted*, namely:

   (b) "other backward classes of citizens' means the "backward classes of citizens specified in Schedule I";

   (c) clauses *(b-I) (b-2)* and *(b-3)* shall be *omitted.*

3. In section 3 of the principle Act,

   (a) *for* sub-section (1*)*, (2) and (3) the following sub-section shall be *substituted* namely :

   "(1) In public services and posts there shall be reserved at the stage of direct recruitment, the following percentage of vacancies to which recruitment are to be made in accordance with the roster referred to in sub-section (5) in favour of the persons belonging to Scheduled Castes, Scheduled Tribes and other Backward Classes of citizens,

   (a) in the case of Scheduled Castes—21 per cent:

   (b) in the case of Scheduled Tribe—2 per cent:

(c) in the case of other Backward Classes citizens—27 percent:
Provided that the reservation under clause *(c)* shall not apply to the category of other Backward Classes of citizens specified in Schedule II:
Provided further that reservation of vacancies for all categories of persons shall not exceed in any year of recruitment fifty per cent of the total vacancies of that year as also fifty per cent of the cadre strength of the service to which the recruitment is to be made.

(2) If, in respect of any year of recruitment any vacancy reserved for any category of persons under sub-section (1) remains unfilled, such vacancy shall be carried forward and be filled through special recruitment in that very year or in succeeding year or years of recruitment as a separate class of vacancy and such-class of vacancy shall not be considered together with the vacancies of the year of recruitment in which it is filled and also for the purpose of determining the ceiling of fifty per cent reservation of the total vacancies of that year notwithstanding anything to the contrary contained in sub-section (1);

(3) Where a vacancy reserved for the Scheduled Tribes remains unfilled even after three special recruitments made under sub-section (2), such vacancy may be filled from amongst the persons belonging to the Scheduled Castes:

(b) (i) sub-section (3-A), (3-B) shall be *omitted;*
(ii) sub-section (4) shall be *omitted;*

(c) *for* sub-section (5), the following sub-section shall be *substituted,* namely :

"(5) The State Government shall for applying the reservation under sub-section (1), by a notified order, issue a roster comprising the total cadre strength of the public service or post indicating therein the reserve points and the roster so issued shall be implemented in the form of a running account from year to year until the reservation for various categories of persons mentioned in sub-section (1) is achieved and the operation of the roster and the running account shall, thereafter, come to an end, and when a vacancy arises thereafter in public service or post the same shall be filled from amongst the persons belonging to the category to which the post belongs in the roster."

4. *For* Schedule-I, to the principal Act, the following Schedule shall be *substituted, n*amely:

SCHEDULE-I
(See section 2 (b))

5. In Schedule-II to the principal Act :

(a) in Article I, the words "or has been" shall be *omitted,*
(b) in Article II in clause (A) in sub-clause (e) for the word *'temporary'* word *'permanent'* shall be substituted;

6. Schedule-III to the principal Act shall be *omitted.*

7. (1) The Uttar Pradesh Public Services (Reservation for Scheduled Castes, Scheduled Tribes and other Backward Classes) (Amendment) Ordinance, 2002 and the Uttar Pradesh Public Services (Reservation for Scheduled Castes, Scheduled Tribes and other Backward Classes) (Second Amendment) Ordinance, 2002 are hereby repealed.

(2) Notwithstanding such repeal, anything done or any action taken under the provisions of the principal Act as amended by the Ordinances referred to in sub-section (1) shall be deemed to have been done or taken under the corresponding provisions of the principal Act as amended by this Act as if the provisions of this Act were in force at all material times.

STATEMENT OF OBJECT AND REASONS

The Uttar Pradesh Public Service (Reservation for Scheduled Castes Scheduled Tribes and Other Backward

Classes Act, 1994 has been enacted to provide for the reservation in public services and post in favour of persons belonging to Scheduled Castes, Scheduled Tribes and other Backward Class citizens and for matters connected therewith and incidental thereto. The said Act was amended by The Uttar Pradesh Public Service (Reservation for Scheduled Castes, Scheduled Tribes and Other Backward Classes Act, 2001 (U.P. Act No. 21 of 2001) to further classify the persons belonging to the Scheduled Castes into two categories and the other Backward Classes into three categories keeping in view their representation in public Services and posts in proportion to their population and to provide for reservation to them in public services and posts and also to preside for,

(a) the reservation in any year of recruitment to the extent of fifty per cent of vacancies of that year or of the cadre; (b) abolition of restrictions of maximum three special recruitments for unfilled vacancies of a reserved category: (c) carrying forward the unfilled vacancies of any reserved categories as a separate class of vacancies until unfilled; (d) issue of roster on the cadre strength by indicating reservation points to various reserved categories.

2. The aforesaid Act of 2001 was challenged in the Supreme Court by a writ petition by the *Akil Bharatvarsh Chhatra Yuwa Berozgar Front* in which the Hon'ble Supreme Court in its interim order dated January 21, 2002 directed that no executive order in pursuance of the aforesaid Act of 2001 shall be passed during the pendency of the writ petition. In view of the said order of Hon'ble Supreme Court, recruitment to fill the vacancies in public services and posts could not be made and a large number of posts in various departments were lying vacant. It was, therefore, decided to restore the provision of the aforesaid Act, 1994 as they stood before amendment by the said U.P. Act No. 21 of 2001.

3. Since the State Legislature was not in session and immediate legislative action was necessary to implement the aforesaid decision, the Uttar Pradesh Public Services (Reservation for Scheduled Castes, Scheduled Tribes and Other

Backward Classes) (Amendment) Ordinance, 2002 (U.P. Ordinance No. 2, 2002) was promulgated by the Governor on June 6, 2002.

4. As the provisions at (a) to referred to in para first above made to include the principle propounded by the Hon'ble Supreme Court in the case of *R.K. Sabbarwal and others* v. *State of Punjab and others* and in the light of the provisions of clause (4-B) of the constitution inserted by the Constitution (Eighty-first Amendment) Act, 2000 were also replaced by the provisions by the aforesaid U.P. Ordinance No. 2 of 2002 it was decided to amend the aforesaid Act of 1994 so as include them therein.

5. Since the State Legislature was not in session and immediate legislative action was necessary to implement the decision referred to in para 4 above, the Uttar Pradesh Public Services (Reservation for Schedule Castes, Schedule Tribes and Other Backward Classes) (Second Amendment) Ordinance, 2002•(U.P. Ordinance No. 7 of 2002) was promulgated by the Governor on June 25, 2002.

This Bill is introduced to replace the aforesaid Ordinances.

APPENDIX 13

OFFICIAL GAZETTE UTTAR PRADESH

Published by U.P. Government
Not Ordinary
Legislative Appendix
Part 4, Section (B)
Lucknow, Monday, 10 October 2005
Notification
No. 4/1/2005

In exercise of powers under section 13 of the Uttar Pradesh Public Service (Reservation for Scheduled Caste, Scheduled Tribes and Other Backward Classes Act, 1994 (UP Act No. 4 of 1994) the governor is pleased to make following amendment in Scheduled-1 of said Act.

AMENDMENT

(1) In scheduled-1 to the aforesaid Act the following entries shall be omitted; viz.

(12) Kahar, Kashyap; (13) Kewat, Mallah, Nishad; (16) Kumhar, Prajapati; (29) Dhivar; (38) Bind; (40) Bhar, Rajbhar.

(2) Entries of the said schedule-1 shall be renumbered as Part-1 thereof and after part 1 of schedule-1 as so renumbered the following parts shall be inserted namely:

PART II

Backward class citizen who shall be deemed to be and entitled to get benefit of Scheduled Castes instead of backward class under the Act :

(1) Kahar, Koshyap; (2) Kewat, Mallah, Nishad; (3) Kumhar, Prajapati; (4) Dhivar; (5) Bind; (6) Bhar, Rajbhar

PART III

Following classes of citizens shall be deemed to be entitled to get benefit of scheduled castes under the Act:

(1) Dhimar; (2) Batham; (3) Turha; (4) Gaud;
(5) Manjhi; (6) Machhua

By order
B.N. Dikshit
Vishesh Sachiv

APPENDIX 14

Percentages of Reservations for SCs/STs and OBCs where Recruitment is made on a Local or Regional Basis*

Name of State/UT	*% of reservation for SC/ST/OBC*
1. Andhra Pradesh	15 SC/6 ST/27 OBC
2. Assam	6 SC/11 ST/27 OBC
3. Bihar	15 SC/9 ST/26 OBC
4. Gujarat	7 SC/14 ST/27 OBC
5. Haryana	19 SC/Nil ST/27 OBC
6. Himachal Pradesh	25 SC/5 ST/20 OBC
7. Jammu & Kashmir	9 SC/13 ST/27 OBC
8. Karnataka	15 SC/5 ST/27 OBC
9. Kerala	10 SC/1 ST/27 OBC
10. Madhya Pradesh	14 SC/23 ST/13 OBC
11. Maharashtra	7 SC/9 ST/27 OBC
12. Manipur	1 SC/27 ST/22 OBC
13. Meghalaya	1 SC/44 ST/5 OBC
14. Mizoram	Nil SC/45 ST/5 OBC
15. Orissa	15 SC/23 ST/12 OBC
16. Punjab	27 SC/Nil ST/23 OBC
17. Rajasthan	17 SC/12 ST/21 OBC
18. Sikkim	6 SC/23 ST/2l OBC
19. Tamil Nadu	19 SC/1 ST/27 OBC
20. Tripura	15 SC/29 ST/6 OBC
21. Uttar Pradesh	21 SC/I ST/27 OBC
22. West BengaI	2 SC 16 ST/22 OBC

*Vide DOP&T.O.M. No. 36012/22/93 Esit. (SCT), dt. 29.12.1993.

Union Territories

1.	Andaman Nicobar Islands	Nil SC/12 ST/27 OBC
2.	Chandigarh	14 SC/Nil ST/27 OBC
3.	Dadra and Nagar Haveli	2 SC/43 ST/5 OBC
4.	Daman & Diu	2 S C/1 ST/27 OBC
5.	Pondichery	16 SC/Nil ST/27 OBC

N.B. :

1. In respect of Arunachal Pradesh, Nagaland and Lakshadweep there is no change in the existing reservation Rosters.
2. For Goa, the reservation Rosters will be the same as is given in respect of the Union Territory of Daman and Diu.
3. For Delhi, the rosters as prescribed for recruitment on All-India basis is to be followed.

SC—Scheduled Castes	15
ST—Scheduled Tribes	7-1/2%
OBC—Other Backward Classes.	27%

APPENDIX 15

OFFICIAL GAZETTE UTTAR PRADESH

Published by U.P. Government
Legislative Section-1
Lucknow, 23 March, 1994
No. 488/XVII-V-1-1(A)-6-1994
Lucknow, October 6, 2001
Notification

THE UTTAR PRADESH PUBLIC SERVICES (RESERVATION FOR SCHEDULED CASTES, SCHEDULED TRIBES AND OTHER BACKWARD CLASSES) (AMENDMENT) ACT, 1994

(U.P. Act No. 4 of 1994)

The Governor of U.P. is pleased to give consent on 22 March 1994 on the Uttar Pradesh Public Services (Reservation for Scheduled Castes, Scheduled Tribes and Other Backward Classes) Act, 1994 enacted by U.P. legislature under Article 200 of Indian Constitution. It is published as Act No. 4, 1994 for the information of the general public.

THE UTTAR PRADESH PUBLIC SERVICES (RESERVATION FOR SCHEDULED CASTES, SCHEDULED TRIBES AND OTHER BACKWARD CLASSES) ACT, 1994

(U.P. Act No. 4 of 1994)
(As passed by the Uttar Pradesh Legislature)
AN ACT

To provide for the reservation in Public Services and posts

in favour of the persons belonging to the Scheduled Castes, Scheduled Tribes and other Backward Classes of citizens and for matters connected therewith or incidental thereto.

IT IS HEREBY enacted in the Fifty-third Year of the Republic of India as follows:

1. (1) This Act may be called the Uttar Pradesh Public Services (Reservation for Scheduled Castes, Scheduled Tribes and other Backward Classes) Act, 1994.
   (2) It shall be deemed to have come into force on December 11, 1993.
2. In this Act:
   (a) "appointing authority' in relation to public services and posts means the authority empowers to make appointment to such services o posts;
   (b) "Other backward classes of citizens" means the backward classes of citizens specified in Schedule I;
   (c) "Public services and posts means the services and posts in connection with the affairs of the State and includes services and posts in :
      (i) a local authority;
      (ii) a Co-operative society as defined in clause (f) of section 2 of the Uttar Pradesh Co-operative Societies Act, 1965 in which not less than fifty-one percent of the share capital of the society is held by the State Government;
      (iii) a Board of a corporation or a statutory body established by or under a central or a Uttar Pradesh Act which is owned and controlled by the State Government or a Government company as defined in section 617 of the Companies Act, 1956 in which not less than fifty-one of the paid up share capital is held by the State Government;
      (iv) an educational institution owned and controlled by the State Government or

which receives grants-in-aid from the State Government including a university established by or under a Uttar Pradesh Act, except an institution established and administered by minorities referred to in clause (1) of Article 30 of the constitution;

(v) respect of which reservation was applicable by Government orders on the date of the commencement of this Act which are not covered under sub-clause (i) to (iv).

(d) "Year of recruitment" in relation to a vacancy means a period of twelve months commencing on the first of July of a year within which the process of direct recruitment against such vacancy is initiated.

3. (1) In public services and posts there shall be reserved at the stage of direct recruitment, the following percentage of vacancies to which recruitments are to be made in accordance with the roster referred to in sub-section (5) in favour of the persons belonging to Scheduled Castes, Scheduled Tribes and other Backward Classes of citizens.

(a) in the case of Scheduled Castes—Twenty-one percent;

(b) in the case of Scheduled Tribes—Two per cent;

(c) in the case of other Backward Classes—Twenty-seven percent;

Provided that the reservation under clause (c) shall not apply to the category of other Backward Classes of citizens specified in Schedule II:

(2) If, even in respect of any year of recruitment any vacancy reserved for any category of persons under sub-section (1) remains unfilled, special recruitment shall made for such number of times, not exceeding three as may be considered necessary to fill such vacancy from amongst the persons belong to that category.

(3) If, in the third such recruitment referred to in sub-section (2) suitable candidates belonging to Scheduled Tribes are not available to fill the vacancies reserved for them such vacancy shall be filled by persons belonging to Scheduled castes.

(4) Where due to non-availability of suitable candidates any of the vacancies reserved under sub-section (1) remains unfilled, even after special recruitment referred to sub-section (2), it may be carried over to the next year commencing on the first of July in which recruitment is to made, subject to the condition that in that year total reservation of vacancies for all categories of persons mentioned in sub-section (1) shall not exceed fifty percent of the total vacancies.

(5) The State Government shall, for applying the reservation under sub-sections by a notified order, issue a roster which shall be continuously applied till it is exhausted.

(6) If a person belonging to any of the categories mentioned in sub-section (1) gets selected on the basis of merit in an open competition with general candidates he shall not be adjusted against the vacancies reserved for such category under sub-section (1).

(7) If, on the date of commencement of this Act, reservation was in force under Government Orders for appointment to posts to be filled by promotion. Such Government Orders shall continue to be applicable till they are modified or revoked.

4. (1) The State Government may, by notified order, entrust the appointing authority or any officer or employee with the responsibility of ensuring the compliance of the provisions of this Act.

(2) The State Government may, in the like manner, invest the appointing authority or officer or employee referred to in sub-section (I) with

such powers or authority as may be necessary for effectively discharging the responsibility entrusted to him under sub-section (I).

5. (1) Any appointing authority or officer or employee entrusted with the responsibility under sub-section (I) of section 4 who wilfully acts in a manner intended to contravene or defeat the purpose of this Act shall on conviction, be punishable with imprisonment which may extend to three months or with fine which may extend to one thousand rupees or with both.

(2) No court shall take cognizance of an offence under this section except with the previous sanction of the State Government or officer authorized in this behalf by the State Government by an order.

(3) An offence punishable under sub-section (I) shall be tried summarily by a Metropolitan Magistrate or a Judicial Magistrate of the first class and the provision of sub-section (I) of section 262, section 263, section 264 and the section 265 of code of criminal Procedure, 1973 shall *mutatis mutandis* apply.

6. If it comes to the notice of the State Government, that any person belonging to any of the categories mentioned in sub-section (l) of section 3 has been adversely affected on account of non-compliance of the provisions of this Act or the rules made thereunder or the Government orders in this behalf by the appointing authority, it may call for such records and take such action as it may considered necessary.

7. The State Government may by order, provide for nomination of officers in Selection giving representation to the Scheduled Castes, Scheduled Tribes, and other backward classes of citizens in the Selection Committee to such extent and in such manner as it may consider necessary where such Committee is constituted either under the service rules or otherwise.

8. The State Government may in favour of the categories of persons mentioned in sub-section (1) Of section 3, by order grant such concessions in respect of fees for any competitive examination or interview and relaxation in upper age limit it as it may consider necessary.

   (2) The State Government orders in force the date of the commencement of this Act, in respect of concessions and relaxations, including concession in fee for any competitive examination or interview and relaxation in upper age limit and those relating to reservation in direct recruitment and promotion, in favour of categories of persons referred to in sub-section (1) which are not in consistent with the provisions of this Act, shall continue to be applicable till they are modified or revoked, as the case may be.
9. For the purpose of reservation provided under this Act caste certificate shall be issued by such authority or officer and in such manner and form as the state Government may, by order provide.
10. If any difficulty arises in giving effect to the provision of this Act, the State Government may by a notified order make such provisions not consistent with the provisions of this Act as appears to it to be necessary or expedient for removing the difficulty.
11. No Suit, prosecution or other legal proceedings shall lie against the State Government or any person for anything which is in good faith done or intended to be done in pursuance of this Act or the rules made thereunder.
12. The State Government may by a notification make rules for carrying out the purposes of this Act.
13. The State government may by a notification amend the Schedules and upon the publication of such notification in the Gazette, the Schedules shall be deemed to be amended accordingly.
14. Every order made sub-section (5) section (3), sub-sections (1) and (2) of section 4 and section 10 and every notification issued under section 13 shall be laid as soon as be before both the houses of State

Legislative and the provisions of sub-section (1) of section 23-A of the Uttar Pradesh General Clauses Act, 1904 shall apply as they apply in respect of rules made by the State Government under any Uttar Pradesh Act;

15. The provisions of this Act shall not apply to the cases in which selections process has been initiated before the commencement of this Act and such cases shall be dealt with in accordance with the provision of law and Government as they stood before commencement;

Explanation (1) : For the purposes of this sub-section the selection process shall be deemed to have been initiated where, under the relevant service rules, recruitment is to be made on the basis of—

(i) Written test or interview only, the written test of the interview, as the case may be, has started, or

(ii) both written test and interview, the written test has started.

(2) The provisions of this Act shall not apply to the appointment, to be made under the Uttar Pradesh Recruitment of Department of Government Servant Dying in Harness Rules, 1974.

16. (1) The Uttar Pradesh Public Services (Reservation for Backward Classes) Act, 1989, The Uttar Pradesh Public Services (Reservation for Scheduled Castes and Scheduled Tribes) Act, 1989 and the Uttar Pradesh Public Services (Reservation for Scheduled Castes, Scheduled Tribes and Backward Classes) Ordinance, 1994 are hereby repealed.

(2) Notwithstanding such repeal, anything done or any action taken under the provisions of the Acts and the ordinance referred to in sub-section (1), shall be deemed to have been done or taken under the corresponding provisions of this Act as if the provisions of this Act were in force at all material times.

SCHEDULED I
See section 2(6)

1. Ahir
2. Arakh
3. Kachehi
4. Kaliar
5. Kewat or Mallah
6. Kisan
7. Koeri
8. Kumhar
9. Kurini
10. Kamboj
11. Kasgar
12. Kunjra or Racen
13. Glosain
14. Gujjar
15. Gadariva
16. Gaddi
17. Giri
18. Chikwa (Qassab)
19. Chhippi
20. Jogi
21. Dhafali
22. Jhoja
23. Tamoli
24. Teli
25. Darji
26. Dhiver
27. Naqqal
28. Nat (not included in SC category)
29. Naik
30. Faqir
31. Banjara
32. Barhai
33. Bari
34. Beragi
35. Bind
36. Biyar
37. Bhar
38. Bhurji or Bharhhunja
39. Bhathiara
40. Mali, Saini
41. Manihar
42. Murao or Mural
43. Momin (Ansaf)
44. Mirasi
45. Muslim, Kavastha
46. Naddaf (Dhuniya, mansoori)
47. Ivlarchcha
48. Rantgrez
49. Lodha, Lodhi, Lot, Lodhi, Rajput,
50. Lohar
51. Lonia
52. Sonar
53. Halwai
54. Sweeper (not included in SC category)
55. Hajjam (Nai)

SCIIEDULED II
See Section 3(b)

1. Son or daughter of—
   (a) a member of Indian Administrative Service, Indian Foreign Service, Indian Police Service, Indian Forest Service or other Central Service whether directly recruited or promoted from any State Service; or
   (b) a member of Uttar Pradesh Civil Service (Executive Branch), Uttar Pradesh Police Service or other State Service, who has been directly recruited to such Service; or
   (c) Such Group A/Class I officer of any Department or Ministry of Government of India or educational, research or other institutions under such Department or Ministry, who is not included in sub-category (a); or
   (d) Such Group A/Class I officer of any Department or institution of the State Government, who is not included in sub-category (b); or
   (e) an officer of the defence forces or para military forces who is not below the rank of a Colonel or equivalent rank:
   Provided that the income from salary of such member or officer of service is Rupees ten thousand or more per mensum, his spouse is at least a graduate and he or his spouse owns a house in an urban area.
2. Son or daughter of a person engaged in profession as a Doctor, Surgeon, Engineers, Lawyer, Architect, Chartered Accountant, media and information professorial, management and other consultant, film artist and other film professional, running educational institution or coaching institute or engaged in the business as share or stock broker or in entertainment business;
   Provided that his average income from all sources for three consecutive financial years is not less than

rupees ten lakh per annum, his spouse is at least a graduate and his family owns immovable property worth at least rupees twenty lakh.

3. Son or daughter of a business man whose average income for three consecutive financial years is not less than rupees ten lakh per annum, his spouse is atleast a graduate and his family owns immovable property worth atleast rupees twenty lakh.
4. Son or daughter of an industrialist whose level of investment in running units is over rupees ten crore and such units are engaged in commercial production for atleast five years and his spouse is atleast a graduate.
5. Son or daughter of a person who has holding within the limit fixed under the Uttar Pradesh imposition of Ceiling on Land Holdings Act, 1960, has an income of rupees ten lakh in a financial year from sources other than agriculture such as salary, business or industry and the like and his spouse is atleast a graduate.
6. Son or daughter of a person not included in any of the aforementioned categories, whose average income from all sources for three consecutive financial years in not less than rupees ten lakh per annum, his spouse is atleast a graduate and his family owns immovable property worth at least rupees twenty lakh.

APPENDIX 16

THE CENTRAL EDUCATIONAL INSTITUTIONS (RESERVATION IN ADMISSION) ACT, 2006

The Central Educational Institutions (Reservation In Admission) Act, 2006 # No. 5 Of 2007, [3rd January, 2007]

An Act to provide for the reservation in admission of the students belonging to the Scheduled Castes, the Scheduled Tribes and the Other Backward Classes of citizens, to certain Central Educational Institutions established, maintained or aided by the Central Government, and for matters connected therewith or incidental thereto. BE it enacted by Parliament in the Fifty-seventh Year of the Republic of India as follows:

1. Short title: This Act may be called the Central Educational Institutions (Reservation in Admission) Act, 2006.

2. Definitions: In this Act, unless the context otherwise requires,

(a) "academic session" means the period in a calendar year, or a part thereof, during which a Central Educational Institution is open for teaching or instruction in any branch of study or faculty;

(b) "annual permitted strength" means the number of seats, in a course or programme for teaching or instruction in each branch of study or faculty authorised by an appropriate authority for admission of students to a Central Educational Institution;

(c) "appropriate authority" means the University Grants Commission, the Bar Council of India, the Medical Council of India, the All India Council for Technical

Education or any other authority or body established by or under a Central Act for the determination, coordination or maintenance of the standards of higher education in any Central Educational Institution;

(d) "Central Educational Institution" means—

(i) a university established or incorporated by or under a Central Act;

(ii) an institution of national importance set-up by an Act of Parliament;

(iii) an institution, declared as a deemed University under section 3 of the University Grants Commission Act, 1956, and maintained by or receiving aid from the Central Government;

(iv) an institution maintained by or receiving aid from the Central Government, whether directly or indirectly, and affiliated to an institution referred to in clause (i) or clause (ii), or a constituent unit of an institution referred to in clause (iii);

(v) an educational institution set up by the Central Government under the Societies Registration Act, 1860;

(e) "faculty" means the faculty of a Central Educational Institution;

(f) "Minority Educational Institution" means an institution established and administered by the minorities under clause (1) of Article 30 of the Constitution and so declared by an Act of Parliament or by the Central Government or declared as a Minority Educational Institution under the National Commission for Minority Educational Institutions Act, 2004;

(g) "Other Backward Classes" means the class or classes of citizens who are socially and educationally backward, and are so determined by the Central Government;

(h) "Scheduled Castes" means the Scheduled Castes notified under Article 341 of the Constitution;

(i) "Scheduled Tribes" means the Scheduled Tribes notified under Article 342 of the Constitution; and
(j) "teaching or instruction in any branch of study" means teaching or instruction in a branch of study leading to three principal levels of qualifications at bachelor (undergraduate) masters (postgraduate) and doctoral levels.

3. Reservation of Seats in Central Educational Institutions: The reservation of seats in admission and its extent in a Central Educational Institution shall be provided in the following manner, namely:

(i) out of the annual permitted strength in each branch of study or faculty, fifteen per cent seats shall be reserved for the Scheduled Castes;
(ii) out of the annual permitted strength in each branch of study or faculty, seven and one-half per cent seats shall be reserved for the Scheduled Tribes;
(iii) out of the annual permitted strength in each branch of study or faculty, twenty-seven per cent seats shall be reserved for the Other Backward Classes.

4. Act not to apply in certain cases: The provisions of section 3 of this Act shall not apply to:

(a) a Central Educational Institution established in the tribal areas referred to in the Sixth Schedule to the Constitution;
(b) the institutions of excellence, research institutions, institutions of national and strategic importance specified in the Schedule to this Act;
Provided that the Central Government may, as and when considered necessary, by notification in the Official Gazette, amend the Schedule;
(c) a Minority Educational Institution as defined in this Act;
(d) a course or programme at high levels of specialisation, including at the post-doctoral level,

within any branch of study or faculty, which the Central Government may, in consultation with the appropriate authority, specify.

5. Mandatory increase of seats: (1) Notwithstanding anything contained in clause (iii) of section 3 and in any other law for the time being in force, every Central Educational Institution shall, with the prior approval of the appropriate authority, increase the number of seats in a branch of study or faculty over and above its annual permitted strength so that the number of seats, excluding those reserved for the persons belonging to the Scheduled Castes, the Scheduled Tribes and the Other Backward Classes, is not less than the number of such seats available for the academic session immediately preceding the date of the coming into force of this Act.

(2) Where, on a representation by any Central Educational Institution, the Central Government, in consultation with the appropriate authority, is satisfied that for reasons of financial, physical or academic limitations or in order to maintain the standards of education, the annual permitted strength in any branch of study or faculty of such institution cannot be increased for the academic session following the commencement of this Act, it may permit by notification in the Official Gazette, such institution to increase the annual permitted strength over a maximum period of three years beginning with the academic session following the commencement of this Act; and then, the extent of reservation for the Other Backward Classes as provided in clause (iii) of section 3 shall be limited for that academic session in such manner that the number of seats available to the Other Backward Classes for each academic session are commensurate with the increase in the permitted strength for each year.

6. Reservation of seats in admissions to begin in calendar year, 2007: The Central Educational Institutions shall take all necessary steps, which are required in giving effect to the provisions of sections 3, 4 and 5 of this Act, for the purposes of reservation of seats in admissions to its academic sessions commencing on and from the calendar year, 2007.

7. Laying of notifications before Parliament: Every notification made under this Act shall be laid, as soon as may be after it is made, before each House of Parliament while it is in session, for a total period of thirty days which may be comprised in one session or in two or more successive sessions, and if, before the expiry of the session immediately following the session or the successive sessions aforesaid, both Houses agree in making any modification in the notification or both Houses agree that the notification should not be made, the notification shall thereafter have effect only in such modified form or be of no effect, as the case may be; so, however, that any such modification or annulment shall be without prejudice to the validity of anything previously done under that notification.

THE SCHEDULE
[See Section 4(b)]

Sl. No. Names of the Institutions of Excellence, etc.

1. Homi Bhabha National Institute, Mumbai and its constituent units, namely:

    (i) Bhabha Atomic Research Centre, Trombay;
    (ii) Indira Gandhi Centre for Atomic Research, Kalpakkam;
    (iii) Raja Ramanna Centre for Advanced Technology, Indore;
    (iv) Institute for Plasma Research, Gandhinagar;
    (v) Variable Energy Cyclotron Centre, Kolkata;
    (vi) Saha Institute of Nuclear Physics, Kolkata;
    (vii) Institute of Physics, Bhubaneshwar;
    (viii) Institute of Mathematical Sciences, Chennai;
    (ix) Harish-Chandra Research Institute, Allahabad;
    (x) Tata Memorial Centre, Mumbai.

2. Tata Institute of Fundamental Research, Mumbai.
3. North-Eastern Indira Gandhi Regional Institute of Health and Medical Science, Shillong.

4. National Brain Research Centre, Manesar, Gurgaon.
5. Jawaharlal Nehru Centre for Advanced Scientific Research, Bangalore.
6. Physical Research Laboratory, Ahmedabad.
7. Space Physics Laboratory, Thiruvananthapuram.
8. Indian Institute of Remote Sensing, Dehradun.

K.N. CHATURVEDI
Secy. to the Govt. of India
Last updated on 01.02.2008

Glossary

A

APAPATRAS: This term used for Chandalas or Untouchables.

B

BRANDIES BRIEF: The term is used for innovative brief submitted by Louis D. Brandeis in Muller *v.* Oregon. The brief was prepared in defence of Oregon ten-hour law for women. In brief only two scant pages were given to conventional legal arguments and over one hundred pages were devoted to the new kind of evidence drawn from hundreds of reports, both domestic and foreign, of committees, statistical bureaux, Commissioners of hygiene and factory inspectors—all providing that, long hours are as a matter of fact dangerous to women's health, safety and morals, and short hours result in social and economic benefits. The brief was a bold innovation making enormously extended the bounds of common knowledge and compelled to Court to take judicial notice of this extension.

C

CARRY FORWARD AND EXCHANGE RULE: If sufficient number of SC and ST candidates fit for appointment against reserved posts are not available, such vacancies can be dereserved to be filled by candidates of other communities and the reservations are carried forward to subsequent three recruitment years, except in case of promotion by selection from Group C to Group B, within Group B and from Group B to the lowest rung of Group A where carrying forward of reservation are not permitted. While filling up reserved posts, the oldest carried forward vacancy will be filled up first. Vacancies reserved for SCs and STs may be exchanged and filled up by candidates from SC and ST candidates, in case no suitable candidates from the respective community, for which the vacancy is reserved, is not available. The normal provision is that the exchange is permissible only for the reservations which have been carried forward to third year of recruitment.

Now unfilled vacancies of reserved quota are not to be filled by general candidates, they have to remain unfilled and have to be carried forward **(Majority judgment in Mandal Case, Para 703).**

CREAMY LAYER OF OBCs: *creamy-layer as when a person has been able to shed-off the attributes of social and educational backwardness and has secured employment or has engaged himself in some trade/profession of high status... at that stage he is normally no longer in need of reservation for himself.* It indicates members of those backward classes who are highly advanced socially as well as economically and educationally among backward class and they constitute the forward section of a particular backward class—as forward as any other forward class.

COMPENSATORY DISCRIMINATION: It indicates a policy to safeguard the interests of the historically disadvantaged section of population.

D

DVIJA: Dvija is symbolic of rebirth or twice-born.

DESERVATION: When sufficient number of candidates of SC/ST is not available to fill up the respective reserved vacancies, it can be filled by general candidates to get the work going on. But a vacancy reserved for SC/ST cannot be filled by a general candidate without first dereserving the reserved vacancy. Dereservation has basically three functions :

(1) It keeps reservations alive for four years while efforts can be made to find suitable SC/ST candidates.
(2) It helps administration as the same does not suffer by keeping reserved vacancies vacant. It can fill up the vacancy by general candidate to get the work done.
(3) It serves public interest where general candidate also gets appointed against reserved vacancy without harming the chances of SC/ST.

E

EKAJATI: Earlier *'Ekajati'* was symbolic of once-born in Buddhist text. Later it denotes ethnic groups or four traditional ones Patanjali text.

H

HINA JATYO: Hina jatyo represents Low tribes, of barbers, potter or weavers, a remnant of the Dasyu tribes on the outskirts of civilization. The lowest of all are the Chandalas and other outcaste tribes.

J

JATI: This term is more often used for the meaning of sub-divisions of the Verna.

P

PROTECTIVE DISCRIMINATION: It indicates a policy which aims at protection of the interests of those who have been oppressed for ages and therefore at present are not in a position to compete with privileged sections of the people.

R

REVERSE DISCRIMINATION: *Reverse* discrimination is discrimination in favour of certain groups in order to rectify the inherent inequality of opportunity experienced by these groups. Protective discrimination is also known as reverse discrimination as it involves discrimination in favour of those who until recently had been victim of discrimination.

Table of Cases

Panchayat Varga Sharmajivi Samudaik Sahakari Khedut Cooperation Society *v.* Haribhai Mevabhai, (1996), 10 SCC 320 (paras 6, 10 & 4). 97
Paradise Printers *v.* Union Territory of Chandigarh, AIR 1988 SC 354. 74
P. Rajendran *v.* State of Madras, AIR 1968 SC, 1012. 78, 146
Peoples Union for Democratic Rights *v.* Union of India, 1982, 3 SCC 161. 96
Poudyal, R.C. *v.* Union of India, 1994, Supp. (1) SCC 324. 99
Prem Chand Garg *v.* Excise Commissioner, AIR 1963 SC 996. 97
P.G.I. M.E. & R. *v.* K.L. Narasimhan (1997) 6 SCC 283. 153
Preeti Srivastava *v.* State of M.P., 1999 7 SCC 120
Purna Chandra Modi *v.* Union of India, 1996 CAT.
Rajendra Kumar Gour and others *v.* Union of India and Others, 2001 CAT.
Rajagopal Ramraj *v.* Union of India, M.P. 1993. 136, 137
Ratilal *v.* State of Bombay, 1954 SCR 1055. 93
Rajendran *v.* Union of India, AIR 1968 SC 507. 78, 85, 88
R. Chitralekha *v.* State of Mysore and Others, AIR 1963, p. 1823. 131, 136
Ramesh Kumar Singh *v.* State of Bihar, AIR 1978 SC 327, 331
Ramana Dayaram Shetty *v.* Union of India, AIR 1979 SC 1628. 73
Ram Bhagat Singh *v.* State of Haryana, AIR 1997 2 SCC 417. 136
Ram Singh *v.* Union of India & Ors., 1999 (CAT—Patna). 155
R.K. Sabharwal & Ors. *v.* Union of India, 1995 (1) ATJ 410. 137, 154
S. Vinod Kumar and Anothers *v.* Union of India & Others (1996) 6 SCC 580. 88, 140
Sheele Barse *v.* State of Maharahshtra, 1983 2 SCC 96. 158
Sharma S.S. *v.* Union of India, AIR 1981 SC 588. 80
Subhash Kumar *v.* State of Bihar, AIR 1991 SC 420. 158
Srinivasa *v.* State of Karnataka, AIR 1987 SC 1518. 96
Sri Srinivasa Theatre *v.* Government of Tamil Nadu, AIR 1992 SC 999, 1004. 73
S. Narayan *v.* District Collector, Salem, 1997 2 SCC 571. 103

Bibliography

Books

Amrik Singh, Caste, Class and Reservation, *EPW*, Vol. 20, 1991.

Andre Beteille, The Backward Classes and the New Social Order, Oxford University Press, New Delhi, 1981.

Andre Bateille, Caste: Old and New, Asia Publishing House, 1969.

Anirudh Prasad, Reservation Justice to OBCs, Deep & Deep Publications, N. Delhi, 1997.

Aruna Sundaresh, Constitutional Law and Reservations, New Frontiers in Education, Vol. 16, No. 2, 1986.

Arvind P. Datar, Datar on Constitution of India, Wadhwa & Company Law Publications, N. Delhi, 2001.

Asghar Ali, Backward Class Benefits and Social Class in India, *EPW*, 1920-70.

A.K. Vakil, Reservation Policy and SC in India, Ashish Publication, N. Delhi, 1985.

B.R. Ambedkar, Annihilation of Castes, Thacker & Co., 1946.

B.R. Ambedkar, Who were the Shudras, Bombay Publication, 1946.

B.R. Ambedkar, The Untouchables, Amrit Book Co., New Delhi, 1948.

B. Sivaramayya, Reservation: Problems and Prospects, Uppal Publishing House, New Delhi, 1984.

Dr. Jayant Lakshmikant Aparjit, Equality and Compensatory Discrimination under the Indian Constitution, Pub. Dalitsons Nagpur, 1992.

Dr. M.C. Jain Kagzi, The Constitution of India, Pub. Metropolitan Book Company Private Ltd., Vol. I & II, 1988.

Dr. Parmanand Singh, Equality, Reservation and Discrimination in India, Deep & Deep Publications, N. Delhi, 1985.

Dr. R. Chandra, Dr. Ambedkar: Science and Society, Indica Publication, Delhi, 2000.

Durga Das Basu, Shorter Constitution of India, Wadhwa and Company Law Publisher, N. Delhi, Reprint 2004.

Ekta Singh, Caste System in India: A Historical Perspective, ed. 2004, Gyan Books Pvt. Publication Ltd., N. Delhi.

G.P. Verma, Caste Reservation in India, Chugh Publications.

Ghanshayam Shah, Caste, Class and Reservation, *EPW*, 19 January 1985.

Ghanshayam Shah, "Caste in Contemporary India", New Delhi, 1985.

Ghanshayam Shah, Caste, Caste-Conflict and Reservation, New Delhi, 1985.

H.M. Seervai, Constitutional Law of India, Universal Law Publisher, N. Delhi, 1999, Vol. I, II and III.

Indian Law Institute, Law and Social Change, 1988.

J.N. Pandey, Constitutional Law of India, Central Law Agency Publication; Allahabad, 1994.

J.R. Kmable, Rising and Awakening of Depressed Classes in India, 1979.

Lelah Dushkin, Caste, Caste-Conflict and Reservation, Ajanta Books International, Delhi, 1979.

M.P. Jain, Indian Constitutional Law, Wadhwa and Company Law Publisher, N. Delhi, 1987; Reprint 1994.

Marc Galanter, Law and Society in Modern India, 1997.

M.L. Mathur, Encyclopedia of Backward Caste (4 Vols.), Gyan Books Pvt. Ltd. Publication, N. Delhi, 2003.

M.N. Srinivasa, Social Change in Modern India, New Delhi, 1982.

Nandu Ram, Encyclopedia of Scheduled Castes in India (5 Vols.), Gyan Books Pvt. Ltd. Publication, N. Delhi, 2004.

Om Prakash Sangwan, Social System and The Dalit Identity, Commonwealth Publication, New Delhi, 1996.

P. Ramanatha Aiyer, Law Laxican, 1997.

P.M. Bakshi, The Constitution of India, Universal Law Publication Co. Pvt. Ltd., N. Delhi, 2002, Rep. 2004.

Prof. Ramesh Chandra and Dr. Sangh Mitra, Dalit Identity in the New Millennium, Commonwealth Publication, New Delhi, Vol. 9, 2003.

Rajni Kothari, Caste in Indian Politics, New Delhi, 1970.

Rajni Kothari, Reservation for Scheduled Castes: Gaps between Policy and Implementation, Uppal Publishing House, New Delhi, 1991.

Ram Ahuja, Indian Social System, Rawat Publication, N. Delhi, 1993.

Ratna, G. Revankar, The Indian Constitution—A Case Study of Backward Classes, Pub. Rutherford, Madison, Teaneck, Fairleigh Dickinson University Press.

S.N. Singh, Reservation Policy for Backward Classes, Rawat Publication, Jaipur, India, 1996.

Shayma Nand Singh, Reservation—Problems and Prospects, Uppal Publishing House, New Delhi, 1991.

Shyama Nand Singh, "Roots of Caste War in Bihar", *Mainstream*, New Delhi, January 16, 1988.

Sanjay Paswan and Paramanshi Jaideva, Encyclopedia of Dalits in India: General Study, Kalpaz Publications, Vol. 1, 14, 2002.

S. Nurul Hasan, Caste System in Medieval Muslim Society, *The Telegraph*, April 1, 1991.

Subhash, C. Kashyap, Welfare of SC and ST, Constitutional Safeguard and Role of Parliament, Government of India Publication, N. Delhi, 1986.

S.V. Ketkar, History of Caste in India, Rawat Publications, Jaipur, 1979.

The Framing of India's Constitution, Universal Law Publishing Co. Pvt. Ltd., N. Delhi, Vol. 2.

Triloki Nath, Politics of the Depressed Classes, Deputy Publications, N. Delhi, 1987.

Upendra Baxi, Caste, Class and Reservation, *EPW*, March 9, 1985.

U. Baxi, The Crisis of Indian System, 1982.

U. Baxi, Law and Poverty : Critical Essays, 1988.

V.P. Singh, History of Reservation-I; History of Reservation-II: Extracts from the Report of the Tamil Nadu Second Backward Classes Commission, 1985.

Articles and Journals

Basavaraju, Constitutional Reservation to SC/ST—A Perspective, ALR 2000, Vol. 27(2), pp. 155-72.

D.K. Bhatt and Dr. P.C. Joshi, Social Justice and Reservation for OBCs: An Analysis of Judicial Response, ALR 2000, Vol. 27(2), pp. 109-24.

Dr. S.K. Singh, Concept of Creamy Layer in Backward Class Reservation under Indian Constitution, AIR 2000 (87), pp. 156-60.

Dr. S.K. Singh, Other Backward Class Reservation and the Concept of Creamy Layer, AIR 2003, Vol. (80), pp. 79-82.

Kamal Jeet Singh and Surendra Singh Jaswal, Glimpses to the History of Jurisprudence of Caste Reservation in India, SCC 1998, Vol. 1.

K.C. Sunny, Creamy Layer Principle: Its Social Relevance and Legal Consequences, ALR 1999, Vol. 23: 1 & 2, pp. 137-74.

Ravi Varma, Caste Reservation in Kerala, Organizer, 20 March, 2005.

S. Viswanathan, The Dalit Causes, a new perspective, *Frontline*, Nov. 2004.

Sheela Rai, Social and Conceptual Background to the Policy of Reservation, *Economic and Political Weekly*, Oct. 19, 2002, pp. 4309-18.

Magazine

Economic and Political Weekly, Oct. 19, 2002.

Frontline, Nov. 2004.

Organizer, 20 March, 2005.

Reports

Constitutional Assembly Debate, Vol. VII, Government of India, N. Delhi.

Kaka Kalelkar Commission, 1953 (First Backward Class Commission).

Mandal Commission Report, 1980 (Second Backward Class Commission).

Websites

www.ambedkar.org, workshop on Reservation Laws, Legal Remedies and Organizing SC/ST/OBC.

www.dalitindia.com.

www.dalits.org, Reservation and Employment: The Unacknowledged Reservation System, National Campaign on Dalit Human Rights.

www.dayafterindia.com.

www.saxakali.com

www.themoronline.com.

www.thehindu.com.

www.tiss.edu.com, Reservation and relaxation in age and work experience for SC/ST/OBC candidates.

www.vedamsbooks.com.

Material Used in Research Methodology
Primary Source Material

1. Constitution of India
2. Constitutional Assembly Debate
3. Government Documents

   (i) Reports of Kaka Kalelkar Backward Class Commission, 1955.

   (ii) Reports of B.P. Mandal Backward Class Commission, 1980.

   (iii) Census of India, 2001.

Secondary Sources Material

1. Books and Articles
2. Magazines
3. News papers
4. Supreme Court Decisions
5. Websites
6. Journals
   1. SCC
   2. AIR
   3. SCR
   4. ALR
   5. Periodicals

Index